Microsoft® Office

PowerPoint® 2003

COMPREHENSIVE

ROBERT T. GRAUER
UNIVERSITY OF MIAMI

MARYANN BARBER
UNIVERSITY OF MIAMI

PEARSON
Prentice Hall

Upper Saddle River,
New Jersey 07458

To Marion —
my wife, my lover, and my best friend

Robert Grauer

To Frank —
I love you

To Holly —
for being my friend

Maryann Barber

Library of Congress Cataloging-in-Publication Data

Grauer, Robert T.
    Microsoft Office PowerPoint 2003 / Robert T. Grauer, Maryann Barber.
        p. cm. -- (The exploring Office series)
    Includes index.
    ISBN 0-13-143487-X
    1. Computer graphics. 2. Microsoft PowerPoint (Computer file). 3. Business presentations
--Graphic methods--Computer programs. I. Barber, Maryann M. II. Title. III. Series.
    T385.G73744 2003
    006.6'862--dc22   2003068937

Executive Acquisitions Editor: Jodi McPherson
VP/ Publisher: Natalie E. Anderson
Senior Project Manager, Editorial: Eileen Clark
Editorial Assistants: Brian Hoehl, Alana Meyers, and Sandy Bernales
Media Project Manager: Cathleen Profitko
Marketing Manager: Emily Williams Knight
Marketing Assistant: Lisa Taylor
Project Manager, Production: Lynne Breitfeller
Production Editor: Greg Hubit
Associate Director, Manufacturing: Vincent Scelta
Manufacturing Buyer: Lynne Breitfeller
Design Manager: Maria Lange
Interior Design: Michael J. Fruhbeis
Cover Design: Michael J. Fruhbeis
Cover Printer: Phoenix Color
Composition and Project Management: The GTS Companies
Printer/Binder: Banta Menasha

Microsoft and the Microsoft Office Specialist logo are trademarks or registered trademarks of Microsoft Corporation in the United States and/or other countries. Prentice Hall is independent from Microsoft Corporation, and not affiliated with Microsoft in any manner. This publication may be used in assisting students to prepare for a Microsoft Office Specialist Exam. Neither Microsoft Corporation, its designated review companies, nor Prentice Hall warrants that use of this publication will ensure passing the relevant Exam.

Use of the Microsoft Office Specialist Approved Courseware Logo on this product signifies that it has been independently reviewed and approved in complying with the following standards:
Acceptable coverage of all content related to the Specialist level Microsoft Office Exams entitled "PowerPoint 2003" and sufficient performance-based exercises that relate closely to all required content based on sampling of text.

10 9 8 7 6 5 4
ISBN 0-13-143487-X spiral
ISBN 0-13-145188-X adhesive

Contents

MICROSOFT® OFFICE POWERPOINT® 2003

one

Introduction to PowerPoint®: Presentations Made Easy   1

two

Gaining Proficiency: Slide Show Tools and Digital Photography   65

three

Animating a Presentation: Diagrams and Charts   121

four

Advanced Techniques: Slide Masters, Narration, and Web Pages   165

Getting Started with Microsoft® Windows® XP

What does this logo mean?

It means this courseware has been approved by the Microsoft® Office Specialist Program to be among the finest available for learning **Microsoft PowerPoint 2003**. It also means that upon completion of this courseware, you may be prepared to take an exam for Microsoft Office Specialist qualification.

What is a Microsoft Office Specialist?

A Microsoft Office Specialist is an individual who has passed exams for certifying his or her skills in one or more of the Microsoft Office desktop applications such as Microsoft Word, Microsoft Excel, Microsoft PowerPoint, Microsoft Outlook, Microsoft Access, or Microsoft Project. The Microsoft Office Specialist Program typically offers certification exams at the "Specialist" and "Expert" skill levels.[*] The Microsoft Office Specialist Program is the only program approved by Microsoft for testing proficiency in Microsoft Office desktop applications and Microsoft Project. This testing program can be a valuable asset in any job search or career advancement.

More Information:

To learn more about becoming a Microsoft Office Specialist, visit www.microsoft.com/officespecialist

To learn about other Microsoft Office Specialist approved courseware from Pearson Education visit www.prenhall.com

---

*The availability of Microsoft Office Specialist certification exams varies by application, application version, and language. Visit www.microsoft.com/officespecialist for exam availability.

Preface

Continuing a tradition of excellence, Prentice Hall is proud to announce the new *Exploring Microsoft Office 2003* series by Robert T. Grauer and Maryann Barber. The hands-on approach and conceptual framework of this comprehensive series helps students master all aspects of the Microsoft Office 2003 software, while providing the background necessary to transfer and use these skills in their personal and professional lives.

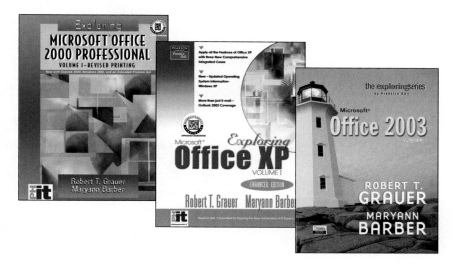

The entire series has been revised to include the new features found in the Office 2003 Suite, which contains Word 2003, Excel 2003, Access 2003, PowerPoint 2003, Publisher 2003, FrontPage 2003, and Outlook 2003.

In addition, this edition includes fully revised end-of-chapter material that provides an extensive review of concepts and techniques discussed in the chapter. Each chapter now begins with an *introductory case study* to provide an effective overview of what the reader will be able to accomplish, with additional *mini cases* at the end of each chapter for practice and review. The conceptual content within each chapter has been modified as appropriate and numerous end-of-chapter exercises have been added.

The new *visual design* introduces the concept of *perfect pages*, whereby every step in every hands-on exercise, as well as every end-of-chapter exercise, begins at the top of its own page and has its own screen shot. This clean design allows for easy navigation throughout the text.

Continuing the success of the website provided for previous editions of this series, Exploring Office 2003 offers expanded resources that include online, interactive study guides, data file downloads, technology updates, additional case studies and exercises, and other helpful information. Start out at <u>www.prenhall.com/grauer</u> to explore these resources!

Organization of the Exploring Office 2003 Series

The new Exploring Microsoft Office 2003 series includes five combined Office 2003 texts from which to choose:

- **Volume I** is Microsoft Office Specialist certified in each of the core applications in the Office suite (Word, Excel, Access, and PowerPoint). Five additional modules (*Essential Computing Concepts, Getting Started with Windows XP, The Internet and the World Wide Web, Getting Started with Outlook,* and *Integrated Case Studies*) are also included. **Volume I Enhanced Edition** adds 18 new chapter-opening case studies, two new integrated case studies, 30 additional end-of-chapter problems, and 20 new mini cases to the existing Volume I.

- **Volume II** picks up where Volume I leaves off, covering the advanced topics for the individual applications. A *Getting Started with VBA* module has been added.

- The **Plus Edition** extends the coverage of Access and Excel to six and seven chapters, respectively (as opposed to four chapters each in Volume I). It also maintains the same level of coverage for PowerPoint and Word as in Volume I so that both applications are Microsoft Office Specialist certified. The Plus Edition includes a new module on XML but does not contain the Essential Computing Concepts or Internet modules.

- The **Brief Microsoft Office 2003** edition provides less coverage of the core applications than Volume I (a total of 10 chapters as opposed to 18). It also includes the *Getting Started with Windows XP* and *Getting Started with Outlook* modules.

- **Getting Started with Office 2003** contains the first chapter from each application (Word, Excel, Access, and PowerPoint), plus three additional modules: *Getting Started with Windows XP, The Internet and the World Wide Web*, and *Essential Computing Concepts*.

Individual texts for Word 2003, Excel 2003, Access 2003, and PowerPoint 2003 provide complete coverage of the application and are Microsoft Office Specialist certified. For shorter courses, we have created brief versions of the Exploring texts that give students a four-chapter introduction to each application. Each of these volumes is Microsoft Office Specialist certified at the Specialist level.

This series has been approved by Microsoft to be used in preparation for Microsoft Office Specialist exams.

The Microsoft Office Specialist program is globally recognized as the standard for demonstrating desktop skills with the Microsoft Office suite of business productivity applications (Microsoft Word, Microsoft Excel, Microsoft PowerPoint, Microsoft Access, and Microsoft Outlook). With a Microsoft Office Specialist certification, thousands of people have demonstrated increased productivity and have proved their ability to utilize the advanced functionality of these Microsoft applications.

By encouraging individuals to develop advanced skills with Microsoft's leading business desktop software, the Microsoft Office Specialist program helps fill the demand for qualified, knowledgeable people in the modern workplace. At the same time, Microsoft Office Specialist helps satisfy an organization's need for a qualitative assessment of employee skills.

Instructor and Student Resources

The **Instructor's CD** that accompanies the Exploring Office series contains:

- Student data files
- Solutions to all exercises and problems
- PowerPoint lectures
- Instructor's manuals in Word format that enable the instructor to annotate portions of the instructor manuals for distribution to the class
- Instructors may also use our *test creation software,* TestGen and QuizMaster. TestGen is a test generator program that lets you view and easily edit test-bank questions, create tests, and print in a variety of formats suitable to your teaching situation. Exams can be easily uploaded into WebCT, BlackBoard, and CourseCompass. QuizMaster allows students to take the tests created with TestGen on a local area network.

Prentice Hall's Companion Website at www.prenhall.com/grauer offers expanded IT resources and downloadable supplements. This site also includes an online study guide for students containing true/false and multiple choice questions and practice projects.

WebCT www.prenhall.com/webct

Gold level customer support available exclusively to adopters of Prentice Hall courses is provided free-of-charge upon adoption and provides you with priority assistance, training discounts, and dedicated technical support.

Blackboard www.prenhall.com/blackboard

Prentice Hall's abundant online content, combined with Blackboard's popular tools and interface, result in robust Web-based courses that are easy to implement, manage, and use—taking your courses to new heights in student interaction and learning.

CourseCompass www.coursecompass.com

CourseCompass is a dynamic, interactive online course management tool powered by Blackboard. This exciting product allows you to teach with marketing-leading Pearson Education content in an easy-to-use, customizable format.

Training and Assessment www2.phgenit.com/support

Prentice Hall offers Performance Based Training and Assessment in one product, Train&Assess IT. The Training component offers computer-based training that a student can use to preview, learn, and review Microsoft Office application skills. Web or CD-ROM delivered, Train IT offers interactive multimedia, computer-based training to augment classroom learning. Built-in prescriptive testing suggests a study path based not only on student test results but also on the specific textbook chosen for the course.

The Assessment component offers computer-based testing that shares the same user interface as Train IT and is used to evaluate a student's knowledge about specific topics in Word, Excel, Access, PowerPoint, Windows, Outlook, and the Internet. It does this in a task-oriented, performance-based environment to demonstrate proficiency as well as comprehension on the topics by the students. More extensive than the testing in Train IT, Assess IT offers more administrative features for the instructor and additional questions for the student.

Assess IT also allows professors to test students out of a course, place students in appropriate courses, and evaluate skill sets.

New! Each chapter now begins with an introductory case study to provide an effective overview of what students will accomplish by completing the chapter.

CHAPTER

1

Getting Started with Microsoft® Windows® XP

OBJECTIVES

After reading this chapter you will:

1. Describe the Windows desktop.
2. Use the Help and Support Center to obtain information.
3. Describe the My Computer and My Documents folders.
4. Differentiate between a program file and a data file.
5. Download a file from the Exploring Office Web site.
6. Copy and/or move a file from one folder to another.
7. Delete a file, and then recover it from the Recycle Bin.
8. Create and arrange shortcuts on the desktop.
9. Use the Search Companion.
10. Use the My Pictures and My Music folders.
11. Use Windows Messenger for instant messaging.

hands-on exercises

1. WELCOME TO WINDOWS XP
   Input: None
   Output: None

2. DOWNLOAD PRACTICE FILES
   Input: Data files from the Web
   Output: Welcome to Windows XP (a Word document)

3. WINDOWS EXPLORER
   Input: Data files from exercise 2
   Output: Screen Capture within a Word document

4. INCREASING PRODUCTIVITY
   Input: Data files from exercise 3
   Output: None

5. FUN WITH WINDOWS XP
   Input: None
   Output: None

CASE STUDY
UNFORESEEN CIRCUMSTANCES

Steve and his wife Shelly have poured their life savings into the dream of owning their own business, a "nanny" service agency. They have spent the last two years building their business and have created a sophisticated database with numerous entries for both families and nannies. The database is the key to their operation. Now that it is up and running, Steve and Shelly are finally at a point where they could hire someone to manage the operation on a part-time basis so that they could take some time off together.

Unfortunately, their process for selecting a person they could trust with their business was not as thorough as it should have been. Nancy, their new employee, assured them that all was well, and the couple left for an extended weekend. The place was in shambles on their return. Nancy could not handle the responsibility, and when Steve gave her two weeks' notice, neither he nor his wife thought that the unimaginable would happen. On her last day in the office Nancy "lost" all of the names in the database—the data was completely gone!

Nancy claimed that a "virus" knocked out the database, but after spending nearly $1,500 with a computer consultant, Steve was told that it had been cleverly deleted from the hard drive and could not be recovered. Of course, the consultant asked Steve and Shelly about their backup strategy, which they sheepishly admitted did not exist. They had never experienced any problems in the past, and simply assumed that their data was safe. Fortunately, they do have hard copy of the data in the form of various reports that were printed throughout the time they were in business. They have no choice but to manually reenter the data. ■

Your assignment is to read the chapter, paying special attention to the information on file management. Think about how Steve and Shelly could have avoided the disaster if a backup strategy had been in place, then summarize your thoughts in a brief note to your instructor. Describe the elements of a basic backup strategy. Give several other examples of unforeseen circumstances that can cause data to be lost.

1

New! A listing of the input and output files for each hands-on exercise within the chapter. Students will stay on track with what is to be accomplished.

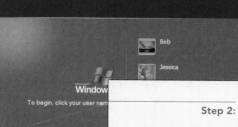

hands-on exercise

1 Welcome to Windows XP

Objective To log on to Windows XP and customize the desktop; to open the My Computer folder; to move and size a window; to format a floppy disk and access the Help and Support Center. Use Figure 7 as a guide.

Step 1: **Log On to Windows XP**

- Turn on the computer and all of the peripheral devices. The floppy drive should be empty prior to starting your machine.
- Windows XP will load automatically, and you should see a login screen similar to Figure 7a. (It does not matter which version of Windows XP you are using.) The number and names of the potential users and their associated icons will be different on your system.
- Click the icon for the user account you want to access. You may be prompted for a password, depending on the security options in effect.

Bob

Jessica

Windows

To begin, click your user name

Turn off Home Computer

Click icon for user account to be accessed

(a) Log On to Windows XP (step 1)

FIGURE 7 Hands-on Exercise 1

USER ACCOUNTS

The available user names are cr...
Windows XP, but you can add or d...
click Control Panel, switch to the Ca...
the desired task, such as creating...
then supply the necessary informati...
user accounts in a school setting.

10   GETTING STARTED WITH MICROSOFT WINDOWS XP

Each step in the hands-on exercises begins at the top of the page to ensure that students can easily navigate through the text.

Step 2: **Choose the Theme and Start Menu**

- Check with your instructor to see if you are able to modify the desktop and other settings at your school or university. If your network administrator has disabled these commands, skip this step and go to step 3.
- Point to a blank area on the desktop, click the **right mouse button** to display a context-sensitive menu, then click the **Properties command** to open the Display Properties dialog box. Click the **Themes tab** and select the **Windows XP theme** if it is not already selected. Click **OK**.
- We prefer to work without any wallpaper (background picture) on the desktop. **Right click** the desktop, click **Properties**, then click the **Desktop tab** in the Display Properties dialog box. Click **None** as shown in Figure 7b, then click **OK**. The background disappears.
- The Start menu is modified independently of the theme. **Right click** a blank area of the taskbar, click the **Properties command** to display the Taskbar and Start Menu Properties dialog box, then click the **Start Menu tab**.
- Click the **Start Menu option button**. Click **OK**.

Click Desktop tab

Click right mouse button to display shortcut menu

Click None

Right click blank area on taskbar

Display Properties

(b) Choose the Theme and Start Menu (step 2)

FIGURE 7 Hands-on Exercise 1 (continued)

IMPLEMENT A SCREEN SAVER

A screen saver is a delightful way to personalize your computer and a good way to practice with basic commands in Windows XP. Right click a blank area of the desktop, click the Properties command to open the Display Properties dialog box, then click the Screen Saver tab. Click the down arrow in the Screen Saver list box, choose the desired screen saver, then set the option to wait an appropriate amount of time before the screen saver appears. Click OK to accept the settings and close the dialog box.

New! Larger screen shots with clear callouts.

Boxed tips provide students with additional information.

GETTING STARTED WITH MICROSOFT WINDOWS XP   11

MINI CASES AND PRACTICE EXERCISES

New!

We've added mini cases at the end of each chapter for expanded practice and review.

MINI CASES

The Financial Consultant

A friend of yours is in the process of buying a home and has asked you to compare the payments and total interest on a 15- and 30-year loan at varying interest rates. You have decided to analyze the loans in Excel, and then incorporate the results into a memo written in Microsoft Word. As of now, the principal is $150,000, but it is very likely that your friend will change his mind several times, and so you want to use the linking and embedding capability within Windows to dynamically link the worksheet to the word processing document. Your memo should include a letterhead that takes advantage of the formatting capabilities within Word; a graphic logo would be a nice touch.

Fun with the If Statement

Open the *Chapter 4 Mini Case—Fun with the If Statement* workbook in the Exploring Excel folder, then follow the directions in the worksheet to view a hidden message. The message is displayed by various If statements scattered throughout the worksheet, but the worksheet is protected so that you cannot see these formulas. (Use help to see how to protect a worksheet.) We made it easy for you, however, because you can unprotect the worksheet since a password is not required. Once the worksheet is unprotected, pull down the Format menu, click the Cells command, click the Protection tab, and clear the Hidden check box. Prove to your professor that you have done this successfully, by changing the text of our message. Print the completed worksheet to show both displayed values and cell formulas.

The Lottery

Many states raise money through lotteries that advertise prizes of several million dollars. In reality, however, the actual value of the prize is considerably less than the advertised value, although the winners almost certainly do not care. One state, for example, recently offered a twenty million dollar prize that was to be distributed in twenty annual payments of one million dollars each. How much was the prize actually worth, assuming a long-term interest rate of five percent? Use the PV (Present Value) function to determine the answer. What is the effect on the answer if payments to the recipient are made at the beginning of each year, rather than at the end of each year?

A Penny a Day

What if you had a rich un[...] salary each day for the n[...] prised at how quickly th[...] use the Goal Seek comm[...] (if any) will your uncle pa[...] uncle pay you on the 31s[...]

The Rule of 72

Delaying your IRA for or[...] on when you begin. Tha[...] a calculator, using the "R[...] long it takes money to [...] money earning 8% annu[...] money doubles again in [...] your IRA at age 21, rathe[...] initial contribution. Use[...] lose, assuming an 8% ra[...] determine the exact ame[...]

New!

Each project in the end-of-chapter material begins at the top of a page—now students can easily see where their assignments begin and end.

PRACTICE WITH EXCEL

1. **Theme Park Admissions:** A partially completed version of the worksheet in Figure 3.13 is available in the Exploring Excel folder as *Chapter 3 Practice 1*. Follow the directions in parts (a) and (b) to compute the totals and format the worksheet, then create each of the charts listed below.

   a. Use the AutoSum command to enter the formulas to compute the total number of admissions for each region and each quarter.

   b. Select the entire worksheet (cells A1 through F8), then use the AutoFormat command to format the worksheet. You do not have to accept the entire design, nor do you have to use the design we selected. You can also modify the design after it has been applied to the worksheet by changing the font size of selected cells and/or changing boldface and italics.

   c. Create a column chart showing the total number of admissions in each quarter as shown in Figure 3.13. Add the graphic shown in the figure for emphasis.

   d. Create a pie chart that shows the percentage of the total number of admissions in each region. Create this chart in its own chart sheet with an appropriate name.

   e. Create a stacked column chart that shows the total number of admissions for each region and the contribution of each quarter within each region. Create this chart in its own chart sheet with an appropriate name.

   f. Create a stacked column chart showing the total number of admissions for each quarter and the contribution of each region within each quarter. Create this chart in its own chart sheet with an appropriate name.

   g. Change the color of each of the worksheet tabs.

   h. Print the entire workbook, consisting of the worksheet in Figure 3.13 plus the three additional sheets that you create. Use portrait orientation for the Sales Data worksheet and landscape orientation for the other worksheets. Create a custom header for each worksheet that includes your name, your course, and your instructor's name. Create a custom footer for each worksheet that includes the name of the worksheet. Submit the completed assignment to your instructor.

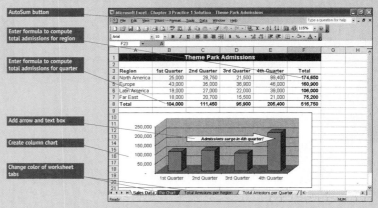

FIGURE 3.13   Theme Park Admissions (exercise 1)

INTEGRATED CASE STUDIES

New!
Each case study contains multiple exercises that use Microsoft Office applications in conjunction with one another.

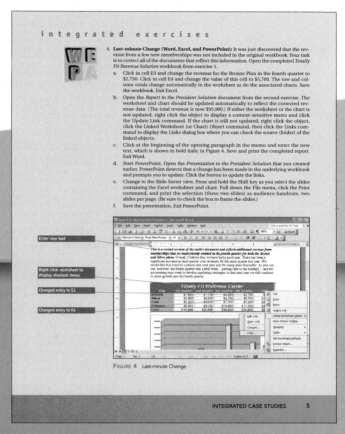

CASE STUDY

1

Integrated Case Study:
The Totally Fit Wellness Center

OBJECTIVES

1. Use the core applications in Office 2003 individually or in conjunction with one another.
2. Link an Excel chart to a Word document and a PowerPoint presentation.
3. Import an Excel worksheet into an Access database.
4. Create Access tables, queries, reports, and forms.
5. Use an Access table as the basis for a mail merge.
6. Use Word to create a Web page for the organization.

integrated exercises

1. Totally Fit Revenue Workbook and Chart (Excel)
2. Report to the President (Word and Excel)
3. Presentation to the President (PowerPoint and Excel)
4. Last-minute Change (Word, Excel, and PowerPoint)
5. Importing Data (Access and Excel)
6. A Relational Database (Access)
7. Access Objects: Forms, Queries, and Reports (Access)
8. An Access Switchboard (Access)
9. Mail Merge (Word and Access)
10. Worksheet References (Excel)
11. Presentation to the Board (PowerPoint and Excel)
12. Letter to the Board (Word and Excel)
13. Create a Home Page (Word)
14. Submission Checklist (Word)

This document provides a series of 13 exercises in Microsoft Office that relate to the Totally Fit Wellness Center, a health center such as might exist at your school or university. Each exercise describes a specific task for the organization to accomplish and typically requires the use of multiple applications within Microsoft Office for solution. Many of the exercises are cumulative in nature. You may, for example, be asked to create an Excel chart in one exercise, and then incorporate that chart into a Word memo and a PowerPoint presentation in subsequent exercises. Other exercises will ask you to create or modify an Access database, to exchange data between Excel and Access, and to create a Web page for the Wellness Center. Collectively, you will gain considerable practice in the core applications of Microsoft Office 2003, and especially in how they work together to accomplish complex tasks.

All of the exercises are based on material from the core application chapters in *Exploring Office 2003 Volume I*. Specific chapter references are deliberately not provided so that the case study is as realistic as possible. Think of this assignment as your first day on the job; you were hired by the Wellness Center because you are proficient in Microsoft Office. This is your chance to show what you know. ■

Your assignment is to follow the directions of your instructor with respect to which of the exercises you are to complete within the case description. You should begin by downloading the practice files from our Web site at www.prenhall.com/grauer. Go to the site, click the book icon for Office 2003, and then click the Students Download tab. Scroll until you can select the link to Integrated Case Studies, and then download the file to your desktop. Double click the file icon and follow the onscreen instructions to install the practice files on your computer. The files you need will be in the Totally Fit folder within the Exploring Integrated Cases folder.

1

4. **Last-minute Change (Word, Excel, and PowerPoint):** It was just discovered that the revenue from a few new memberships was not included in the original workbook. Your task is to correct all of the documents that reflect this information. Open the completed *Totally Fit Revenue Solution* workbook from exercise 1.

a. Click in cell E3 and change the revenue for the Bronze Plan in the fourth quarter to $2,750. Click in cell E4 and change the value of this cell to $5,700. The row and column totals change automatically in the worksheet as do the associated charts. Save the workbook. Exit Excel.

b. Open the *Report to the President Solution* document from the second exercise. The worksheet and chart should be updated automatically to reflect the corrected revenue data. (The total revenue is now $95,900.) If either the worksheet or the chart is not updated, right click the object to display a context-sensitive menu and click the Update Link command. If the chart is still not updated, right click the object, click the Linked Worksheet (or Chart) Object command, then click the Links command to display the Links dialog box where you can check the source (folder) of the linked objects.

c. Click at the beginning of the opening paragraph in the memo and enter the new text, which is shown in bold italic in Figure 4. Save and print the completed report. Exit Word.

d. Start PowerPoint. Open the *Presentation to the President Solution* that you created earlier. PowerPoint detects that a change has been made in the underlying workbook and prompts you to update. Click the button to update the links.

e. Change to the Slide Sorter view. Press and hold the Shift key as you select the slides containing the Excel worksheet and chart. Pull down the File menu, click the Print command, and print the selection (these two slides) as audience handouts, two slides per page. (Be sure to check the box to frame the slides.)

f. Save the presentation. Exit PowerPoint.

FIGURE 4 Last-minute Change

INTEGRATED CASE STUDIES   5

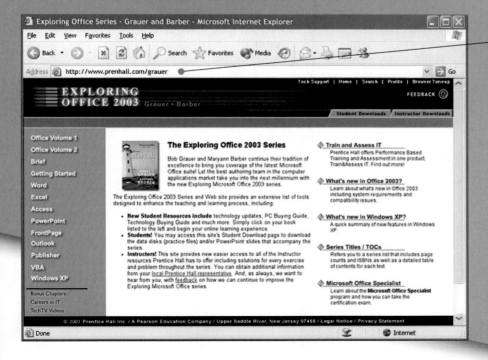

Companion Web site

New!
Updated and enhanced Companion Web site. Find everything you need— student practice files, PowerPoint lectures, online study guides, and instructor support (solutions)!

www.prenhall.com/grauer

Acknowledgments

We want to thank the many individuals who have helped to bring this project to fruition. Jodi McPherson, executive acquisitions editor at Prentice Hall, has provided new leadership in extending the series to Office 2003. Cathi Profitko did an absolutely incredible job on our Web site. Shelly Martin was the creative force behind the chapter-opening case studies. Emily Knight coordinated the marketing and continues to inspire us with suggestions for improving the series. Greg Hubit has been masterful as the external production editor for every book in the series from its inception. Eileen Clark coordinated the myriad details of production and the certification process. Lynne Breitfeller was the project manager and manufacturing buyer. Lori Johnson was the project manager at The GTS Companies and in charge of composition. Chuck Cox did his usual fine work as copyeditor. Melissa Edwards was the supplements editor. Cindy Stevens, Tom McKenzie, and Michael Olmstead wrote the instructor manuals. Michael Fruhbeis developed the innovative and attractive design. We also want to acknowledge our reviewers who, through their comments and constructive criticism, greatly improved the series.

Gregg Asher, Minnesota State University
Lynne Band, Middlesex Community College
Don Belle, Central Piedmont Community College
Stuart P. Brian, Holy Family College
Carl M. Briggs, Indiana University School of Business
Kimberly Chambers, Scottsdale Community College
Jill Chapnick, Florida International University
Alok Charturvedi, Purdue University
Jerry Chin, Southwest Missouri State University
Charles Cole, East Stroudsburg University
Dean Combellick, Scottsdale Community College
Cody Copeland, Johnson County Community College
Larry S. Corman, Fort Lewis College
Janis Cox, Tri-County Technical College
Douglas Cross, Clackamas Community College
Martin Crossland, Southwest Missouri State University
Bill Daley, University of Oregon
Paul E. Daurelle, Western Piedmont Community College
Shawna DePlonty, Sault College of Applied Arts and Technology
Carolyn DiLeo, Westchester Community College
Judy Dolan, Palomar College
David Douglas, University of Arkansas
Carlotta Eaton, Radford University
Cheryl J. Fetterman, Cape Fear Community College
Judith M. Fitspatrick, Gulf Coast Community College
James Franck, College of St. Scholastica
Raymond Frost, Central Connecticut State University
Susan Fry, Boise State University
Midge Gerber, Southwestern Oklahoma State University
James Gips, Boston College
Vernon Griffin, Austin Community College
Ranette Halverson, Midwestern State University
Michael Hassett, Fort Hays State University
Mike Hearn, Community College of Philadelphia
Wanda D. Heller, Seminole Community College

Bonnie Homan, San Francisco State University
Ernie Ivey, Polk Community College
Walter Johnson, Community College of Philadelphia
Mike Kelly, Community College of Rhode Island
Jane King, Everett Community College
Rose M. Laird, Northern Virginia Community College
David Langley, University of Oregon
John Lesson, University of Central Florida
Maurie Lockley, University of North Carolina at Greensboro
Daniela Marghitu, Auburn University
David B. Meinert, Southwest Missouri State University
Alan Moltz, Naugatuck Valley Technical Community College
Kim Montney, Kellogg Community College
Bill Morse, DeVry Institute of Technology
Kevin Pauli, University of Nebraska
Mary McKenry Percival, University of Miami
Marguerite Nedreberg, Youngstown State University
Dr. Francisca Norales, Tennessee State University
Jim Pruitt, Central Washington University
Delores Pusins, Hillsborough Community College
Gale E. Rand, College Misericordia
Judith Rice, Santa Fe Community College
David Rinehard, Lansing Community College
Marilyn Salas, Scottsdale Community College
Herach Safarian, College of the Canyons
John Shepherd, Duquesne University
Barbara Sherman, Buffalo State College
Robert Spear, Prince George's Community College
Michael Stewardson, San Jacinto College—North
Helen Stoloff, Hudson Valley Community College
Margaret Thomas, Ohio University
Mike Thomas, Indiana University School of Business
Suzanne Tomlinson, Iowa State University
Karen Tracey, Central Connecticut State University
Antonio Vargas, El Paso Community College
Sally Visci, Lorain County Community College
David Weiner, University of San Francisco
Connie Wells, Georgia State University
Wallace John Whistance-Smith, Ryerson Polytechnic University
Jack Zeller, Kirkwood Community College

A final word of thanks to the unnamed students at the University of Miami who make it all worthwhile. Most of all, thanks to you, our readers, for choosing this book. Please feel free to contact us with any comments and suggestions.

Robert T. Grauer   Maryann Barber
rgrauer@miami.edu   mbarber@miami.edu
www.prenhall.com/grauer

1

Introduction to PowerPoint:
Presentations Made Easy

CASE STUDY
GAME WORLD

Dave Moles and Cathi Profitko started Game World five years ago. Their vision was, and still is, to create a chain of stores that offers its customers a complete collection of video games for sale, trade, or rent. The two friends struggled initially until they realized that they should focus on the three top players in the market: PlayStation, Xbox, and Nintendo. Sales and profits have climbed steadily ever since. Last year, they broke through the one million dollar barrier as they recorded a 50% increase in sales over the previous year.

Dave and Cathi have already rejected several offers to sell their growing business and are looking to expand. They have demonstrated that their concept is successful and are seeking to franchise their operation, but realize they will need a substantial amount of cash to do so. Thus, they have decided to seek venture capital from outside. One potential source has asked that they create a PowerPoint presentation for their initial meeting that provides a comparison of quarterly revenues between this year and last year. The budding entrepreneurs have asked you to create the presentation and have provided some content in the form of an Excel workbook with financial data, as well as a partially completed presentation. This is an excellent opportunity—you love video games and you have the chance to get in on the ground floor. ■

Your assignment is to read the chapter and then complete the presentation for Dave and Cathi. The Exploring PowerPoint folder contains the two files you will need: the *Chapter 1 Case Study – Game World* presentation and an Excel workbook by the same name. The workbook contains several worksheets, so be sure to link the correct worksheet to the appropriate slide in the presentation. You have also been asked to insert at least one clip art image on slide two and/or slide six for interest. Add transition or animation effects as you see fit. Print the completed presentation as audience handouts.

This chapter introduces you to PowerPoint, one of the four major applications in Microsoft Office (Microsoft Word, Microsoft Excel, and Microsoft Access are the other three). PowerPoint enables you to create a professional presentation without relying on others, then it lets you deliver that presentation in a variety of ways. You can show the presentation on the computer, on the World Wide Web, or even on overhead transparencies.

PowerPoint is easy to learn because it is a Windows application and follows the conventions associated with the common user interface. Thus, if you already know one Windows application, it is that much easier to learn PowerPoint because you can apply what you know. It's even easier if you use Word, Excel, or Access since there are over 100 commands that are common to Microsoft Office.

The chapter begins by showing you an existing PowerPoint presentation so that you can better appreciate what PowerPoint is all about. We discuss the various views within PowerPoint and the advantages of each. We describe how to modify an existing presentation and how to view a presentation on the computer. You are then ready to create your own presentation, a process that requires you to focus on the content and the message you want to deliver. We show you how to enter the text of the presentation, how to add and/or change the format of a slide, and how to apply a design template. We also explain how to animate the presentation to create additional interest. The last portion of the chapter describes how to enhance a presentation through the inclusion of other objects such as a Word table or an Excel chart.

A PowerPoint presentation consists of a series of slides such as those in Figure 1.1. The various slides contain different elements (such as text, photographs, and WordArt), yet the presentation has a consistent look with respect to its overall design and color scheme. You might think that creating this type of presentation is difficult, but it isn't. It is remarkably easy, and that is the beauty of PowerPoint. In essence, PowerPoint allows you to concentrate on the content of a presentation without worrying about its appearance. You supply the text and supporting elements and leave the formatting to PowerPoint.

In addition to helping you create the presentation, PowerPoint provides a variety of ways to deliver it. You can show the presentation on a computer using animated transition effects as you move from one slide to the next. You can include sound and/or video in the presentation, provided your system has a sound card and speakers. You can also automate the presentation and distribute it on a disk for display at a convention booth or kiosk. If you cannot show the presentation on a computer, you can easily convert it to overhead transparencies.

PowerPoint also gives you the ability to print the presentation in various ways to distribute to your audience. You can print one slide per page, or you can print miniature versions of each slide and choose among two, three, four, six, or even nine slides per page. You can prepare notes for yourself consisting of a picture of each slide together with notes about the slide. You can also print the text of the presentation in outline form. Giving the audience a copy of the presentation (in any format) enables them to follow it more closely, and to take it home when the session is over.

POLISH YOUR DELIVERY

The speaker is still the most important part of any presentation, and a poor delivery will kill even the best presentation. Look at the audience as you speak to open communication and gain credibility. Don't read from a prepared script. Speak slowly and clearly and try to vary your delivery. Pause to emphasize key points, and be sure the person in the last row can hear you.

Introduction to PowerPoint

Robert Grauer and Maryann Barber

(a) Title Slide

The Essence of PowerPoint

- ☐ You focus on content
  - ■ Enter your thoughts in an outline or directly on the individual slides
  - ■ Add additional elements such as tables and charts
- ☐ PowerPoint takes care of the design
  - ■ Professionally designed templates
  - ■ Preformatted slide layouts
- ☐ Flexibility in delivery and presentation

(b) Bullet Slide

Flexibility in Output

- ☐ Web-based presentations (HTML documents)
- ☐ Computer presentations (slide show)
- ☐ Print in a variety of formats
  - ■ Audience handouts
  - ■ Outline
  - ■ Speaker notes
- ☐ Traditional - Overhead transparencies

(c) Bullet Slide

Add Objects for Interest

- ☐ Include photographs, clipart, and other objects as appropriate
- ☐ Use animation and sound to add variety
- ☐ Meet Bob and Maryann

(d) Photographs

PowerPoint is Easy to Learn

- ☐ PowerPoint uses the same menus and commands as other Office applications
- ☐ The Standard and Formatting toolbars contain many of the same icons as other applications
- ☐ Common keyboard shortcuts such as **Ctrl+B** and **Ctrl+I** for boldface and italics also apply
- ☐ Help is only a mouse click away

(e) Bullet Slide with Animation

(f) WordArt

FIGURE 1.1   A PowerPoint Presentation

The Common User Interface

The desktop in Figure 1.2 should look somewhat familiar even if you have never used PowerPoint, because PowerPoint shares the common user interface of every Windows application. You should recognize, therefore, the two open windows in Figure 1.2—the application window for PowerPoint and the document window for the current presentation.

The PowerPoint window contains the Minimize, Maximize (or Restore), and Close buttons. The document window, however, contains only a Close button for the current presentation, allowing you to close the presentation, but keep PowerPoint open. The title bar indicates the application (Microsoft PowerPoint) as well as the name of the presentation on which you are working (Introduction to PowerPoint). The *menu bar* appears immediately below the title bar and provides access to the pull-down menus within the application. The presentation appears within the document window and shows the outline of the entire presentation, a graphical image of one slide (the title slide in this example), and speaker notes for the selected slide.

The Standard and Formatting toolbars are displayed below the menu bar and are similar to those in Word and Excel. Hence, you may recognize several buttons from those applications. The *Standard toolbar* contains buttons for the most basic commands in PowerPoint such as opening, saving, and printing a presentation. The *Formatting toolbar*, under the Standard toolbar, provides access to formatting operations such as boldface, italic, and underlining.

The vertical *scroll bar* is seen at the right of the document window and indicates that the presentation contains additional slides that are not visible. This is consistent with the *status bar* at the bottom of the window that indicates you are working on slide 1 of 6. The *Drawing toolbar* appears above the status bar and contains additional tools for working on the slide. The view buttons above the Drawing toolbar are used to switch between the different views of a presentation. PowerPoint views are discussed in the next section.

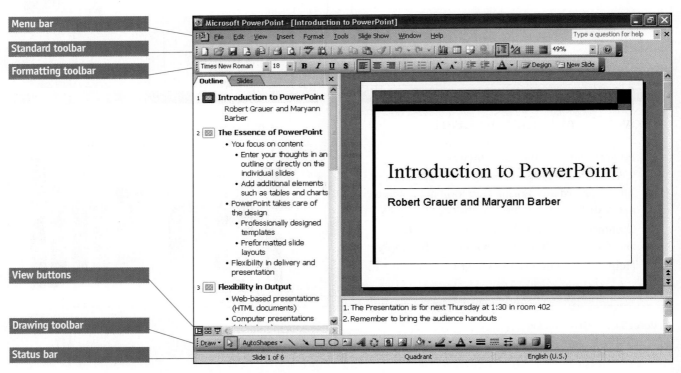

FIGURE 1.2 Introduction to PowerPoint

PowerPoint Views

PowerPoint offers multiple views in which to create, modify, and/or deliver a presentation. Each view represents a different way of looking at the presentation, and each view has unique capabilities. (There is some redundancy among the views in that certain tasks can be accomplished from multiple views.) The View menu and/or the View buttons at the bottom of the presentation enable you to switch from one view to another.

The ***Normal view*** in Figure 1.3a divides the screen into three panes containing an outline of the presentation, an enlarged view of one slide, and the associated speaker notes (if any) for the selected slide. The ***outline*** provides the fastest way to enter or edit text for the presentation. You type directly into the outline and can move easily from one slide to the next. The outline can also be used to move and copy text from one slide to another and/or to rearrange the order of the slides within a presentation. The outline is limited, however, in that it does not show graphic elements that may be present on individual slides. Thus, you may want to switch to the Normal view in Figure 1.3b that contains ***thumbnail images*** (slide miniatures) rather than the outline. This view also lets you change the order of the slides by clicking and dragging a slide to a new position. The Outline and Slides tabs in the left pane let you switch between the two variations of the Normal view.

The Normal view also provides access to the individual slides and/or speaker notes, each of which appears in its own pane. The size of the individual panes in the Normal view can be changed by dragging the border that separates one pane from another. The Normal view is all that you will ever need, but many individuals like to close the left pane completely to see just an individual slide as shown in Figure 1.3c. The individual slide, whether it is in the Normal view or displayed in a window by itself, is where you change text or formatting, add graphical elements, or apply various animation effects.

You can also elect to work in the Notes Page and/or Slide Sorter view. The ***Notes Page view*** in Figure 1.3d is redundant in that speaker notes can be entered from the Normal view. It is convenient, however, to print audience handouts of this view, since each page will contain a picture of the slide plus the associated speaker notes. The notes do not appear when the presentation is shown, but are intended for use by the speaker to help him or her remember the key points about each slide.

The ***Slide Sorter view*** in Figure 1.3e offers yet another view in which to reorder the slides within a presentation. It also provides a convenient way to delete one or more slides and/or to set transition effects for multiple slides simultaneously. Anything that you do in one view is automatically reflected in the other view. If, for example, you change the order of the slides in the Slide Sorter view, the changes will be automatically reflected in the outline or thumbnail images within the Normal view.

The ***Slide Show view*** in Figure 1.3f is used to deliver the completed presentation to an audience, one slide at a time, as an electronic presentation on the computer. The show may be presented manually where the speaker clicks the mouse to move from one slide to the next. The presentation can also be shown automatically, where each slide stays on the screen for a predetermined amount of time, after which the next slide appears automatically. Either way, the slide show may contain various transition effects from one slide to the next.

THE TASK PANE

All views in PowerPoint provide access to a task pane, which facilitates the execution of subsequent commands. The task pane serves many functions. It can be used to open an existing presentation, apply clip art to a slide, change the layout of the elements on a slide, apply transition and animation effects, or change the template of the entire presentation.

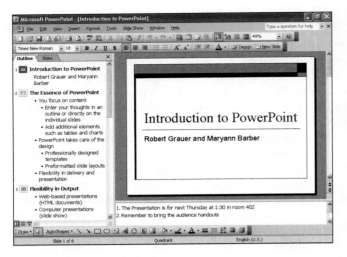

(a) Normal View with Outline

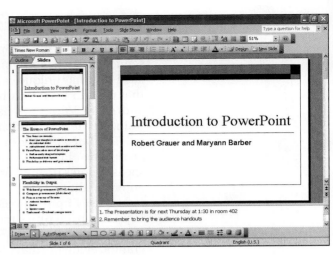

(b) Normal View with Thumbnail Images

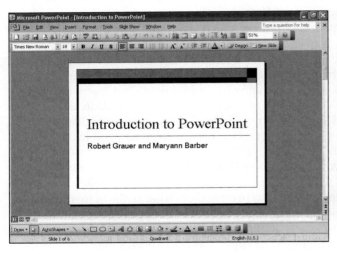

(c) Individual Slide

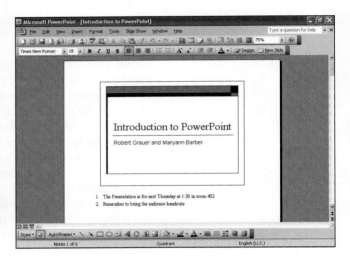

(d) Notes Page View

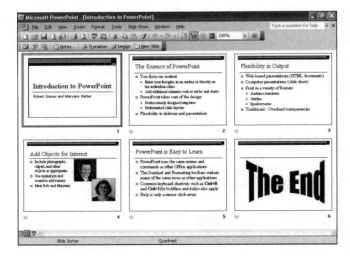

(e) Slide Sorter View

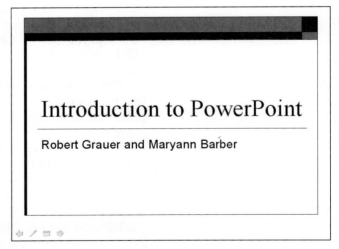

(f) Slide Show View

FIGURE 1.3 Multiple Views

The File Menu

The **File menu** is a critically important menu in virtually every Windows application. It contains the Save and Open commands to save a presentation on disk, then retrieve (open) that presentation at a later time. The File menu also contains the **Print command** to print a presentation, the **Close command** to close the current presentation but continue working in the application, and the **Exit command** to quit the application altogether.

The **Save command** copies the presentation that you are working on (i.e., the presentation that is currently in memory) to disk. The command functions differently the first time it is executed for a new presentation, in that it displays the Save As dialog box as shown in Figure 1.4a. The dialog box requires you to specify the name of the presentation, the drive (and an optional folder) in which the presentation is to be stored, and its file type. All subsequent executions of the command save the presentation under the assigned name, replacing the previously saved version with the new version.

The **file name** (e.g., My First Presentation) can contain up to 255 characters including spaces, commas, and/or periods. (Periods are discouraged, however, since they are too easily confused with DOS extensions.) The Save In list box is used to select the drive (which is not visible in Figure 1.4a) and the folder (e.g., Exploring PowerPoint) in which the file will be saved. The **Places bar** provides shortcuts to frequently used folders without having to search through the Save In list box. Click the Desktop icon, for example, and the file is saved on the Windows desktop. The **file type** defaults to a PowerPoint presentation. You can, however, choose a different format, such as an RTF (Rich Text Format) outline that can be imported into Microsoft Word. You can also save any PowerPoint presentation as a Web page (or HTML document).

The **Open command** is the opposite of the Save command as it brings a copy of an existing presentation into memory, enabling you to work with that presentation. The Open command displays the Open dialog box in which you specify the file name, the drive (and optionally the folder) that contains the file, and the file type. PowerPoint will then list all files of that type on the designated drive (and folder), enabling you to open the file you want.

The Save and Open commands work in conjunction with one another. The Save As dialog box in Figure 1.4a, for example, saves the file My First Presentation in the Exploring PowerPoint folder. The Open dialog box in Figure 1.4b loads that file into memory so that you can work with the file, after which you can save the revised file for use at a later time.

The toolbars in the Save As and Open dialog boxes have several buttons in common that facilitate the execution of either command. The Views button lets you display the files in different views. The Details view (in Figure 1.4a) shows the file size as well as the date and time that the file was last modified. The Preview view (in Figure 1.4b) shows the first slide in a presentation, without having to open the presentation. The List view displays only the file names, and thus lets you see more files at one time. The Properties view shows information about the presentation, including the date of creation and number of revisions.

FILE MANAGEMENT AT YOUR FINGERTIPS

Use the toolbar in the Open and/or Save As dialog boxes to perform basic file management within an Office application. You can select any existing file, and delete it or rename it. You can create a new folder, which is very useful when you begin to work with a large number of documents. You can also use the Views button to change the way the files are listed within the dialog box. Point to any tool to display a ScreenTip indicative of its function.

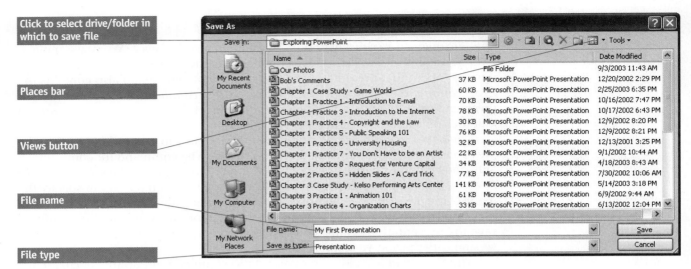

Click to select drive/folder in which to save file

Places bar

Views button

File name

File type

(a) Save As Dialog Box (Details view)

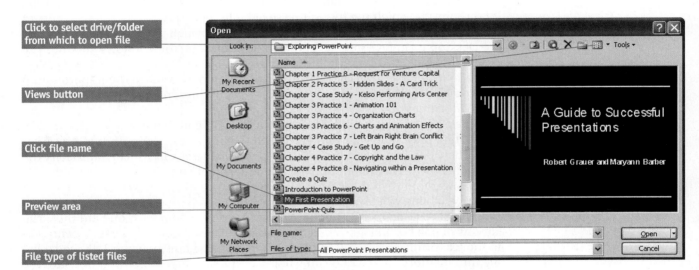

Click to select drive/folder from which to open file

Views button

Click file name

Preview area

File type of listed files

(b) Open Dialog Box (Preview view)

FIGURE 1.4   The Save and Open Commands

SORT BY NAME, DATE, OR FILE SIZE

The files in the Save As and Open dialog boxes can be displayed in ascending or descending sequence by name, date modified, or size. Change to the Details view, then click the heading of the desired column; for example, click the Modified column to list the files according to the date they were last changed. Click the column heading a second time to reverse the sequence—that is, to switch from ascending to descending, and vice versa.

1 Introduction to PowerPoint

Objective To start PowerPoint, open an existing presentation, and modify the text on an existing slide; to show an existing presentation and print handouts of its slides. Use Figure 1.5 as a guide in the exercise.

Step 1: **Log on to Windows XP**

- Turn on the computer and all of its peripherals. The floppy drive should be empty prior to starting your machine.

- Your system will take a minute or so to get started, after which you should see a logon screen similar to Figure 1.5a. Do not be concerned if the appearance of your desktop is different from ours.

- Click the icon for the user account you want to access. You may be prompted for a password, depending on the security options in effect.

- You should be familiar with basic file management and very comfortable moving and copying files from one folder to another. If not, you may want to review the material in the Windows XP section of this text.

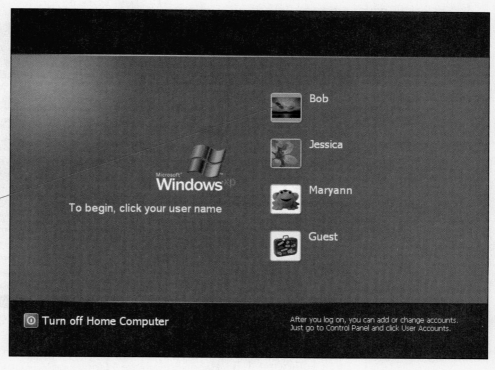

Click icon for your user account

(a) Log on to Windows XP (step 1)

FIGURE 1.5 Hands-on Exercise 1

USER ACCOUNTS

The available user names are created automatically during the installation of Windows XP, but you can add or delete users at any time. Click the Start button, click Control Panel, switch to the Category view, and select User Accounts. Choose the desired task, such as creating a new account or changing an existing account. Do not expect, however, to be able to modify accounts in a school setting.

Step 2: Obtain the Practice Files

- Start Internet Explorer and go to **www.prenhall.com/grauer**. Click the book for **Office 2003**, which takes you to the Office 2003 home page. Click the **Student Downloads tab** (near the top of the window) to go to the Student Downloads page as shown in Figure 1.5b.

- Select the appropriate file to download.
  - ❑ Choose **Exploring PowerPoint** (or **PowerPoint Volume I**) if you are using a stand-alone PowerPoint text.
  - ❑ Choose **Office 2003 Volume I** (for regular or **Enhanced Edition**), **Office 2003 Plus**, or **Office 2003 Brief** if you have an Office text.

- Click the link to download the file. You will see the File Download box asking what you want to do. Click the **Save button**. The Save As dialog box appears.

- Click the **down arrow** in the Save In list box and select the drive and folder where you want to save the file. Click **Save**.

- Start Windows Explorer, select the drive and folder where you saved the file, then double click the file and follow the onscreen instructions.

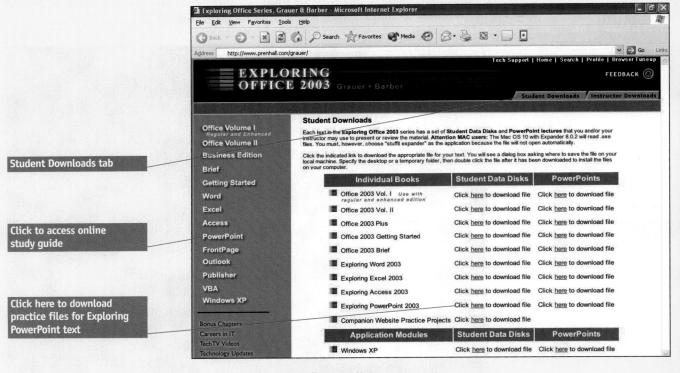

Student Downloads tab

Click to access online study guide

Click here to download practice files for Exploring PowerPoint text

(b) Obtain the Practice Files (step 2)

FIGURE 1.5 Hands-on Exercise 1 (*continued*)

EXPLORE OUR WEB SITE

The Exploring Office Series Web site offers an online study guide (multiple-choice, true/false, and matching questions) for each individual textbook to help you review the material in each chapter. You can take practice quizzes by yourself and/or e-mail the results to your instructor. These online study guides are available via the tabs in the left navigation bar. You can return to the Student Downloads page at any time by clicking the tab toward the top of the window and/or you can click the link to Home to return to the home page for the Office 2003 Series. And finally, you can click the Feedback button at the top of the screen to send a message directly to Bob Grauer.

Step 3: Open a Presentation

- Click the **Start button** to display the Start menu. Click (or point to) the **All Programs button**, click **Microsoft Office**, then click **Microsoft Office PowerPoint 2003** to start the program. Close the task pane.

- Pull down the **File menu** and click the **Open command** (or click the **Open button** on the Standard toolbar).

- You should see an Open dialog box similar to the one in Figure 1.5c. Click the **drop-down arrow** on the Look In list box. Click the appropriate drive, drive C or drive A, depending on the location of your data.

- Double click the **Exploring PowerPoint folder** within the Look In box to make it the active folder. This is the folder from which you will retrieve and into which you will save the presentation.

- Click the **Views button** repeatedly to cycle through the different views. We selected the Preview view in Figure 1.5c.

- Double click **Introduction to PowerPoint** to open the presentation and begin the exercise.

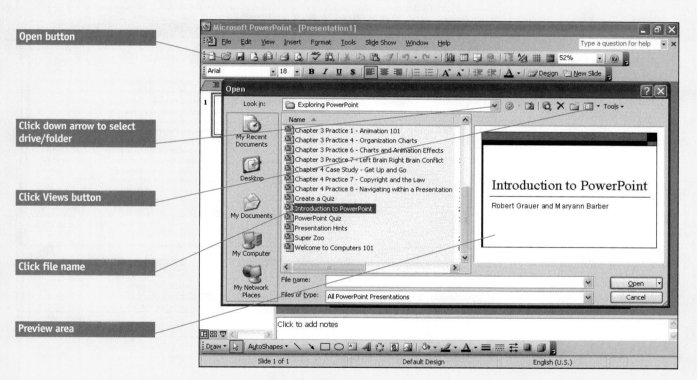

(c) Open a Presentation (step 3)

FIGURE 1.5 Hands-on Exercise 1 (*continued*)

SEPARATE THE TOOLBARS

You may see the Standard and Formatting toolbars displayed on one row to save space within the application window. If so, we suggest you separate the toolbars, so that you see all of the buttons on each. The easiest way to do this is to click the down arrow at the end of any toolbar, then click the option to show the buttons on two rows. You can click the down arrow a second time to show the buttons on one row if you want to return to the other configuration.

Step 4: The Save As Command

- If necessary, click the **Maximize button** in the application window so that PowerPoint takes the entire desktop.

- Pull down the **File menu**. Click the **Save As command** to display the dialog box shown in Figure 1.5d.

- Enter **Introduction to PowerPoint Solution** as the name of the new presentation. Click the **Save button**.

- There are now two identical copies of the file on disk, "Introduction to PowerPoint", which is the original presentation that we supplied, and "Introduction to PowerPoint Solution", which you just created.

- The title bar shows the latter name, as it is the presentation currently in memory. All subsequent changes will be made to this version. (You can always return to the original presentation if necessary.)

Create New Folder button

Click down arrow to select drive/folder

Enter file name

(d) The Save As Command (step 4)

FIGURE 1.5 Hands-on Exercise 1 (*continued*)

CREATE A NEW FOLDER

All Office documents are stored in the My Documents folder by default. It's helpful, however, to create additional folders, especially if you work with a large number of different documents. You can create one folder for school and another for work, and/or you can create different folders for different applications. To create a folder, pull down the File menu, click the Save As command, then click the Create New Folder button to display the New Folder dialog box. Enter the name of the folder, then click OK to create the folder. Once the folder has been created, use the Look In box to change to that folder the next time you open or save a presentation.

Step 5: Modify a Slide

- Click the *Outline tab* in the left pane. Click and drag the border separating the outline from the slide to give yourself more room to work.

- Press and hold the left mouse button as you drag the mouse over the presenters' names, **Robert Grauer and Maryann Barber**. You can select the text in either the outline or the slide pane.

- Release the mouse. The names should be highlighted (selected) as shown in Figure 1.5e. The selected text is affected by the next command.

- Type your name, which automatically replaces the selected text in both the outline and the slide pane. Press **Enter**.

- Type your class on the next line and note that the entry is made in both the slide and the outline panes.

- Pull down the **File menu** and click the **Save command** (or click the **Save button** on the Standard toolbar).

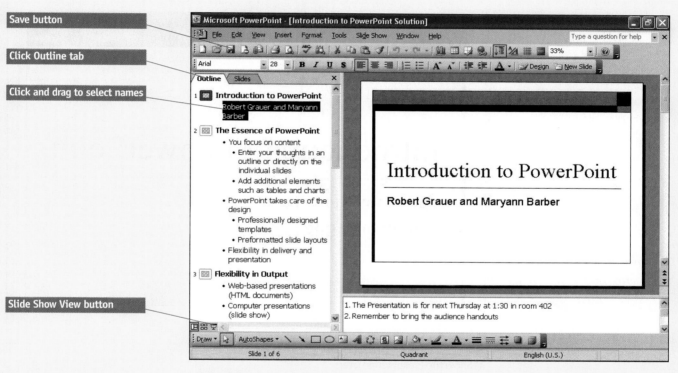

(e) Modify a Slide (step 5)

FIGURE 1.5   Hands-on Exercise 1 (*continued*)

THE AUTOMATIC SPELL CHECK

A red wavy line under a word indicates that the word is misspelled, or in the case of a proper name, that the word may be spelled correctly, but that it is not in the dictionary. In either event, point to the underlined word and click the right mouse button to display a shortcut menu. Select the appropriate spelling from the list of suggestions or add the word to the supplementary dictionary. To enable (disable) the automatic spell check, pull down the Tools menu, click the Options command, click the Spelling and Style tab, then check (clear) the option to check spelling as you type.

Step 6: Show the Presentation

- Press **Ctrl+Home** to return to the first slide. Click the **Slide Show button** above the status bar, or pull down the **View menu** and click **Slide Show**.

- The presentation will begin with the first slide as shown in Figure 1.5f.

- Click the mouse to move to the second slide. The first slide exits to the left, which is one of several transition effects used to add interest to a presentation.

- Click the mouse to go to the next (third) slide, which illustrates an animation effect. This requires you to click the mouse to display each succeeding bullet.

- Continue to view the show until you come to the end of the presentation. You can press the **Esc key** at any time to cancel the show and return to the PowerPoint window. Note the transition effects and the use of sound (provided you have speakers on your system) to enhance the presentation.

- Do you see how PowerPoint will help you to become a better public speaker?

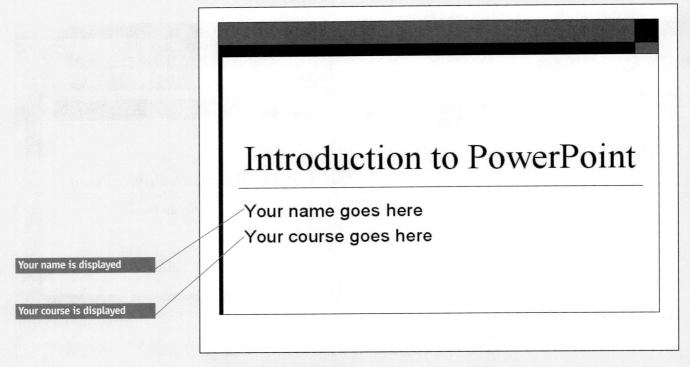

(f) Show the Presentation (step 6)

FIGURE 1.5 Hands-on Exercise 1 (*continued*)

ANNOTATE A SLIDE

Press Ctrl+P to change the mouse pointer to a point, then click and drag on the slide during the presentation to annotate the slide in much the same way your favorite football announcer diagrams a play. Use the PgDn and PgUp keys to move forward and back in the presentation while the annotation is in effect. The annotations will disappear when you exit the slide show unless you elect to keep them permanently when prompted at the end of the show. You can also type the letter E at any time to erase the annotations from a specific slide. Press Ctrl+A to change the mouse pointer back to an arrow.

Step 7: **Print the Presentation**

- Pull down the **File menu**. Click **Print** to display the Print dialog box in Figure 1.5g. (Clicking the Print button on the Standard toolbar does not display the Print dialog box.)

- Click the **down arrow** in the **Print what** drop-down list box, click **Handouts**, and specify **6** slides per page as shown in Figure 1.5g.

- Check the box to **Frame Slides**. Check that the **All option button** is selected under Print range. Click the **OK command button** to print the handouts for the presentation.

- Pull down the **File menu** a second time and click the **Print command**. Click the **down arrow** in the Print what list box and select **Outline View** to print the presentation in outline form. Click **OK**.

- Execute the **File Print command** a third and final time. Click the **Slides option button**, then type **1** in the associated text box to print only the first slide. Click the **down arrow** in the Print what list box and select **Slides** to print the first slide as a cover sheet. Click **OK**.

Click All

Specify 6 slides per page

Click down arrow on Print what box and click Handouts

Check box to Frame slides

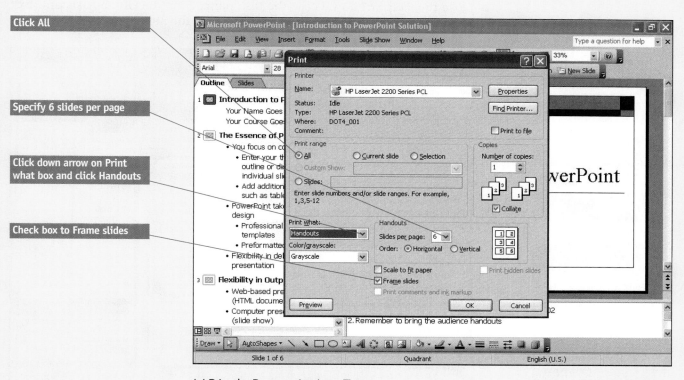

(g) Print the Presentation (step 7)

FIGURE 1.5   Hands-on Exercise 1 (*continued*)

SHOW THE KEYBOARD SHORTCUT IN A SCREENTIP

You can expand the ScreenTip associated with any toolbar button to include the equivalent keyboard shortcut. Pull down the View menu, click Toolbars, then click Customize to display the Customize dialog box. Click the Options tab and check the box to show the shortcut keys in the ScreenTips. Close the dialog box, then point to any toolbar button, and you should see the name of the button as well as the equivalent keyboard shortcut. There is no need to memorize the shortcuts, but they are useful.

Step 8: **Help With PowerPoint**

- The best time to obtain help is when you don't need any. Try either of the following:
  - ❏ Pull down the **Help menu** and click the command to **Show the Office Assistant**. Click the **Assistant**, then enter the question, **"How do I get help?"** in the Assistant's balloon and click **Search**, or
  - ❏ Type the question directly in the **Ask a Question box** in the upper right of the PowerPoint window and press **Enter**.

- Regardless of the technique you choose, PowerPoint will display a message indicating that it is searching the Office Web site. (Help is not available locally, and this can be a problem with a slow Internet connection.)

- You should see a task pane with the results of the search as shown in Figure 1.5h. Click the link that is most appropriate (e.g., About getting help while you work in this example).

- A new window opens containing the detailed help information. Click the **Print button** in the Help window to print the help topic for your instructor.

- Close the Help window. Close the task pane. Hide the Office Assistant. Exit PowerPoint if you do not want to continue with the next exercise at this time.

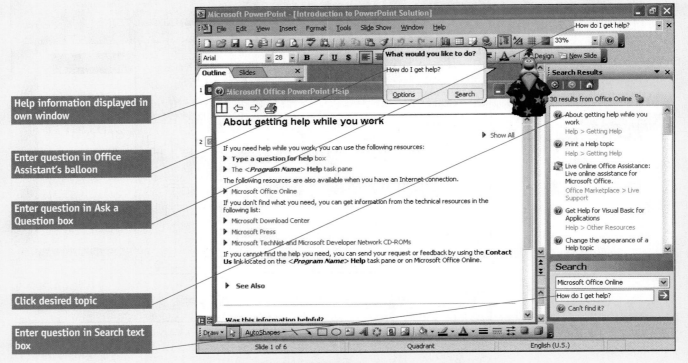

(h) Help with PowerPoint (step 8)

FIGURE 1.5 Hands-on Exercise 1 (*continued*)

TIP OF THE DAY

Pull down the Help menu, click the command to show the Office Assistant, click the Office Assistant when it appears, then click the Options button to display the Office Assistant dialog box. Click the Options tab, check the box to Show the Tip of the Day at Startup, then click OK. The next time you start PowerPoint, you will be greeted by the Assistant, who will offer you the tip of the day.

You are ready to create your own presentation, a process that requires you to develop its content and apply the formatting through the use of a template or design specification. You can do the steps in either order, but we suggest you start with the content. Both steps are iterative in nature, and you are likely to go back and forth many times before you are finished.

You will also find yourself switching from one view to another as you develop the presentation. It doesn't matter which view you use, as long as you can accomplish what you set out to do. You can, for example, enter text one slide at a time in the Slide Normal view. You can also use the outline as shown in Figure 1.6, to view the text of many slides at the same time and thus gain a better sense of the overall presentation.

Each slide in the outline contains a title, followed by bulleted items, which are indented one to five levels, corresponding to the importance of the item. The main points appear on level one. Subsidiary items are indented below the main point to which they apply. Any item can be **promoted** to a higher level or **demoted** to a lower level, either before or after the text is entered. Each slide in the outline is numbered, and the numbers adjust automatically for the insertion or deletion of slides as you edit the presentation.

Consider, for example, slide 4 in Figure 1.6a. The title of the slide, *Develop the Content*, appears immediately after the slide number and icon. The first bullet, *Use the outline*, is indented one level under the title, and it in turn has two subsidiary bullets. The next main bullet, *Review the flow of ideas*, is moved back to level one, and it, too, has two subsidiary bullets.

The outline is (to us) the ideal way to create and edit the presentation. The **insertion point** marks the place where new text is entered and is established by clicking anywhere in the outline. (The insertion point is automatically placed at the title of the first slide in a new presentation.) Press Enter after typing the title or after entering the text of a bulleted item, which starts a new slide or bullet, respectively. The new item may then be promoted or demoted as necessary.

Editing is accomplished through the same techniques used in other Windows applications. For example, you can use the Cut, Copy, and Paste commands in the Edit menu (or the corresponding buttons on the Standard toolbar) to move and copy selected text, or you can simply drag and drop text from one place to another. You can also use the Find and Replace commands that are found in every Office application.

Note, too, that you can format text in the outline by using the **select-then-do** approach common to all Office applications; that is, you select the text, then you execute the appropriate command or click the appropriate button. The selected text remains highlighted and is affected by all subsequent commands until you click elsewhere in the outline.

Figure 1.6b displays a collapsed view of the outline, which displays only the title of each slide. The advantage to this view is that you see more slides on the screen at the same time, making it easier to move slides within the presentation. The slides are expanded or collapsed using tools on the **Outlining toolbar**.

CRYSTALLIZE YOUR MESSAGE

Every presentation exists to deliver a message, whether it's to sell a product, present an idea, or provide instruction. Decide on the message you want to deliver, then write the text for the presentation. Edit the text to be sure it is consistent with your objective. Then, and only then, should you think about formatting, but you should always keep the message foremost in your mind. The success of any presentation will ultimately depend on its content.

1 ▦ **A Guide to Successful Presentations**
    Robert Grauer and Maryann Barber

2 ▦ **Define the Audience**
    - Who is in the audience
        - Managers
        - Coworkers
        - Clients
    - What are their expectations

3 ▦ **Create the Presentation**
    - Develop the content
    - Format the presentation
    - Animate the slide show

4 ▦ **Develop the Content**
    - Use the outline
        - Demote items (Tab)
        - Promote items (Shift+Tab)
    - Review the flow of ideas
        - Cut, copy, and paste text
        - Drag and drop

5 ▦ **Format the Presentation**
    - Choose a design template
    - Customize the template
        - Change the color scheme
        - Change the background shading
    - Modify the slide masters

6 ▦ **Animate the Slide Show**
    - Transitions
    - Animations
    - Hidden slides

7 ▦ **Tips for Delivery**
    - Rehearse timings
    - Arrive early
    - Maintain eye contact
    - Know your audience

(a) The Expanded Outline

1 ▦ **A Guide to Successful Presentations**

2 ▦ **Define the Audience**

3 ▦ **Create the Presentation**

4 ▦ **Develop the Content**

5 ▦ **Format the Presentation**

6 ▦ **Animate the Slide Show**

7 ▦ **Tips for Delivery**

(b) The Collapsed Outline

FIGURE 1.6 The Presentation Outline

Slide Layouts

New slides are typically created as text slides, consisting of a slide title and a single column of bullets. The layout of a text (or any other) slide can be changed, however, to include clip art or other objects, and/or to display a double column of bullets. The new elements can be added manually by using the various tools on the Drawing toolbar or by letting PowerPoint change the layout for you.

PowerPoint provides a set of predefined *slide layouts* that determine the nature and position of the objects on a slide. The layouts are displayed by default within the task pane whenever the Insert menu is used to add a slide. Just insert the slide, then select the desired layout from the task pane. You can also change the layout of an existing slide by selecting the slide and choosing a different layout from the task pane. (Use the View menu to toggle the task pane open, then click the down arrow within the task pane to display the slide layouts.)

Figure 1.7 illustrates the creation of a two-column text slide, which in turn has three *placeholders* that determine the position of each object. Once the layout has been selected, you simply click the appropriate placeholder to add the title or text. Thus, you would click on the placeholder for the title and enter the text of the title as indicated. In similar fashion, you click the placeholder for either column of bullets and enter the associated text.

Other layouts include clip art, organization charts, and other objects. There are additional content layouts for a table, picture, diagram, or media clip. (You can change the size and/or position of the placeholders by moving and sizing the placeholders just as you would any other object.) It's easy, as you will see in the hands-on exercise, which follows shortly.

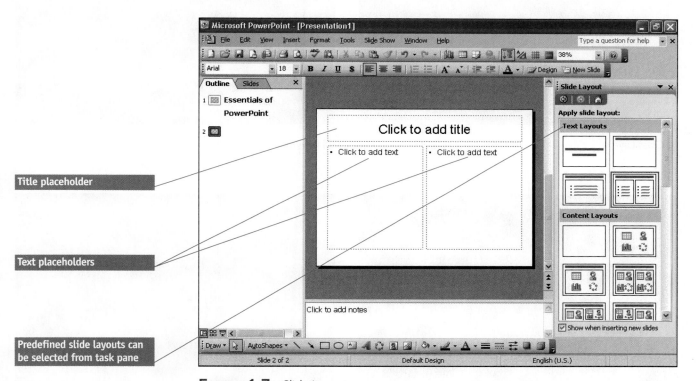

FIGURE 1.7 Slide Layouts

PowerPoint enables you to concentrate on the content of a presentation without concern for its appearance. You focus on what you are going to say, and trust in PowerPoint to format the presentation attractively. The formatting is implemented automatically by selecting one of the many templates that are supplied with PowerPoint.

A *template* is a design specification that controls every element in a presentation. It specifies the color scheme for the slides and the arrangement of the different elements (placeholders) on each slide. It determines the formatting of the text, the fonts that are used, and the size and placement of the bulleted text.

Figure 1.8 displays the title slide of a presentation in four different templates. Just choose the template you like, and PowerPoint formats the entire presentation according to that template. And don't be afraid to change your mind. You can use the Slide Design command at any time to select a different template and change the look of your presentation.

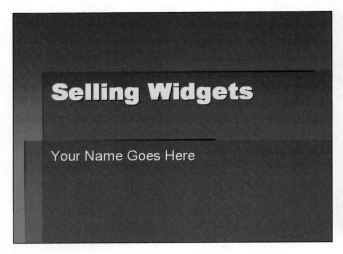

(a) Glass Layers

(b) Fireworks

(c) Maple

(d) Ocean

FIGURE 1.8 Templates

2 Creating a Presentation

Objective   To create a new presentation; to apply a design template to a presentation. Use Figure 1.9 as a guide.

Step 1:   **Create a New Presentation**

- Click the **Start button**, click the **All Programs button**, click **Microsoft Office**, then click **Microsoft PowerPoint** to start PowerPoint. PowerPoint opens with a new blank presentation.

- If necessary, pull down the **View menu** and switch to the **Normal view** and click the **Outline tab** as shown in Figure 1.9a.

- Hide the Office Assistant if it appears. You can get help without the Assistant by using the Ask a Question box.

- Close the task pane.

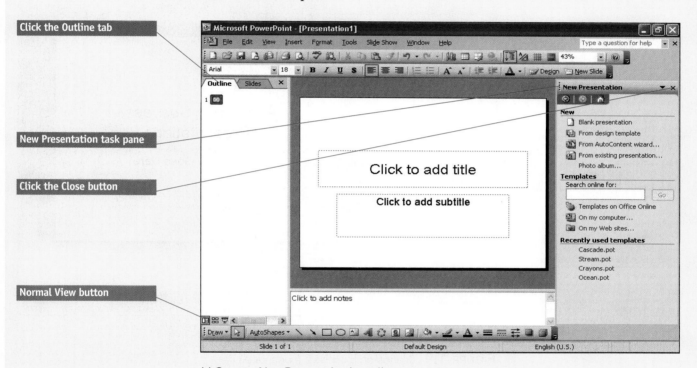

(a) Create a New Presentation (step 1)

FIGURE 1.9   Hands-on Exercise 2

EXPLORE THE TASK PANE

Different task panes are displayed at different times, depending on what you want to accomplish. The Getting Started task pane is displayed when PowerPoint is started initially, and it contains links to the last several presentations that were opened. The New Presentation task pane suggests different ways to create a presentation; e.g., by using the AutoContent Wizard, which is discussed in Chapter 2. Other task panes are displayed automatically according to the selected command. You can also use the Ctrl+F1 keyboard shortcut to open (close) the task pane at any time.

Step 2: Create the Title Slide

■ Click anywhere in the box containing **Click to add title**, then type the title, **A Guide to Successful Presentations**, as shown in Figure 1.9b. The title will automatically wrap to a second line.

■ Click anywhere in the box containing **Click to add subtitle** and enter your name. Click outside the subtitle placeholder when you have entered your name on the slide.

■ The outline now contains the title of the presentation as well as your name. You can use the outline to change either element.

■ Click in the Notes pane and enter a note that pertains to the title slide—for example, the date and time that the presentation is scheduled. The notes are primarily for the speaker, but can also be distributed to the audience.

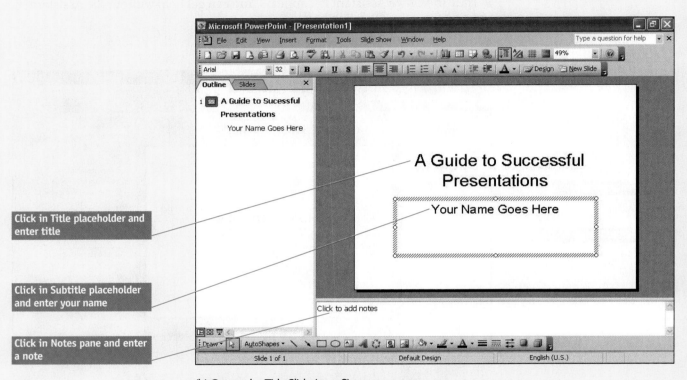

Click in Title placeholder and enter title

Click in Subtitle placeholder and enter your name

Click in Notes pane and enter a note

(b) Create the Title Slide (step 2)

FIGURE 1.9 Hands-on Exercise 2 (*continued*)

THE UNDO AND REDO COMMANDS

Click the drop-down arrow next to the Undo button to display a list of your previous actions, then click the action you want to undo, which also undoes all of the preceding commands. Undoing the fifth command in the list, for example, will also undo the preceding four commands. The Redo command works in reverse and cancels the last Undo command.

Step 3: **Save the Presentation**

- Pull down the **File menu** and click **Save** (or click the **Save button** on the Standard toolbar). You should see the Save As dialog box in Figure 1.9c. If necessary, click the **down arrow** on the **Views button** and click **Details**.

- To save the file:
  - ❏ Click the **drop-down arrow** on the Save In list box.
  - ❏ Click the appropriate drive, drive C or drive A, depending on whether or not you installed the data disk on your hard drive.
  - ❏ Double click the **Exploring PowerPoint folder** to make it the active folder (the folder in which you will save the document).
  - ❏ Enter **My First Presentation** as the name of the presentation.

- Click **Save** or press the **Enter key**. The title bar changes to reflect the name of the presentation.

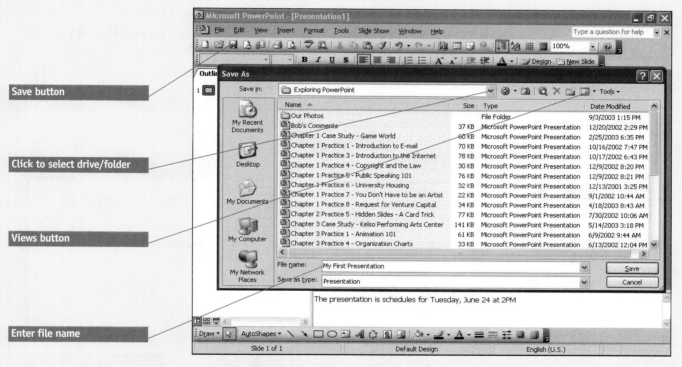

(c) Save the Presentation (step 3)

FIGURE 1.9   Hands-on Exercise 2 (*continued*)

CHANGE THE DEFAULT FOLDER

The default folder is where PowerPoint goes initially to open an existing presentation or to save a new presentation. If you have your own machine, however, you may find it useful to change the default folder. Pull down the Tools menu, click the Options command, then click the Save tab within the Options dialog box. Click in the text box that contains the default file location, enter a new folder, and click OK. The next time you open or save a file, PowerPoint will go automatically to that location.

Step 4: Enter the Text

- Check that the Outlining toolbar is displayed. If not, pull down the **View menu**, click the **Toolbars command**, then click **Outlining** to show the toolbar.

- Click and drag the border between the outline pane and the slide pane to enlarge the outline pane.

- Click after your name in the outline pane. Press **Enter** to begin a new item, then press **Shift+Tab** to promote the item and create slide 2. Type **Define the Audience**. Press **Enter**.

- Press the **Tab key** (or click the **Demote button** on the Outlining toolbar) to enter the first bullet. Type **Who is in the audience** and press **Enter**.

- Press the **Tab key** to enter the second-level bullets. Type **Managers**. Press **Enter**. Type **Coworkers**. Press **Enter**. Type **Clients**. Press **enter**.

- Press **Shift+Tab** (or click the **Promote button** on the Outlining toolbar) to return to the first-level bullets. Type **What are their expectations**. Press **Enter**.

- Press **Shift+Tab** to enter the title of the third slide. Type **Tips for Delivery**. Press **Enter**, then press the **Tab key** to create the first bullet.

- Add the remaining text for this slide and for slide 4 as shown in Figure 1.9d.

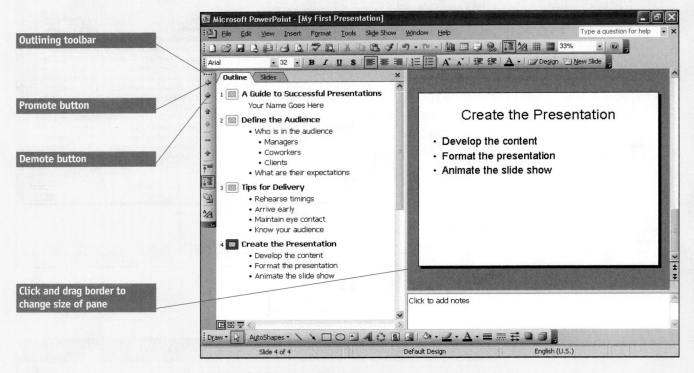

(d) Enter the Text (step 4)

FIGURE 1.9 Hands-on Exercise 2 (*continued*)

JUST KEEP TYPING

The easiest way to enter the text for a presentation is to type continually in the outline. Just type an item, then press Enter to move to the next item. You will be automatically positioned at the next item on the same level, where you can type the next entry. Continue to enter text in this manner. Press the Tab key as necessary to demote an item (move it to the next lower level). Press Shift+Tab to promote an item (move it to the next higher level).

Step 5: **The Thesaurus and Spell Check**

■ Enter the text of the remaining slides as shown in Figure 1.9e. Do *not* press Enter after entering the last bullet on the last slide or else you will get a blank bullet.

■ Click anywhere within the word "**Hidden**" that appears on the last slide. Pull down the **Tools menu** and click the **Thesaurus command** to open the research task pane, which automatically displays synonyms for the selected word.

■ Point to the desired replacement (e.g., concealed), click the **drop-down arrow** to display a menu, and click **Insert** to replace "hidden" with "concealed". Click the **Undo button** to return to the original text if you prefer the original word.

■ Click the **Spelling button** on the Standard toolbar to check for spelling. The result of the spell check depends on how accurately you entered the text of the presentation. We deliberately misspelled the word *Transitions*.

■ Continue to check the document for spelling errors. Click **OK** when PowerPoint indicates it has checked the entire presentation.

■ Click the **Save button** on the Standard toolbar to save the presentation.

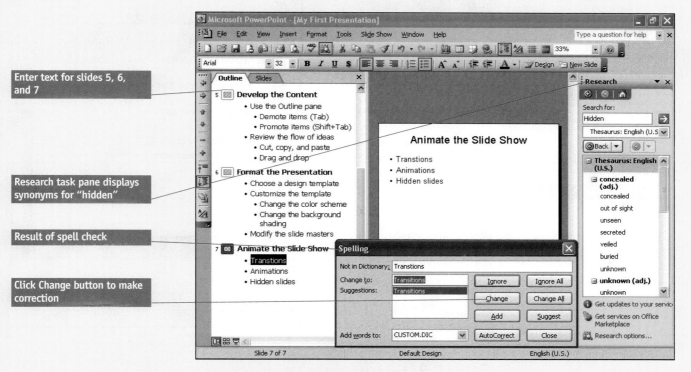

(e) The Thesaurus and Spell Check (step 5)

FIGURE 1.9 Hands-on Exercise 2 (*continued*)

THE RESEARCH TASK PANE

Microsoft Office 2003 brings the resources of the Web directly into the application. Pull down the Tools menu and click the Research command to open the Research task pane. Type the entry you are searching for, click the down arrow to choose a reference book, then click the green arrow to initiate the search. You have access to a dictionary, thesaurus, and encyclopedia. You even have an online bilingual dictionary. Research has never been easier.

Step 6: **Drag and Drop**

- Press **Ctrl+Home** to move to the beginning of the presentation. (If you don't see the Outlining toolbar, pull down the **View menu**, click the **Toolbars command**, and check **Outlining** to display the toolbar.)

- Click the **Collapse All button** on the Outlining toolbar to collapse the outline as shown in Figure 1.9f.

- Click the **icon** for **slide 3** (Tips for Delivery) to select the slide. Point to the **Slide icon** (the mouse pointer changes to a four-headed arrow), then click and drag to move the slide to the end of the presentation.

- All of the slides have been renumbered. The slide titled Tips for Delivery has been moved to the end of the presentation and appears as slide 7. Click the **Expand All button** to display the contents of each slide.

- Click anywhere in the presentation to deselect the last slide.

- Save the presentation.

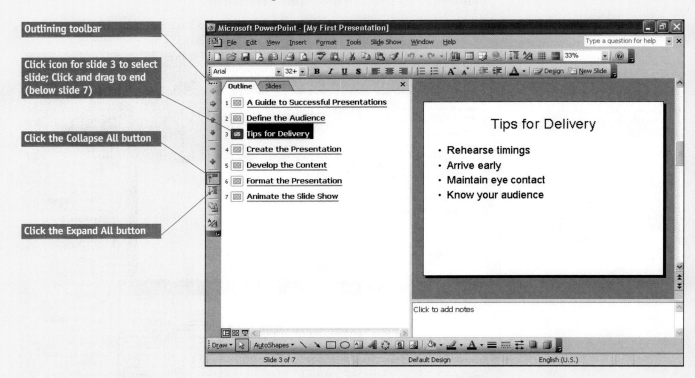

(f) Drag and Drop (step 6)

FIGURE 1.9 Hands-on Exercise 2 (*continued*)

SELECTING SLIDES IN THE OUTLINE

Click the slide icon or the slide number next to the slide title to select the slide. PowerPoint will select the entire slide (including its title, text, and any other objects that are not visible in the outline). Click the first slide, then press and hold the Shift key as you click the ending slide to select a group of sequential slides. Press Ctrl+A to select the entire outline. You can use these techniques to select multiple slides regardless of whether the outline is collapsed or expanded. The selected slides can be copied, moved, expanded, collapsed, or deleted as a unit.

Step 7: **Choose a Design Template**

■ Pull down the **Format menu** and click the **Slide Design command** to open the task pane as shown in Figure 1.9g. (This command will change the contents of the task pane if the task pane is already open.)

■ Click the **down arrow** on the scroll bar within the task pane to scroll through the available designs until you find one that you like. (We chose the Ocean design.) Click the selected design in the task pane to apply this template to your presentation.

■ Select a different design to see how your presentation looks when set in another template.

■ Click the **Undo button** to cancel the last command and return to the previous design. Click the **Redo button** to reverse the undo operation.

■ Spend a few minutes (and *limit* yourself to a few minutes) until you have the design you like.

■ Save the presentation.

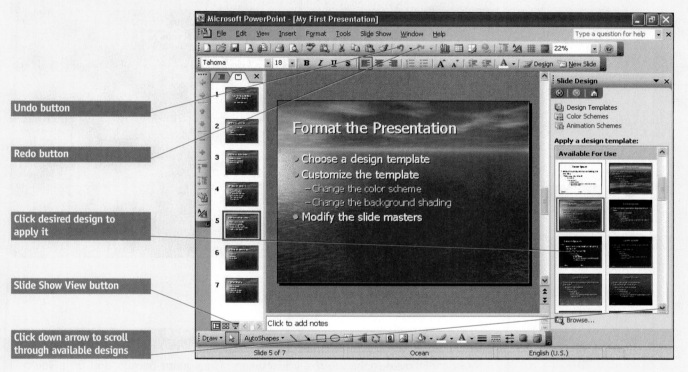

(g) Choose a Design Template (step 7)

FIGURE 1.9   Hands-on Exercise 2 (*continued*)

CUSTOMIZE THE SELECTED TEMPLATE

PowerPoint offers a wide variety of professional templates that are suitable for virtually every presentation. Even so, you will find yourself wanting to customize a template, perhaps by adding a unifying corporate logo, modifying a placeholder, changing a font style or size, or moving a placeholder. You could change every slide individually, but it is much easier to modify the underlying slide master, which controls the formatting and other elements that appear on the individual slides. Any change to the slide master is automatically reflected in every slide except the title slide. See practice exercise 9 at the end of the chapter.

Step 8: **View the Presentation**

- Press **Ctrl+Home** to move to the beginning of the presentation. Click the **Slide Show button** on the status bar to view the presentation as shown in Figure 1.9h.
  - ❑ To move to the next slide: Click the **left mouse button**, type the letter **N**, or press the **PgDn key**.
  - ❑ To move to the previous slide: Type the letter **P** or press the **PgUp key**.

- Continue to move from one slide to the next until you come to the end of the presentation and are returned to the Normal view.

- Save the presentation. Exit PowerPoint if you do not want to continue with the next exercise at this time.

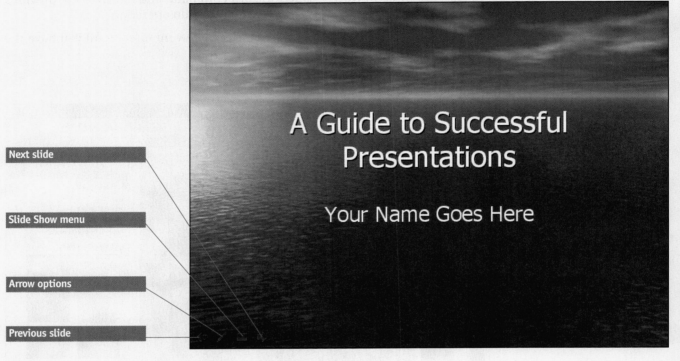

Next slide

Slide Show menu

Arrow options

Previous slide

A Guide to Successful Presentations

Your Name Goes Here

(h) View the Presentation (step 8)

FIGURE 1.9 Hands-on Exercise 2 (*continued*)

BACK UP YOUR WORK

We cannot overemphasize the importance of adequate backup and urge you to back up your important files at every opportunity. Exit PowerPoint, start Windows Explorer, then copy the presentation from drive C to a floppy disk. If the presentation is too large, you can compress the file before you copy it, and/or you can burn a CD. You can also e-mail the presentation to yourself as an attachment. Remember, you can always get another copy of Microsoft Office, but your data files are irreplaceable. Make duplicate copies of any files that you cannot afford to lose, and then store those files away from your computer.

You have successfully created a PowerPoint presentation, but the most important step is yet to come—the delivery of the presentation to an audience. This is best accomplished through a computerized slide show (as opposed to using overhead transparencies or 35mm slides). The computer becomes the equivalent of a slide projector, and the presentation is called a slide show.

PowerPoint can help you add interest to the slide show in two ways, transitions and animations. *Transitions* apply to the slide as a whole and control the way a slide moves on and off the screen. *Animations* control the entrance and/or exit of individual elements on a single slide. Transitions and animations are applied from the task pane within the Normal view as shown in Figure 1.10. (Pull down the Slide Show menu and select the Slide Transition or Custom Animation command to open the task pane with the appropriate options.)

The task pane in Figure 1.10a contains a list box with the available *transition effects*. Slides may move on to the screen from the left or right, be uncovered by horizontal or vertical blinds, fade, dissolve, and so on. You select a slide, choose the effect, select a speed and sound, then indicate when you want to advance the slide (either on a mouse click or after a specified number of seconds). Click the Play button at the bottom of the pane to preview the transition, or click the Slide Show button to move directly to a complete show. (Transition effects can also be applied from the Slide Sorter view, where you can apply the same transition to multiple slides by selecting the slides prior to applying the effect.)

Figure 1.10b shows the application of animation effects to a specific slide. You can select a predefined animation scheme for the slide as a whole, or you can animate each object individually. The animation schemes are divided into subtle, moderate, and exciting, and it is fun to experiment with the various effects. *Custom animation* requires you to select an animation effect for each object on the slide, then specify the order in which the objects are to appear. The slide in Figure 1.10b, for example, displays the title, the four bullets in succession, and the clip art in that order. Look closely at the icons in the task pane and you will see that different effects are chosen for the various objects.

Delivering the Presentation

PowerPoint can help you to create attractive presentations, but the content and delivery are still up to you. You have worked hard to gain the opportunity to present your ideas and you want to be well prepared for the session. Practice aloud several times, preferably under the same conditions as the actual presentation. Time your delivery to be sure that you do not exceed your allotted time. Everyone is nervous, but the more you practice, the more confident you will be.

Arrive early. You need time to gather your thoughts as well as to set up the presentation. Start PowerPoint and open your presentation prior to addressing the audience. Be sure that your notes are with you and check that water is available for you during the presentation. Look at the audience to open communication and gain credibility. Speak clearly and vary your delivery. Try to relax. You'll be great!

QUESTIONS AND ANSWERS (Q & A)

Indicate at the beginning of your talk whether you will take questions during the presentation or collectively at the end. Announce the length of time that will be allocated to questions. Rephrase all questions so the audience can hear. If you do receive a hostile question, rephrase it in a neutral way and try to disarm the challenger by paying a compliment. If you don't know the answer, say so.

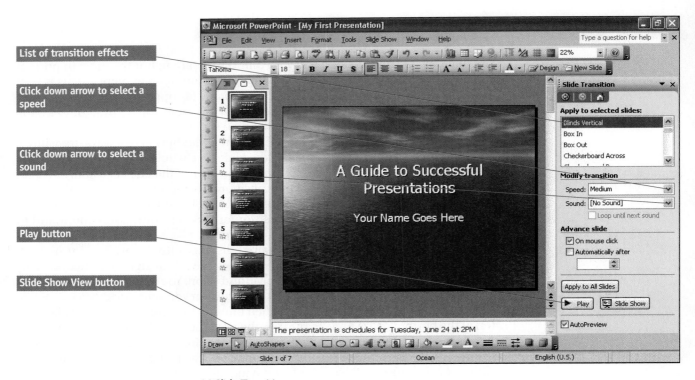

List of transition effects

Click down arrow to select a speed

Click down arrow to select a sound

Play button

Slide Show View button

(a) Slide Transition

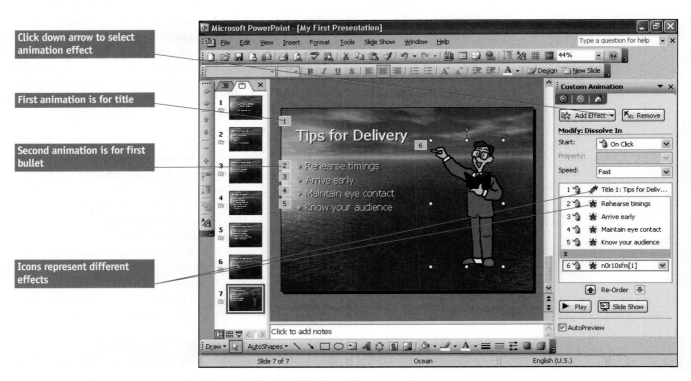

Click down arrow to select animation effect

First animation is for title

Second animation is for first bullet

Icons represent different effects

(b) Custom Animation

FIGURE 1.10 Transition and Animation Effects

3   Animating a Presentation

Objective   To change the layout of an existing slide; to establish transition and animation effects. Use Figure 1.11 as a guide in the exercise.

Step 1:   **Change the Slide Layout**

- Start PowerPoint. There are two basic ways to open an existing presentation. You can use the Open command in the File menu, or you can open the presentation from the task pane.

- Pull down the **View menu** and click the **Task pane command** to display the task pane, then (if necessary) click the **down arrow** in the task pane to select **Getting Started**.

- You should see My First Presentation from the previous exercise since the most recently used presentations are listed automatically.

- Click **My First Presentation**. (Click the link to **More** if the presentation is not listed, to display the Open dialog box, where you can select the drive and folder to locate your presentation.)

- Click the **Outline tab**, then scroll in the left pane until you can select the **Tips for Delivery slide**.

- Open the task pane. Click the **down arrow** on the task pane to select **Slide Layout** as shown in Figure 1.11a. Now scroll in the task pane until you can select the **Title, Text & Clip Art layout** as shown in Figure 1.11a. Click the layout to apply it to the current slide.

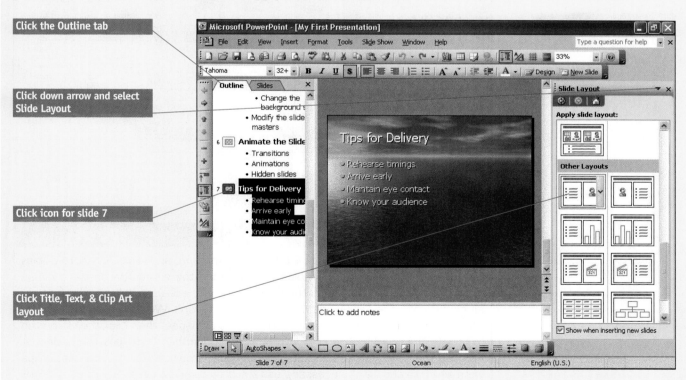

(a) Change the Slide Layout (step 1)

FIGURE 1.11   Hands-on Exercise 3

Step 2: Add the Clip Art

- Double click the **placeholder** on the slide to add the clip art. You will see the Select Picture dialog box as shown in Figure 1.11b, although the size, position, and content will be different on your screen.

- Click in the **Search** text box and enter the keyword **education**, then click the **Go button** to look for clip art that is described by this term.

- Select (click) the clip art you want and click **OK**. The clip art should appear on the slide.

- The clip art is sized automatically. You can, however, move and size the clip art just like any other Windows object.

- Save the presentation.

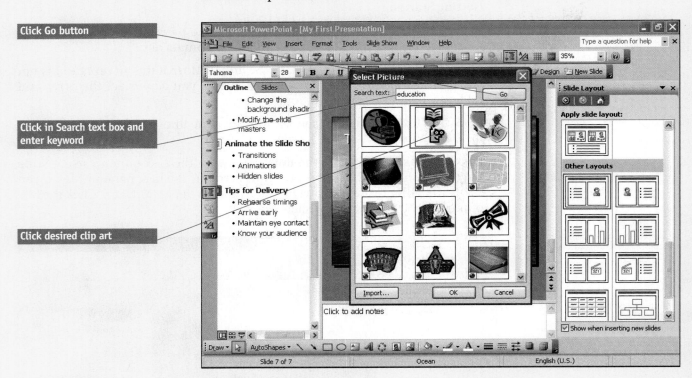

(b) Add the Clip Art (step 2)

FIGURE 1.11   Hands-on Exercise 3 (*continued*)

THE INSERT PICTURE COMMAND

Pull down the Insert menu, click the Picture command, and click Clip Art to display the Clip Art task pane that enables you to extend the search parameters for an appropriate media object. Click the down arrow in the Search in list box and select all of the collections including those on the Microsoft Web site. Click the down arrow in the Results list box and choose All media types, then click the Go button to initiate the search. The search may take longer than it did previously since it includes the Web, but you should have a much larger selection of potential clips from which to choose. If necessary, use the drop-down arrow on either search box to limit the search as you see fit.

Step 3: Add Transition Effects

- You can apply transitions either in the Normal view (with the thumbnail images) or in the Slide Sorter view. We chose the latter. Thus, click the **Slide Sorter View button** above the status bar to change to this view.

- Select (click) the first slide. Click the **Transition button** on the Slide Sorter toolbar to display the transition effects in the task pane.

- Click in the list box to select the **Blinds Vertical** transition effect (a preview plays automatically) as shown in Figure 1.11c.

- A Transition icon appears under the slide after the effect has been applied. Change the speed to **Medium**.

- Select (click) slide 2 and apply the **Checkerboard Across** transition effect to this slide. Change the speed to **Medium**.

- Apply different transition effects to the other slides in the presentation.

- Save the presentation.

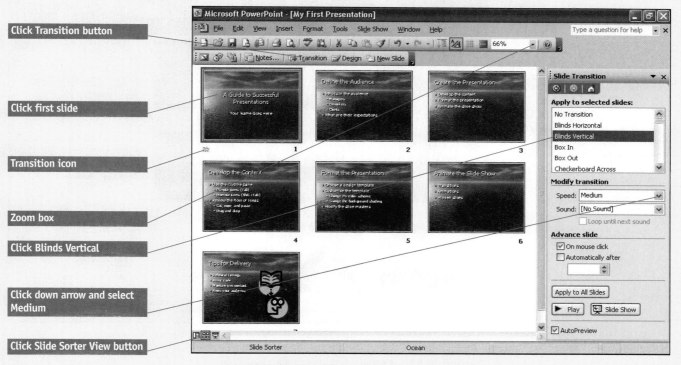

(c) Add Transition Effects (step 3)

FIGURE 1.11 Hands-on Exercise 3 (*continued*)

CHANGE THE MAGNIFICATION

Click the down arrow on the Zoom box to change the display magnification, which in turn controls the size of individual slides. The higher the magnification, the easier it is to read the text of an individual slide, but the fewer slides you see at one time. Conversely, changing to a smaller magnification decreases the size of the individual slides, but enables you to see more of the presentation.

Step 4: **Create a Summary Slide**

■ Pull down the **Edit menu** and press **Select All** to select every slide in the presentation. (You can also press **Ctrl+A** or press and hold the **Ctrl key** as you click each slide in succession.)

■ Click the **Summary Slide button** on the Slide Sorter toolbar to create a summary slide containing a bullet with the title of each selected slide. The new slide appears at the beginning of the presentation as shown in Figure 1.11d.

■ Click and drag the **Summary Slide** to the end of the presentation. (As you drag the slide, the mouse pointer changes to include the outline of a miniature slide, and a vertical line appears to indicate the new position of the slide.)

■ Release the mouse. The Summary Slide has been moved to the end of the presentation, and the slides are renumbered automatically.

■ Save the presentation.

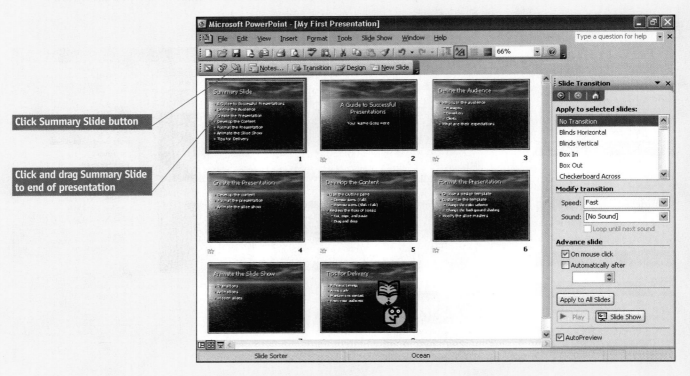

(d) Create a Summary Slide (step 4)

FIGURE 1.11 Hands-on Exercise 3 (*continued*)

SELECTING MULTIPLE SLIDES

You can apply the same transition or animation effect to multiple slides with a single command. Change to the Slide Sorter view, then select the slides by pressing and holding the Ctrl key as you click the slides. Use the task pane to choose the desired transition when all the slides have been selected. Click anywhere in the Slide Sorter view to deselect the slides and continue working.

Step 5: **Create Animation Effects**

- Double click the **Summary Slide** to change to the Normal view. The task pane should still be open. Click the **down arrow** on the task pane to choose **Slide Design—Animation Schemes**.

- Scroll in the Open list box to the **Moderate category**, and choose **Spin** as shown in Figure 1.11e. You will automatically see a preview of the effect.

- Scroll in the Open list box to the **Exciting category** and choose a different effect. (We're not sure who rates the effects and why one is deemed to be exciting, while the other is only moderate.)

- Click the **Undo button** if you prefer the original animation scheme.

- Save the presentation.

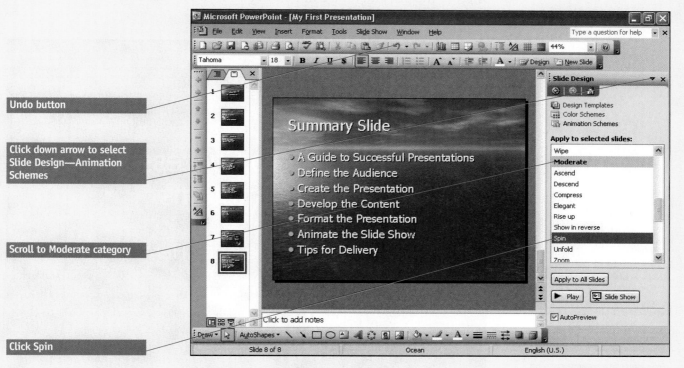

(e) Create Animation Effects (step 5)

FIGURE 1.11 Hands-on Exercise 3 (*continued*)

CUSTOMIZE THE ANIMATION

You can modify the effects of a predefined animation scheme for selected slides and/or objects on those slides. Click the down arrow in the task pane and choose Custom Animation. Select the slide, select the object on the slide that is to receive special treatment, click the Add Effect button to display a menu, choose the category (Entrance, Emphasis, etc.), and choose the effect, which will preview automatically. (Click the Remove button if you do not like the result.) Set a time limit because PowerPoint gives you virtually unlimited flexibility.

Step 6: **Show the Presentation**

■ Press **Ctrl+Home** to return to the first slide, then click the **Slide Show button** above the status bar to view the presentation. You should see the opening slide in Figure 1.11f.

■ Click the **left mouse button** to move to the next slide (or to the next bullet on the current slide when animation is in effect).

■ Click the **right mouse button** to display the Shortcut menu and return to the previous slide (or to the previous bullet on the current slide when an animation is in effect).

■ Continue to view the presentation until you come to the end. Click the **left mouse button** a final time to return to the regular PowerPoint window.

■ Close the presentation. Exit PowerPoint if you do not want to continue with the next exercise at this time.

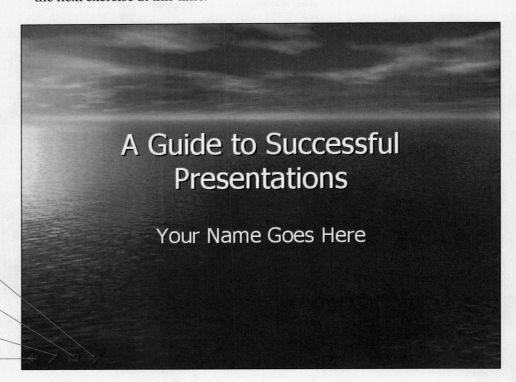

(f) Show the Presentation (step 6)

FIGURE 1.11 Hands-on Exercise 3 (*continued*)

CREATE A CUSTOM SHOW

Many presenters have to create nearly identical shows for different audiences. You could create multiple presentations and store each presentation in its own file, but it is much more efficient to create custom shows within a single presentation. Pull down the Slide Show menu, click the Custom Shows command, and click the New button to select the slides for the first custom show. Repeat the process to create additional custom shows, then select the show you want to view from the Custom Show dialog box.

Thus far we have focused on presentations that consisted largely of text. PowerPoint also enables you to include a variety of visual elements that add impact to a presentation as can be seen in Figure 1.12. (This is the presentation that we will create in the next hands-on exercise.) You can add clip art, sound, or animated clips that are stored on your computer and/or you can download additional objects from the Microsoft Web site. You can also use the supplement applications that are included with Microsoft Office to add organization charts and WordArt. You can insert objects that were created in other applications, such as a chart from Microsoft Excel or a table from Microsoft Word.

A chart or table is inserted into a presentation through linking or embedding. The essential difference between the two techniques is that embedding places the object into the presentation, whereas linking does not. In other words, an ***embedded object*** is stored within the presentation. A ***linked object***, on the other hand, is stored in its own file, and the presentation is one of many potential documents that are linked to that object. The advantage of linking over embedding is that the presentation is updated automatically if the original object is changed.

Linking is also preferable if the same object is referenced in many documents, so that any change to the object has to be made in only one place (the source document). An Excel chart, for example, may be linked to a Word document and a PowerPoint presentation. You can subsequently change the chart, and both the document and presentation are updated automatically.

You can also add ***comments*** to any presentation to explain your thoughts to colleagues who may review the presentation prior to delivery. The comments appear on a slide during editing, but not during delivery as you will see in the hands-on exercise that follows shortly.

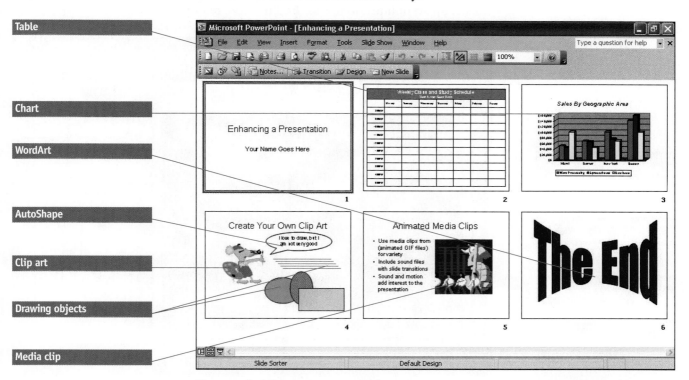

FIGURE 1.12 Enhancing a Presentation

The Microsoft Clip Organizer

The *Insert Picture command* displays a task pane through which you can insert clip art, photographs, sounds, and movies (collectively called clips). The clips can come from a variety of sources. They may be installed locally in the My Collections folder, they may have been installed in conjunction with Microsoft Office in the Office Collections folder, and/or they may have been downloaded from the Web and stored in the Web Collections folder. You can insert a specific clip into a document if you know its location. You can also search for a clip that will enhance the document on which you are working.

The search is made possible by the *Microsoft Clip Organizer*, which brings order out of potential chaos by cataloging the clips that are available to you. You enter a keyword that describes the clip you are looking for, specify the *collections* that are to be searched, and indicate the type of clip(s) you are looking for. The results are displayed in the task pane as shown in Figure 1.13, which returns the clips that are described by the keyword "artist". Our example is searching all collections for all media types in order to return the greatest number of potential clips. When you see a clip that you want to use, all you have to do is point to the clip, click the down arrow that appears, and then click the Insert command from the resulting menu.

You can access the Microsoft Clip Organizer (to view the various collections) by clicking the Organize clips link at the bottom of the task pane. You can also access the Clip Organizer outside of PowerPoint by clicking the Start button on the task bar, and then clicking All Programs, Microsoft Office, Microsoft Office Tool, and Microsoft Clip Organizer. Once in the Organizer, you can search through the clips in the various collections, reorganize the existing collections, add new collections, and even add new clips (with their associated keywords) to the collections. The other links at the bottom of the task pane in Figure 1.13 provide access to additional clip art online and tips for finding more relevant clips.

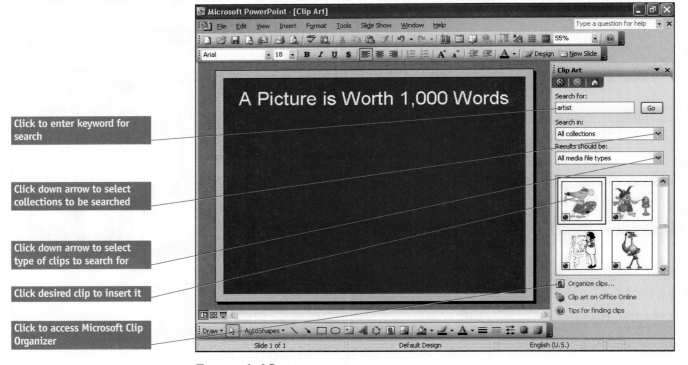

FIGURE 1.13 The Insert Picture Command

Office Art

Everyone likes *clip art*, but relatively few individuals think in terms of enhancing it. It takes a lot of talent to create original clip art, but it takes only a little imagination to create a drawing from existing clip art as shown in Figure 1.14. There is no way that we could have drawn the artist, but it was very easy to copy the artist and create the slide, given the original clip art.

Any piece of clip art is an object that can be copied, moved, and sized like any other Windows object. Thus, we clicked on the original clip art (the artist in the upper right of the slide) to display the sizing handles, clicked the copy and paste buttons to duplicate the object, then moved and sized the copied image to the bottom of the slide. We then copied the smaller artist across the bottom of the slide.

Next we used various tools on the Drawing toolbar to complete the slide. Select the Line tool, for example, then click and drag to create a line. Once the line has been created, you can select it and change its properties (such as thickness, style, or color) by using other tools on the Drawing toolbar. The oval and rectangle tools work the same way. The AutoShapes button on the Drawing toolbar provides access to the balloon and other callouts in which you enter the text.

There are other techniques you can use as well. You can, for example, select multiple objects simultaneously and group them together to move and/or size those objects with a single mouse click. Press and hold the Shift key to select multiple objects (e.g., the large artist, the balloon, and the three circles), click the Draw button, then click the Group command. The five objects have been combined into one larger object with a single set of sizing handles.

All it takes is a little imagination and a sense of what you can do. Use different clip art images on the same slide and you get something entirely different. It is fun and it is easy. Just be flexible and willing to experiment. We think you will be pleased with the results.

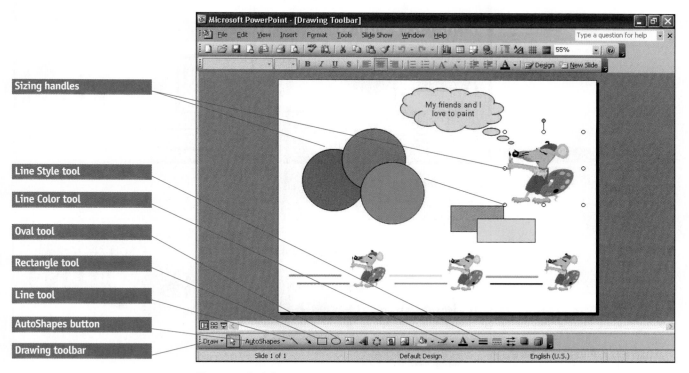

FIGURE 1.14 Office Art

Microsoft WordArt

Microsoft WordArt is an application within Microsoft Office that creates decorative text that can be used to add interest to a document. You can use WordArt in addition to clip art within a document, or in place of clip art if the right image is not available. You can rotate text in any direction, add three-dimensional effects, display the text vertically down the page, slant it, arch it, or even print it upside down. In short, you are limited only by your imagination.

WordArt is intuitive and easy to use. In essence, you choose a style for the text from among the selections in Figure 1.15a. Then you enter the specific text in a subsequent dialog box, after which the result is displayed in Figure 1.15b. The finished WordArt is an object that can be moved and sized within a presentation.

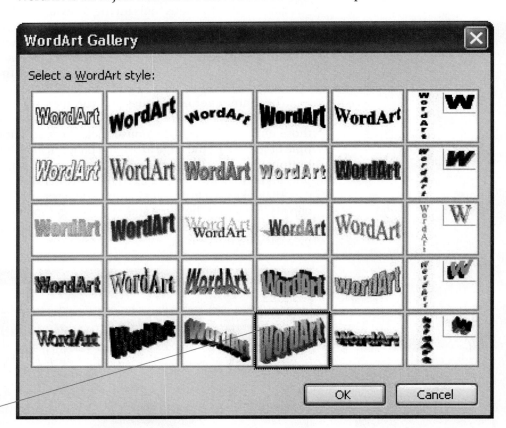

Click WordArt style

(a) Choose the Style

(b) Completed Entry

FIGURE 1.15 Microsoft WordArt

4 Enhancing a Presentation

Objective To include a Word table and an Excel chart in a presentation; to modify existing clip art and create a WordArt object. Use Figure 1.16 as a guide.

Step 1: **Insert a Comment**

■ Start PowerPoint. Click the **New button** on the Standard toolbar to begin a new presentation. Close the task pane. Enter the title of the presentation and your name on the title slide. Save the presentation as **Enhancing a Presentation** in the **Exploring PowerPoint folder**.

■ Click the **Normal View button** above the status bar if you are not in the Normal view. Click the **Slides tab** to display the slides in the left pane.

■ Pull down the **Insert menu** and click the **Comment command** to insert a comment onto the slide as shown in Figure 1.16a.

■ You will see an empty balloon that contains the name of the person who has registered this copy of Office, together with today's date. Enter any text at all as a comment.

■ Click anywhere outside the comment. The balloon closes, and you see a comment marker. Click the marker, and the comment reappears.

■ The Reviewing toolbar appears automatically whenever you are working with comments. The Markup button at the extreme left of the toolbar toggles the comment markers on and off.

■ Click the **New Slide button** on the Formatting toolbar. (This will open the task pane if it is not already open.) Scroll down in the task pane until you can select a **blank layout**.

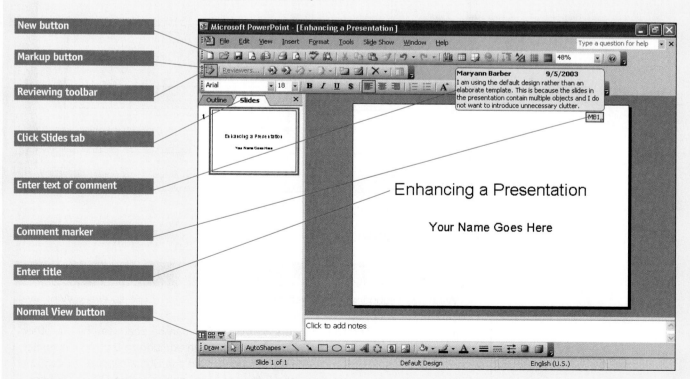

(a) Insert a Comment (step 1)

FIGURE 1.16 Hands-on Exercise 4

Step 2: **Copy the Word Table**

- Start Word. Open the **My Study Schedule** Word document in the **Exploring PowerPoint folder** as shown in Figure 1.16b. The document consists entirely of a Word table.

- Click and drag to select the text **Your Name Goes Here** that appears at the top of the table. Type your first and last name, which automatically replaces the selected text.

- You can click in any cell and enter an activity. The text will automatically flow from one line to the next within the cell. Limit the entry to two lines, however, or else the table may not fit on one page (or one slide). Save the document.

- Point to the table. Click the tiny square at the upper left of the table to select the entire table. Be sure that every cell is highlighted, or else the table will not be copied successfully. Click the **Copy button** to copy the table to the clipboard.

- Exit Word. The copied text remains in the clipboard even though Microsoft Word is no longer open.

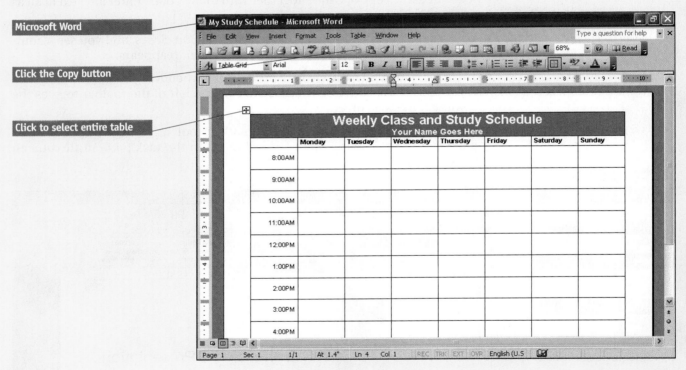

(b) Copy the Word Table (step 2)

FIGURE 1.16 Hands-on Exercise 4 (*continued*)

THE WINDOWS CLIPBOARD

The Windows clipboard is an area of memory that is available to every Windows application. Execution of the Copy command in one application places the copied text (or other object) on the clipboard from where it can be accessed by any other application. Microsoft Office has its own clipboard (in addition to the Windows clipboard) that can hold up to 24 objects. You can open the Office clipboard from any Office application by pulling down the Edit menu and selecting the Office Clipboard command.

Step 3: Insert the Table

- You should be back in PowerPoint as shown in Figure 1.16c. (If not, click the **PowerPoint button** on the Windows taskbar.)

- Click anywhere on the second slide to select this slide. Click the **Paste button** on the Standard toolbar to paste (embed) the Word table onto this slide.

- Pull down the **Insert menu** and click the **Comment command**. Enter the text of the comment shown in the figure, which indicates that the table has been embedded (rather than linked) into the presentation.

- Click anywhere outside the comment after you have finished.

- Click the **Previous Item button** on the Reviewing toolbar to move to the previous comment. Click the **Next Item button** to return to this comment.

- Save the presentation.

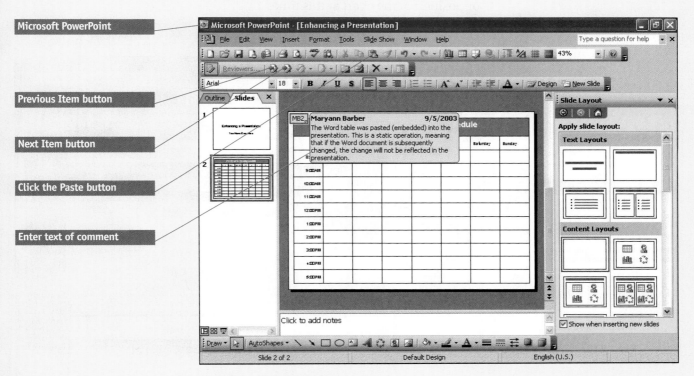

(c) Insert the Table (step 3)

FIGURE 1.16   Hands-on Exercise 4 (*continued*)

SEND SLIDES TO A WORD DOCUMENT

You can embed and/or link Word documents and PowerPoint presentations in either direction; that is, you can insert a Word document into a PowerPoint presentation as was done here, and/or you can send PowerPoint slides to a Word document. Pull down the File menu and click the Send To command, then choose Microsoft Word to display the associated dialog box. You will be given the choice of how to arrange the PowerPoint slides in the resulting Word document.

Step 4: **Insert the Excel Chart**

- Start Excel. Open the **Software Sales** workbook in the **Exploring PowerPoint folder**. The workbook consists of a single sheet that contains data and a chart.

- Click anywhere in the chart background to select the entire chart. You should see sizing handles around the white border of the chart. Click the **Copy button** on the Standard toolbar to copy the chart to the clipboard. Do not close the workbook as we will return to it momentarily.

- Click the **PowerPoint button** on the Windows taskbar to return to the PowerPoint presentation. Click the **New slide button** and use the Slide Layout task pane to insert a blank slide into the presentation. Close the task pane.

- Pull down the **Edit menu** and click the **Paste Special command** to display the Paste Special dialog box in Figure 1.16d. Click the **Paste link option button**. Click **OK** to insert the chart onto the slide. Do not be concerned about the size or position of the chart at this time.

- Save the presentation.

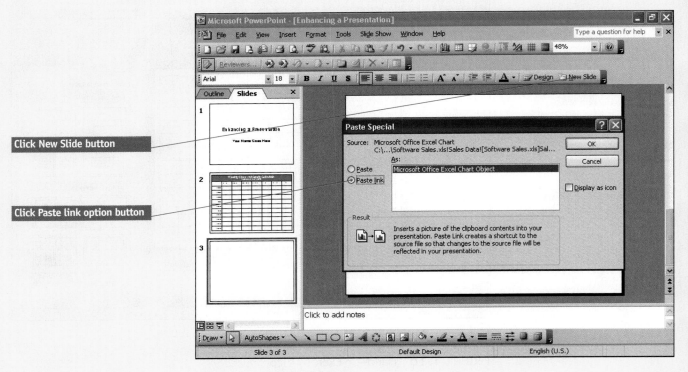

(d) Insert the Excel Chart (step 4)

FIGURE 1.16 Hands-on Exercise 4 (*continued*)

LINKING VERSUS EMBEDDING

Linking is very different from embedding as it provides a dynamic connection to the source document. A linked object, such as an Excel chart, is tied to its source, so that any changes to the source file are reflected in the PowerPoint presentation. Linking is especially useful when the same object is inserted into multiple documents, as changes to the object are made in only one place (in the source file). A linked object must always be saved in its file.

Step 5: **Update the Chart**

■ You should see the chart as shown in Figure 1.16e. The sizing handles indicate that the chart is currently selected and can be moved and sized like any other Windows object.

■ Click and drag a corner handle (the pointer changes to a two-headed arrow) to proportionally increase (decrease) the size of the chart. Point to any border (the pointer changes to a four-headed arrow) to move the chart on the slide.

■ Note that the database sales for Miami are very low ($12,000). Double click the chart to return to Excel (or click the **Excel button** on the Windows taskbar). Click in **cell B4** and change the database sales for Miami to **$100,000**. Save the workbook. Exit Excel.

■ Return to PowerPoint. The chart may automatically reflect the change in database sales. If not, right click the chart and select the **Update Link command**.

■ Pull down the **Insert menu** and click the **Comment command** to insert an appropriate comment indicating that the chart in the presentation is linked to an Excel workbook. Close the Reviewing toolbar. Save the presentation.

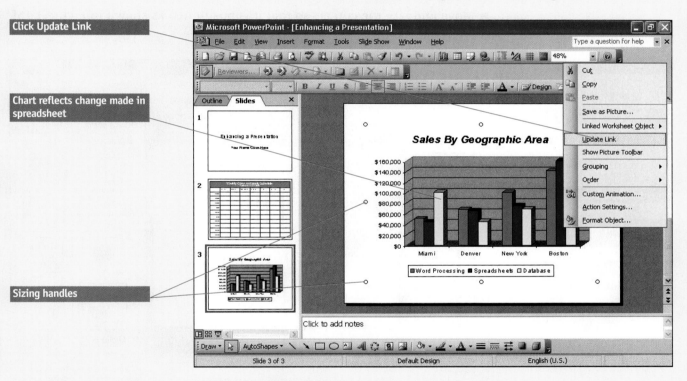

(e) Update the Chart (step 5)

FIGURE 1.16 Hands-on Exercise 4 (*continued*)

UPDATING LINKS

The next time you open this presentation you will see a message indicating that links are present and further, that the links can be updated. You should respond by clicking the Update Links command button, which in turn will bring in the most current version of the chart to the presentation. This assumes that the Excel workbook is still in the same folder where it was created initially. If there is a problem, perhaps because the workbook has been moved or renamed, pull down the Edit menu and click the Links command to modify the link.

Step 6:   **Insert the Clip Art**

- Click the **New Slide button** and select the **Title Only** layout. Click in the title placeholder and type **Create Your Own Clip Art**.

- Pull down the **Insert menu**, click **Picture**, and then click **Clip Art** (or click the **Insert Clip Art button** on the Drawing toolbar). The contents of the task pane change automatically.

- Type **Artist** in the Search text box. Be sure the list boxes show you are searching all collections and are looking for all media types. Click the **Go button** to initiate the search.

- The system pauses, then starts to return all objects that satisfy the search criteria.

- Click the **down arrow** in the task pane to scroll through the images until you find the one that you want. Point to the right side of the image, then click the **down arrow** that appears to display a menu. Click **Insert**.

- Click the mouse to select our artist. Click the **Draw button**, click **Rotate or Flip**, then click the **Flip Horizontal command** to turn the artist around.

- Move and size the clip art so that it is positioned as shown in Figure 1.16f. Close the task pane. Save the presentation.

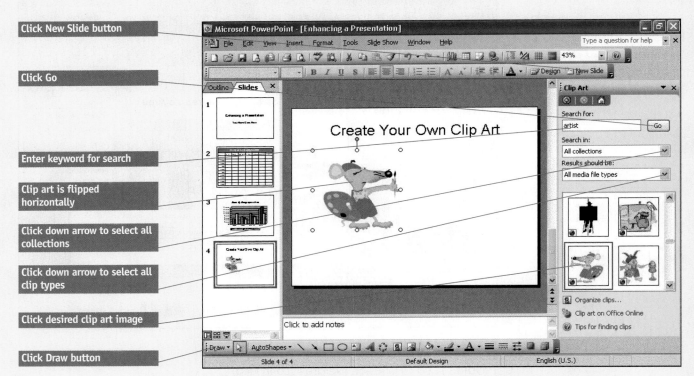

(f) Insert the Clip Art (step 6)

FIGURE 1.16   Hands-on Exercise 4 (*continued*)

THE SHIFT KEY

The Shift key has special significance when used in conjunction with the Line, Rectangle, and Oval tools. Press and hold the Shift key as you drag the line tool horizontally or vertically to create a perfectly straight line in either direction. Press and hold the Shift key as you drag the Rectangle and Oval tool to create a square and circle, respectively.

Step 7: **Use the Drawing Toolbar**

- Click the **AutoShapes button** on the Drawing toolbar, click **Callouts**, then click the desired balloon. The mouse pointer changes to a tiny crosshair.

- Click and drag on the slide where you want the balloon to go. Release the mouse. The balloon is selected automatically, and the sizing handles are displayed. If necessary, click and drag the balloon to adjust its size or position.

- Type the phrase shown in the figure. You can select the text, then change its font, size, or alignment. Click elsewhere on the slide to deselect the balloon.

- Click the **Line tool** on the Drawing toolbar, then click and drag to draw a line on the slide. To change the color or thickness, select the line (the sizing handles appear), click the appropriate tool on the Drawing toolbar, then select a new color or thickness.

- Select the completed line, click the **Copy button**, then click the **Paste button** several times to copy the line. Use the **Oval** or **Rectangle tools** to draw additional shapes, then use the **Fill Color tool** to change their color.

- Move and size the objects as necessary. Save the presentation.

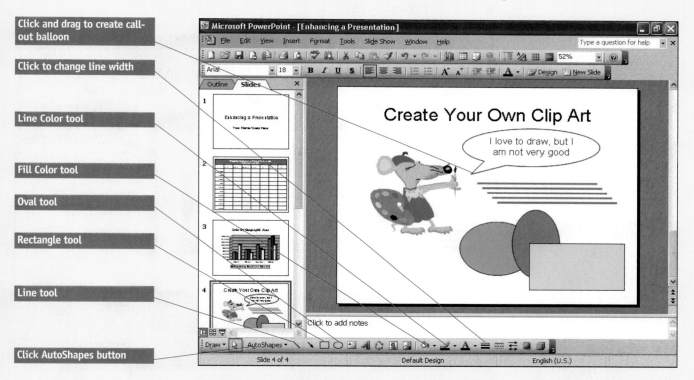

(g) Use the Drawing Toolbar (step 7)

FIGURE 1.16 Hands-on Exercise 4 (*continued*)

AUTOSHAPES

An AutoShape is a predefined shape that is drawn automatically when you select its icon from the AutoShapes toolbar, then click and drag in the slide. (To display the AutoShapes menu, click the AutoShape button on the Drawing toolbar.) To place text inside an AutoShape, select the shape and start typing. You can also change the fill color or line thickness by selecting the shape, then clicking the appropriate button on the Drawing toolbar.

Step 8: **Add a Media Clip**

- Click the **New Slide button** and select the **Title**, **Text & Media Clip** layout. Enter **Animated Media Clips** as the title of the slide. Enter the bulleted text as shown in Figure 1.16h.

- Double click the Media placeholder to add the media clip, which in turn displays the Media Clip dialog box.

- Select any clip that appeals to you. (The clip in the figure is available in the Exploring PowerPoint folder as **CashRegister**.)

- Click **OK** to insert the clip onto the slide. Size the media clip art after it appears on the slide.

- Pull down the **Slide Show menu** and click **Slide Transition** to display these options in the task pane. Click the **down arrow** in the Sound list box and select **Cash Register**. Check the box to **Loop until next sound**.

- Click the **Play button** to preview the effect. You should see the men passing an object to the sound of a cash register. (You need a sound card and speakers to hear the sound.)

- Save the presentation.

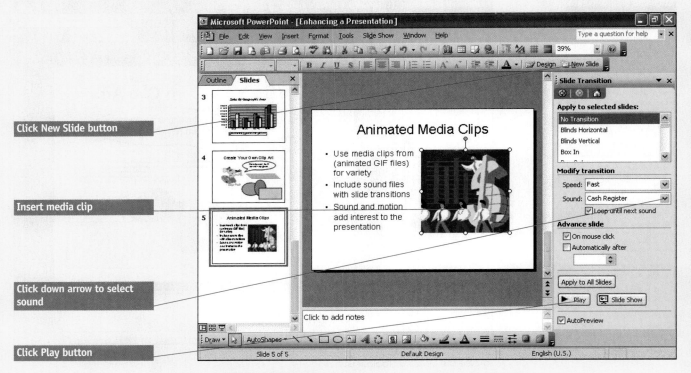

(h) Add a Media Clip (step 8)

FIGURE 1.16   Hands-on Exercise 4 (*continued*)

INSERT SLIDES FROM OTHER PRESENTATIONS

You work hard to develop individual slides and thus you may find it useful to reuse a slide from one presentation to the next. Pull down the Insert menu, click the Slides from Files command to display the Slide Finder dialog box, and click the Browse button to locate the presentation that contains the slides you want. Press and hold the Ctrl key to select multiple slides from this presentation, then click the Insert button to bring the selected slides into the current presentation.

Step 9: **Add the WordArt**

- We're ready to add the sixth and final slide. Click the **New Slide button** and select the **blank slide layout**. Close the task pane.

- Click the **Insert WordArt button** on the Drawing toolbar to display the WordArt Gallery dialog box as shown in Figure 1.16i. Choose any style you like (we took the fourth style from the left in the first row). Click **OK.**

- You should see the Edit WordArt text box. Enter **The End** as the text for your WordArt object. Click **OK** to close the Edit WordArt text box and insert the WordArt into your presentation.

- Move and size the WordArt object just as you would any other Windows object. Click and drag a corner sizing handle to increase the size of the WordArt until it takes the entire slide.

- Point to the middle of the WordArt object (the mouse pointer changes to a four-headed arrow), then click and drag to position the WordArt in the middle of the slide.

- Save the presentation.

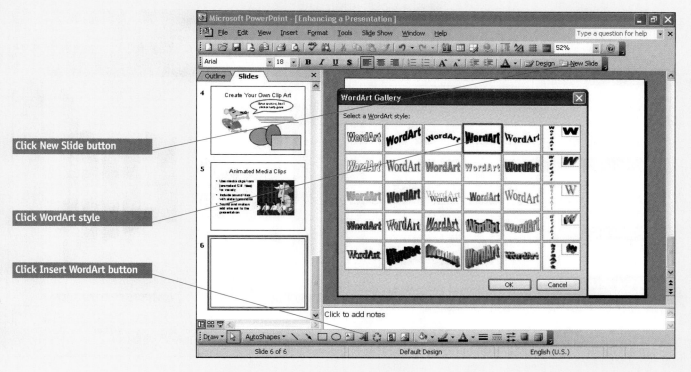

(i) Add the WordArt (step 9)

FIGURE 1.16 Hands-on Exercise 4 (*continued*)

THE WORDART TOOLBAR

The WordArt toolbar is the easiest way to change an existing WordArt object. It is displayed automatically when a WordArt object is selected and is suppressed otherwise. As with any other toolbar, you can point to a button to display a ScreenTip containing the name of the button, which is indicative of its function. You will find buttons to display the text vertically, change the style or shape, and/or edit the text.

Step 10: Complete the WordArt

- You should see the WordArt as shown in Figure 1.16j. You can click and drag the yellow diamond to change the slope of the text and/or you can click and drag the green circle to rotate the text.

- Click the WordArt object. Click the **down arrow** for the **Fill Color tool** on the Drawing toolbar to display the available fill colors. Select (click) **blue** to change the color of the WordArt object.

- Experiment with other tools on the Drawing and/or WordArt toolbars to enhance the WordArt image. Set a time limit. (Use the Undo command if the results are not what you intended.)

- Pull down the **Slide Show menu** and click **Slide Transition** to display these options in the task pane. Click the **down arrow** in the Sound list box and select **Applause**.

- Click the **Play button** to preview the effect. (You will need a sound card and speakers to hear the sound.)

- Close the task pane. Save the presentation.

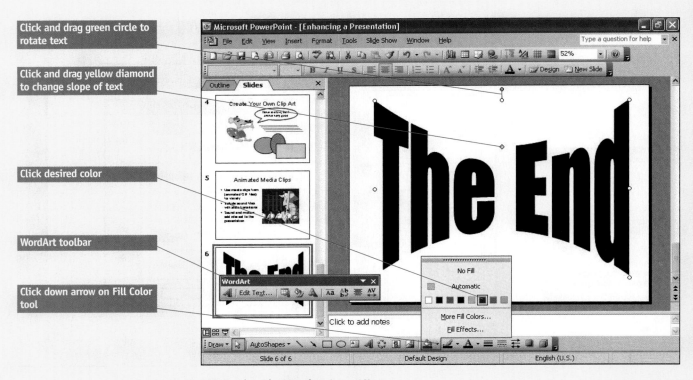

(j) Complete the WordArt (step 10)

FIGURE 1.16 Hands-on Exercise 4 (*continued*)

THE THIRD DIMENSION

You can make your WordArt images even more dramatic by adding 3-D effects. You can tilt the text up or down, right or left, increase or decrease the depth, and change the shading. Pull down the View menu, click Toolbars, click Customize to display the complete list of available toolbars, then check the box to display the 3-D Settings toolbar. Select the WordArt object, then experiment with various tools and special effects. The results are even better if you have a color printer.

Step 11: Print the Comments Pages

- Click the **Print Preview button** to preview the presentation. Click the **down arrow** on the Print What list box to select **Handouts (6 per page)**.

- Click the **down arrow** on the Options list box and toggle **Print Comments and Ink Markup** on, as shown in Figure 1.16k.

- The status bar indicates that you are on the first of two pages. Page 1 contains the six handouts. Page 2 contains the comments you entered earlier. Press the **PgDn key** to move to the second page, then scroll to the top of the page to see the comments.

- Click the **Print button** to display the Print dialog box, which contains the same information as the Print Preview screen; that is, you are printing audience handouts and will include comments. Click **OK** to print the presentation. Close the Print Preview window.

- Press **Ctrl+Home** to move to the first slide in the presentation, then click the **Slide Show button** to view the presentation.

- Save the presentation a final time. Exit PowerPoint. Well done!

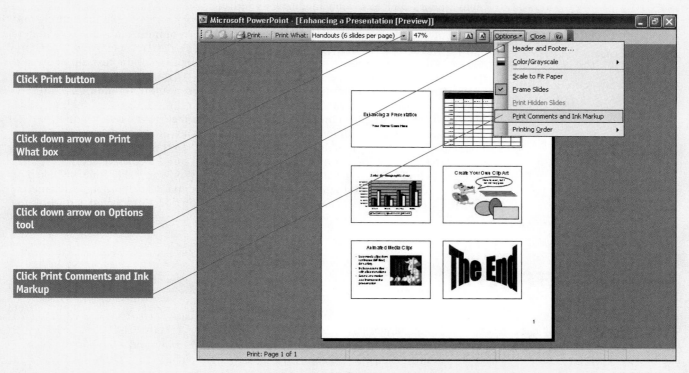

(k) Print the Comments Pages (step 11)

FIGURE 1.16 Hands-on Exercise 4 (*continued*)

THE PAGE SETUP COMMAND

The Print command determines what you will print—e.g., slides, an outline or note pages—but it does not control how the information appears on the printed page. This is controlled by the Page Setup command, which is present in virtually every Windows application. Pull down the File menu and click the Page Setup command to display the associated dialog box. This enables you to change the orientation (portrait or landscape) and/or the paper size.

SUMMARY

Microsoft PowerPoint enables you to focus on the content of a presentation without worrying about its appearance. You supply the text and supporting elements and leave the formatting to PowerPoint. The resulting presentation consists of a series of slides with a consistent design and color scheme. The presentation can be delivered in a variety of ways, such as a computer slide show, via the Web, or using overhead transparencies. It can also be printed in a variety of formats.

PowerPoint has different views, each with unique capabilities. The Normal view displays the Slide, Outline or Thumbnail images, and Notes Page views in a single window. The Slide Sorter view displays multiple slides on one screen (each slide is in miniature) and lets you see the overall flow of the presentation. The Notes Page view is best suited to printing audience handouts that display the slide and the associated speaker notes. The Slide Show view displays one slide at a time with transition and animation effects.

The outline is the easiest way to enter the text of a presentation. Text is entered continually in the outline, then promoted or demoted so that it appears on the proper level in the slide. The outline can be collapsed to show multiple slides on one screen, thus enabling you to change the order of the slides and/or move text from one slide to another.

The Insert Picture command displays a task pane in which you enter a keyword that describes the clip you are looking for. The search is made possible by the Microsoft Clip Organizer, which organizes the media files available to you into collections, then enables you to limit a search to specific media types and/or specific collections.

PowerPoint provides a set of predefined slide layouts that determine the nature and position of the objects on a slide. Each layout contains one or more placeholders to determine the position of the associated object. A template is a design specification that controls every aspect of a presentation. It specifies the formatting of the text, the fonts and colors that are used, and the design, size, and placement of the bullets.

Transitions and animations can be added to a presentation for additional interest. Transitions control the way in which one slide moves off the screen and the next slide appears. Animations control the appearance of individual elements on a single slide.

Clip art may be copied, moved, and/or sized to create modified drawings known as Office Art. The Drawing toolbar contains various tools to further enhance the clip art. WordArt is an application within Microsoft Office that creates decorative text.

Objects from other applications such as Excel charts or Word tables may be linked or embedded into a PowerPoint presentation. Linking is a dynamic technique, which means that if the underlying object changes, that change is automatically reflected in the presentation. Embedding, however, is static, and subsequent changes are not reflected in the presentation.

KEY TERMS

MULTIPLE CHOICE

1. How do you save changes to a PowerPoint presentation?

   (a) Pull down the File menu and click the Save command
   (b) Click the Save button on the Standard toolbar
   (c) Either (a) and (b)
   (d) Neither (a) nor (b)

2. Which of the following can be printed in support of a PowerPoint presentation?

   (a) Audience handouts
   (b) Notes
   (c) An outline
   (d) All of the above

3. Which toolbars are typically displayed in the Normal view?

   (a) The Standard toolbar
   (b) The Formatting toolbar
   (c) The Drawing toolbar
   (d) All of the above

4. Ctrl+Home and Ctrl+End are keyboard shortcuts that move to the beginning or end of the presentation in the:

   (a) Outline view
   (b) Slide Sorter view
   (c) Either (a) or (b)
   (d) Neither (a) nor (b)

5. The predefined slide formats in PowerPoint are known as:

   (a) View
   (b) Slide layouts
   (c) Audience handouts
   (d) Speaker notes

6. Which menu contains the commands to save the current presentation, or to open a previously saved presentation?

   (a) The Tools menu
   (b) The File menu
   (c) The View menu
   (d) The Edit menu

7. The Open command:

   (a) Brings a presentation from disk into memory
   (b) Brings a presentation from disk into memory, then erases the presentation on disk
   (c) Stores the presentation in memory on disk
   (d) Stores the presentation in memory on disk, then erases the presentation from memory

8. The Save command:

   (a) Brings a presentation from disk into memory
   (b) Brings a presentation from disk into memory, then erases the presentation on disk
   (c) Stores the presentation in memory on disk
   (d) Stores the presentation in memory on disk, then erases the presentation from memory

9. Which of the following can be displayed in the task pane?

   (a) Animation and transition effects
   (b) Design templates and slide layouts
   (c) Both (a) and (b)
   (d) Neither (a) nor (b)

10. Where will the insertion point be after you complete the text for a bullet in the outline and press the Enter key?

    (a) On the next bullet at the same level of indentation
    (b) On the next bullet at a higher level of indentation
    (c) On the next bullet at a lower level of indentation
    (d) It is impossible to determine

11. Which of the following is true about an Excel chart that is linked to both a Word document and a PowerPoint presentation?

    (a) The chart cannot be linked to any other presentations or Word documents
    (b) The chart cannot be modified since it is already linked to two documents
    (c) The chart can be modified, but any changes have to be made in two places, once in the Word document and once in the PowerPoint presentation
    (d) Any changes to the chart will be reflected automatically in both the Word document and the PowerPoint presentation.

... continued

12. What advantage, if any, is there to collapsing the outline so that only the slide titles are visible?

    (a) More slides are displayed at one time, making it easier to rearrange the slides in the presentation

    (b) Transition and build effects can be added

    (c) Graphic objects become visible

    (d) All of the above

13. Which of the following is a true statement regarding transition and build effects?

    (a) Every slide must have the same transition effect

    (b) Every bullet must have the same build effect

    (c) Both (a) and (b)

    (d) Neither (a) nor (b)

14. Which of the following is true?

    (a) Slides can be added to a presentation after a template has been chosen

    (b) The template can be changed after all of the slides have been created

    (c) Both (a) and (b)

    (d) Neither (a) nor (b)

15. Which of the following is a true statement regarding the Microsoft Clip Organizer?

    (a) The search may be limited to a specific media type

    (b) The search may be limited to specific collections

    (c) Both (a) and (b)

    (d) Neither (a) nor (b)

16. You are working on a PowerPoint presentation called First Presentation. You pull down the File menu, click the Save As command, and save the file with a new name, First Presentation Solution. Which of the following statements is true?

    (a) The title bar at the top of the PowerPoint window shows First Presentation Solution

    (b) There are two files on disk, First Presentation and First Presentation Solution

    (c) Both (a) and (b)

    (d) Neither (a) nor (b)

17. What is the effect of executing two successive Undo commands, one right after the other?

    (a) The situation is not possible because the Undo command is not available

    (b) The situation is not possible because the Undo command cannot be executed twice in a row

    (c) The Undo commands cancel each other out; that is, the document is the same as it was prior to the first Undo command

    (d) The last two commands prior to the first Undo command are reversed

18. Which of the following is a true statement about the Windows and Office clipboards?

    (a) Both clipboards can hold only a single item

    (b) Both clipboards can hold multiple items

    (c) The Windows clipboard holds only a single item; the Office clipboard can hold multiple items

    (d) The Office clipboard can hold only a single item; the Windows clipboard can hold multiple items

ANSWERS

1. c	**7.** a	**13.** d
2. d	**8.** c	**14.** c
3. d	**9.** c	**15.** c
4. d	**10.** a	**16.** c
5. b	**11.** d	**17.** d
6. b	**12.** a	**18.** c

PRACTICE WITH POWERPOINT

1. **Introduction to E-Mail:** The presentation in Figure 1.17 reviews the basics of e-mail and simultaneously provides practice with modifying an existing PowerPoint presentation. The presentation also contains two slides on computer viruses and reminds you that your computer is at risk whenever you receive an e-mail message with an attachment. Open the partially completed presentation in *Chapter 1 Practice 1* within the Exploring PowerPoint folder and do the following:

    a. Modify the title slide to include your name and your e-mail address. Replace the sample e-mail address with your address on slide 4.

    b. Boldface and italicize the four basic capabilities in any e-mail program (Send, Compose, Reply, and Forward) on slide 2. Boldface and italicize the name of each e-mail folder on slide 3.

    c. Move the last two slides (Be Aware of Computer Viruses and Protect Yourself) to the indicated positions in Figure 1.17. Read the content of these two slides very carefully. Which antivirus program do you use?

    d. Set a limit of five minutes to experiment with different design templates, and then choose a template for the completed presentation.

    e. Add transition effects throughout the presentation as you see fit.

    f. Print the presentation in multiple ways. Print the title slide as a slide (full page) to serve as a cover page. Print the outline of the presentation, then print audience handouts for the entire presentation (six per page). Be sure to frame the individual slides.

    g. View the completed presentation, paying special attention to slide 6, which contains hyperlinks to the Norton and McAfee Web sites. Visit both sites. What is the cost of each program and the associated cost of an annual update? How do the sites provide protection against new viruses? When was the last time you updated your antivirus program?

    h. Be prepared to present your findings in a class discussion.

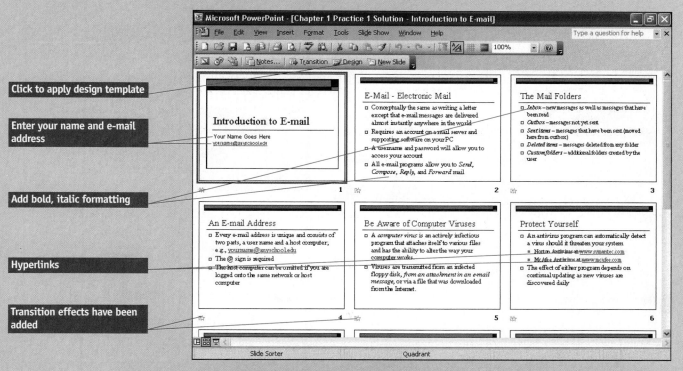

FIGURE 1.17 Introduction to E-mail (exercise 1)

2. **What's New in Windows® XP?:** Windows XP is the newest and most powerful version of the Windows operating system. It has a slightly different look than earlier versions, but it maintains the conventions of its various predecessors. The Windows XP Home Edition is intended for entertainment and home use. It includes a media player, support for digital photography, and an instant messenger. The Windows XP Professional Edition has all of the features of the Home Edition plus additional security to encrypt files and protect data.

a. Go to the Exploring Office Web site at www.prenhall.com/grauer; click the link to Office 2003, then click the link to "What's New in Windows XP?"

b. Read the summary description of Windows XP, then click the link to download the PowerPoint presentation. Save the file to your desktop, then go to your desktop, double click the file that you just downloaded, and follow the onscreen instructions to unzip the presentation in Figure 1.18.

c. Start PowerPoint. Pull down the File menu, click the Open command, and change to the drive and folder where you just unzipped the "What's New in Windows XP?" presentation. Open the presentation.

d. Pull down the Slide Show menu and click the View Show command to view the presentation. There are 25 slides in all, and it should take you no more than 10 or 15 minutes to go through the entire presentation. We think you will learn something, even if you have been using Windows XP for several months.

e. Go to the title slide, add your name after Bob's, and replace Bob's e-mail address with your own.

f. Create a new slide immediately after the title slide. Choose the Title and Text layout, title the slide "My Favorite New Features", then list at least three new features in Windows XP.

g. Print the presentation in multiple ways. Print the title slide as a slide (full page) to serve as a cover page for the assignment. Print the audience handouts for the entire presentation (six per page). Be sure to frame the individual slides.

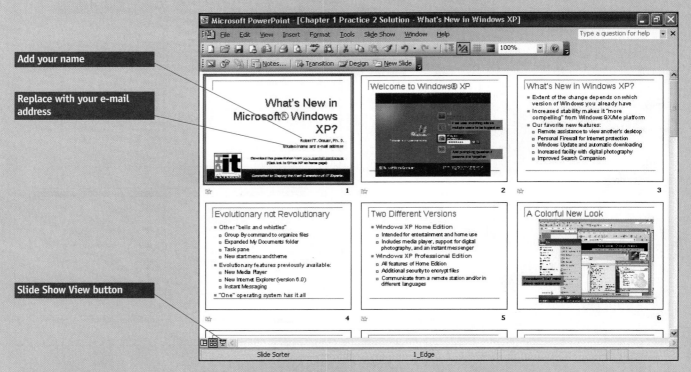

FIGURE 1.18   What's New in Windows XP? (exercise 2)

3. **Introduction to the Internet:** The presentation in Figure 1.19 is intended to review the basics of the Internet and provide practice with modifying an existing PowerPoint presentation. Open the partially completed presentation in *Chapter 1 Practice 3* within the Exploring PowerPoint folder and do the following:

a. Add your name to the title slide as indicated. Add a note to this slide to identify your class and your professor.

b. Search the presentation to find the slide containing the acronyms HTTP, HTTPS, HTML, and ISP (all of the terms are on the same slide). Boldface and italicize these acronyms.

c. Delete the clip art on the "Connecting to the Internet" slide. Change the layout of this slide to a two-column bulleted slide, and then describe your Internet connection(s) in the second column.

d. Add a bulleted slide after slide 6 (The Uniform Resource Locator). The new slide should list five specific Web sites. The first bullet should reference your school or professor. The second bullet should reference the Exploring Office Web site. Each bullet should name the site followed by its URL, e.g., The Exploring Office Web site at www.prenhall.com/grauer.

e. Set a limit of five minutes to experiment with different design templates, and then choose a template for the completed presentation.

f. Add transition effects throughout the presentation as you see fit.

g. Print the presentation in multiple ways. Print the title slide as a slide (full page) to serve as a cover page. Print the notes for the first slide. Print the audience handouts for the entire presentation (six per page). Be sure to frame the individual slides. And finally, print the presentation in outline form.

h. Go through the presentation one slide at a time to learn and/or review the material. Did you learn anything new? Are you surprised at the age of the Internet? What additional material (if any) would you include in the presentation? Summarize your thoughts in a brief note to your instructor.

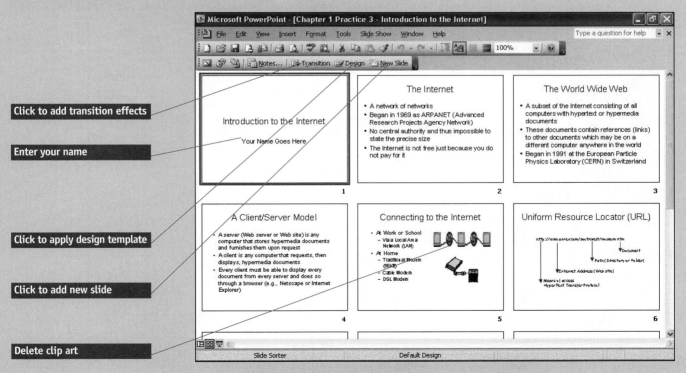

FIGURE 1.19 Introduction to the Internet (exercise 3)

4. **Copyright and the Law:** The presentation in Figure 1.20 is intended to review basic copyright law and software licensing and also to provide practice with modifying an existing PowerPoint presentation. Open the partially completed presentation in *Chapter 1 Practice 4* within the Exploring PowerPoint folder and do the following:

a. Add a copyright logo to the title slide. Our logo is actually a piece of clip art, which has a built-in animation effect. Pull down the Insert menu, click Picture, click Clip Art to display the Insert Clip Art task pane, and then search on the keyword, copyright. (We have included the clip art image as a GIF file in the Exploring PowerPoint folder if your search is unsuccessful.) Add your name to the title slide as indicated.

b. Boldface and italicize the terms "copyright" on slide 2 (first bullet only), "End User License Agreement" and "Site License" on slide 4, and "public domain" and "fair use exclusion" on slide 7.

c. Set a limit of five minutes to experiment with different design templates, and then choose a template for the completed presentation.

d. Add transition effects throughout the presentation as you see fit.

e. Insert a new slide immediately before the last slide that contains the following text. *Individuals who violate copyright law and/or software licensing agreements may be subject to criminal or civil action by the copyright or license owners. This means you!* Choose a font size and style so that the text fills the entire slide.

f. Visit one or more of the Web sites that are indicated on the last slide to obtain additional information. How do you feel about the copyright law with respect to downloading music from the Web? Be prepared to discuss the content of these sites in class.

g. Print the presentation in multiple ways. Print the title slide as a slide (full page) to serve as a cover page for the assignment. Print audience handouts for the entire presentation (six per page). Be sure to frame the individual slides. And finally, print the presentation in outline form.

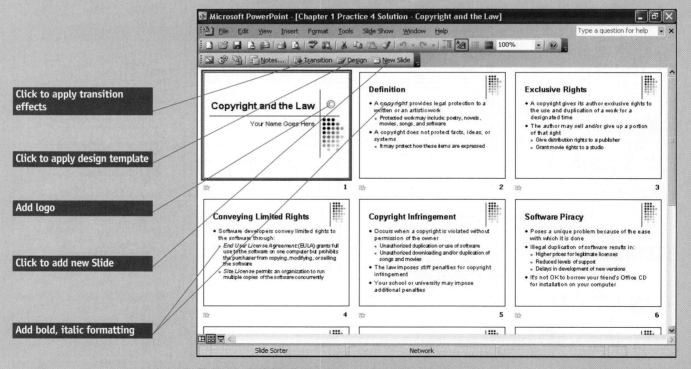

FIGURE 1.20 Copyright and the Law (exercise 4)

5. **Public Speaking 101:** PowerPoint will help you to create an attractive presentation, but the delivery is still up to you. It's easier than you think, and you should not be intimidated at the prospect of facing an audience. You can become an effective speaker by following the basic tenets of good public speaking as described in the presentation of Figure 1.21.

a. Open the *Chapter 1 Practice 5* presentation that describes the basics of good public speaking. Add your name to the title slide.

b. Print the notes for the presentation, then view the slide show, looking at the appropriate notes for each slide.

c. Which slides have notes attached? Are the notes redundant, or do they add something extra? Do you see how the notes help a speaker to deliver an effective presentation?

d. What different delivery styles were referenced in the learning activity slide? Was the class able to see the problem inherent with the ineffective delivery of each topic?

e. Which slide contains the phrase, "Common sense is not common practice"? In what context is the phrase used within the presentation?

f. Which personality said, "You can observe a lot by watching"? In what context is the phrase used during the presentation?

g. Public speaking is like any other skill; the more you practice, the better you become. All you need is a friendly audience. Ask your instructor to create groups of four or five students, and then practice delivering the presentation to your classmates. Were you able to follow the tenets of good public speaking?

h. What suggestions were made in the presentation to create a positive learning environment? Do you have any additional suggestions?

i. Summarize your thoughts about this presentation in a short note to your instructor.

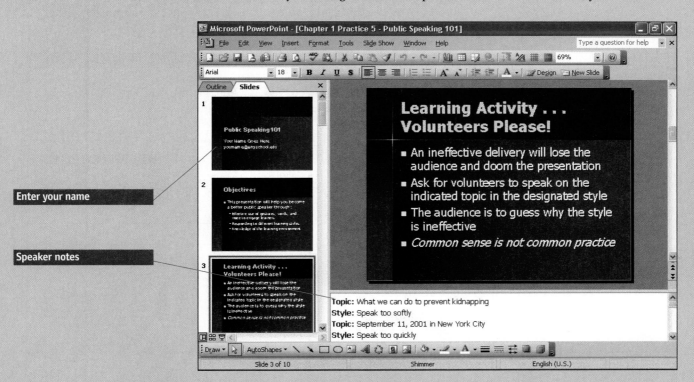

FIGURE 1.21   Public Speaking 101 (exercise 5)

6. **University Housing:** A partially completed version of the presentation in Figure 1.22 has been saved as the *Chapter 1 Practice 6* presentation in the Exploring PowerPoint folder. Open this presentation and save it as *Chapter 1 Practice 6 Solution* so that you can return to the original presentation if necessary.

   a. Insert a new slide that contains a mission statement as the fifth slide in the presentation. The mission statement should read as follows: *The mission of the **University Housing Office** is to provide a total environment that will enrich the educational experience of its residents. It seeks to promote increased interaction between faculty and students through resident masters, special programs, and intramural activities.*

   b. Open the *Chapter 1 Practice 6* workbook that is in the Exploring PowerPoint folder. Click the worksheet tab containing the side-by-side column chart. If necessary, click the Zoom button and change the magnification so that you can select the entire chart. Click the Copy button. Return to PowerPoint and go to the fourth slide. Pull down the Edit menu, click Paste Special, select Microsoft Excel Chart Object, click Paste Link, and click OK.

   c. The chart should appear in the presentation. The only tricky part (if any) is to display the entire chart (it may be cropped initially). Select the chart, then click and drag a corner sizing handle to make the chart smaller. Right click the chart and click the command to display the Picture toolbar. Select the Crop tool, then click and drag the side handle at the right of the chart to show the portion of the chart that may have been cropped initially. Move and size the chart as necessary.

   d. Use the same technique as in steps b and c to link the worksheet for room and meal revenues to the appropriate slide in the presentation. Move and/or size these objects after they have been added to the presentation.

   e. Add your name to the title slide. Print the audience handouts of the completed presentation (six per page) for your instructor. Be sure to frame the slides. Exit PowerPoint. Close the Excel workbook and exit Excel.

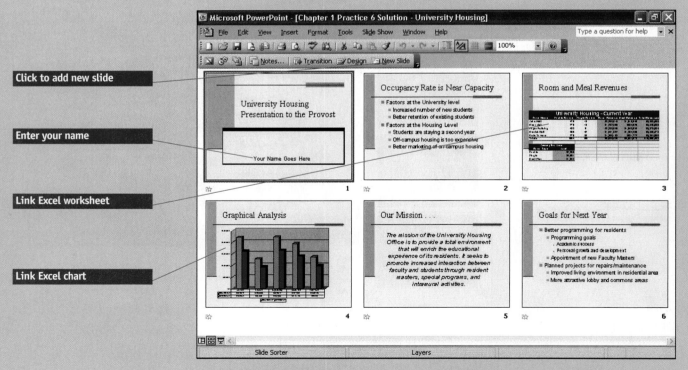

FIGURE **1.22** University Housing (exercise 6)

7. **You Don't Have to Be an Artist:** Figure 1.23 illustrates how you can modify existing clip art to create entirely different images. Open the presentation in *Chapter 1 Practice 7*. Add your name to the title slide. Change to the Slide Sorter view. Select the second slide (The Original Clip Art), click the Copy button, then click the Paste button to duplicate the original slide.

   a. Double click the copied slide (slide 3) to return to the Normal view. Select The Original Clip Art. Click the down arrow on the Draw button, and then click the Ungroup command. Click Yes to convert the picture to a Microsoft Office Drawing Object. Click on the clip art, and then ungroup it a second time. You should see two sets of sizing handles, one around the duck, and one around the computer and table.

   b. Click in the background area of the slide to deselect both objects. Now click on the duck and experiment with the various tools on the Drawing toolbar to flip the image horizontally or vertically. Change the title of the slide to describe the modification.

   c. Click in the outline pane, click on slide 2 (the slide that contains The Original Clip Art), click the Copy button, then click on slide 3 and click the paste button three times. Select (click) slide 4 and use the appropriate tools on the Drawing toolbar to create this slide. Change the title of slide 4 to reflect the modification. Create slides 5 and 6 in similar fashion, changing the title each time.

   d. Add a seventh slide of your own design, then copy the clip art from that slide to the title slide. You will have to group the objects on the seventh slide in order to move the clip art as a unit. Pull down the Edit menu, click Select All to select all of the objects, then press and hold the Ctrl key as you click the title to deselect the title. Now, right click the selected clip art, click Grouping from the context-sensitive menu, then click the Group command. You can now select the image (consisting of multiple ducks) as a single object and copy it to the title slide.

   e. Print the completed presentation for your instructor. Print the title slide as a full page, then print audience handouts of slides 2 through 7.

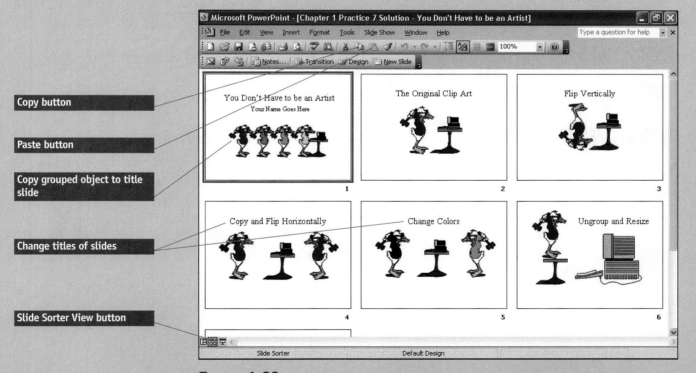

FIGURE 1.23 You Don't Have to Be an Artist (exercise 7)

8. **Request for Venture Capital:** Definitely Needlepoint is a successful retail store owned by four close friends who enjoy needlepoint. The store has been in operation for three years and has increased its revenue and profit for each year. The partners are looking to expand their operation by requesting venture capital. They have an important meeting scheduled for next week and have decided to use PowerPoint to present their case. Your assignment is to open the partially completed version of the *Chapter 1 Practice 8* presentation that is displayed in Figure 1.24 and proceed as follows:

a. Insert a new slide containing the mission statement as the second slide in the presentation. The mission statement should read as follows: *Definitely Needlepoint provides an intimate setting in which to stitch. Our customers are our friends and participate in a variety of social and educational activities that encourage and develop the art of needlepoint.*

b. Open the *Chapter 1 Practice 8* workbook in the Exploring PowerPoint folder. Select the worksheet that contains sales data for last year, and link that data to the slide containing the year-to-year comparison (slide 4). Now select the worksheet with sales data for the current year and link this data to the same slide. Move and/or size the worksheets after they have been added to the presentation.

c. Locate the worksheet containing the chart that shows the sales increase by category. Link this chart to slide 5.

d. Locate the chart that shows the sales increase by quarter and link the chart to slide 6.

e. Add your name to the title slide in the indicated position. Print the audience handouts of the completed presentation (six per page) for your instructor. Print the outline. Print the title slide as a full slide to use as a cover page for the assignment.

f. Save the completed presentation. Exit PowerPoint. Close the Excel workbook. Exit Excel.

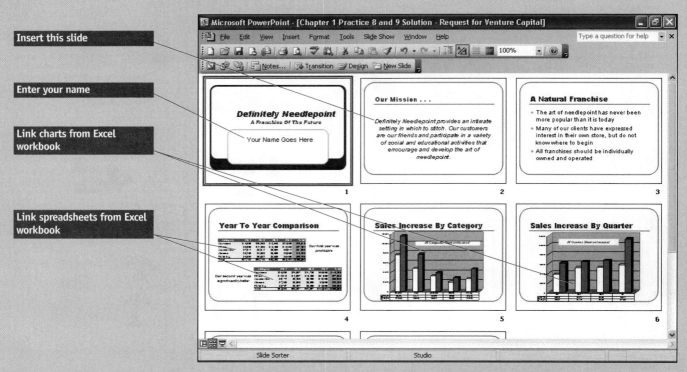

FIGURE 1.24 Request for Venture Capital (exercise 8)

9. **A Look Ahead—Action Buttons and Slide Masters:** The presentation in Figure 1.25 appears to be identical to the presentation in the previous exercise. Look closely, however, and you will see a set of four action buttons at the bottom of the second and third slides in the presentation. (The buttons are used during the slide show to provide easy navigation to the first, previous, next, and last slides in the presentation.) The buttons are on every slide except for the title slide, but the additional slides are not visible in Figure 1.25. The buttons are added to the slide master, which in turn displays them on every slide. Proceed as follows:

a. Open the completed presentation from the previous exercise. Pull down the View menu, click the Master command, then select the Slide Master. (Be sure the bulleted slide is selected, as opposed to the title slide.) Pull down the Slide Show menu, click the Action Buttons command, and select (click) the beginning |◄ button that indicates the first slide.

b. The mouse pointer changes to a tiny crosshair. Click in the footer area at the bottom of the slide, then drag the mouse to create an action button. Release the mouse. The Action Settings dialog box is displayed automatically. The Hyperlink to Option button is selected and First Slide is specified in the associated list box. Click OK to accept the default settings and close the Action Settings dialog box. Repeat this process three additional times to create action buttons for the previous, next, and ending slides in that sequence.

c. Click and drag the individual action buttons so that there is sufficient space between the buttons to increase their size to ½ inch each. Press and hold the Shift key as you click each action button to select all four buttons. Point to any button, click the right mouse button to display a context-sensitive menu, then click Format AutoShape to display the Format AutoShape dialog box. Click the Size tab, then enter .35 and .5 as the height and width of each button. Click OK to accept the settings and close the dialog box.

d. Change to the Slide Sorter view. The action buttons should appear on every slide.

e. Save the presentation. Press Ctrl+Home to move to the first slide. Pull down the Slide Show menu and click the View Show command. Test the action buttons to be sure that they work as intended.

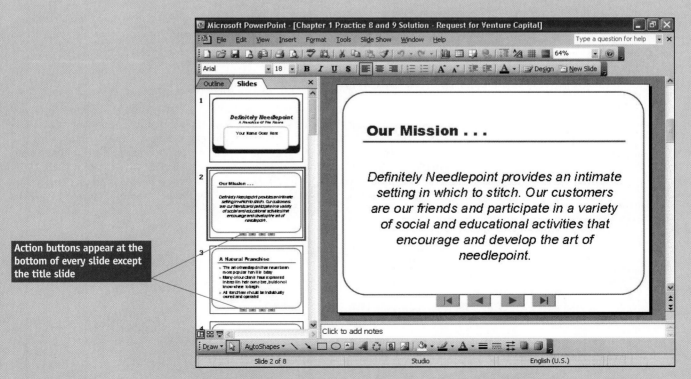

FIGURE 1.25 A Look Ahead—Action Buttons and Slide Masters (exercise 9)

MINI CASES

Planning for Disaster

This case has nothing to do with presentations per se, but it is perhaps the most important case of all, as it deals with the question of backup. Do you have a backup strategy? Do you even know what a backup strategy is? This is a good time to learn, because sooner or later you will need to recover a file. The problem always seems to occur the night before an assignment is due. You accidentally erased a file, are unable to read from a floppy disk, or worse yet, suffer a hardware failure in which you are unable to access the hard drive. The ultimate disaster is the disappearance of your computer, by theft or natural disaster. Describe in 250 words or fewer the backup strategy you plan to implement in conjunction with your work in this class.

Changing Menus and Toolbars

Office 2003 lets you switch to a series of short menus that contain only basic commands. The additional commands are made visible by clicking the double arrow that appears at the bottom of the menu. New commands are added to the menu as they are used, and conversely, other commands are removed if they are not used. A similar strategy is followed for the Standard and Formatting toolbars, which are displayed on a single row, and thus do not show all of the buttons at one time. The intent is to simplify Office 2003 for the new user by limiting the number of commands that are visible. The consequence, however, is that the individual is not exposed to new commands, and hence may not use Office to its full potential. Which set of menus do you prefer? How do you switch from one set to the other?

Be Creative

One interesting way of exploring the potential of presentation graphics is to imagine it might have been used by historical figures had it been available. Choose any historical figure or current personality and create at least a six-slide presentation. You could, for example, show how Columbus might have used PowerPoint to request funding from Queen Isabella, or how Elvis Presley might have pleaded for his first recording contract. The content of your presentation should be reasonable, but you don't have to spend an inordinate amount of time on research. Just be creative and use your imagination. Use clip art as appropriate, but don't overdo it. Place your name on the title slide as technical adviser.

The National Debt

The national debt is staggering—more than $6 trillion, or approximately $20,000 for every man, woman, and child in the United States. The annual budget is approximately $2 trillion. Use the Internet to obtain exact figures for the current year, then use this information to create a presentation on income and expenditures. Do some additional research and obtain data on the budget, the deficit, and the national debt for the years 1945, 1967, and 1980. The numbers may surprise you. For example, how does the interest expense for the current year compare to the total budget in 1967 (at the height of the Vietnam War)? To the total budget in 1945 (at the end of World War II)?

Gaining Proficiency:
Slide Show Tools and Digital Photography

CASE STUDY
FEATURE FILMS, INC.

Shelly Daniels has a bright, creative, and energetic personality. She is currently a senior majoring in Motion Pictures within the Communication Department and studying for her bachelor's degree. She hopes to become a producer or director for a major film company, following the footsteps of her grandfather, Norman A. Daniels.

This term she is taking COM400: Administration of Studio Operations. The capstone project requires every student to create their own feature film company and present an overview of their company to the class. The presentation is to be in the form of an employee orientation; it should include a description of the company's history, organizational structure, past and present projects, corporate policies, and employee benefits. The assignment was given at the beginning of the semester with the understanding that it would be developed as the topics were presented. It is now the end of the semester, and Shelly, a procrastinator by nature, is in a real bind. She has 24 hours to complete the entire assignment before presenting it to the class. In a flash of inspiration, she turns to the AutoContent Wizard for help and finds the *Employee Orientation* template, which is the perfect place to start her presentation. ■

Your assignment is to read the chapter, paying special attention to Hands-on Exercise 4, which describes the AutoContent Wizard. Put yourself in Shelly's shoes and create a presentation based on the Employee Orientation template. You will, however, have to add your own content to comply with the requirements of the assignment. You will also be graded on how well you present to the class. Thus, you should practice several times to rehearse your timing and delivery. Use animation and/or transition effects to add interest. Add notes throughout the presentation and then print the completed presentation in multiple ways. Print audience handouts (six per page). Print an outline of the presentation. Print at least one slide to show the notes that you have added. Print the title slide as a slide (full page) to serve as a cover page.

PowerPoint provides a series of slide show tools to help you deliver a presentation effectively. The tools are discussed briefly in conjunction with the presentation in Figure 2.1, and then described in detail in a hands-on exercise. The text on the second slide is worthy of special mention as it was entered into a table, as an alternative to the standard bulleted text slide. The table was created through the ***Insert Table command*** to provide variety within a presentation.

Each slide in the presentation (except for the title slide) contains the identical text that was entered through the ***Header and Footer command***. The inclusion of a header or footer personalizes a presentation by adding items such as the date, place of the presentation, and/or the slide number. You can also include a clip art or logo to create additional interest.

Look carefully under each slide and you will see a number that represents the amount of time the presenter intends to devote to the slide. The timings were entered through the ***Rehearse Timings*** feature that lets you time a presentation as you practice your delivery. The Rehearse Timings feature can also be used with the ***Set Up Show command*** to automate a presentation so that each slide will be shown for the set time period.

The icon under slide number 5 indicates that it is a ***hidden slide***, which prevents the slide from appearing during a regular slide show. This is a common practice among experienced speakers who anticipate probing questions that may arise during the presentation. The presenter prefers not to address the topic initially, but creates a slide to hold in reserve should the topic arise. The hidden slide can be displayed during a slide show by right clicking the slide and choosing the Go To Slide command.

The ability to annotate slides by drawing on the slide (just like your favorite football announcer) is not visible in Figure 2.1, since the annotation takes place during the actual slide show. This is a favorite technique and one we will illustrate in the next hands-on exercise.

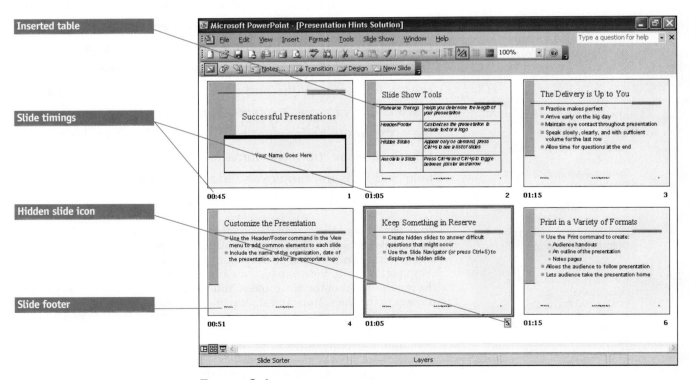

FIGURE 2.1 Presentation Tools

The American workplace is team oriented, with many people typically collaborating on the same document. Microsoft Office XP facilitates this process by enabling the revisions to be stored and accepted (or rejected) electronically. In PowerPoint the process works as follows. You create the initial presentation, then use the ***Send To command*** to send the presentation to one or more people for review. PowerPoint automatically links to your e-mail program and sends the presentation as an attachment.

Each reviewer receives a copy of the presentation, enters his or her changes, then returns the revised presentation as an attachment in an e-mail message. You save each reviewer's attachment as its own file (such as Bob's Comments), then you use the ***Compare and Merge Presentations command*** to open all of the reviewers' presentations and optionally merge the comments with the original presentation. You can merge the comments from multiple reviewers in a single session.

Figure 2.2 shows the suggested changes to the first slide in the selected presentation. The ***revisions pane*** at the right shows how the title slide would look according to the changes for each reviewer. Robert Grauer changes the title to "Successful Presentations", but retains the current template. Maryann Barber, on the other hand, retains the title, but modifies the template. You can accept either or both changes by checking the box next to each reviewer's name in the revisions pane. You can expand any proposed changes in text (such as Bob's change in title) and accept or reject the suggestions individually. You can also use the Undo command to cancel your changes.

The developer of the presentation goes from one slide to the next, accepting or rejecting the changes, as he or she sees fit. The ***Reviewing toolbar*** contains several buttons to aid in this process, such as the Next and Previous Item buttons to move from one revision to the next. The toolbar also provides buttons to insert, edit, or delete comments. The reviewer ends the review, which in turn closes the revisions pane and removes the reviewers' presentations from memory. You can then send the revised presentation as an e-mail attachment.

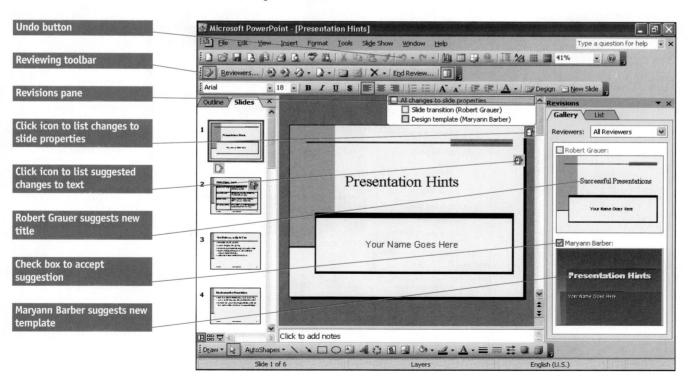

FIGURE 2.2 Reviewing Changes

Objective	To use the Rehearse Timings feature to practice your delivery; to use the Slide Navigator and pen during a presentation; to send a presentation for review; to compare and merge documents. Use Figure 2.3 as a guide in the exercise.

Step 1:   Create the Table

- Start PowerPoint. Open **Presentation Hints** in the **Exploring PowerPoint folder**. Click on the placeholder for the subtitle and add your name to the title slide.

- Pull down the **File menu**, click the **Save As command** to display the File Save dialog box, then save the presentation as **Presentation Hints Solution**.

- Pull down the **Insert menu** and click the **New Slide command** (or click the **New Slide button** on the Formatting toolbar). The task pane opens as shown in Figure 2.3a with a text slide selected by default.

- Click the **Title Only layout** to change the layout of the new slide. Click in the Title placeholder and enter the title **Slide Show Tools** as shown in the figure.

- Click outside the title placeholder. Pull down the **Insert menu** and click the **Table command** to display the Insert Table dialog box in Figure 2.3a.

- Enter **2** as the number of columns and **4** as the number of rows. Click **OK**. The table will be inserted into the document.

- Close the task pane. Save the presentation.

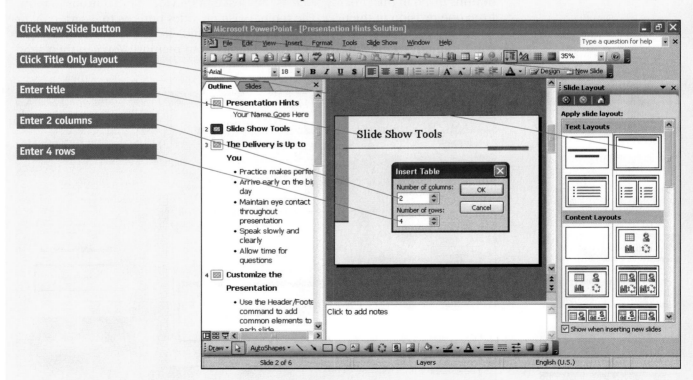

Click New Slide button
Click Title Only layout
Enter title
Enter 2 columns
Enter 4 rows

(a) Create the Table (step 1)

FIGURE 2.3   Hands-on Exercise 1

Step 2: **Complete the Table**

- Click anywhere in the table to select the table and display a hashed border.

- Click and drag the vertical line dividing the two columns to the left so that the first column is narrower and the second column is wider. Drag the left and/or right border to make the table larger or smaller as necessary.

- Enter the text into the table as shown in Figure 2.3b. Text is entered into each cell independently of the other cells.

- Click in a cell, type the appropriate text, then press the **Tab key** to move to the next cell. Complete the table as shown in the figure.

- Click and drag to select multiple cells simultaneously, then use the various buttons on the Formatting toolbar to format the text in these cells as you see fit. Click outside the table to deselect it.

- Save the presentation.

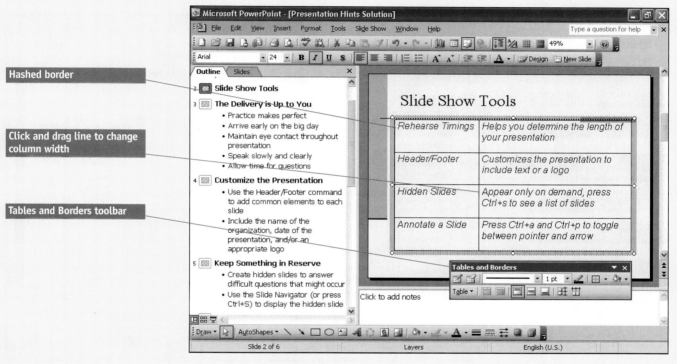

(b) Complete the Table (step 2)

FIGURE 2.3 Hands-on Exercise 1 (*continued*)

THE TABLES AND BORDERS TOOLBAR

The Tables and Borders toolbar contains a variety of tools for use in creating and/or modifying a table. Click the Border Color button (to change the color) or click the Border Width down arrow (to change the thickness), then use the mouse (the pointer changes to a pencil) to paint the table borders according to the new settings. Click the down arrow on the Table button to see the commands that are available. If you do not see the toolbar, pull down the View menu, click (or point to) the Toolbars command, then click the Tables and Borders toolbar.

Step 3: **Add the Slide Footer**

- Pull down the **View menu** and click the **Header and Footer command** to display the Header and Footer dialog box in Figure 2.3c.

- Click the **Slide tab**. Click the check box for the Date and time, then click the **Option button** to Update the date automatically. The presentation will always show the current date when this option is in effect. (Alternatively, you can choose the option to enter a fixed date.)

- Check the Slide number and Footer check boxes as shown. Click in the text box associated with the footer and enter the appropriate text to reflect your school or university.

- Check the box, **Don't show on title slide**, to suppress the footer on the first slide. Click the **Apply to All button** to accept these settings and close the Header and Footer dialog box.

- Save the presentation.

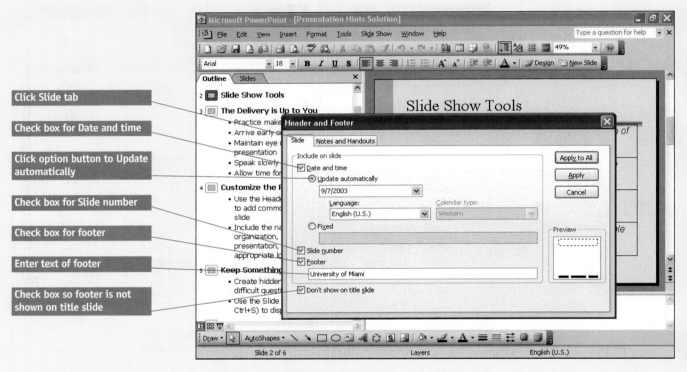

(c) Add the Slide Footer (step 3)

FIGURE 2.3 Hands-on Exercise 1 (*continued*)

CUSTOMIZE THE TABLE LAYOUT

Click and drag to select one or more cells within a table, then pull down the Format menu and click the Tables command to display the Format Table dialog box. You can change the border, fill, or text alignment by clicking the appropriate tab within the dialog box, then executing the appropriate command. Click the Undo command if the result is different from what you intended. You might also want to set a time limit, because there are almost too many options from which to choose.

Step 4:   Send for Review

- Pull down the **File menu**, click (or point to) the **Send To command**, then choose **Mail Recipient (for Review)**. Your e-mail program will open automatically and display a new message as shown in Figure 2.3d. (Skip this step if your e-mail program does not appear, as might happen in a computer lab.)

- The subject, attachment, and text of the note are entered automatically for you. The name of the current presentation, "Presentation Hints Solution" appears in both the subject line and the attachment.

- Enter the e-mail address of a recipient (e.g., a fellow student). You can enter the addresses of multiple individuals if you want more than one person to review the presentation. Sign your name in the message area and click the **Send button**.

- Normally, you would need the reviewer to return the presentation to you with his or her comments.

- We have, however, supplied a presentation for you with comments from our reviewer, so that you do not have to wait for a response.

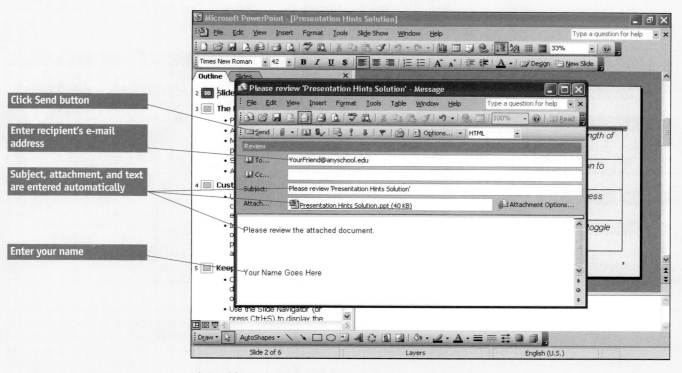

(d) Send for Review (step 4)

FIGURE 2.3   Hands-on Exercise 1 (*continued*)

SEND THE PRESENTATION AS AN ATTACHMENT

Send the completed presentation as an attachment, as opposed to sending it for review. Pull down the File menu, click the Send To command, then choose the second option to send the open presentation as an attachment to an e-mail message. This is an option with which you are probably familiar and is similar in concept to mailing a Word document or Excel workbook. (PowerPoint presentations are generally large files, and thus you may want to compress the file before sending it.)

Step 5: **Compare and Merge Presentations**

- Pull down the **Tools menu** and click the **Compare and Merge Presentations command**. Select the **Bob's Comments** presentation (which represents a review of your presentation) in the Exploring PowerPoint folder. Click the **Merge button**.

- Click **Continue** if you see a message indicating that one presentation was not sent for review. The Revisions Pane opens as shown in Figure 2.3e. Click the **Outline** and **Gallery tabs** in the left and right panes, respectively.

- Select the title slide. Click the icon to the right of the title slide to see suggestions from the reviewer (Robert Grauer in this example). Check the box to accept all changes to the title slide.

- Click the **Next Item button** on the Reviewing toolbar to move to the next revision. This takes you to the third slide, titled "The Delivery is Up to You". Check the box to accept all changes on this slide.

- Continue to click the **Next Item button** and accept all suggested changes until you reach the last slide. PowerPoint indicates that you have reached the end of the presentation and asks if you want to continue. Click **Cancel** since you have reviewed all of the changes.

- Click the **End Review button** on the Reviewing toolbar. Click **Yes** when asked whether to end the review. Save the presentation.

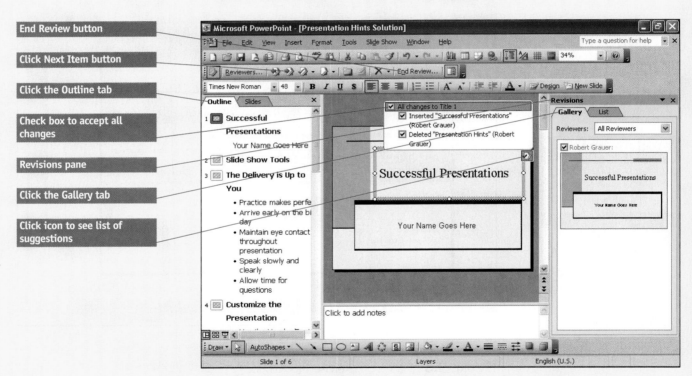

(e) Compare and Merge Presentations (step 5)

FIGURE 2.3 Hands-on Exercise 1 (*continued*)

INSERT COMMENTS INTO THE PRESENTATION

Pull down the Insert menu and click the Comment command (or click the Insert Comment button on the Reviewing toolbar) to insert a comment. The comments are for information only and do not change the actual presentation. Click the Markup button on the Reviewing toolbar to toggle the comment (and reviewer remarks) on and off.

Step 6: Rehearse the Presentation

- Press **Ctrl+Home** to return to the first slide. Pull down the **Slide Show menu** and click the **Rehearse Timings command**.

- The first slide appears in the Slide Show view. The Rehearsal toolbar is displayed in the upper-left corner of the screen. Speak as though you were presenting the slide, then click the mouse to register the elapsed time for that slide and move to the next slide.

- The second slide in the presentation should appear as shown in Figure 2.3f. Speak as though you were presenting the slide and, as you do, watch the Rehearsal toolbar:
  - ❑ The time for the specific slide (1 minute and 5 seconds) is displayed in the Slide Time box. The cumulative time for the presentation (1 minute and 50 seconds) is also shown.
  - ❑ Click the **Repeat button** to redo the timing for the slide.
  - ❑ Click the **Pause button** to (temporarily) stop the clock. Click the **Pause button** a second time to resume the clock.
  - ❑ Click the **Next button** to record the timing and move to the next slide.

- Continue rehearsing the show until you reach the end of the presentation. You should see a dialog box at the end of the presentation that indicates the total time of the slide show.

- Click **Yes** when asked whether you want to record the new timings. PowerPoint returns to the Slide Sorter view and records the timings under each slide.

- Pull down the **Slide Show menu** and click the **Set Up Show command** to display the Set Up Show dialog box.

- Check the option button to advance slides **Manually** (otherwise the slides will be automatically advanced according to the times you just recorded). Click **OK** to accept the settings and close the dialog box.

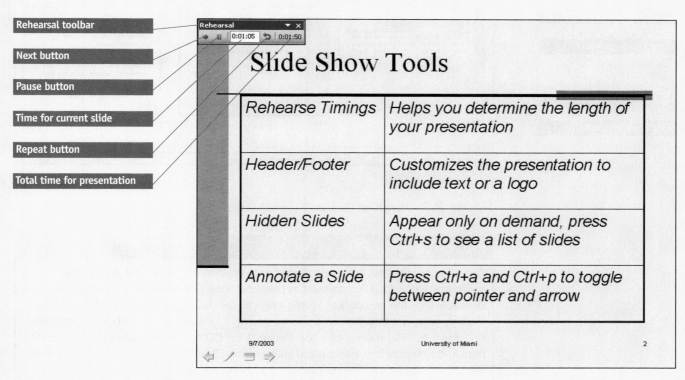

(f) Rehearse the Presentation (step 6)

FIGURE 2.3   Hands-on Exercise 1 (*continued*)

Step 7: **Hide a Slide**

■ If necessary, click the **down arrow** on the Zoom box to zoom to 100%. The slides are larger and easier to read.

■ Select (click) the fifth slide (Keep Something in Reserve) then click the **Hide Slide button** as shown in Figure 2.3g. The slide remains in the presentation, but it will *not* be displayed during the slide show.

■ The Hide Slide button functions as a toggle switch. Click it once and the slide is hidden. Click the command a second time and the slide is no longer hidden. Leave the slide hidden.

■ Click Slide 1, then click the **Slide Show View button** and move quickly through the presentation. You will not see the slide titled Keep Something in Reserve because it has been hidden. (You can still access this slide during the presentation as described in the next step.)

■ Save the presentation.

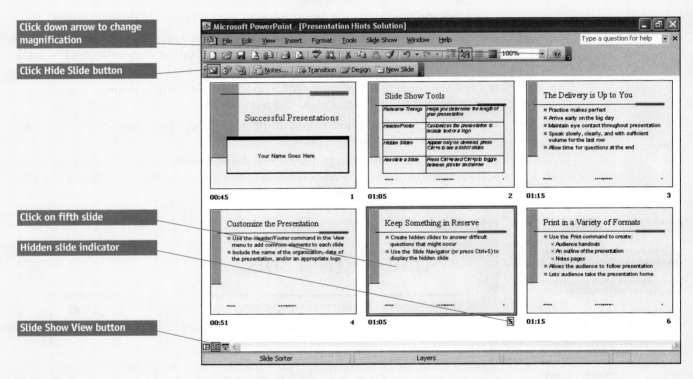

(g) Hide a Slide (step 7)

FIGURE 2.3 Hands-on Exercise 1 (*continued*)

PACKAGE FOR CD

Will your presentation fit on a floppy disk so that you can take it with you to the computer you will use to deliver the presentation? Are you positive that PowerPoint is installed on the computer? Either way, you can use the Package for CD command to copy your presentation to a CD (providing you have the appropriate hardware). Pull down the File menu, click the Package for CD command, and click the options button to display the associated dialog box. Check the box for the PowerPoint Viewer to play presentations without using PowerPoint.

Step 8: **Display the Hidden Slide**

- Press **Ctrl+Home** to move to the first slide in the presentation. Click the **Slide Show View button** above the status bar to show the presentation. You should see the title slide.

- Click the **left mouse button** or press the **PgDn key** to move from one slide to the next. Look at the slide number in the lower-right corner of each slide as the show progresses. You will see slides, 1, 2, 3, 4, and 6; i.e., you will skip slide 5 because it is hidden.

- Right click anywhere on the slide to display a context-sensitive menu as shown in Figure 2.3h. (You can also click the **up arrow** in the lower-left portion of the screen).

- Click the **Go to Slide command** to display a list of the slides in your presentation. Click the **fifth slide** to display the hidden slide. (Note the parentheses around the number 5 to indicate the slide is hidden.)

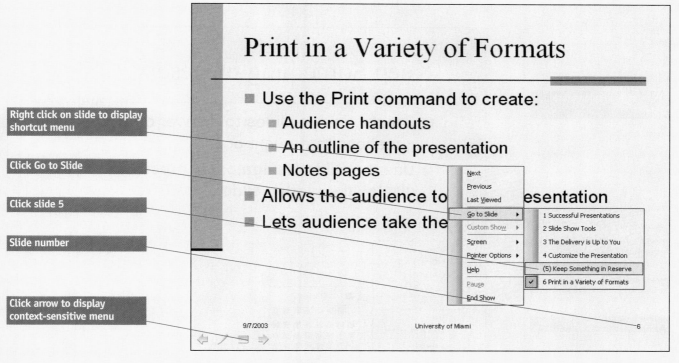

(h) Display the Hidden Slide (step 8)

FIGURE 2.3 Hands-on Exercise 1 (*continued*)

SETTING UP A SLIDE SHOW

You can start a slide show on any slide, advance the slides automatically according to preset timings (established through the Rehearse Timings command), and/or loop through the slide show continually until the user presses the Esc key. Pull down the Slide Show menu, click the Set Up Show command to display the associated dialog box, then experiment with the various options. Click OK to accept the settings and close the dialog box.

Step 9: **Annotate a Slide**

- You should see slide 5. Press **Ctrl+P** to change the mouse arrow to a point, then click and drag to annotate the slide as shown in Figure 2.3i. Type the letter **E**. The annotation disappears.

- Click the **pen icon** (at the lower left of the slide) to display the pointer options, and then click any of the available options. You can change the pointer thickness and/or change the annotation color.

- Draw a new annotation on the slide, then use the **PgDn key** to move to the last slide in the presentation. (Clicking with either the left or right mouse button has no effect when the mouse is set for annotation.)

- Press **Ctrl+A** to return the mouse to an arrow. Click the left mouse button repeatedly to finish the show, then click **Discard** when asked whether to keep the annotations.

- Exit PowerPoint if you do not want to continue with the next hands-on exercise at this time.

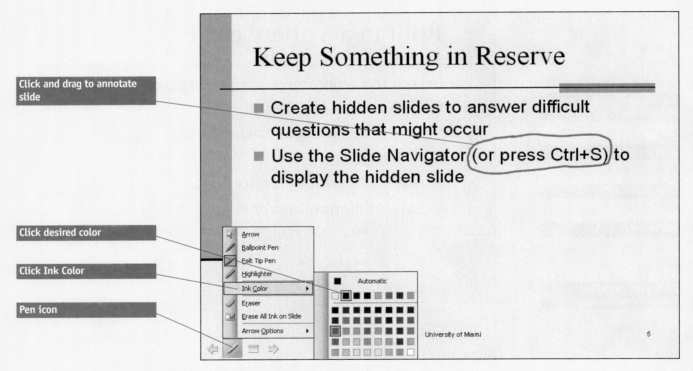

(i) Annotate a Slide (step 9)

FIGURE 2.3 Hands-on Exercise 1 (*continued*)

USE KEYBOARD SHORTCUTS DURING THE SLIDE SHOW

Press Ctrl+S to display a list of the slides in a presentation, including the hidden slides, then double click the slide you want to view. You can also type a number plus the Enter key to go to a specific slide, or press the letter H plus the Enter key to display the next hidden slide. Use Ctrl+P to change the mouse pointer to a point to annotate the slide, then press E to erase the annotations. Press Ctrl+A to change the mouse pointer back to an arrow. If you can't remember these shortcuts, press the F1 key to see the entire list.

The **Internet** and **World Wide Web** are thoroughly integrated into all applications in Microsoft Office in three important ways. First, you can download resources from any Web page for inclusion in a PowerPoint presentation, as you will see in our next hands-on exercise. Second, you can insert hyperlinks into any Office document, then click those links to display the associated Web page in your Web browser. And finally, you can convert any Office document into a Web page for display on your Web server or local area network.

Figure 2.4 illustrates how resources from the Internet can be used to enhance a PowerPoint presentation. The title slide in Figure 2.4a displays a photograph that was downloaded from the Smithsonian Institution's collection of online photographs. The photograph is displayed as an object on a slide and is typical of how most people use a photograph within a presentation. The slide in Figure 2.4b is much more dramatic, and indeed does not even look like a PowerPoint slide. It too displays a photograph, but as background, rather than an object. The text has been entered into a **text box** using the appropriate tool on the Drawing toolbar. (You can right click the text box after it has been created, so that the box will expand and wrap text automatically if additional text is entered.)

Regardless of how you choose to use a photograph, your first task is to access the Web and locate the resource. Thus, you start your Web browser, then you use a search engine to locate the required information (e.g., a photograph of a dinosaur). Once this is done, right click on the photograph to display the context-sensitive menu in the figure, then click the Save Picture As command to download the file to your hard drive. Next, you start PowerPoint where you use the **Insert Picture command** to insert the picture that was just downloaded into a presentation. You can also use the **Insert Hyperlink command** to insert a **hyperlink** onto a slide, which you can click during the slide show, and provided you have an Internet connection, your Web browser will display the associated page.

Copyright Protection

A **copyright** provides legal protection to a written or artistic work, including literary, dramatic, musical, and artistic works such as poetry, novels, movies, songs, and computer software and architecture. It gives the author of a work the exclusive right to the use and duplication of that work. A copyright does not, however, protect facts, ideas, systems, or methods of operation, although it may protect the way these things are expressed.

The owner of the copyright may sell or give up a portion of his or her rights; for example, an author may give distribution rights to a publisher and/or grant movie rights to a studio. **Infringement of a copyright** occurs any time a right reserved by the copyright owner is violated without permission of the owner. Anything on the Internet should be considered copyrighted unless the document specifically says it is in the **public domain**, in which case the author is giving everyone the right to freely reproduce and distribute the material. Does copyright protection prevent you from quoting a document found on the Web in a research paper? Does copyright protection imply that you cannot download an image for inclusion in a term paper? (Facts themselves are not covered by copyright, so you can use statistical data without fear of infringement.)

The answer to what you can use from the Web depends on the amount of the information you reference, as well as the intended use of that information. It is considered **fair use**, and thus not an infringement of copyright, to use a portion of a work for educational, nonprofit purposes, or for the purpose of critical review or commentary. In other words, you can use a quote, downloaded image, or other information from the Web, provided you cite the original work in your footnotes and/or bibliography.

Extinction of the Dinosaurs

Your Name Goes Here

Photograph inserted as object on slide

Text box

Photo by Chip Clark - Catalogue number: USNM 2580

Photo by Chip Clark/National Museum of Natural History

(a) Title Slide

Photograph as slide background

Text boxes

Edmontosaurus annectens

Photo by Chip Clark - Catalogue number: USNM 241

Photo by Chip Clark/National Museum of Natural History

(b) Photograph as Background

FIGURE 2.4   The Web as a Resource

2 The Internet as a Resource

Objective To import slides from an outline; to download a picture from the Internet and use it in a PowerPoint presentation. Use Figure 2.5 as a guide.

Step 1: **Insert the Word Outline**

- Start PowerPoint, which in turn opens a new blank presentation with the title slide already selected. Close the task pane. Click the **Outline tab** in the left pane.

- Enter **Extinction of the Dinosaurs** as the title of the presentation and your name as the author. Save the presentation as **Extinction of the Dinosaurs**.

- Pull down the **Insert menu** and click the **Slides from Outline command** to display the Insert Outline dialog box in Figure 2.5a.

- Click the **drop-down arrow** on the Look in list box to select the Exploring PowerPoint folder. Select the **Extinction of the Dinosaurs** Word document.

- Click the **Insert button**. The Word document is imported into the presentation and converted to individual slides.

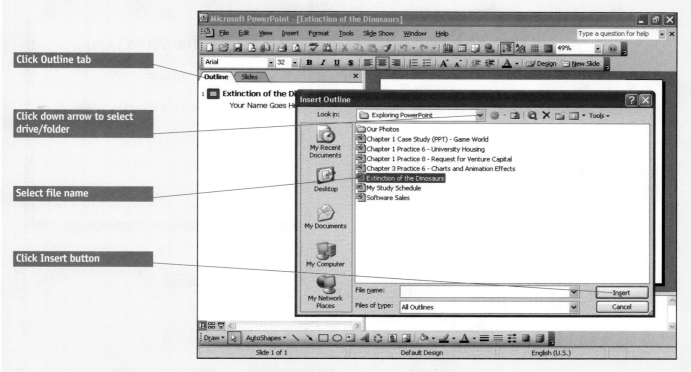

(a) Insert the Word Outline (step 1)

FIGURE 2.5 Hands-on Exercise 2

DISPLAY THE FULL MENUS

Pull down any menu to see if there is a double arrow at the bottom of the menu. If you see the arrow, PowerPoint is displaying only the commands it thinks you need, and we suggest that you display the full menus instead. Pull down the View menu, click the Toolbars command, and click the Customize command. Click the Options tab and check the box to Always show full menus. Pull down any menu; the double arrow has disappeared, and you see the full set of available commands.

Step 2: **Complete the Outline**

- You should see the text of the presentation as shown in Figure 2.5b. Click on the fourth slide that describes the origin of the word *dinosaur*.

- Right click the word "deinos" that is flagged as a misspelling because it is not in the English dictionary. Click **Ignore All** to accept the term without flagging it as a misspelling. Accept the spelling of "sauros" in similar fashion.

- Select (double click) **deinos**, then click the **Bold** and **Italic buttons** on the Formatting toolbar. (You can also use the Ctrl+B and Ctrl+I keyboard shortcuts that apply to all Office applications.)

- Use the **Format Painter** (see boxed tip) to copy this formatting to "sauros" and to "Sir Richard Owen".

- Click outside the placeholder to continue working.

- Save the presentation.

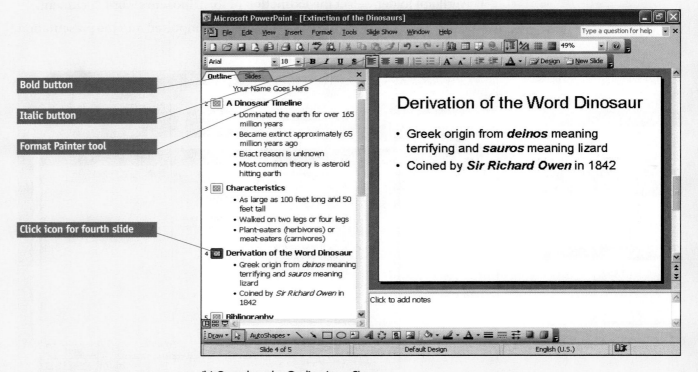

(b) Complete the Outline (step 2)

FIGURE 2.5 Hands-on Exercise 2 (*continued*)

THE FORMAT PAINTER

The Format Painter copies the formatting of the selected text to other places in a presentation. Select the text with the formatting you want to copy, then click or double click the Format Painter button on the Standard toolbar. Clicking the button will paint only one selection. Double clicking the button will paint multiple selections until the feature is turned off by again clicking the Format Painter button. Either way, the mouse pointer changes to a paintbrush, which you can drag over text to give it the identical formatting characteristics as the original selection.

Step 3: **Search the Web**

■ Start Internet Explorer. Click the **Search button** on the Internet Explorer toolbar to open the Search pane as shown in Figure 2.5c. Enter **Smithsonian+ dinosaur** then click the **Search button**.

■ The results of our search are displayed, but you will undoubtedly see a different set of links.

■ Click the link to the **National Museum of Natural History** if it appears. Alternatively, you can click any link that seems promising.

■ Try to find a page that contains one or more photographs. You can also enter the address (**www.nmnh.si.edu/paleo/dino**) directly to duplicate the remainder of the exercise.

■ Click the **Close button** for the Search pane.

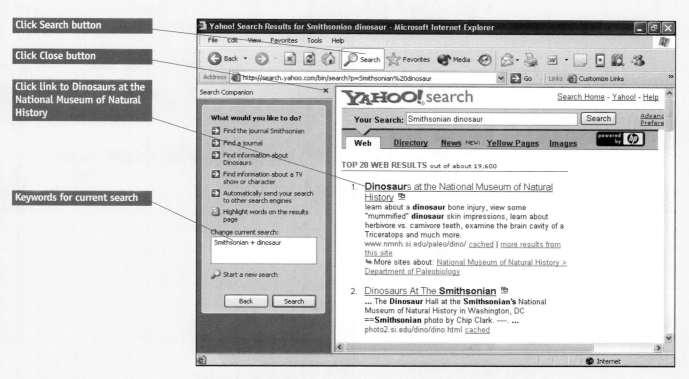

(c) Search the Web (step 3)

FIGURE 2.5 Hands-on Exercise 2 (*continued*)

ABOUT INTERNET EXPLORER

Which version of Internet Explorer are you using? It probably doesn't matter since all recent versions have essentially the same commands, except for slight variations in the toolbar and associated buttons. If your screen does not match ours, it is most likely because you are using a different version of the program. Pull down the Help menu and click the Help Internet Explorer command to see the version of Internet Explorer that is currently installed on your computer. The Help About command works for all Windows applications.

Step 4:   Download the Photograph

- Select any picture on the site, click the **right mouse button** to display a short-cut menu, then click the **Save Picture As command** to display the Save As dialog box in Figure 2.5d.

- Click the **drop-down arrow** in the Save in list box to specify the drive and folder in which you want to save the graphic (e.g., the Exploring PowerPoint folder on drive C).

- The file name and file type are entered automatically. You can change the name, but do not change the file type.

- Click the **Save button** to download the image. Remember the file name and location, as you will need to access the file later in the exercise. The Save As dialog box closes automatically as soon as the picture has been downloaded.

- You need to download at least two pictures for your presentation; thus, repeat the process to download a second picture.

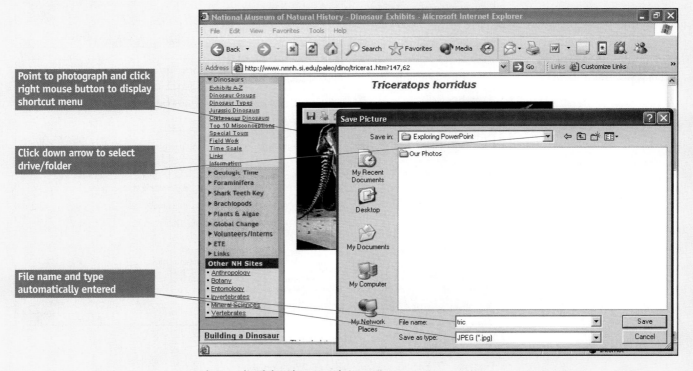

(d) Download the Photograph (step 4)

FIGURE 2.5   Hands-on Exercise 2 (*continued*)

MULTITASKING

Multitasking, the ability to run multiple applications at the same time, is one of the primary advantages of the Windows environment. Switching from one application to another is easy—just click the appropriate button on the Windows taskbar. (If the taskbar is not visible on your screen, it is because the Auto Hide feature is in effect—just point to the bottom edge of the window, and the taskbar will come into view.) You can also use the classic Alt+Tab shortcut. Press and hold the Alt key as you click the Tab key repeatedly to display icons for the open applications, then release the Tab key when the desired application is selected.

Step 5: **Insert the Photograph**

- Click the **PowerPoint button** on the taskbar, then press **Ctrl+Home** to display the first slide. Click below the placeholder for your name in the title slide.

- Pull down the **Insert menu**, point to (or click) **Picture**, then click **From File** to display the Insert Picture dialog box shown in Figure 2.5e.

- Click the **down arrow** on the Views button to select the **Preview view**. Click the **down arrow** on the Look in text box to select the drive and folder where you previously saved the pictures (for example, the Exploring PowerPoint folder on drive C).

- Select (click) one of the photographs you downloaded and a preview should appear within the Insert Picture dialog box. Click the **Insert button**.

- Click and drag the photograph to the bottom-right side of the slide. Click the slide title and drag the placeholder to the top of the slide.

- Click the placeholder for your name and drag it underneath the title. Click and drag the picture underneath your name. Size the picture as necessary.

- Save the presentation.

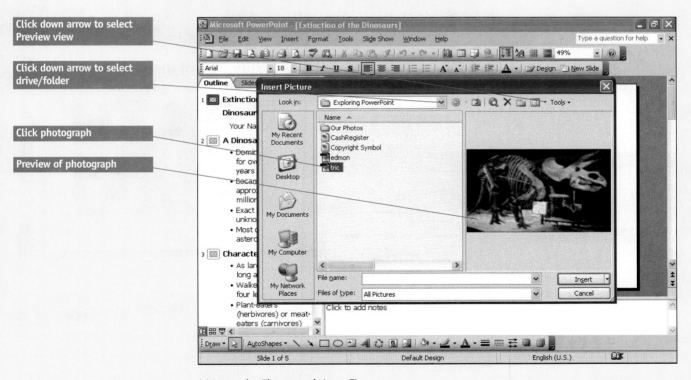

Click down arrow to select Preview view

Click down arrow to select drive/folder

Click photograph

Preview of photograph

(e) Insert the Photograph (step 5)

FIGURE 2.5 Hands-on Exercise 2 (*continued*)

CROPPING A PICTURE

The Crop tool lets you eliminate (crop) part of a picture. Select (click) the picture to display the Picture toolbar and sizing handles. (If you do not see the Picture toolbar, pull down the View menu, click the Toolbars command, then click the Picture toolbar.) Click the Crop tool (the ScreenTip will display the name of the tool), then click and drag a sizing handle to crop the part of the picture you want to eliminate.

Step 6: Move and Size the Objects

- Your title slide should be similar to Figure 2.5f. Click the **Text Box tool**, then click and drag below the picture to create a text box. Enter text to cite the source for your picture as shown in Figure 2.5f. If necessary, change to an appropriate font and point size.

- Move and size the objects on the slide as necessary. To size an object:
  - ❑ Click the object to display the sizing handles.
  - ❑ Drag a corner handle (the mouse pointer changes to a double arrow) to change the length and width of the object simultaneously.
  - ❑ Drag a handle on the horizontal or vertical border to change one dimension.

- To move an object:
  - ❑ Click the object to display the sizing handles.
  - ❑ Point to any part of the border except a sizing handle (the mouse pointer changes to a four-sided arrow), then click and drag to move the object.

- Save the presentation.

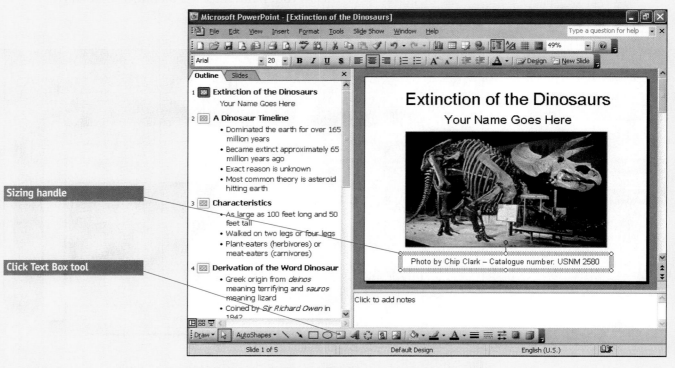

(f) Move and Size the Objects (step 6)

FIGURE 2.5 Hands-on Exercise 2 (*continued*)

ENTER THE URL AUTOMATICALLY

Use the Copy command to enter the URL into a presentation and ensure that it is entered correctly. Click in the Address bar of Internet Explorer to select the URL, then pull down the Edit menu and click the Copy command (or use the Ctrl+C shortcut). Switch to the PowerPoint presentation, click on the slide where you want to insert the URL, then pull down the Edit menu and click Paste (or press Ctrl+V). (The Cut command does not apply here, but it can be executed by the Ctrl+X keyboard shortcut. The "X" is supposed to remind you of a pair of scissors.)

Step 7: **The Picture as Background**

■ Click the **New Slide button** to display slide layouts in the task pane. Click the blank slide layout.

■ Pull down the **Format menu** and click the **Background command** to display the Background dialog box in Figure 2.5g.

■ Click the **down arrow** in the Background fill list box, click **Fill Effects** to display the Fill Effects dialog box, click the **Picture tab**, then click the **Select Picture button** to display the Select Picture dialog box.

■ Click the **down arrow** on the Look in text box to select the drive and folder where you saved the picture, select the photograph, then click the **Insert button** so that the photograph appears in the Fill Effects dialog box.

■ Click **OK** to accept the picture and close the Fill Effects dialog box. Click the **Apply button** on the Background dialog box. The photograph should now appear as the background for your slide.

■ Save the presentation.

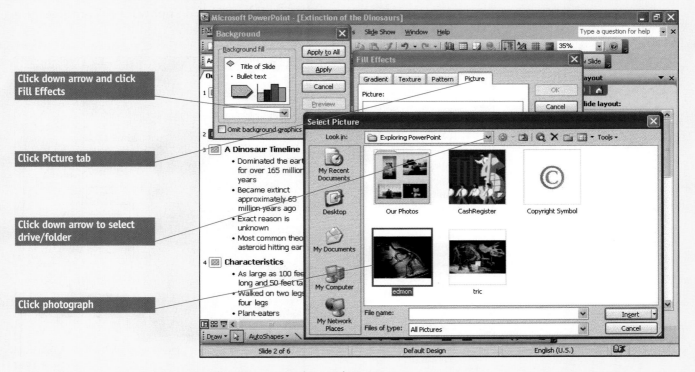

(g) The Picture as Background (step 7)

FIGURE 2.5   Hands-on Exercise 2 (*continued*)

IT'S A DIFFERENT LOOK

The slide you just created does not look like a PowerPoint slide, but it is, and it will make a tremendous impact during your next presentation. Use your imagination to expand the technique to an entire presentation. You could, for example, do a report on Impressionist paintings and show one painting per slide. You can also add a second (and smaller) photograph (perhaps of the artist) on the slide that will show both artist and painting. See practice exercise 2 at the end of the chapter.

Step 8: Add a Text Box

- Click the **Text Box tool** on the Drawing toolbar, then click and drag on the slide to create a text box. Enter the dinosaur name as shown in Figure 2.5h. If necessary, change to an appropriate font, color, and point size, such as **48 point red Times New Roman bold**. Size the text box as necessary.

- Click the **Text Box tool** a second time, then click and drag to create a second text box. Enter text to cite the source as shown in the figure. We used the same font as in the previous text box (Times New Roman), but chose a smaller size (**24 point**).

- You may need to change the font color and/or move the text box to read the text more easily. Save the presentation.

- Pull down the **File menu** and click the **Print command** to display the Print dialog box. Select **Handouts** in the Print What dialog box and choose **6 slides per page**. Click **OK**.

- Pull down the **File menu** a second time and click the **Print command**. Print an outline of the presentation.

- Close Internet Explorer. Exit PowerPoint if you do not want to continue with the next exercise at this time.

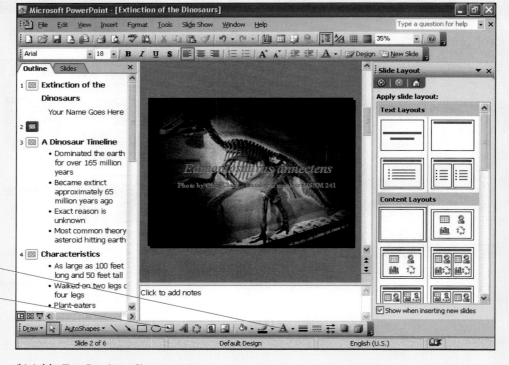

(h) Add a Text Box (step 8)

FIGURE 2.5   Hands-on Exercise 2 (*continued*)

CHANGE THE ALIGNMENT

Use the Left, Center, or Right-Align buttons to change the alignment of any bullet, slide title, or text box. Just click anywhere in the item, then click the appropriate button on the Formatting toolbar. You can also use the corresponding keyboard shortcuts (Ctrl+L, Ctrl+E, Ctrl+R), for left, center, or right alignment. The shortcuts also work in Microsoft Word.

Figure 2.6 displays multiple slides from our first presentation, which illustrates how to work with photographs. The presentation is created from a series of pictures that are stored in their own folder from where they are inserted into the presentation. Each slide in Figure 2.6 illustrates a different capability.

The *photo album* in Figure 2.6a imports multiple photographs into a presentation, without having to format each picture individually. The photos may be taken from your hard disk, a scanner, or a digital camera. Regardless of the origin or file format of the photographs, you can specify how many pictures you want per slide (one, two, or four), choose from a variety of picture frames (rounded corners are used in our figure), and/or insert a caption below each picture.

Figure 2.6b displays cropped versions of two pictures in the original album. Compare these photographs to their counterparts in Figure 2.6a to see how we eliminated part of the background in order to focus on the happy couple. This was accomplished through the *Crop tool* on the *Picture toolbar*, which also contains additional tools to rotate a photograph and/or change the color or brightness. You can also compress a photograph (generally without a loss in quality) within a presentation to reduce the file size.

Figure 2.6c illustrates one of our favorite techniques, which is to use a photograph as a fill effect for the background of the slide. The slide itself is "empty"; it does not contain a photograph or even a title (although a title could be added to describe the photograph). Instead, the *Format Background command* was used to select the photograph as a background for the slide, in effect, creating a presentation that bears no resemblance to a typical PowerPoint presentation.

Figure 2.6d applies a custom animation effect to dissolve a black-and-white photograph into its color counterpart. The original color photograph is duplicated and saved as a black-and-white photograph, with the latter placed directly on top. An exit effect (dissolve out) is applied to the black-and-white picture, thus creating the transition. It's a simple and effective technique that adds variety to a presentation.

Figure 2.6e combines WordArt with a picture background. WordArt was used to create the initial object (the word "love"), after which the *Format WordArt command* was used to apply the photograph as fill. The only tricky part (if any) is to choose the photograph and text in such a way as to not obscure an essential portion of the underlying picture. The crop tool may be useful, therefore, to alter a picture prior to selecting it as fill.

Figure 2.6f uses animation in conjunction with a sound file to create a musical ending in which the photographs scroll continuously on the slide while the music plays in the background. The four original photographs are arranged one on top of another, extending above and below the slide. All four photographs are selected, and the custom animation command is applied. The sound (music) file is inserted independently and timed to play simultaneously with the scrolling of the pictures.

Photographs, File Formats, and File Folders

A photograph may be stored anywhere on a hard disk, although beginners typically store all photographs in the *My Pictures folder* within their My Documents folder. You may create additional folders (within the My Pictures folder and/or anywhere on your system) to hold groups of pictures. You can move and copy photographs from one folder to another, or from one device to another, such as from a hard disk to a zip drive, floppy disk, or CD (provided you have the software to write to the CD).

A photograph has the same attributes as any other file, which include the file name, type, file size, and date the file was created or last modified. There are many different file types for graphic work. The *Joint Photographic Experts Group* (*JPEG*, pronounced "jpeg") *format* is the most common for photographs. The *Graphics Interchange Format* (*GIF*, pronounced "jif") is used for clip art and similar images.

(a) Photo Album

(b) Revised (cropped) Photos

(c) Photo as Background

(d) Black-and-white Transition

(e) WordArt

(f) Credits and Sound

FIGURE 2.6 Fun with Photographs

Transitions and Animations

Transitions and animations are similar in that both add interest to a presentation through movement and (optionally) sound. A *transition* applies to the slide as a whole and controls the way the entire slide moves on and off the screen. An *animation* controls the appearance of individual elements on a single slide. PowerPoint includes a selection of animation schemes that can be applied to selected slides and/or to the presentation as a whole. PowerPoint also gives you the ability to create a *custom animation*, which requires that you determine when (in what sequence) the objects appear and how the objects make their entrance (e.g., whether they fly in from the top or bottom). You can also control how long the objects are to remain on the screen and if (how) they are to exit. The objects on a slide may include text boxes, clip art, photographs, and so on.

Each slide in Figure 2.7 has its own entrance and exit effect, denoted by a green and red icon, respectively. (The effects from which you can choose are divided into subtle, moderate, and exciting, and it is fun to experiment.) The sequence and duration of the individual animations are seen in the associated timeline. The entrance of the Los Angeles photo is triggered by clicking the mouse during the slide show. This is followed automatically by the exit of this object, followed by the entrance of the next photo, followed by the exit of the photo. Each effect takes two seconds (medium speed) as indicated on the timeline. Most animation options include an optional sound effect; for example, you can specify the sound of a clicking camera as each photograph makes its appearance.

Any animated slide can be thought of as a theatrical production unto itself. The objects on a PowerPoint slide, just like the actors in a Broadway show, must be thoroughly scripted so that the performance is as effective as possible. You can select multiple objects at the same time in order to apply the same effects in a single command. You can resequence an animation by clicking the reorder arrows up or down within the custom animation task pane. You can change and/or remove effects as necessary. It's fun, it's easy, and as you may have guessed, it's time for our next hands-on exercise.

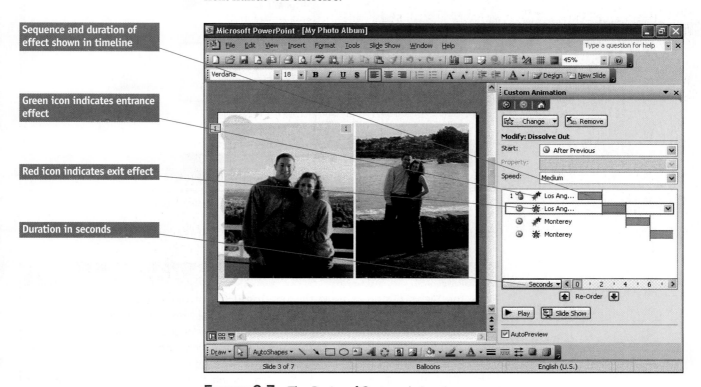

FIGURE 2.7   The Basics of Custom Animation

3   Fun with Photographs

Objective   Create a photo album; use cropping and other techniques to enhance individual photographs; apply custom animation to various slides. Use Figure 2.8 as a guide.

Step 1:   **Create a Photo Album**

■ Start PowerPoint. Close the task pane and any open presentations. Pull down the **Insert menu**, click **Picture**, then click **New Photo Album** to display the Photo Album dialog box.

■ Click the **File/Disk command button** to select from existing photos on your computer. You can use your own photos or you can use our pictures, which are in the **Our Photos folder** within the **Exploring PowerPoint folder**.

■ Press and hold the **Ctrl key** as you select the four pictures in Figure 2.8a. (Be sure to include **Los Angeles** and **Monterey** as we will crop these photos in a later step.) Click the **Insert button**.

Views button

Click File/Disk command button

Click first picture, then press Ctrl as you click remaining pictures

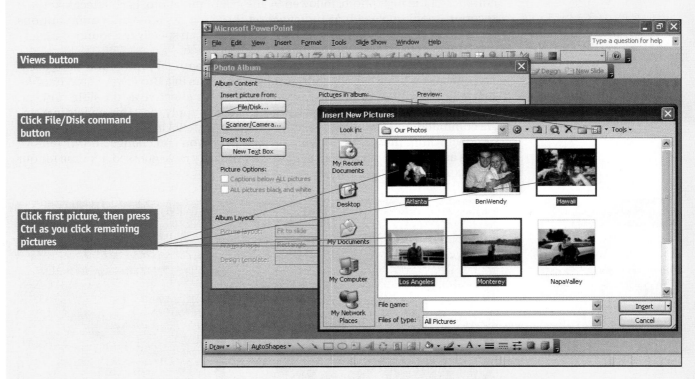

(a) Create a Photo Album (step 1)

FIGURE 2.8   Hands-on Exercise 3

CHANGE THE VIEW

Use the Views button to cycle through the different views that are available with photographs. The Thumbnails view is ideal for selecting a picture as it displays a miniature version of the photograph. The Details view provides the most information, and further, it enables you to sequence your files according to any attribute. Click the Size column, for example, and you arrange the pictures according to file size. Click the column a second time to switch from ascending to descending sequence and vice versa.

Step 2: **Choose the Album Layout**

■ You should see the Photo Album dialog box as shown in Figure 2.8b. You can change the order of the photos within the album by selecting a photo, then pressing the **up** or **down arrow** as necessary.

■ Look toward the bottom of the dialog box (in the Album Layout area) and make the indicated selections. We chose **4 pictures** for the layout and **Rounded Rectangle** for the Frame shape.

■ Click the **Browse button**, double click the **Presentation Designs folder**, select a design template (we chose **Balloons**), then click **Select** to close the dialog box. Click the **Create button** to create the album.

■ You should see a presentation consisting of two slides. The first slide is the title slide. The second slide contains the four pictures you selected.

■ If your layout is different from ours, pull down the **Format menu**, click the **Photo Album command** to display the associated dialog box, and enter the correct parameters. Click the **Update button**.

■ If necessary, change the title slide to include your name. Save the presentation as **My Photo Album**.

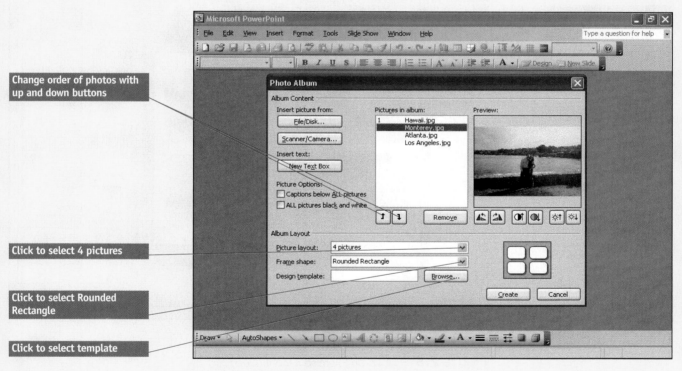

(b) Choose the Album Layout (step 2)

FIGURE **2.8**   Hands-on Exercise 3 (*continued*)

TOUCH UP YOUR PHOTOS

It's not PhotoShop, but the Format Photo Album command provides limited capability to modify a photograph. Select the appropriate picture within the Format Photo Album dialog box, then use the appropriate tool within the dialog box. You can rotate a picture left or right, increase or decrease the contrast, and/or increase or decrease the brightness. You can also point to any tool to display a ScreenTip that is indicative of its function.

Step 3: Add Custom Animation

■ Change to the **Normal view** if necessary. Click the **Slides tab** in the left pane. Pull down the **Slide Show menu** and click **Custom Animation** to open the task pane as shown in Figure 2.8c.

■ Select the second slide. Press and hold the **Ctrl key** as you select all four photos. Click the **Add Effect button**, click **Entrance**, then select **Dissolve In** for the effect. (Click the **More Effects subcommand** if you do not see the Dissolve In effect.) Click the **down arrow** in the **Speed list box** and select **Slow**.

■ Click a **down arrow** next to any effect and click **Start After Previous** so that the pictures are displayed one after another, without having to click the mouse.

■ Be sure that all four animation effects are still selected, then click a **down arrow** next to any effect, and click **Effect Options** to display the Dissolve In dialog box. Click the **Effect tab**, click the **down arrow** for the **Sound list box** and (scroll if necessary to) choose **Camera**.

■ Click **OK** to accept the sound and close the dialog box. Save the presentation.

(c) Add Custom Animation (step 3)

FIGURE 2.8 Hands-on Exercise 3 (*continued*)

COMPRESS YOUR PICTURES

Use the Compress Pictures command to (attempt to) reduce the size of a presentation. Save the presentation before you begin because the command cannot be undone. Select any picture, then click the Compress Pictures tool on the Picture toolbar to display the associated dialog box. Check the options to compress pictures and to delete the cropped areas of pictures. Click OK, then click the Apply button when warned that you might reduce the quality of the photographs. Review the presentation. If the quality is significantly less (it rarely is), exit the presentation without saving to return to the original.

Step 4: Crop a Picture

- Click the **New Slide button** to insert a new slide. Change the slide layout to a blank slide. Close the task pane.

- Pull down the **Insert menu**, click **Picture**, click **From File**, then select the **Monterey picture** from the **Our Photos folder** in the **Exploring PowerPoint folder**. Click **Insert** and move it to the right side of the slide.

- Insert the **LA picture** in similar fashion and move it to the left of the slide. (You must insert the original pictures; you cannot copy the photographs from slide 2 because the Photo Album command disables cropping.)

- Select the LA photo as shown in the figure. The Picture toolbar should be visible, but if not, pull down the **View menu**, click **Toolbars**, then click the **Picture toolbar**. Use the **cropping tool** to crop the picture as shown in Figure 2.8d.

- Once you are satisfied with the result, click off the picture, then click and drag a corner to resize (enlarge) the cropped image. Crop the Monterey photo in similar fashion. Add animation as you see fit.

- Try to size the resulting photos identically for symmetry on this slide. Save the presentation.

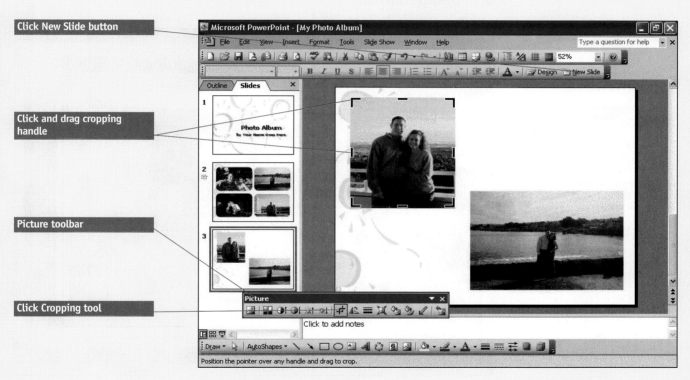

(d) Crop a Picture (step 4)

FIGURE 2.8 Hands-on Exercise 3 (*continued*)

SAVE THE NEW PICTURE

Once you have modified a picture, by cropping, shading, or any other technique, you can save the new picture as a replacement for the original. Right click the photo to display a context-sensitive menu. Choose the Save as Picture command, specify JPEG or GIF as the file format, then choose the folder where you want to save the photo. Click the Save button. You can now use the modified picture in all subsequent photo albums.

Step 5: **Set a Picture as the Background**

■ Our favorite technique is to create presentations that do not look as though they were created in PowerPoint. One way to accomplish this is to create a blank slide that contains nothing other than a single photograph as the slide background.

■ Insert a blank slide at the end of the presentation. Close the task pane. Pull down the **Format command** and click the **Background command** to display the Background dialog box in Figure 2.8e.

■ Click the **down arrow** in the **Background Fill** area, click **Fill Effects** to display the associated dialog box, then click the **Picture tab**.

■ Click the **Select Picture command button**, then select the desired photo (e.g., **BenWendy** in the **Our Photos folder**).

■ Click **Insert** to select the picture, click **OK**, then click the **Apply button** to set the photograph as the background for this slide.

■ It's easy and effective. The only "trick" is to choose a photo that has the approximate proportions of the slide.

■ Save the presentation.

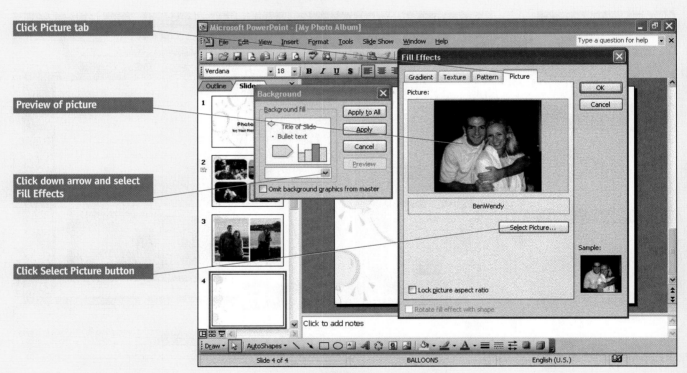

(e) Set a Picture as the Background (step 5)

FIGURE 2.8 Hands-on Exercise 3 (*continued*)

PRINTING THE PRESENTATION

We're not sure why, but the slide background may not print on a black-and-white printer. If this is true on your configuration (click the Print Preview button to find out), pull down the File menu, click the Print command, then choose Color in the Color/Grayscale list box even if you have a black-and-white printer.

Step 6: From Black and White to Color

- Insert a blank slide at the end of the presentation. Pull down the **Insert menu**, click **Picture**, click **From File**, then select the **BenWendy picture** from the **Our Photos folder**. Click **Insert**.

- Ben and Wendy should appear on a blank slide, with the picture selected. Size the picture, press **Ctrl+C** to copy it, then press **Ctrl+V** to duplicate it.

- Right click the top picture, then click the **Format Picture command** to display the associated dialog box. Click the **Picture tab**, then click the **down arrow** on the **Color list box** in the Image control area. Select **Black and White** and click **OK**.

- Check that the top picture is still selected, pull down the **Slide Show menu**, and click **Custom Animation** to open the task pane as shown in Figure 2.8f. Click the **Add Effect button**, click **Exit**, then click **Dissolve Out**. Change the speed to **Very slow**. Close the task pane.

- Click and drag the black-and-white photo so that it is directly on top of the color photo (see the boxed tip for additional hints). Click the **Slide Show button** to see the finished slide, then click the black-and-white photograph to dissolve to color. Press **Esc**.

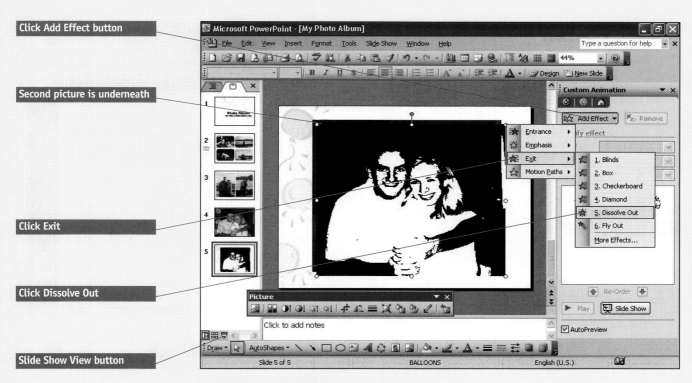

Click Add Effect button

Second picture is underneath

Click Exit

Click Dissolve Out

Slide Show View button

(f) From Black and White to Color (step 6)

FIGURE 2.8 Hands-on Exercise 3 (*continued*)

PLACE ONE PHOTO ON TOP OF ANOTHER

Press and hold the Ctrl key to select both pictures, pull down the Format menu, and click Picture to display the Format Picture dialog box. Click the Size tab, then enter the appropriate dimensions (e.g., a width of 7 inches for Ben and Wendy). Check the box to lock the aspect ratio so as not to distort the picture. Click the Position tab and enter horizontal and vertical distances from the left corner. Click OK. Both photos are still selected, and you can click and drag to "fine tune" the size and position.

Step 7: Create the WordArt

- Insert a blank slide at the end of the presentation, then close the task pane. Click the **Insert WordArt button** on the Drawing toolbar to display the WordArt Gallery dialog box. Choose any style you like (we took the first style in the first row). Click **OK**.

- You should see the Edit Text box. Enter **LOVE** (in uppercase) as the text for your WordArt object. Click **OK** to insert the WordArt into your presentation. Move and size the WordArt object so that it takes the entire slide as shown in Figure 2.8g.

- Pull down the **Format menu** and click **WordArt** to display the Format WordArt dialog box. Click the **Colors and Lines tab**, click the **down arrow** in the **Color list box** (in the Fill section), and select **Fill Effects** to display the dialog box.

- Click the **Picture tab**. Click the **Select Picture button**. Select the **BenWendy photo** and click **Insert**. Click **OK** to close the Fill Effects dialog box. Click **OK** a second time to close the Format WordArt dialog box.

- You should see the completed WordArt object with the photo as the fill for the letters. (You may have to resize the WordArt and/or use a cropped photo to better position the photo inside the text.) Save the presentation.

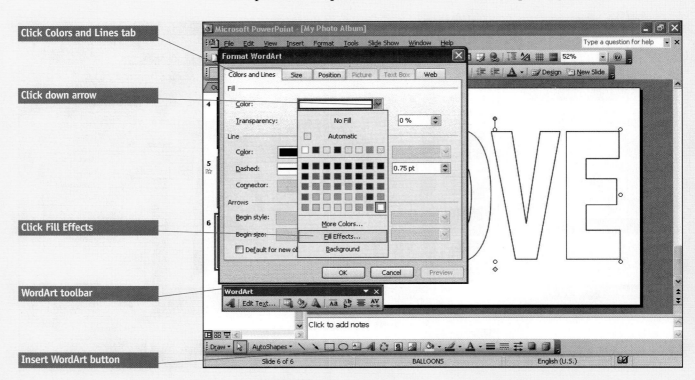

(g) Create the WordArt (step 7)

FIGURE 2.8   Hands-on Exercise 3 (*continued*)

THE WORDART TOOLBAR

The WordArt toolbar provides the easiest way to change an existing WordArt object. It is displayed automatically when a WordArt object is selected (and suppressed otherwise). As with any toolbar, you can point to a button to display a ScreenTip containing the name of the button, which is indicative of its function. You will find buttons to display the text vertically, change the style or shape, and/or edit the text.

Step 8: **Create the Credits Slide**

- Press **Ctrl+Home** to move to the beginning of the presentation. Select (click) the second slide, which is the original "photo album" that contains the four photographs. Press **Ctrl+C** to copy the slide.

- Press **Ctrl+End** to move to the end of the presentation. Press **Ctrl+V** to paste the slide at the end of the presentation.

- Arrange the photographs in a filmstrip. The end result will have a picture above and below the actual slide as shown in Figure 2.8h. Give yourself additional room in which to work by changing the zoom percentage and/or making the notes pane smaller.

- Pull down the **Slide Show menu** and click **Custom Animation**. Delete all of the existing animation effects. (The existing effects are the transition to the sound of a camera that we added at the beginning of the presentation.)

- Press and hold the **Ctrl key** to select all four pictures. Click the **Add Effect button**, click **Entrance**, click **More Effects**, scroll to the **Exciting category**, then choose **Credits**.

- You should see a preview of the effect in which the pictures scroll onto the screen just as in a list of movie credits. Click **OK**. Save the presentation.

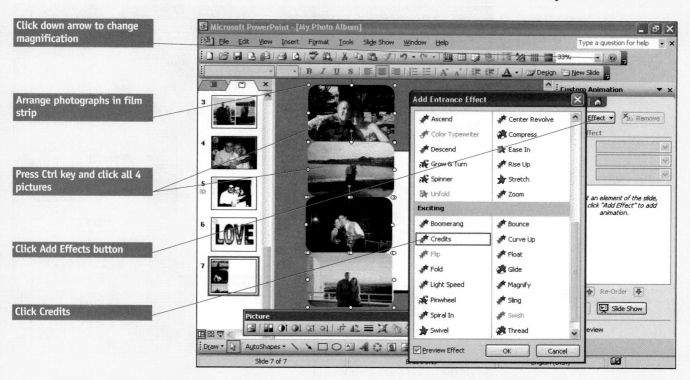

(h) Create the Credits Slide (step 8)

FIGURE 2.8 Hands-on Exercise 3 (*continued*)

USE THE GRID FOR EASY ALIGNMENT

Pull down the View menu, click the Grid and Guides command to display the associated dialog box, then check the boxes to snap objects to the grid and to display the grid on screen. The grid is visible when you work in PowerPoint, but it does not appear during a slide show or on the printed version of a presentation. Use the grid to align objects more precisely on a slide, especially in relation to one another.

Step 9: Add the Sound and Animation

■ Pull down the **Insert menu**, click **Movies and Sounds**, then choose **Sound from File** to display the Insert Sound dialog box. Change to the **Our Photos folder**, specify **All Files** as the file type, then insert **Beethoven's Symphony 9**. Click **OK**.

■ Click **Automatically** when asked how you want the sound to start during the show. Click and drag the animation for Beethoven's symphony to the top of the Custom animation list as shown in Figure 2.8i. (The zero next to the effect indicates that the sound will play automatically.)

■ Click the animation for the first rounded rectangle (photograph), then press and hold the **Ctrl key** as you select the transition effects for the other photographs. Click the **down arrow** next to the last rectangle, then click **Start With Previous**.

■ Click the **down arrow** next to the last effect, click **Timing** to display the Credits list box, then set the Repeat list box **Until Next Click** so that the pictures scroll continually. Click **OK**. Move the pictures to the middle of the slide.

■ Turn up the sound on your computer, then click the **Play button**. Close the task pane. Click and drag the **Sound icon** to the lower-right portion of the slide.

■ Save the presentation.

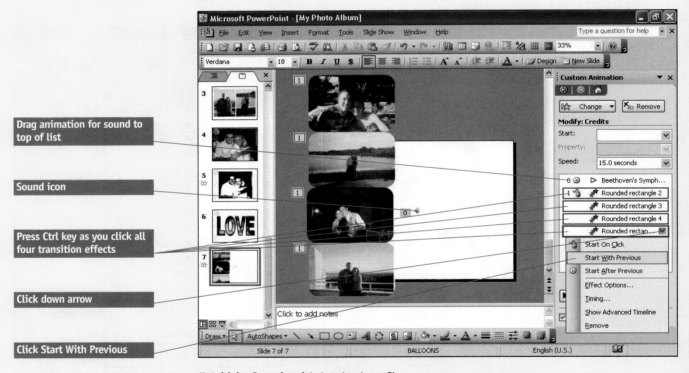

(i) Add the Sound and Animation (step 9)

FIGURE 2.8 Hands-on Exercise 3 (*continued*)

PRESENTATION PROPERTIES

How long did it take you to create this presentation? What was the total editing time? How many words does the presentation contain? How many slides have speaker notes? The answers to these and other questions are found in the presentation properties. Pull down the File menu, click the Properties command, and click the Statistics tab to see this information. Explore the other tabs to see what other information is (can be) stored to describe your presentation.

Step 10: **Show Time**

- Press **Ctrl+Home** to move to the first slide. Print the presentation in the form of audience handouts for your instructor. Save the presentation a final time.

- Click the **Slide Show button** (at the bottom of the window) to show the presentation as shown in Figure 2.8j. Think about the various techniques that were used to create the slides:
  - Slide 2 (the four photographs) was created initially as a photo album. The animation effects (the click of the camera) were added manually.
  - Slide 3 contains two photos that were cropped for better composition.
  - Slide 4 displays a photo as the background for a slide.
  - Slide 5 uses a transition effect to colorize a black-and-white photograph.
  - Slide 6 uses a photograph as the background for a WordArt object.
  - Slide 7 uses sound and the credits animation effect.

- Press **Esc** to end the presentation. Exit PowerPoint if you do not want to continue with the next exercise at this time.

(j) Show Time (step 10)

FIGURE 2.8   Hands-on Exercise 3 (*continued*)

USE YOUR PICTURES AS A SCREEN SAVER

Right click the desktop to display a context-sensitive menu, click Properties to display the Properties dialog box, click the Screen Saver tab, and choose My Picture Slide Slideshow. Click the Settings tab, click the Browse button, and select the folder containing your photographs. We suggest that you change the picture every seven seconds, that the pictures take the entire screen, and that you use transition effects between pictures. Click OK to accept the settings you have chosen, then click the Preview button to view the screen saver. [This tip works in Windows XP and may not work in previous versions.]

THE AUTOCONTENT WIZARD

One of the hardest things about creating a presentation is getting started. You have a general idea of what you want to say, but the words do not come easily to you. The ***AutoContent Wizard*** offers a potential solution. It eliminates writer's block and moves you immediately into a presentation. The wizard asks you a series of questions, then it uses your answers to suggest a presentation. The presentation is not complete, but it does provide an excellent beginning.

The AutoContent Wizard is accessed through the New Presentation view in the task pane and is illustrated in Figure 2.9. The wizard prompts you for the type of presentation in Figure 2.9a, for the style of the presentation in Figure 2.9b, and for additional information in Figure 2.9c. The wizard then has all the information it needs and proceeds to create a presentation for you. It even chooses a design template as illustrated by the title slide in Figure 2.9d. The template contains a color scheme and custom formatting to give your presentation a certain "look." You can change the design at any time to give your presentation a completely different look while retaining its content.

The real benefit of the wizard, however, is the outline shown in Figure 2.9e, which corresponds to the topic you selected earlier (Marketing Plan). The outline is very general, as it must be, but it provides the essential topics to include in your presentation. You work with the outline provided by the AutoContent Wizard just as you would with any other outline. You can type over existing text, add or delete slides, move slides around, promote or demote items, and so on. In short, you don't use the AutoContent outline exactly as it is presented; instead you use the outline as a starting point, then modify it to fit the needs of your presentation. The wizard has accomplished its goal, however, by giving you a solid beginning.

The presentation created by the AutoContent Wizard is based on one of several presentations that are provided with PowerPoint. You can use the wizard as just described, or you can bypass the wizard entirely and select the outline directly from the presentation templates on your computer in the New Presentation task pane. Either way, you wind up with a professional presentation with respect to design and content. Naturally, you have to modify the content to fit your needs, but you have jump-started the creative process. You simply open the presentation, then you modify the existing text as necessary, while retaining the formatting in the selected template.

Figure 2.10 displays the title slides of several sample presentations that are included with PowerPoint. The presentations vary considerably in content and design. There is a presentation for recommending a strategy in Figure 2.10a, a business plan in Figure 2.10b, and even a presentation to communicate bad news in Figure 2.10c. The presentation in Figure 2.10d contains an award certificate that is also suitable for printing. The presentations in Figure 2.10e and 2.10f are for an employee orientation and a project overview, respectively. Animation and branching are also built into several of the presentations. The AutoContent Wizard is an excellent way to start a presentation, as you shall see in our next exercise.

CHOOSE AN APPROPRIATE DESIGN

A design should enhance a presentation without calling attention to itself. It should be consistent with your message, and as authoritative or informal as the situation demands. Choosing the right template requires common sense and good taste. What works in one instance will not necessarily work in another. You would not, for example, use the same template to proclaim a year-end bonus as you would to announce a fourth-quarter loss and impending layoffs. Set a time limit, or else you will spend too much time on the formatting and lose sight of the content.

(a) Presentation Type

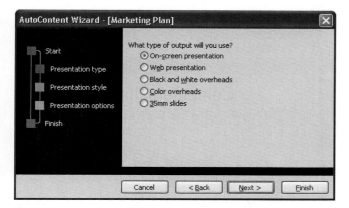

(b) Presentation Style

(c) Presentation Options

FIGURE 2.9 The AutoContent Wizard

(d) Title Slide and Selected Template

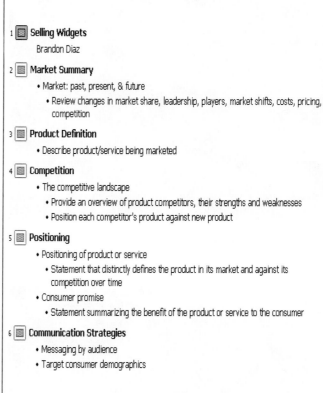

(e) Suggested Outline (additional slides not shown)

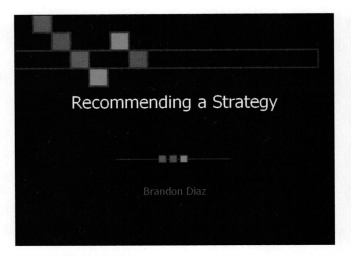

(a) Recommending a Strategy

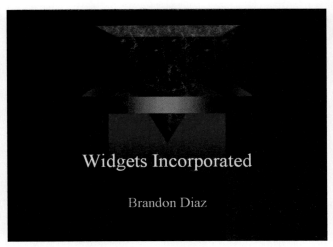

(b) Business Plan

(c) Communicating Bad News

(d) Award Certificate

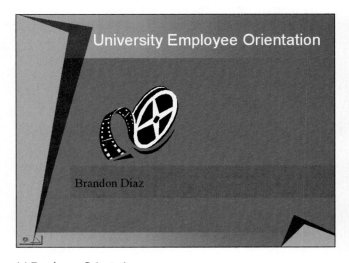

(e) Employee Orientation

(f) Project Overview

FIGURE 2.10 Suggested Presentations

4   The AutoContent Wizard

Objective   Use the AutoContent Wizard to create a generic presentation for subsequent modification; insert a hyperlink on a presentation slide. Use Figure 2.11.

Step 1:   **The AutoContent Wizard**

- Start PowerPoint and if necessary open the task pane. Click the **down arrow** in the task pane and select **New Presentation.** Click the **From AutoContent Wizard** link in the New Presentation area. You should see the first screen in the AutoContent Wizard.

- Click the **Next button** (within the wizard's dialog box) to select the presentation type. Click the **General button** as shown in Figure 2.11a.

- Select the **Communicating Bad News presentation**. Click **Next**. The option button for Onscreen presentation is selected by default. Click **Next**.

- Click in the Presentation title text box and enter **Our First Exam** as the name of the presentation. Check the boxes for **Date last updated** and **Slide Number**. Click **Next**.

- The wizard indicates it has all the answers. Click **Finish**.

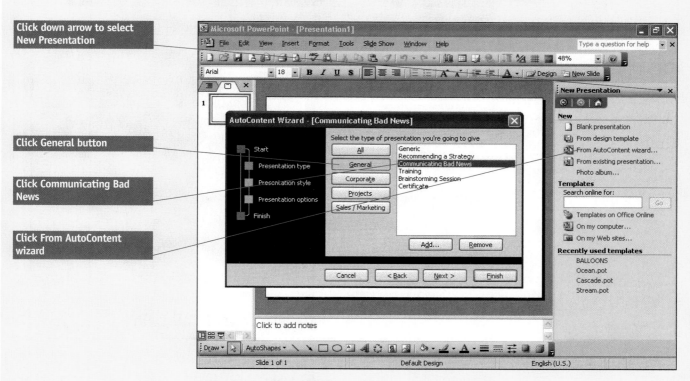

Click down arrow to select New Presentation

Click General button

Click Communicating Bad News

Click From AutoContent wizard

(a) The AutoContent Wizard (step 1)

FIGURE 2.11   Hands-on Exercise 4

THE HEADER AND FOOTER COMMAND

The Header and Footer command provides an easy way to display the same information on every slide. Pull down the View menu, click the Header and Footer command, then enter the date of the presentation, a descriptive footer, and/or the slide number. Click the Apply to All button to display these fields on every slide (or check the box to suppress the information on the title slide).

Step 2: **Modify the Presentation**

- Your presentation should be displayed in the Normal view. Note that each slide contains a footer, with the date and slide number, according to the settings you entered within the AutoContent Wizard when you created the presentation.

- Modify the title slide to include **your name**, **your e-mail address**, and **your instructor's name**.

- The AutoContent Wizard creates a generic presentation for communicating bad news. It is up to you, however, to change the text to make it relevant to the specific presentation as shown in Figure 2.11b.
  - ❑ Change the second slide (Our Situation) to describe the need for an exam.
  - ❑ Click the icon next to the third slide to select the entire slide. Press the **Del key** to delete the slide.
  - ❑ Change the fourth slide (Alternatives Considered) as shown in Figure 2.11b.

- Change the last slide (Summary) to a single item that says **Study for the Exam**. Click the **Bullets button** on the Formatting toolbar to remove the bullet from this item. Click the **Center button** to center the text.

- Save the presentation as **Our First Exam** in the **Exploring PowerPoint folder**.

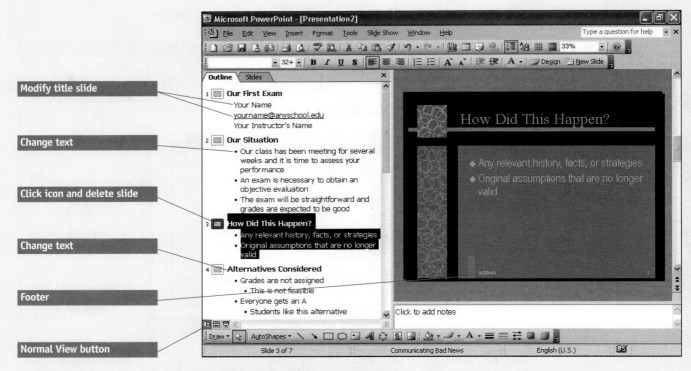

(b) Modify the Presentation (step 2)

FIGURE 2.11 Hands-on Exercise 4 (*continued*)

DELETING SLIDES

Slides may be deleted in either the Normal (tri-pane) view or the Slide Sorter view. Select (click) the Slide icon in the Outline pane of the Normal view to select one slide (or press and hold the Shift key as you click to select multiple slides), then press the Del key. You can also click the Slides tab in the Normal view, then press and hold the Ctrl key to select multiple slides prior to pressing the Delete key. Use the same technique in the Slide Sorter view.

Step 3: **Insert a Hyperlink**

- Change the text on slides 4 and 5 as shown in Figure 2.11c. Click and drag to select **Class Web Site** (the displayed text for the hyperlink you will add).

- Click the **Insert Hyperlink button** on the Standard toolbar (the button is not visible in Figure 2.11c) or pull down the **Insert menu** and click the **Hyperlink command**. Either way, you will see the Insert Hyperlink dialog box.

- The link to **Existing File or Web Page** is selected. Click the **Browsed Pages Button** at the left of the dialog box, then click in the **Address list box** and enter **www.prenhall.com/grauer**. (The http:// is entered automatically for you.)

- Click **OK** to create the link and close the Insert Hyperlink dialog box. Click outside the placeholder.

- Save the presentation.

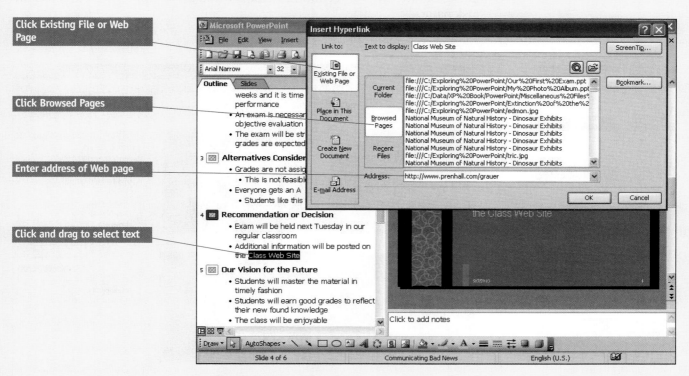

(c) Insert a Hyperlink (step 3)

FIGURE 2.11   Hands-on Exercise 4 (*continued*)

AUTOFORMAT AS YOU TYPE

Type any Web or e-mail address, then press the Enter key and the address is automatically converted to a hyperlink. (The Web address must begin with www or http:). Both conversions are performed through the AutoFormat as you Type command within Microsoft Office. If this does not work for you, pull down the Tools menu, click AutoCorrect Options, then click the AutoFormat as You Type tab. Check the box for Internet and network paths with hyperlinks, then click OK to accept the settings and close the dialog box.

Step 4: Customize the Presentation

- Change to the **Slide Sorter view** to view your presentation as shown in Figure 2.11d. (The task pane is not yet open.) Look closely at slides 1 and 4 to note that the hyperlinks have been added.

- Click the **Transition button** on the Slide Sorter toolbar to open the task pane. Click the **down arrow** on the Speed list box and change the speed to **Medium**. Click the **Apply to All Slides button** to change the speed on every slide.

- Click the **Design button** on the Slide Sorter toolbar to display the Design templates in the task pane. (You can also double click the name of the template, "Communicating Bad News", that appears in the middle of the status bar at the bottom of the window.)

- Choose a different design template (we chose the **Slit design**, which has a red background). Choose yet another design if you are still not satisfied. Close the task pane.

- Save the presentation.

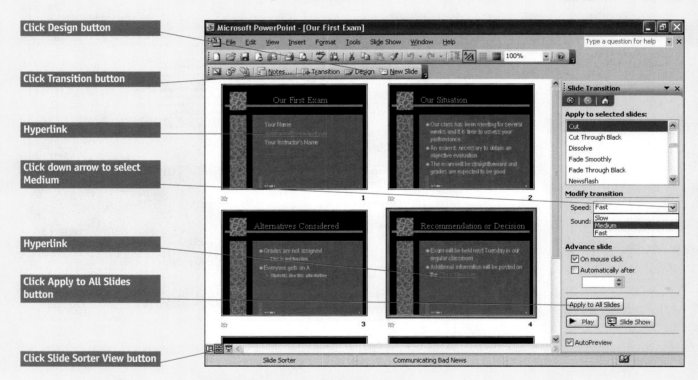

(d) Customize the Presentation (step 4)

FIGURE 2.11 Hands-on Exercise 4 (continued)

SET A TIME LIMIT

It's addictive, but it's not always productive, and while it's fun to experiment with different templates and animation effects, it is all too easy to spend too much time fine-tuning your presentation. It's much more important to focus on the content of your presentation rather than subtle changes in its appearance. Impose a time limit on the amount of time you will spend on this activity, and end the session when the limit is reached.

Step 5: Add Speaker Notes

- Return to the **Normal view**. Click the **Slides tab** in the left pane. The template of the presentation has changed to the Slit design as shown in Figure 2.11e.

- If necessary, press **Ctrl+Home** to go to the first slide. Click in the speaker notes area and enter an appropriate note. You can use our text, or make up your own. Save the presentation a final time.

- Print the presentation in multiple ways.
  - ❏ Print the **Notes Page** for the title slide to serve as a cover page.
  - ❏ Print the **outline** of the presentation.
  - ❏ Print **audience handouts** for the entire presentation (six per page).
  - ❏ Be sure to frame the individual slides.
  - ❏ Submit the various printouts to your instructor.

- Press **Ctrl+Home** to return to the first slide, then click the **Slide Show button** to view the presentation. Press **Esc** at the end of the show. Close the presentation. Exit PowerPoint.

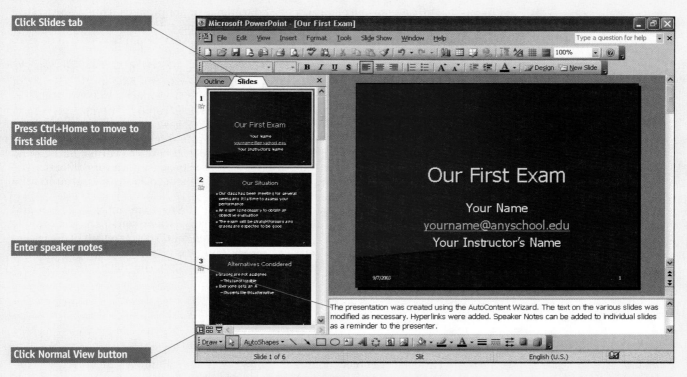

(e) Add Speaker Notes (step 5)

FIGURE 2.11 Hands-on Exercise 4 (*continued*)

ADD NUMBERED OR GRAPHICAL BULLETS

Why settle for simple bullets when you can have numbers or pictures? Click and drag to select the bulleted text on a slide, then click the Numbering button on the formatting toolbar to change to numbered bullets. You can also right click the selected text to display a context-sensitive menu, then click the Bullets and Numbering command to display the associated dialog box, where you can customize the bullets by selecting symbols, pictures, and/or special characters.

SUMMARY

A presentation can be sent electronically to multiple individuals for review. Each reviewer receives a copy of the presentation, enters his or her changes, and then returns the revised presentation as an attachment in an e-mail message. Comments from multiple reviewers can be merged in a single session.

The Header and Footer command is used to personalize a presentation by inserting a common element on every slide, such as the date, time, and/or place of the presentation. The Rehearse Timings feature times each slide as you practice your delivery so that you can estimate the duration of your presentation. Other tools are provided for use during the actual presentation. Slides can be hidden (prior to the presentation) then displayed by right clicking any slide during a slide show, clicking the Go To command, then choosing the hidden slide from a list of slides.

The new Package for CD command copies your presentation to a CD (providing you have the appropriate hardware). The command also gives you the option to save the presentation with the PowerPoint Viewer, so that the presentation may be viewed on computers that do not have PowerPoint installed.

Photographs and other resources can be downloaded from the Web for inclusion in a PowerPoint presentation. Information on the Web is protected by copyright, but you are permitted to use a portion of the work for educational or nonprofit uses under the fair use exclusion. Be sure to cite the work appropriately. The Insert Hyperlink command adds a hyperlink to a slide, which can be accessed during a presentation, provided you have an Internet connection.

A photo album imports multiple photographs into a presentation, without having to format each picture individually. The photos may be taken from a hard disk, a scanner, or a digital camera. The Joint Photographic Experts Group (JPEG, pronounced "jpeg") format is the most common file type for photographs. The Graphics Interchange Format (GIF, pronounced "jif") is used for clip art and similar images.

Photographs may be cropped using the appropriate tool on the Picture toolbar and/or special effects can be applied to enhance a presentation. The Format Background command uses a photograph as the background for a slide, creating a very different type of Powerpoint presentation. A photograph may also be used as the background for a WordArt object.

The AutoContent Wizard facilitates the creation of a new presentation. The wizard asks a series of questions, then it uses the answers to suggest a presentation based on one of several general presentations included within PowerPoint. The end result of the wizard is an outline based on the topic you selected. The outline is very general, as it must be, but it provides the essential topics to include in your presentation. The AutoContent Wizard is the best way to jump-start the creative process.

KEY TERMS

MULTIPLE CHOICE

1. How do you insert a hyperlink into a PowerPoint presentation?

   (a) Pull down the Insert menu and click the Hyperlink command
   (b) Click the Insert Hyperlink button on the Standard toolbar
   (c) Both (a) and (b)
   (d) Neither (a) nor (b)

2. Which of the following is true about hidden slides?

   (a) Hidden slides are invisible in every view
   (b) Hidden slides cannot be accessed during a slide show
   (c) Both (a) and (b)
   (d) Neither (a) nor (b)

3. Which view displays the timings for individual slides after the timings have been established by rehearsing the presentation?

   (a) Slide view
   (b) Outline view
   (c) Slide Sorter view
   (d) All of the above

4. Which of the following is true about annotating a slide?

   (a) The annotations are permanent; that is, once entered on a slide, they cannot be erased
   (b) The annotations are entered using the pen during the slide show
   (c) Both (a) and (b)
   (d) Neither (a) nor (b)

5. Which of the following can be printed for a presentation?

   (a) Audience handouts
   (b) An outline
   (c) Notes
   (d) All of the above

6. Which of the following is a true statement regarding the review of a presentation?

   (a) A presentation must have multiple reviewers
   (b) The review process is initiated outside of PowerPoint by sending a presentation as an ordinary e-mail attachment
   (c) Each reviewer's comments must be examined in a separate session
   (d) The comments of multiple reviewers can be merged in a single session

7. Which of the following *cannot* be accomplished directly by using the Format Photo Album command?

   (a) Changing the number of photographs on a slide
   (b) Changing the shape of the photographs
   (c) Inserting captions below the photographs
   (d) Adding custom animation to the individual photos

8. How do you crop a picture and then enlarge the result?

   (a) Select the crop tool, click and drag any border away from the center, click off the picture, then click and drag any corner inward
   (b) Select the crop tool, click and drag any border toward the center, click off the picture, then click and drag any corner inward
   (c) Select the crop tool, click and drag any border toward the center, click off the picture, then click and drag any corner outward
   (d) It cannot be done

9. Which of the following is *not required* to dissolve a black-and-white photograph into a color photograph?

   (a) Copy the original color photograph, then change the copied photograph to black and white
   (b) Place the black-and-white photograph on top of the color photograph
   (c) Apply the "dissolve out" exit effect to the black-and-white photograph
   (d) Apply the "dissolve in" entrance effect to the color photograph

... continued

10. Which of the following can be applied to a given object on a specific slide?

(a) An entrance effect, but not an exit effect

(b) An exit effect, but not an entrance effect

(c) Both an entrance and an exit effect

(d) Neither an entrance nor an exit effect

11. Which entrance effect(s) should be applied to multiple objects on a slide so that the objects appear one after another without having to click the mouse?

(a) Any entrance effect starting after the previous object

(b) Any entrance effect starting with the previous object

(c) Any entrance effect starting with a mouse click

(d) It cannot be done

12. Which of the following parameters can be set for the "fly in" entrance effect?

(a) The direction (left, right, top, or bottom)

(b) The speed (e.g., fast, medium, or slow)

(c) The starting time (e.g., automatically after the previous object appears)

(d) All of the above

13. Where can you store photographs for use in a subsequent presentation?

(a) In the My Pictures folder

(b) In a folder within the My Pictures folder

(c) In any folder on drive C

(d) All of the above

14. The AutoContent Wizard:

(a) Creates a generic presentation that can be customized as necessary

(b) Inserts a clip art image on every slide according to its content

(c) Inserts the author's name on every slide

(d) All of the above

15. Which of the following can be done to customize a presentation created by the AutoContent Wizard?

(a) Insert or delete a slide

(b) Change the template

(c) Change the transition effect

(d) All of the above

16. Which of the following provides legal protection to the author for a written or artistic work?

(a) Public domain

(b) Copyright

(c) Fair use exclusion

(d) Footnote

17. Which of the following keyboard shortcuts is correct with respect to animating a presentation?

(a) Press Ctrl+P to change the mouse pointer to a pen to animate the slide

(b) Press Ctrl+A to change the mouse pointer back to an arrow

(c) Both (a) and (b)

(d) Neither (a) nor (b)

18. Which format is most commonly associated with photographs?

(a) Joint Photograph Experts Group (JPEG), which is pronounced "jpeg"

(b) Graphics Interchange Format (GIF), which is pronounced "gif"

(c) Both (a) and (b)

(d) Neither (a) nor (b)

ANSWERS

1. c		**7.** d		**13.** d	
2. d		**8.** c		**14.** a	
3. c		**9.** d		**15.** d	
4. b		**10.** c		**16.** b	
5. d		**11.** a		**17.** c	
6. d		**12.** d		**18.** a	

PRACTICE WITH POWERPOINT

1. **Composite Photographs:** The presentation in Figure 2.12 builds on the first hands-on exercise to create two additional slides, each of which contains multiple photographs. You can add these slides to the original presentation and/or you can create a new presentation as shown. As with the original presentation, you can use our photographs or substitute your own.

   a. Start a new presentation. Change the slide layout to a blank slide, and then insert the photographs of Brian and Jessica (in the Our Photos folder) onto a single slide. Arrange the photographs in an attractive overlapping fashion. You can use your own pictures instead of ours.

   b. Select all of the photographs, then use the Format Picture command to apply a black 4 point border around every picture.

   c. Check that all of the photographs are still selected. Click the Compress tool on the Picture toolbar to compress the pictures and reduce their file size.

   d. Click outside the slide to deselect all of the pictures. Now select the pictures individually, pull down the Slide Show menu, click Custom Animation, and apply an entrance effect to each photograph. Set the timing for each entrance effect so that it begins automatically after the previous animation.

   e. You can create a composite picture from the individual photographs for use in any Office document. Click anywhere on the slide and press Ctrl+A to select all of the photographs. Right click the slide to display a context-sensitive menu, click the Grouping command, and then click Group. The sizing handles appear on the border of the slide to indicate a single object. Right click the slide once again; click the Save as Picture command, then save the slide as a JPEG image.

   f. Insert a new slide for the wordArt. Create four separate WordArt objects, each of which is a single letter, (L, O, V, and E), and each of which has a fill based on a different photograph.

   g. Use custom animation so that the objects appear in sequence, one after the other. Include the sound of applause in conjunction with the letter E.

   h. Print the presentation as an audience handout (two slides per page) for your instructor. Be sure to frame the individual slides.

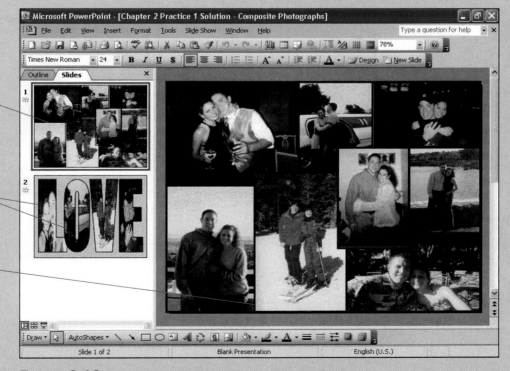

FIGURE 2.12 Composite Photographs (exercise 1)

2. **Impressionist Paintings:** The paintings in Figure 2.13 may be viewed at the Web Museum (www.ibiblio.org/wm), which currently welcomes over 200,000 visitors per week from all over the world. The museum is maintained by Nicolas Pioch and is one of our favorite sites on the Web. Start Internet Explorer to go to the museum, click the link to Famous Artworks (or search for Impressionist paintings), and then to the main page for impressionist paintings. Use that page as the basis for this assignment.

a. Choose any artist and any painting by that artist. Click the thumbnail image of the painting you select to enlarge the painting, then right click the painting and save the image in a new folder called Impressionist Paintings. If necessary, change the name of the file to include the artist and the name of the painting. Repeat this process to download five to ten paintings.

b. Start PowerPoint. Use the Insert Picture command to create a new photo album. Insert the paintings into the presentation, so that the paintings are displayed one painting per slide. Display a caption under each painting as shown in Figure 2.12.

c. Change the title of the presentation to Impressionist Paintings and include your name on the title slide. Add a hyperlink on the title slide that points to the Web Museum. (Pull down the Insert menu, click the Hyperlink command, specify "The Web Museum" as the text to display, and enter the corresponding Web address.)

d. View the completed presentation and enjoy a private showing of priceless art. Print the completed presentation as audience handouts (six per page) for your instructor.

e. Create your own screen saver based on the impressionist paintings that you saved earlier. (This technique works in Windows XP and has to be modified for earlier versions of Windows.) Right click the desktop to display a context-sensitive menu, click Properties, then click the Screen Saver tab and choose the My Picture Slideshow from the Screen Saver list box. Click the Settings button, click the Browse button, and select the folder containing the impressionist paintings. Check the boxes to use transition effects and to include file names (to see the name of the artist with the painting).

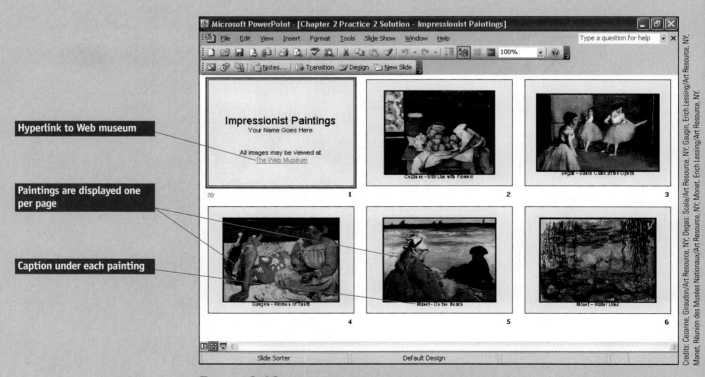

FIGURE 2.13 Impressionist Paintings (exercise 2)

3. **My Favorite Presidents:** Create a presentation similar to the one in Figure 2.14. The presentation contains six slides. The title slide contains your name and provides a hyperlink to the White House Web site (www.whitehouse.gov), which is the source of our photographs. Each additional slide contains a photograph and quote from one of our favorite presidents. Start a new presentation and create the title slide.

a.   Start Internet Explorer, go to the White House Web site, and locate the list of past presidents. Select any president, point to his picture, click the right mouse button to display a shortcut menu, and save the picture on your PC. Be sure you remember the location of the file when you save it on your local machine.

b.   Use the Windows taskbar to switch to PowerPoint. Insert a new slide and select the Title, Text, and Content layout. Click in the title area of this slide and add the president's name and years in office. Click in the text area, press the backspace key to delete the bullet that appears automatically, and then enter a quotation or short sentence pertaining to this president.

c.   Click the Insert Picture icon in the Content placeholder (the first icon in the second row) to display the Insert Picture dialog box. Select the folder where you saved the file in part (a). Select the picture, then click the Insert button to insert the picture onto the slide. Move and size the picture as appropriate. Save the presentation.

d.   Repeat these steps for the additional presidents. Print the title slide as a full slide to serve as a cover sheet for your assignment, then print the completed presentation as audience handouts (six per page). Be sure to frame the slides.

e.   Create your own screen saver based on the pictures of the presidents that you saved earlier. (This technique works in Windows XP and has to be modified for earlier versions of Windows.) Right click the desktop to display a context-sensitive menu, click Properties, then click the Screen Saver tab and choose the My Picture Slideshow from the Screen Saver list box. Click the Settings button, click the Browse button, and select the folder containing the presidents. Check the boxes to use transition effects and to include file names.

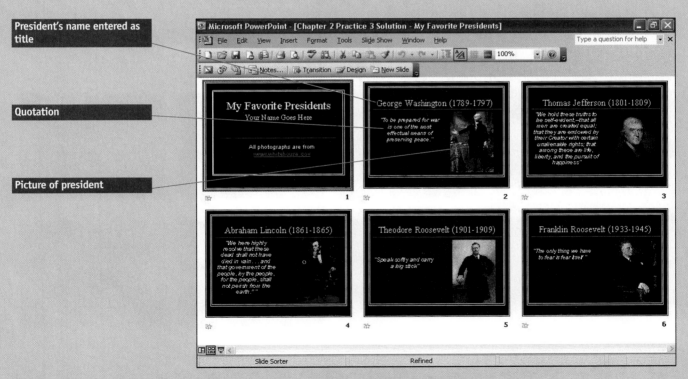

FIGURE 2.14   My Favorite Presidents (exercise 3)

4. **My State or Country:** Create (at least) a six-slide presentation that describes your home state or country of origin, similar to the presentation in Figure 2.15. You do not have to duplicate our presentation exactly, but you are required to include the equivalent information. Proceed as follows:

   a. Start a new presentation. Enter the name of your state or country on the title slide. Add your name to the title slide as well.

   b. Add notes to the title slide that contain the name of the course you are taking, your instructor's name, and the days and times your class meets. Boldface the name of your course as well as the name of your instructor.

   c. Add four additional slides that describe the history, government (include the name of the current governor, president, or prime minister), fun facts (include the population and area), and various symbols pertaining to your state or country.

   d. Add a fifth slide on major attractions that contains hyperlinks to each listed attraction. Visit at least two of the associated Web sites and print a page from each site for your instructor.

   e. Add clip art and/or photographs to the various slides as you see fit.

   f. Apply an appropriate design template to the presentation.

   g. Apply transition effects to all slides.

   h. Print the presentation in multiple ways. Print the title slide as a slide (full page) to serve as a cover page for the assignment. Print the title slide a second time, this time with speaker notes. Print audience handouts for the entire presentation (six per page). Be sure to frame the individual slides. And finally, print the presentation in outline form.

   i. Exchange your assignment with another classmate to learn more about that person. Your instructor may also use the assignment to learn more about the class as a whole; e.g., how many states are represented in your class? How many countries are represented? Which classmates are bilingual? Do any of your classmates speak more than two languages?

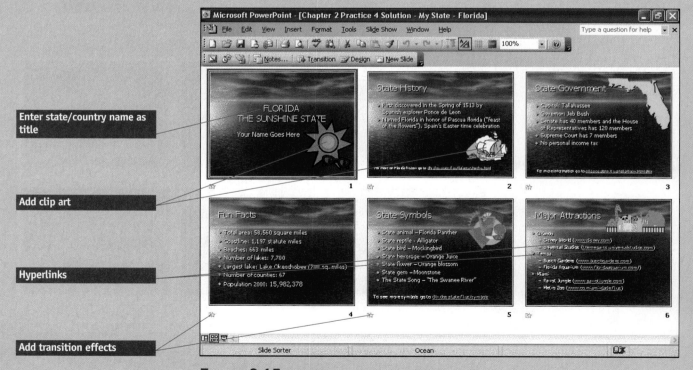

FIGURE 2.15   My State or Country (exercise 4)

5. **Hidden Slides (a card trick):** You didn't expect a card trick in a book on PowerPoint, but we think you will enjoy this exercise. Open the presentation in *Chapter 2 Practice 5*, pull down the Slide Show menu and click the View Show command (or simply press the F5 key to start the show).

a. You will see the title slide, followed by the slide in Figure 2.16. Choose a card and then click the mouse as instructed.

b. Concentrate as directed and then click the mouse to move to the next slide. The card you chose originally will be removed from the stack and only five cards will remain. Try it as often as you like, choosing a different card each time. We will continue to "read your mind" and will always remove your card from the pile.

c. The solution is contained within the original presentation as a hidden slide. Change to the Slide Sorter view, locate the hidden slide, and then double click the slide to return to the Normal view so that you can read the solution. Run through the slide show once again. You can see how easy it is to perform the card trick once you know the answer.

d. Insert a hyperlink on the title slide that will display the slide containing the solution. (You need to specify that the hyperlink is to a place in this document—that is, to an existing slide, as opposed to an external Web page.) Clicking the newly inserted hyperlink during the slide show will display the slide even if it is a hidden slide.

e. Insert a hyperlink on the solution slide that takes you to the second slide in the presentation that describes the card trick. (Once again, specify that the hyperlink is to a place in this document, as opposed to a Web page.)

f. View the presentation a final time to be sure it works as intended.

g. Print the title slide as a full slide to serve as a cover sheet for your assignment. Print the completed presentation as audience handouts (six per page). Be sure to frame the individual slides.

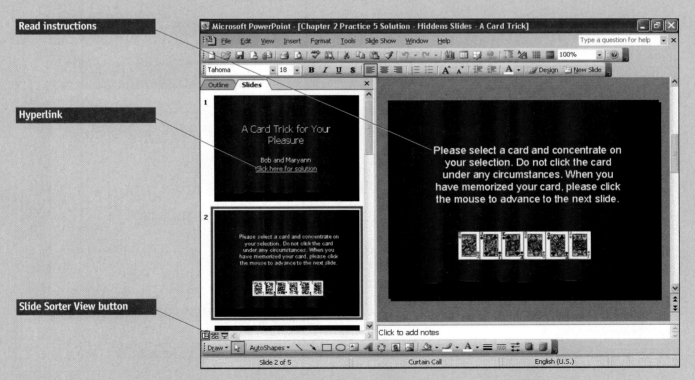

FIGURE 2.16 Hidden Slides (exercise 5)

6. **Creating a Timeline:** The presentation in Figure 2.17 displays a timeline that contains milestones for a hypothetical event. The slide looks quite impressive and is very easy to create. Choose a real or hypothetical event, then create a timeline with at least four milestones. Proceed as follows:

a. Start PowerPoint and create a new presentation. Enter your name and an appropriate title on the title slide.

b. Insert a second slide in the Title and Content layout. Click the icon to insert a table. Enter 12 and 2, for the number of columns and rows, respectively. Click OK to create the table.

c. Click and drag the line separating the two rows, so that the first row is much narrower than the second. Drag the bottom border of the table down to increase the depth of the second row.

d. Select all of the cells in the first row. Change the font size to 17 or 18 points, and then enter the months of the year. Center and boldface the text, then select an appropriate fill color.

e. Click the AutoShapes tool and then create a block arrow for the first milestone. Enter appropriate text to describe the milestone.

f. Use the same fill color as for the months in the first row. Copy the block arrow for the additional milestones, changing the text as necessary for each milestone.

g. You can add a header and/or a footer to the audience handouts by modifying the handout master. Pull down the View menu, click the Master command, and then click Audience Handout. Insert your instructor's name at the upper left of the handout master and today's date at the upper right. Put your name at the lower left of the handout master, and put the page (slide) number on the lower right.

h. Print the completed presentation as audience handouts, two slides per page. Be sure to frame the slides.

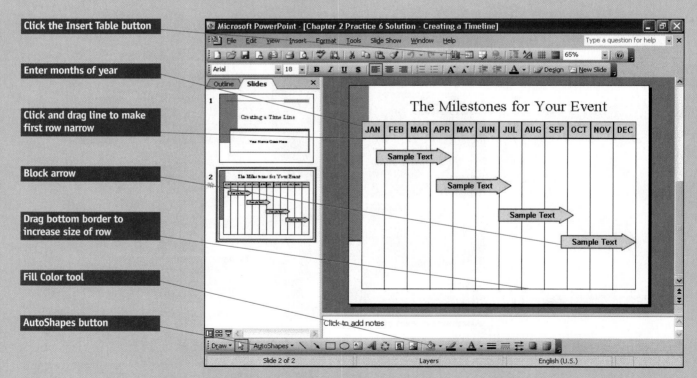

FIGURE 2.17   Creating a Timeline (exercise 6)

7. **Look Ahead—Creating a Web Page:** A PowerPoint presentation can be converted to a Web page so that it can be viewed within an Internet browser. In the early days of the Internet, the only way to create a Web page was to learn HTML. Today, however, it's much easier. You can create a presentation (Word document or Excel workbook), then use the Save as Web Page command to convert the document to a Web page.

a. Open the *Our First Exam* presentation that was created in the fourth hands-on exercise. Pull down the File menu and click the Save As Web Page command to display the Save As dialog box. The file name (Our First Exam) is specified by default. Check that the file type is Single File Web Page (as opposed to Web Page) so that all of the HTML elements are stored in a single document. (The Single File Web Page format was introduced in PowerPoint 2003 and was not available in previous versions of Microsoft Office.)

b. Select the Exploring PowerPoint folder, then click the Save button. The presentation does not change in any noticeable way. Close PowerPoint.

c. Start Windows Explorer and switch to the Exploring PowerPoint folder. Look closely and you will see two files with the same name (Our First Exam). The file types are different, however. You have the original PowerPoint presentation as well as a new MHTML document.

d. Double click the MHTML document to view the presentation as a Web page as shown in Figure 2.18. Experiment with the various controls at the bottom of the Internet Explorer window to view the presentation. How do you go to a specific slide? What happens if you click the Outline button? What happens if you click the Slide Show button in Internet Explorer?

e. Print the title slide from Internet Explorer to prove to your instructor that you have created the Web page.

f. The address bar in Figure 2.18 indicates that you are viewing the Web page locally (from your C drive). What additional steps are necessary if you want to place your presentation on the Web so that it can be viewed by others?

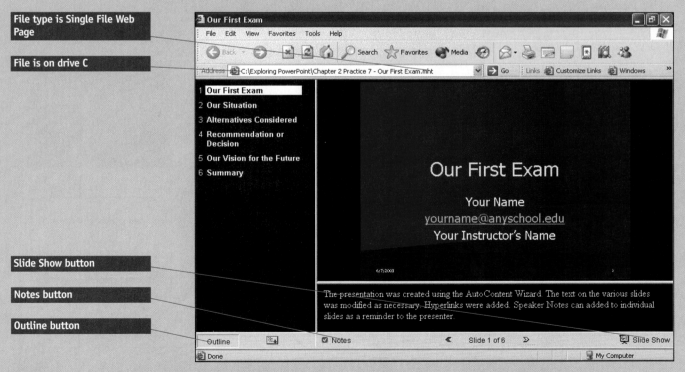

FIGURE 2.18   Look Ahead—Creating a Web Page (exercise 7)

8. **A Look Ahead—Templates and Color Schemes:** The ability to include multiple design templates in a single presentation was first introduced in Office XP. Start a new presentation and enter "Templates and Color" as the title of the presentation. Add your name to the title slide in the indicated placeholder. Choose a design template (we selected the Layers design) and add that information to the title slide. Proceed as follows to create the remainder of the presentation.

   a. Go to the Slide Sorter view as shown in Figure 2.19, copy the title slide, and then change the color scheme in the second slide. Try to use contrasting color schemes— that is, light text on a dark background, versus dark text on a light background. Which color scheme do you prefer? What does PowerPoint suggest? (See the tip for new users that appears on the Standard tab within the Edit Color Scheme dialog box.)

   b. Copy the original title slide, change to the Blends design, and modify the information in the appropriate placeholder. Duplicate this slide and change the color scheme. Repeat this process at least one additional time, so that your complete presentation has a minimum of six slides.

   c. Print the completed presentation as audience handouts (six per page) for your instructor. Use a color printer if possible to appreciate the different color schemes within the presentation.

   d. How many colors comprise a color scheme? How do you change a specific color within a particular color scheme? Be prepared to answer these questions in a class discussion.

   e. Search the Web for additional templates that are not provided in the default installation of Microsoft Office. How much do these templates cost? Are they superior to those provided with Office?

   f. Print the title slide as a full slide to use as a cover sheet for this assignment. Include written answers to the various discussion questions and submit the entire assignment to your instructor.

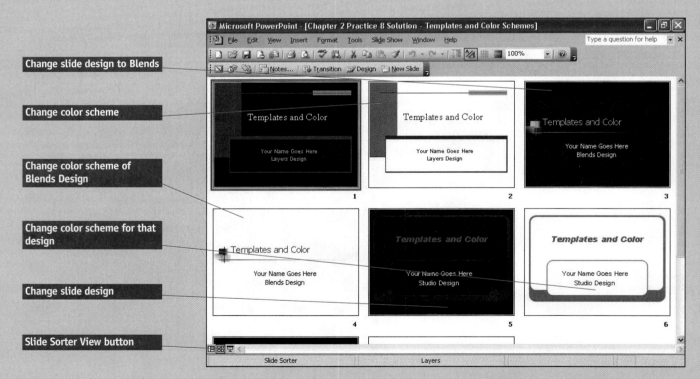

FIGURE 2.19   A Look Ahead—Templates and Color Schemes (exercise 8)

9. **A Look Ahead—Scheduling an Online Broadcast:** Any presentation, even one including video and audio, can be delivered as a Web broadcast. The broadcast can be live or recorded. A live broadcast is scheduled at a precise time, and invitations are sent to a designated list of attendees. A recorded broadcast is uploaded to a Web server and configured for on-demand viewing. Either type of broadcast is ideal for reaching large and/or geographically dispersed audiences. PowerPoint alone is sufficient to broadcast to groups of ten or fewer. Additional software, such as Microsoft Windows Media Server, is required to reach larger audiences. Check with your instructor about the facilities available to you, then proceed as follows:

a. Choose any presentation for your broadcast. It need not be long and it need not include video or audio files, as your objective at this time is to schedule the broadcast and establish basic settings.

b. Pull down the Slide Show menu, click the Online Broadcast command, then click Schedule a Live Broadcast to display the associated dialog box in Figure 2.20. Enter the requested information, which will appear on the lobby page (opening screen) of your broadcast.

c. Click the Tips for Broadcast button to display a help window with detailed information about scheduling a broadcast. Print this information for your instructor. Close the Help window.

d. Click the Settings button in the Schedule Presentation Broadcast dialog box to display the Broadcast Settings dialog box. Click the Presenter tab and then test your video and/or audio devices as necessary.

e. Click the Advanced tab to establish additional settings; e.g., the URL of a chat room, or whether you will use the Windows Media server. Click the Help button in the Broadcast Settings dialog box to learn more. Print the associated information for your instructor. Close the Help window. Close the dialog box.

f. Click the Schedule button to display the associated dialog box and schedule the actual broadcast (if possible). Notify your instructor when your broadcast is to take place in order to get credit for the assignment.

g. Summarize your thoughts about scheduling a broadcast in a short note to your instructor. Add a cover sheet to complete the assignment.

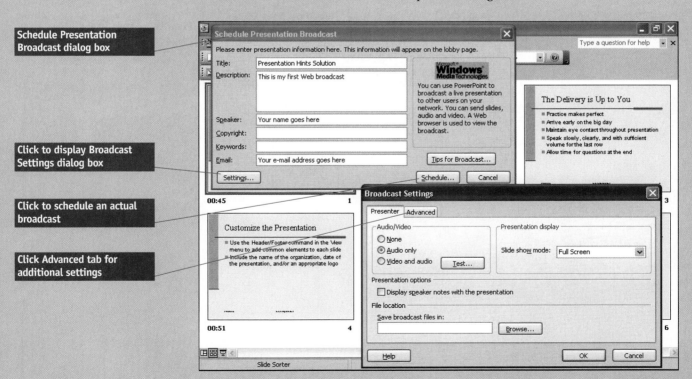

FIGURE 2.20   A Look Ahead—Scheduling an Online Broadcast (exercise 9)

MINI CASES

Digital Cameras

As with all technology, the price of a digital camera has come down significantly while performance has gone up dramatically. What are the most significant capabilities in a digital camera? What is the least amount of money you have to spend to purchase (what you consider) a worthwhile camera? What are the parameters and cost of your ideal camera? Be sure to consider the size and weight of the camera—the more functionality, the larger the camera. The worst picture is the one you do not take because the camera is too big to take with you.

The Annual Report

Corporate America spends a small fortune to produce its annual reports, which are readily available to the public. Choose any company and obtain a copy of its most recent annual report. Use your imagination on how best to obtain the data. You might try a stockbroker, the 800 directory, or even the Internet. Use the information in the annual report as the basis for a PowerPoint presentation. PowerPoint is one step ahead of you and offers a suggested financial report through the AutoContent Wizard.

Two Different Clipboards

The Office clipboard is different from the Windows clipboard, but both clipboards share some functionality. Thus, whenever you copy an object to the Office clipboard, it is also copied to the Windows clipboard. However, each successive copy operation *adds* an object to the Office clipboard (up to a maximum of 24 objects), whereas it *replaces* the contents of the Windows clipboard. The Office clipboard also has its own task pane. Experiment with the Office clipboard from different applications, then summarize your findings in a brief note to your instructor.

Director of Marketing

Congratulations on your appointment as Director of Marketing. The company into which you have been hired has 50 sales representatives across the United States. Laptop computers have just been ordered for the entire sales staff and will be delivered at next week's annual sales meeting. Your job is to prepare a PowerPoint presentation that can be used by the sales staff in future sales calls. It's short notice, but it is a critical assignment. Use the Selling a Product template provided by the AutoContent Wizard as the basis for your presentation.

3

Animating a Presentation:
Diagrams and Charts

OBJECTIVES

After reading this chapter you will:

1. Describe the diagrams that are available in the Diagram Gallery

2. Create a pyramid, a target diagram, and an organization chart

3. Use custom formatting to change the appearance of various diagrams

4. Use Microsoft Graph to create and edit a chart

5. Distinguish between charts with data series in rows versus columns.

6. Add custom animation to individual objects on a slide

7. Animate an organization chart so objects appear by level or branch.

8. Animate a chart so that data appears by category or series.

hands-on exercises

1. DIAGRAMS AND ORGANIZATION CHARTS
   Input: None
   Output: Diagrams and Organization Charts

2. MICROSOFT GRAPH
   Input: None
   Output: Introduction to Charts

3. CUSTOM ANIMATION
   Input: Super Zoo; Diagrams and Organization Charts (from exercise 1); Introduction to Charts (from exercise 2)
   Output: Super Zoo Solution

CASE STUDY
THE KELSO PERFORMING ARTS CENTER

An appreciation for the arts is essential to the quality of life in any society, but the recent budget shortfall at every level of government has put cultural programs in jeopardy throughout the country. The city of Kelso is no exception as its residents have tried unsuccessfully for several years to persuade the city council to build a Performing Arts Center. This year there is a renewed sense of optimism because the political climate has changed, and there is a strong focus on revitalizing the downtown area. In addition, the Kelso family, for whom the city is named, has agreed to donate a prime five-acre site if the council will approve a $30 million bond issue to fund construction.

You are civic minded and a patron of the arts. Kenneth Kelso is also a close personal friend, and he has asked you to spearhead the effort to secure the funding. You and two colleagues from the Chamber of Commerce Leadership Committee are to go before the council on Monday evening to present your case. The Kelso family has worked for several hours to prepare the contents of the presentation, but it is not yet finished. Ken is counting on you to add the finishing touches. He is seeking an eye-catching, attention-grabbing, interest-keeping presentation, which you will also submit to your instructor for his or her entertainment. ■

Your assignment is to read the chapter, taking note of the many ways a presentation can be enhanced through the use of animation, charts, diagrams, and sound. You will then open the partially completed *Chapter 3 Case Study—Kelso Performing Arts Center* presentation and add the objects indicated below, together with the associated animations. Start by modifying the opening slide to include your name and the sound of a drum roll.

Add animation to the existing chart for revenue projection, as well as to the slide that shows the project's time table. Copy the existing pyramid on the fifth slide, modify the copy to create a target diagram on the same slide, and then animate both the pyramid and the target diagram. Create an organization chart on the penultimate (next-to-last) slide, and then animate the chart so that the blocks appear one at a time. You have done a good job, so be sure to include the sound of applause on the last slide. Print the completed presentation as audience handouts for your records.

Figure 3.1 displays a six-slide presentation for a hypothetical "Super Zoo." The presentation is interesting in and of itself; what you cannot see, however, is the animation that is associated with every slide. The giraffe in slide 1, for example, is made to walk across the slide, and then disappear. The boxes in the organization chart on slide 2 appear one branch at a time, as do the columns in the chart on slide 3. There are "exploding fireworks" on the last slide.

The presentation also includes additional objects that we have not seen previously. The organization chart in slide 2 is created through the Diagram Gallery (as described below). The chart in slide 3 is created through Microsoft Graph, a charting program that is built into Microsoft Office. (Charts can also be imported from Microsoft Excel.)

The timeline in slide 4 is developed from a table. Look closely, and you should see the structure of an underlying 2×12 table (two rows and 12 columns, the latter corresponding to the months of the year). Clip art and block arrows were placed on top of the table to create the timeline. Animation was added at the end, so that the arrows (milestones in the project) appear sequentially.

The drawing in slide 5 was created using various tools on the Drawing toolbar. Clip art was placed on top of the various shapes, after which animation was applied to the individual objects. Slide 6 uses the AutoShapes tool to create an exploding slide in conjunction with sound and animation.

As indicated, animation is the common element in every slide and the driving concept throughout this chapter. Before we can apply the animation, however, we must first describe how to create the various objects on the slides. We begin with the organization chart on slide 2.

The Diagram Gallery

An organization chart is one of six types of diagrams that can be created using the **Diagram Gallery** in Microsoft Office. Each diagram is intended to convey a different type of relationship that may exist within an organization. We focus on the organization chart, but it is useful to mention all six diagram types. Thus, we use

- **Organization chart** to show hierarchical relationships

- **Cycle diagram** to show a process with a continuous cycle

- **Radial diagram** to show elements revolving around a core

- **Pyramid diagram** to show foundation relationships

- **Venn diagram** to show overlap between elements

- **Target diagram** to show steps toward a goal

All diagrams are developed within the **drawing canvas** (an area enclosed within hashed lines) that appears when you first create the diagram. Every diagram has a default format, which contains a limited number of entries (shapes). You can insert additional shapes, such as subordinate or coworker boxes on an organization chart. You can also delete existing shapes (e.g., a specific box on an organization chart) by selecting the box and pressing the Del key.

You can change the appearance of a diagram as well as its structure. All diagrams provide access to the **AutoFormat tool** that displays a Style Gallery, which formats the diagram as a whole. Alternatively, you can select individual (and/or multiple) shapes within a diagram and format them independently. You can change the style of the connecting lines in an organization chart as well as their color. You can also change the font and/or alignment of the text within the individual shapes. It's easy, it's fun, and as you might have guessed, it is time for our next hands-on exercise.

(a) Title Slide

(b) Organization Chart
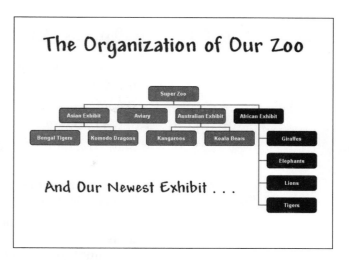

(c) Chart
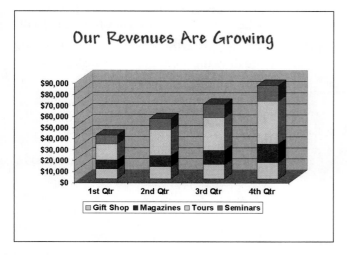

(d) Timeline (table)
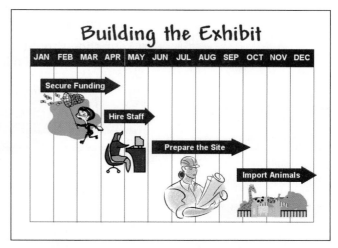

(e) Drawing
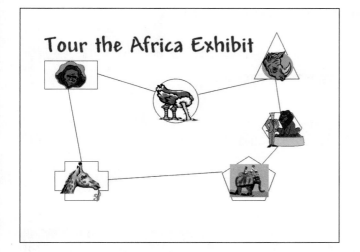

(f) AutoShape

FIGURE 3.1   The Super Zoo Presentation

1 Diagrams and Organization Charts

Objective To create and format an organization chart; to create a pyramid and target using the Diagram Gallery. Use Figure 3.2 as a guide in the exercise.

Step 1: Insert a Diagram

- Start PowerPoint. Click the **New button** to begin a new presentation. Enter the title **Diagrams and Organization Charts** and your name on the title slide.

- Save the presentation as **Diagrams and Organization Charts** in the **Exploring PowerPoint folder**.

- Click the **New Slide button** to insert a new slide. If necessary, click the **down arrow** at the top of the task pane and select **Slide Layout**. Scroll in the task pane until you can select (click) the **Title and Diagram or Organization Chart layout**.

- Double click the icon to **add diagram or organization chart** to display the Diagram Gallery as shown in Figure 3.2a. Select **Organization Chart**. Click **OK**.

- Your slide should contain the default organization chart surrounded by a nonprinting hashed line to indicate the drawing area. Close the task pane.

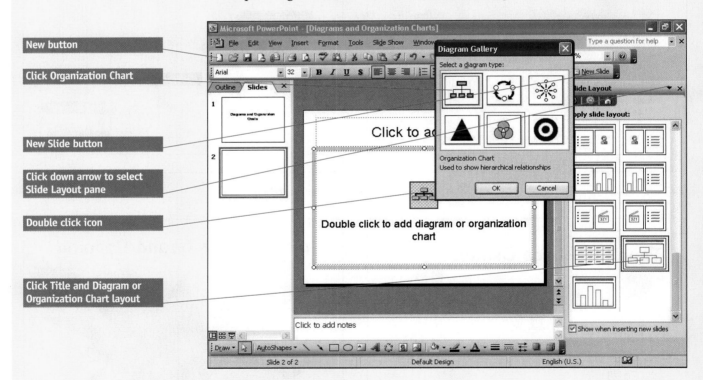

(a) Insert a Diagram (step 1)

FIGURE 3.2 Hands-on Exercise 1

USE THE TOOLBAR BUTTONS

You don't have to change the slide layout to insert a diagram onto an existing slide. Just select the slide, and then click the Insert Diagram or Organization Chart button on the Drawing toolbar. The Drawing toolbar also contains buttons to insert WordArt or clip art.

Step 2: **Create the Organization Chart**

- Click the **title place holder** and enter the title of this slide, **The Organization of Our Zoo**, as shown in Figure 3.2b.

- Click in the top box of the organization chart and type **Super Zoo**. (Do not press the Enter key or you will create an extra line and unnecessarily increase the depth of the box.)

- Click in the **leftmost box** on the second line and type **Asian Exhibit**. Stay in the box after you have entered the text, click the **down arrow** on the **Insert Shape tool** in the Organization Chart toolbar, and click **Subordinate**.

- Click in the newly created box (which appears under the Asian Exhibit) and type **Bengal Tigers** as shown in Figure 3.2b.

- Add **Komodo Dragons** as a second subordinate for **Asian Exhibit**. Enter the text for the remaining boxes as shown in Figure 3.2b. (The remaining boxes in the second row are **Aviary** and **Australian Exhibit**. **Kangaroos** and **Koala Bears** are subordinates for the **Australian Exhibit**.)

- Save the presentation.

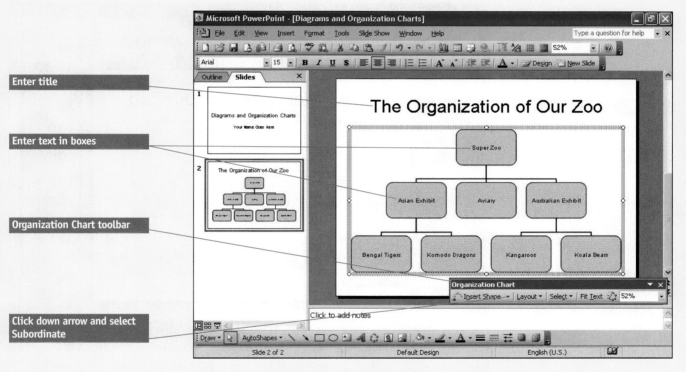

(b) Create the Organization Chart (step 2)

FIGURE 3.2 Hands-on Exercise 1 (*continued*)

IF YOU MAKE A MISTAKE

You can delete any box in the organization chart by selecting the box and pressing the Del key. If necessary, you can delete the entire chart (and start over) by clicking the hashed line surrounding the drawing area and pressing the Del key. You can also cancel (reverse) the last command(s) by clicking the Undo button or using the Ctrl+Z keyboard shortcut.

Step 3: Add the African Exhibit

- Close the left pane to give yourself additional room in which to work. (You can reopen the left pane at any time by clicking the **Normal View button** above the status bar.)

- Add the **African Exhibit** in one of two ways:
  - ❑ Click at the top of the organization chart and insert a **subordinate**, *or*
  - ❑ Click in the rightmost box on the second level and insert a **coworker**.

- Type **African Exhibit** in the box that appears at the end of the second line. Enter **Giraffes** and **Elephants** as subordinates for this box. Do not be concerned that the organization chart is becoming awkward due to its increased width.

- Click the **African Exhibit box**, click **Layout** on the Organization Chart toolbar to display the available layouts as shown in Figure 3.2c, and select **Right Hanging**. The subordinate boxes appear one under the other, as opposed to horizontally.

- Add **Lions** and **Tigers** as additional subordinates to the African Exhibit. Save the presentation.

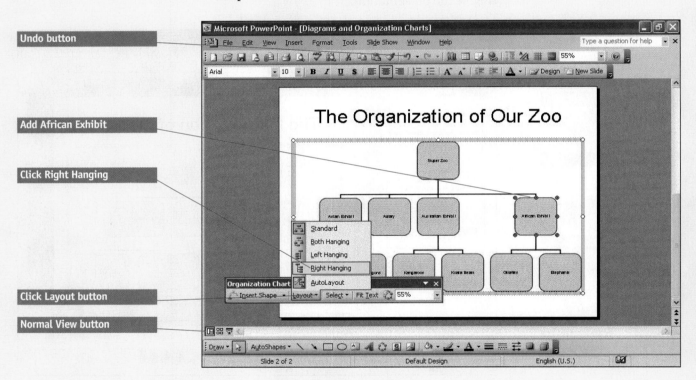

(c) Add the African Exhibit (step 3)

FIGURE 3.2 Hands-on Exercise 1 (*continued*)

THE ORGANIZATION CHART TOOLBAR

The Organization Chart toolbar appears automatically when the chart is selected and disappears when the chart is no longer active. The Insert Shape tool adds a subordinate (a box on the level below the selected box), a coworker (a box on the same level as the selected box), or an assistant (a staff position). The Layout tool changes the design of the chart, the size of the drawing area, or the size of chart within the drawing area. Experiment with the different options. Use the Undo command if the results are unexpected or different from what you intended.

Step 4: **Format the Chart**

- Right click in the background area of the organization chart to display a context-sensitive menu, and, if necessary, toggle the **Use AutoFormat command** off (the check should disappear).

- Click the **Super Zoo box** at the top of the organization chart. Click the **down arrow** next to the **Select tool** in the Organization Chart toolbar and click **Branch** to select the entire organization chart as shown in Figure 3.2d.

- Pull down the **Format menu**. Click **AutoShape** to display the associated dialog box. Click the **Colors and Lines tab**, then click the **down arrow** next to the **color box** (in the fill area) and select **red**. Click **OK**.

- Click off the chart, click the **African Exhibit box**, click the **down arrow** next to the **Select tool** and click **Branch**. Use the **Format AutoShape command** to change the color of this branch to blue.

- Reselect all of the boxes in the organization chart. Click the **Font Size list box** on the Formatting toolbar and enter **11 point** type. Click the **Bold button** to change the font to bold. Click the **down arrow** next to the **Font color box** on the Formatting toolbar. Click **White**. Save the presentation.

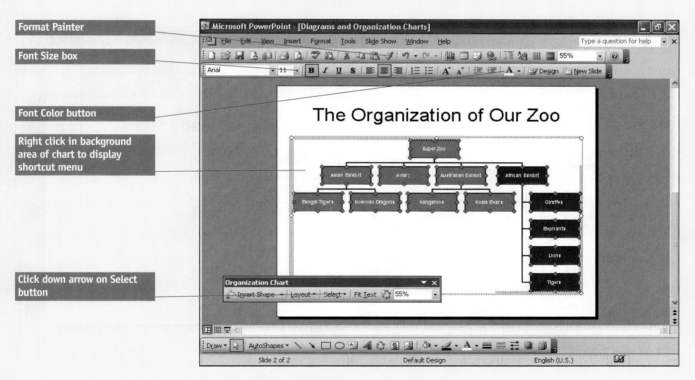

Format Painter

Font Size box

Font Color button

Right click in background area of chart to display shortcut menu

Click down arrow on Select button

(d) Format the Chart (step 4)

FIGURE 3.2 Hands-on Exercise 1 (*continued*)

THE FORMAT PAINTER

The Format Painter copies the formatting of the selected text to other places in a presentation. Select the text with the formatting you want to copy, then click or double click the Format Painter. Clicking the button will paint only one selection. Double clicking the button will paint multiple selections until the feature is turned off by again clicking the button. Either way, the mouse pointer changes to a paintbrush, which you can drag over text to give it the formatting characteristics of the original selection.

Step 5: **Create a Pyramid Diagram**

- Click the **Normal View button** above the status bar and then click the **Slides tab** to check your progress. You should see the newly created organization chart as the second slide in your presentation.

- Click the **New Slide button**, then scroll in the Slide Layout task pane until you can select (click) the **Title and Diagram or Organization Chart layout**. Close the task pane.

- Double click the icon to **add diagram or organization chart** to display the Diagram Gallery. Click the **Pyramid Diagram icon**. Click **OK**. The default pyramid is created with three components.

- Click (select) the top triangle. Click the **Insert Shape button** on the Diagram toolbar twice in a row so that the pyramid has five components. Enter the text of each component as shown in Figure 3.2e.

- Click the **AutoFormat button** on the Diagram toolbar to display the Diagram Style Gallery. Select (click) the **Primary Colors** design, then click the **Apply button** to implement this design. Each block on the pyramid is now a different color.

- Click in the title placeholder and enter **Sponsorship Levels** as the title of the slide. Save the presentation.

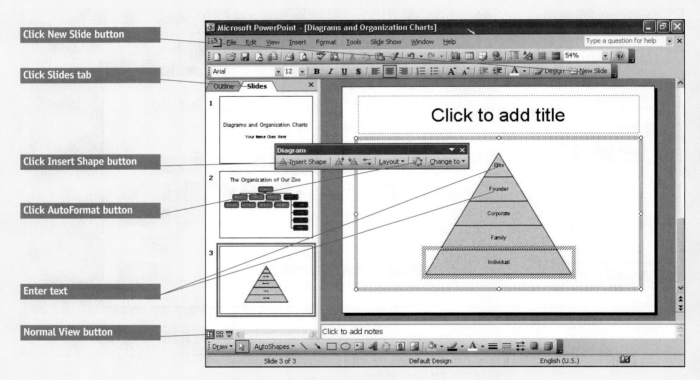

(e) Create a Pyramid Diagram (step 5)

FIGURE 3.2 Hands-on Exercise 1 (*continued*)

AUTOFORMAT ON AND OFF

You can format individual elements within a diagram, provided that auto formatting is not in effect. Right click any element (e.g., a shape in a pyramid or a box in a hierarchy chart), toggle the Use AutoFormat command off (the check should disappear), then use the Format AutoShape command to display the associated dialog box. Click the Colors and Lines tab, change the fill color, line color, and/or thickness as desired, then click OK.

Step 6: **Create a Target Diagram**

- Select (click) any element on the pyramid. Click the **Layout button** on the Diagram toolbar, then click **Fit Diagram to Contents**.

- The size of the drawing canvas shrinks to more closely surround the pyramid. Click and drag the canvas to the left side of the slide.

- Click the **Copy button** on the Standard toolbar (or use the **Ctrl+C** keyboard shortcut). Click the **Paste button** (or press **Ctrl+V**). You should now have two pyramids side by side as shown in Figure 3.2f.

- Select the second pyramid, click the **Change to button** on the Diagram toolbar, and select **Target** to change the second pyramid to a target.

- Move and size the two diagrams as necessary, so that they both fit comfortably on the slide.

- Save the presentation.

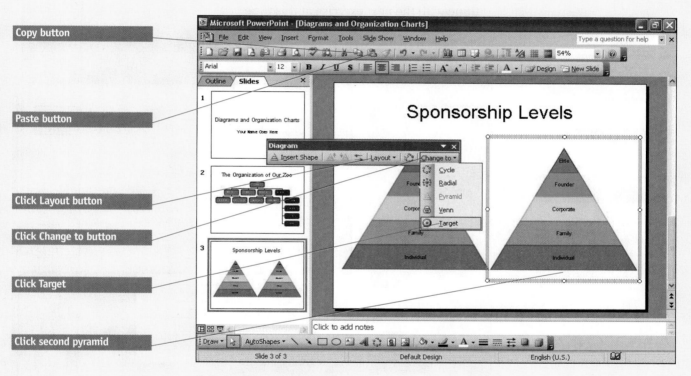

(f) Create a Target Diagram (step 6)

FIGURE 3.2 Hands-on Exercise 1 (*continued*)

THE DIAGRAM TOOLBAR

Start with one of five diagram types (radial, cycle, pyramid, Venn, or target), then click the Change to button to convert to a different type, while retaining all of your text and formatting information. Each diagram type has a unique strength, and you can experiment to find the best diagram type to deliver your message. (Organization charts have their own toolbar and are not convertible to another diagram type.) Use the Insert Shape button to add the appropriate shape to any diagram. You can also use the AutoFormat button to display the Diagram Style Gallery to format the diagram as a whole.

Step 7: Print the Audience Handouts

- Pull down the **File menu** and click the **Print command** to display the Print dialog box. Click the **down arrow** in the **Print What** area and select **Handouts**. Specify **three slides** per page. Check the box to **Frame slides**.

- Click the **Preview button** to display a screen similar to Figure 3.2g. The complete presentation consists of three slides. The target diagram is on the last slide. A series of ruled lines appears next to each slide.

- Click the **Options button**, then click the **Header and Footer command** to display the associated dialog box. Check the box to include **Date and time**, then choose the option to **Update automatically**.

- Enter **your name and class** as the header. Uncheck the boxes for page number and footer. Click the **Apply to All button**, then click the **Print button** and click **OK** to print the audience handouts for your instructor. Close the Preview window.

- Save the presentation a final time. Exit PowerPoint if you do not want to continue with the next exercise at this time.

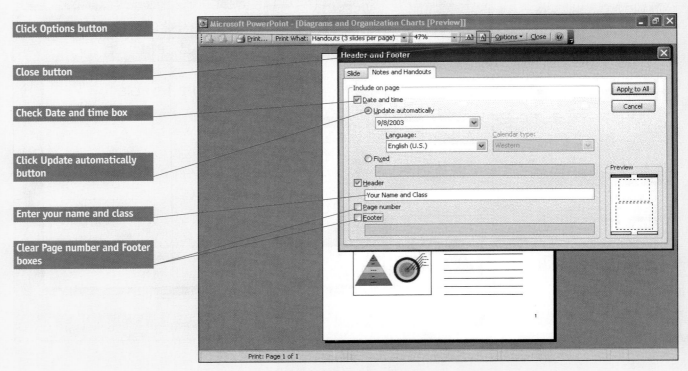

(g) Print the Audience Handouts (step 7)

FIGURE 3.2 Hands-on Exercise 1 (*continued*)

PRINT IN A VARIETY OF FORMATS

Use the flexibility inherent in the Print command to print a presentation in a variety of formats. Pull down the File menu, click the Print command to display the Print dialog box, and then select the desired output. Print handouts for your audience that contain the slide miniatures, or give your audience an outline containing the text of the entire presentation. Print the Notes Pages for yourself as a guide in preparing for the presentation. And finally, you can print the slides themselves, one per page, on overhead transparency masters as backup in case the computer is not available.

MICROSOFT GRAPH

A **chart** (or graph) is a graphic representation of data. You can import an Excel chart into a PowerPoint presentation, and/or you can create a chart from scratch. The latter is accomplished through **Microsoft Graph**, the default charting program for Microsoft Office that is installed automatically with PowerPoint. The program has many of the same capabilities as the charting component of Microsoft Excel.

All charts are based on numeric values called **data points** and descriptive entries called **category labels**. The data points are grouped into one or more **data series** that appear in rows or columns on the worksheet. This terminology is illustrated in Figure 3.3. The **datasheet** in Figure 3.3a contains 16 data points that are divided into four data series. The data represents revenue that has been raised through various funding sources in each of four quarters. Figure 3.3b displays the associated side-by-side column chart when the data series are plotted in rows. Figure 3.3c displays a comparable chart except that the data series are in columns.

Both charts plot a total of 16 data points (four revenue categories over four quarters), but they group the data differently. Figure 3.3b displays the data by quarter whereas Figure 3.3c displays the data by funding source. The choice between the two charts depends on your message and whether you want to emphasize revenue by quarter or by funding source. It sounds complicated, but it's not, and Microsoft Graph will create either chart for you according to your specifications.

- If you specify that the data series are in rows (Figure 3.3b), Microsoft Graph will
  - ❏ Use the first row in the datasheet for the category labels on the X axis.
  - ❏ Use the remaining rows for the four data series (each funding source represents a different series).
  - ❏ Use the first column for the legend text (the legend appears below the chart).

- If you specify that the data series are in columns (Figure 3.3c) the wizard will
  - ❏ Use the first column in the datasheet for the category labels on the X axis.
  - ❏ Use the remaining columns for the four data series (each quarter represents a different series).
  - ❏ Use the first row for the legend text (the legend appears below the chart).

Stacked Column Charts

Multiple data series are typically plotted as one of two chart types—**side-by-side column charts** or **stacked column charts**. Once again, the choice depends on the intended message. If, for example, you want to emphasize the individual revenue amounts in each quarter or revenue category, then the side-by-side columns in Figures 3.3b and 3.3c are more appropriate. If, on the other hand, you want to emphasize the total revenue for each quarter or category, the stacked columns in Figures 3.3d and 3.3e are preferable. The advantage of the stacked column is that the totals are clearly shown and can be easily compared. The disadvantage is that the segments within each column do not start at the same point, making it difficult to determine the actual sales for the individual categories.

Note, too, that the scale on the Y axis in the charts is different for charts with side-by-side columns versus charts with stacked columns. The side-by-side columns in Figure 3.3 show the revenue of each category or quarter, and so the Y axis goes only to $40,000. The stacked columns, however, reflect the total revenue in each quarter or category, and thus the scale goes to $90,000 or $120,000, respectively. Realize, too, that for a stacked column chart to make sense, its numbers must be additive; you shouldn't automatically convert a side-by-side column chart to its stacked column equivalent. It would not make sense, for example, to convert a column chart that plots unit sales and dollar sales side by side, to a stacked column chart that adds the two, because units and dollars represent different physical concepts, and do not make sense when added together.

Introduction to Charts - Datasheet

		A	B	C	D	E
		1st Qtr	2nd Qtr	3rd Qtr	4th Qtr	
1	Gift Shop	$9,000	$11,000	$13,000	$15,000	
2	Magazines	$8,000	$10,000	$13,000	$17,000	
3	Tours	$15,000	$24,000	$30,000	$39,000	
4	Seminars	$8,000	$10,000	$12,000	$14,000	
5						

(a) Datasheet

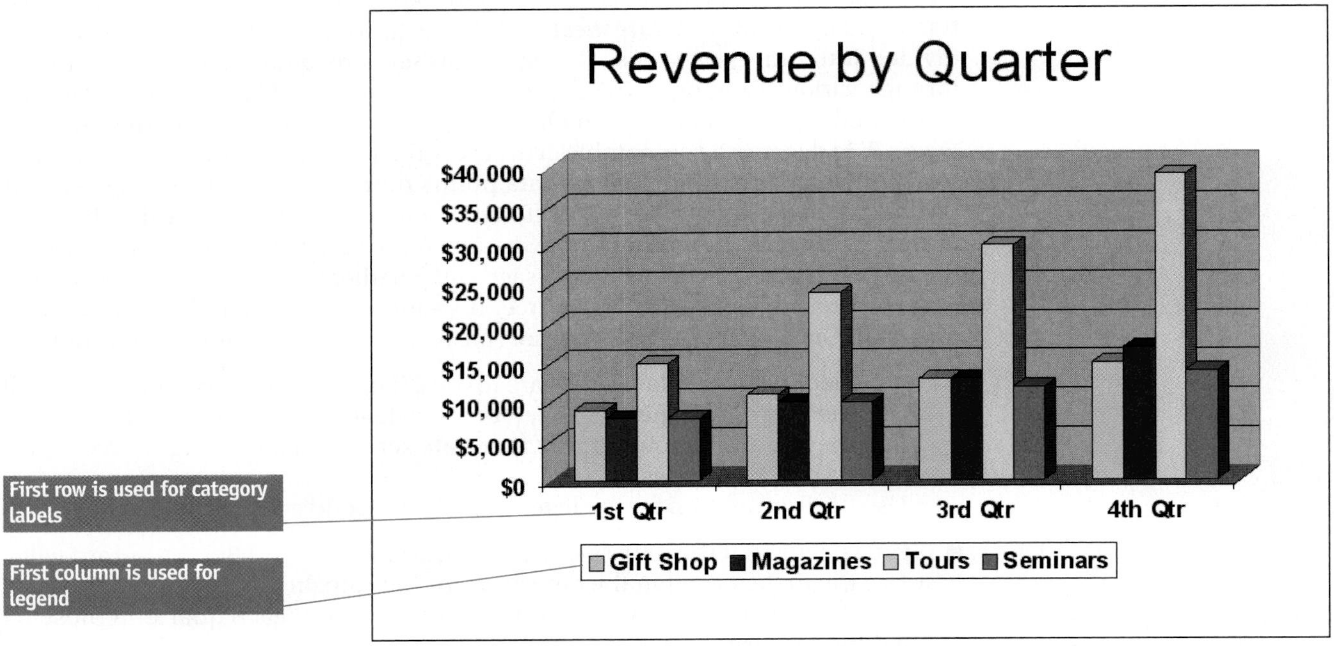

Revenue by Quarter
$40,000
$35,000
$30,000
$25,000
$20,000
$15,000
$10,000
$5,000
$0
1st Qtr
2nd Qtr
3rd Qtr
4th Qtr
Gift Shop
Magazines
Tours
Seminars
First row is used for category labels
First column is used for legend

(b) Side-by-side Column Chart (data in rows)

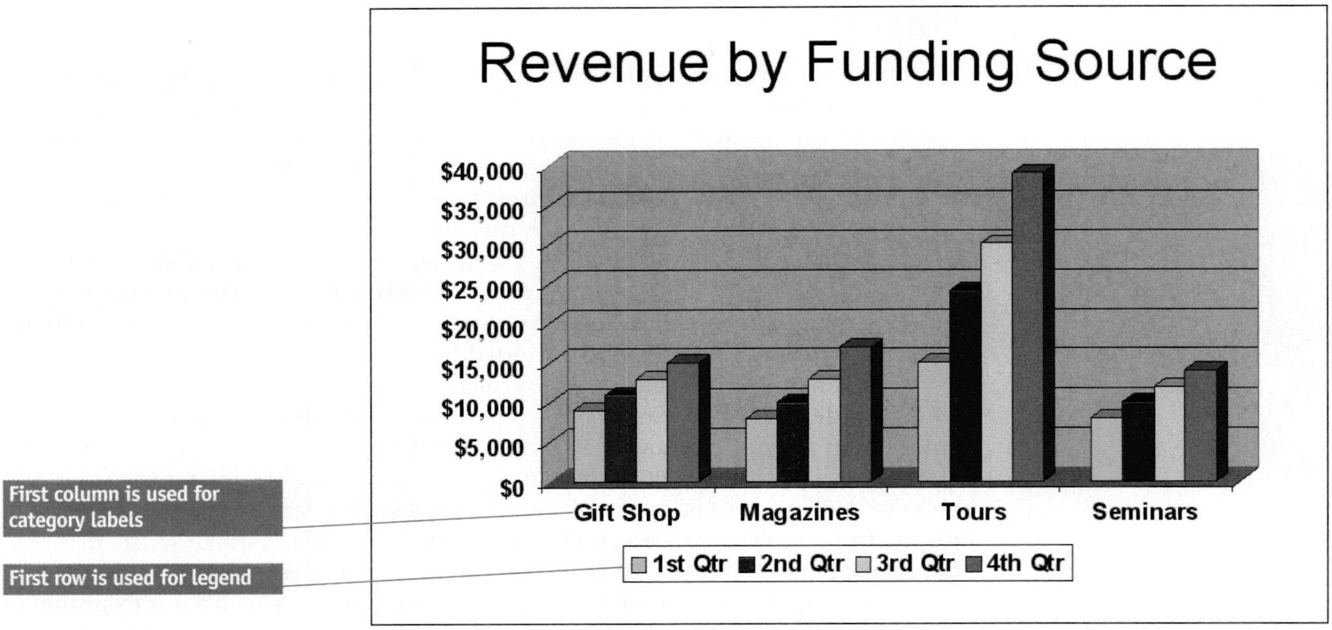

Revenue by Funding Source
$40,000
$35,000
$30,000
$25,000
$20,000
$15,000
$10,000
$5,000
$0
Gift Shop
Magazines
Tours
Seminars
1st Qtr
2nd Qtr
3rd Qtr
4th Qtr
First column is used for category labels
First row is used for legend

(c) Side-by-side Column Chart (data in columns)

FIGURE 3.3 Microsoft Graph

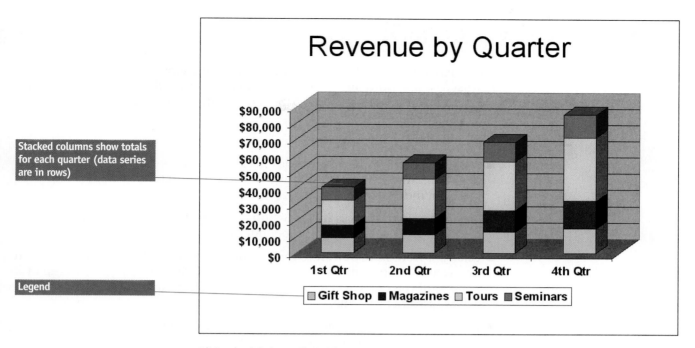

Stacked columns show totals for each quarter (data series are in rows)

Legend

(d) Stacked Column Chart (data in rows)

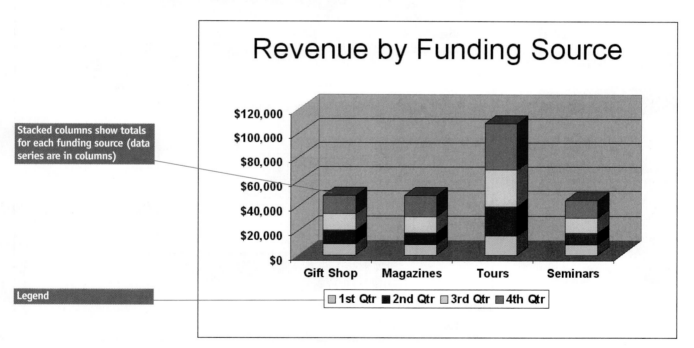

Stacked columns show totals for each funding source (data series are in columns)

Legend

(e) Stacked Column Chart (data in columns)

FIGURE 3.3 Microsoft Graph (*continued*)

EMPHASIZE YOUR MESSAGE

A chart exists to deliver a message, and you want that message to be as clear as possible. One way to help put your point across is to choose a title that leads the audience. A neutral title such as *Revenue by Quarter* does nothing and requires the audience to reach its own conclusion. A better title might be *Our Revenues Are Growing*, which conveys an optimistic sense of a growing business.

2   Microsoft Graph

Objective   Use Microsoft Graph to insert a graph into a presentation; modify the graph to display the data in rows or columns; change the graph format and underlying data. Use Figure 3.4 as a guide in the exercise.

Step 1:   Start Microsoft Graph

- Start PowerPoint. If necessary, click the **New button** on the Standard toolbar to begin a new presentation. Enter the title **Introduction to Charts** and your name on the title slide.

- Save the presentation as **Introduction to Charts** in the **Exploring PowerPoint folder** you have been using throughout the text.

- Click the **New Slide button** to insert a new slide. If necessary, click the **down arrow** at the top of the task pane and select **Slide Layout**. Scroll in the task pane until you can select (click) the **Title and Chart layout** as shown in Figure 3.4a. Close the task pane.

- Double click the icon to **add chart** to start Microsoft Graph.

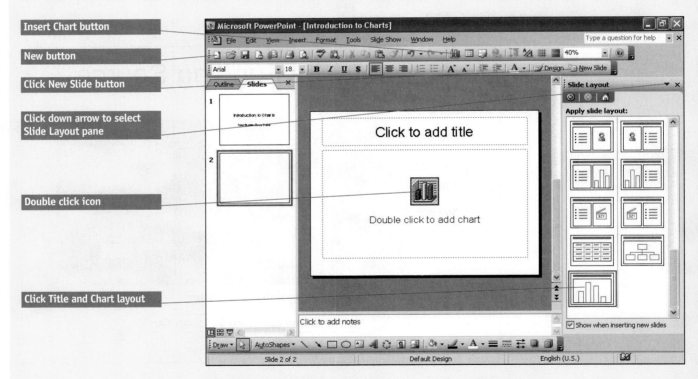

(a) Start Microsoft Graph (step 1)

FIGURE 3.4   Hands-on Exercise 2

INSERTING A CHART

There are several different ways to insert a chart into a presentation. You can insert a new slide and choose one of several slide layouts that contain a place-holder for a chart. You can pull down the Insert menu and select the Chart command, or you can click the Insert Chart button on the Standard toolbar. You can also link or embed a chart from an Excel workbook.

Step 2: The Default Chart

- The default datasheet and chart should be displayed on your monitor. The menus and toolbar have changed to reflect the Microsoft Graph application.

- Click and drag the **title bar** to move the datasheet so that you can see more of the chart, as shown in Figure 3.4b. Click and drag the borders of the datasheet to enlarge (shrink) the datasheet as appropriate. Do not be concerned if the values in your datasheet are different from those in the figure.

- Click in the cell containing "East". Type **Gift Shop** and press **Enter**. The legend changes to reflect the new entry. (We complete the data entry in the next step.)

- Click the **View Datasheet button** on the (Microsoft Graph) Standard toolbar to close the datasheet. Click the **View Datasheet button** a second time to open the datasheet.

- Click the **Legend button** on the Standard toolbar to suppress the legend on the graph. Click the **Legend button** a second time to display the legend.

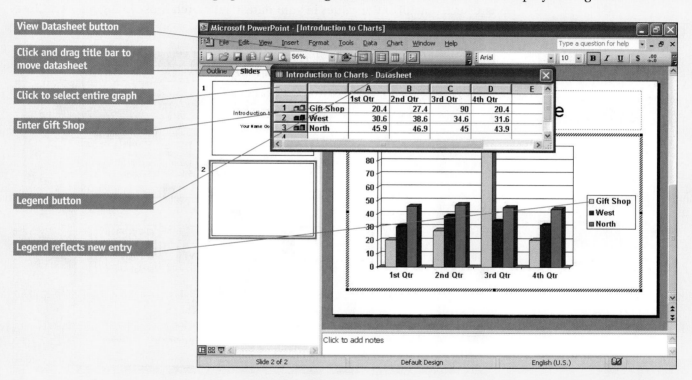

(b) The Default Chart (step 2)

FIGURE 3.4 Hands-on Exercise 2 (*continued*)

IMPORT THE DATA

Microsoft Graph enables you to import data from Microsoft Excel and use that data as the basis for the chart. (You should know the name of the workbook, the appropriate worksheet in that workbook, and the cell range in that worksheet prior to importing the data.) Start Microsoft Graph, click in the upper left square (the area above row 1 and to the left of column A) to select the entire datasheet, then click the Import File button on the Microsoft Graph toolbar to display the Import File dialog box. Select the appropriate drive and folder containing the workbook you want to import, select the file, specify the worksheet and associated range, then click OK. (See practice exercise 6 at the end of the chapter.)

Step 3: Change the Data

- Close the left pane and give yourself more room in which to work. (You can reopen the left pane at any time by clicking the **Normal View button** above the status bar.)

- Click in **cell A1**, the cell containing the gift shop data for the first quarter. Type **9000** and press the **Tab** or **right arrow key** to move to cell B1. The chart changes automatically to reflect the new data.

- Complete the data for the first data series (**Gift Shop**). Enter data for the next two series, (**Magazines** and **Tours**) as shown in Figure 3.4c. Enter data for the fourth series (**Seminars**) to complete the datasheet. Size the datasheet as necessary.

- Click and drag to select all of the numeric data as shown in Figure 3.4c. Click the **Currency Style button** to display a dollar sign next to each value, then click the **Decrease Decimal button** twice to eliminate the cents. Adjust the column width as necessary.

- Check that all of the values in your datasheet match those in Figure 3.4c. Close the datasheet. Save the presentation.

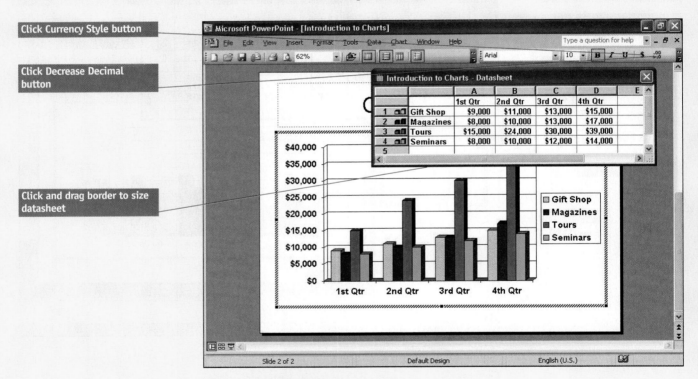

(c) Change the Data (step 3)

FIGURE 3.4 Hands-on Exercise 2 (*continued*)

REMOVING (HIDING) A DATA SERIES

Open the datasheet, right click the row number or column header of the data series you want to delete, and click the Delete command. The series disappears from both the datasheet and the associated chart. Alternatively, you can leave the data series in the datasheet, but can exclude (hide) it from the chart. Click the row number or column header to select the data series, pull down the Data menu, and select the Exclude Row/Column command. To restore the data series in the graph, select the series, pull down the Data menu, and select the Include Row/Column command.

Step 4: **Change the Orientation and Chart Type**

- Click the **By Column button** on the Standard toolbar to change the data series from rows to columns as shown in Figure 3.4d. The X axis changes to display the funding sources. The legend indicates the quarter.

- Click the **By Row button** on the Standard toolbar to change the data series back to rows. Click the **By Column button** a second time to match the orientation in Figure 3.4d.

- Pull down the **Chart menu** and click **Chart Type** to display the associated dialog box. Click the **Standard Types tab**, click **Column**, then select **Stacked column with a 3-D visual effect**.

- Check the box to preserve the **Default formatting**. Click **OK** to accept the settings and close the dialog box.

- The chart changes to a stacked column chart, which more clearly shows the total revenue from each funding source.

- Save the presentation.

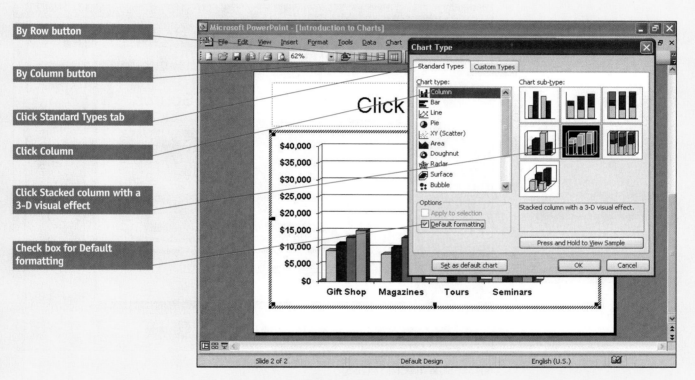

(d) Change the Orientation and Chart Type (step 4)

FIGURE 3.4   Hands-on Exercise 2 (*continued*)

TO CLICK OR DOUBLE CLICK

Once created, a chart becomes an object in a presentation that retains its connection to Microsoft Graph for easy editing. Click any object on the slide other than the chart to deselect the chart. Now click the chart once to select the chart and display the conventional sizing handles to move or size the chart just as you would any other Windows object. Double click the chart (it will be surrounded with a hashed border) to restart Microsoft Graph to edit the chart.

Step 5: Complete the Chart

- The chart should still be selected. Pull down the **Chart menu**, click the **Chart Options command** to display the associated dialog box, then click the **Legend tab**.

- Click the option to display the legend on the **Bottom**, then click **OK**.

- **Right click** the top section on any stacked column to display a context-sensitive menu and click the command to **Format Data Series** to display the associated dialog box.

- Click the **Patterns tab**, click **Red**, then click **OK** to change the color of this data series (the amounts for the fourth quarter) to **red**. Change the color of the next data series (the 3rd quarter) to **yellow**.

- Click outside the hashed area, then click in the title placeholder to enter the title of the slide, **Revenue by Funding Source**, as shown in Figure 3.4e.

- Save the presentation.

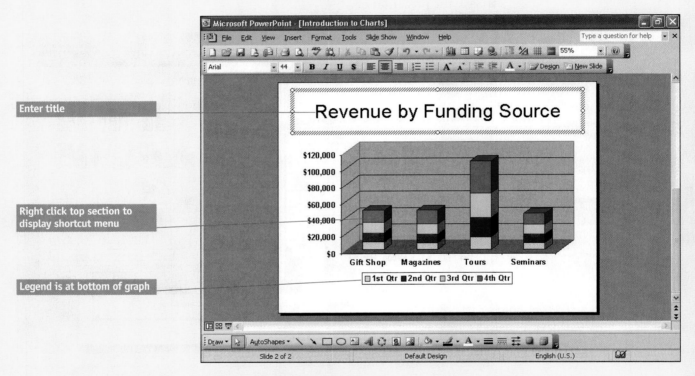

Enter title

Right click top section to display shortcut menu

Legend is at bottom of graph

(e) Complete the Chart (step 5)

FIGURE 3.4 Hands-on Exercise 2 (*continued*)

SET A TIME LIMIT

Microsoft Graph gives you (almost too much) control over the appearance of a chart. Save the presentation before you begin, then use the Format Data Series command to change the color, shape, and pattern and/or add labels to columns within a chart. Use the Undo command if the results are different from what you expected. (If the Undo command is inoperative, you can always use the Chart Type command to return to the default formatting.) It is fun to experiment, but set a time limit and stick to it! Remember, too, that the type of chart is more important than the formatting.

Step 6: Copy the Chart

- Click the **Normal View button** to restore the left pane in Figure 3.4f. Click (select) the slide containing the chart. Click the **Copy button** (or press **Ctrl+C**) to copy the slide to the clipboard.

- Click the **Paste button** (or press **Ctrl+V**) to complete the copy operation. The presentation should contain two identical charts. We will now modify the copied chart by changing its orientation.

- Select (click) the third slide if necessary. Double click the chart to start Microsoft Graph, then click the **By Row button** to display the data series by rows. The name of each quarter appears on the X axis, and the funding sources appear in the legend as shown in Figure 3.4f.

- Click outside the chart area, then click in the placeholder for the title. Change the title to **Our Revenues Are Growing**.

- Print the completed presentation for your instructor (print the slides as handouts, with three slides per page).

- Save the presentation. Exit PowerPoint if you do not want to continue with the next exercise at this time.

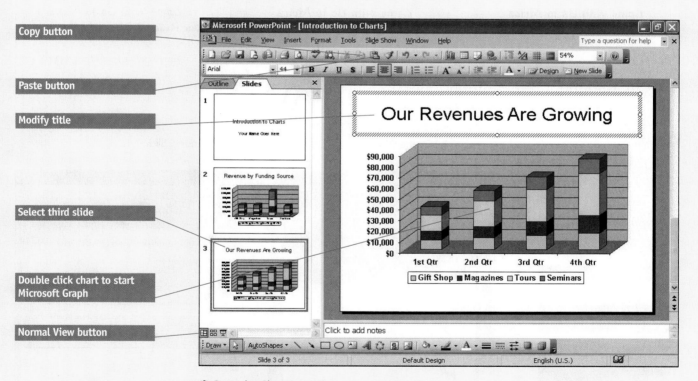

(f) Copy the Chart (step 6)

FIGURE 3.4   Hands-on Exercise 2 (*continued*)

DON'T FORGET HELP

Microsoft Graph includes its own Help system, which functions identically to the Help system in any other application. Pull down the Help menu, click Microsoft Graph Help, and search on any topic for which you want additional information. Remember, too, that you can print the contents of a help screen by clicking the Printer icon at the top of the Help window.

Custom animation determines when and how objects appear on a slide, what they do after they appear on the screen, and how the objects are to exit. It's difficult to describe animation on a static page, but we do our best in Figure 3.5. The sequence begins in Figure 3.5a with the appearance of the title and giraffe, who walks across the screen in Figure 3.5b, after which the author's name appears on the slide. The giraffe makes his exit in Figure 3.5c, and the author's name increases in size.

The ***animation*** is accomplished through the effects specified in the task pane of Figure 3.5d. The icons are color coded—green, red, and yellow to indicate an ***entrance effect***, an ***exit effect***, and an ***emphasis effect***, respectively. The custom animation for the title is selected. The effect is "fly in," which starts on a mouse click. The object enters from the top at medium speed. Look closely and you will see a Mouse icon next to the selected animation within the task pane. Look further and you see a Clock icon next to all subsequent animations to indicate that the animations take place automatically one after another. The ***advanced timeline*** shows the sequence and duration of each effect.

(a) Giraffe Entering

(b) Giraffe Walking

(c) Ending Slide

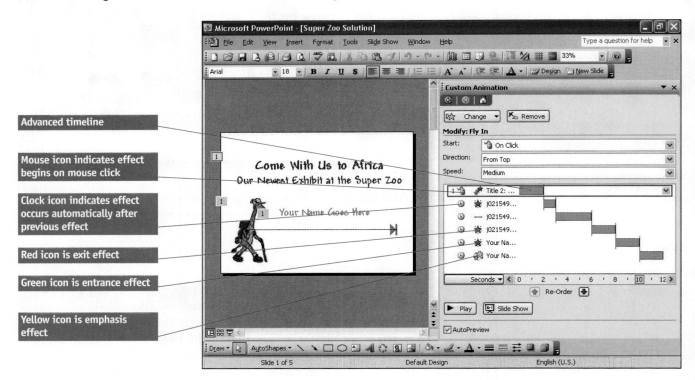

(d) Custom Animation Task Pane

FIGURE 3.5 Custom Animation (title slide)

Animating a Chart

Figure 3.6 displays an animation series in conjunction with a chart. The various categories (the stacked columns) appear sequentially upon a series of mouse clicks, after which the title increases in size. Figure 3.6a shows the slide with just the title, Figure 3.6b shows the slide after two columns have appeared, and Figure 3.6c shows the completed slide, with an enlarged title. The corresponding animation task pane is shown in Figure 3.6d. The green and yellow icons indicate entrance and emphasis effects, respectively.

The Mouse icons within the task pane indicate that the entrance of each column (category) takes place in conjunction with a mouse click. The Clock icon next to the title object, however, indicates that this effect follows automatically after the previous effect—i.e., the title appears automatically after the last column is displayed. The title animation is selected in the task pane and the details for the animation appear toward the top of the task pane. The title will grow to 150% of its size at a medium speed. Note, too, that you can select any effect, then use the up and down arrows to reorder the sequence in which the objects appear.

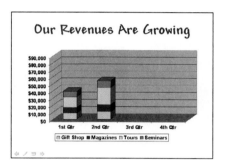

(a) Title Only

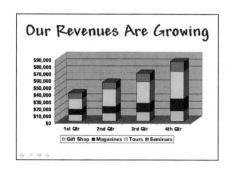

(b) After Two Categories

(c) Ending Slide

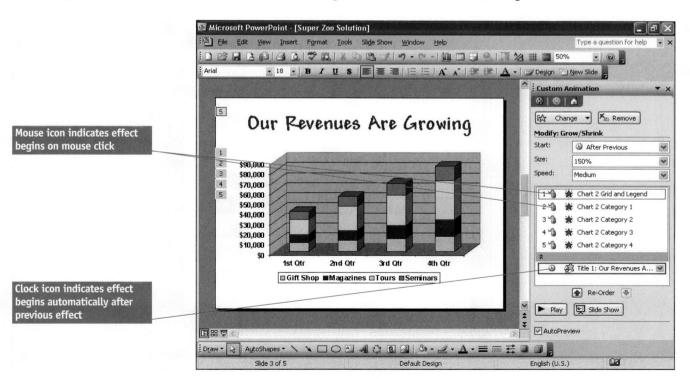

(d) Custom Animation Task Pane

FIGURE 3.6 Custom Animation (the chart)

Animating an Organization Chart

Figure 3.7 displays an animation sequence in conjunction with an organization chart for the Super Zoo. (The chart contains the same boxes as previously, but the coloring is different to illustrate the variation that is possible within a specific chart.) The intent of this example is to show the organization of the zoo, one level at a time. Figure 3.7a displays the title of the chart with a single box to represent the zoo as a whole. Figure 3.7b introduces the second level, with the African exhibit shown in a different color. Figure 3.7c displays the third (and last) level of the organization chart.

The task pane to create this animation is shown in Figure 3.7d. The Mouse icon indicates that each level enters on a mouse click. Thus, the mouse is clicked once to display the highest-level box (Super Zoo). The mouse is clicked a second time to bring in the boxes at the second level (Asian Exhibit, Aviary, Australian Exhibit, and African Exhibit). The mouse is clicked a third and last time to bring in the third (lowest) level. Note, too, that each branch of the organization chart is shown in a different color to emphasize the different exhibits within the zoo.

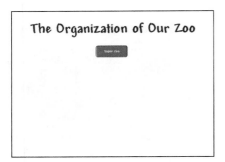

(a) Level 1

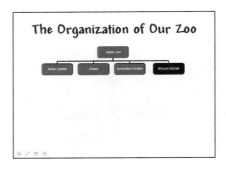

(b) Level 2

(c) Level 3

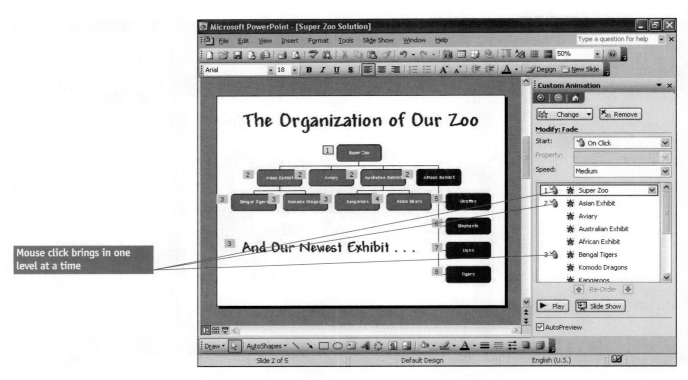

(d) Custom Animation Task Pane

FIGURE 3.7   Custom Animation (organization chart)

3 Custom Animation

Objective Add custom animation to individual objects on a slide; use custom animation to animate an organization chart and a graphical chart.

Step 1: Insert a Slide

- Start PowerPoint. Open the **Super Zoo presentation** in the **Exploring PowerPoint folder**. Add your name to the title slide.

- Pull down the **Insert menu**, click the **Slides from Files command** to display the Slide Finder dialog box in Figure 3.8a.

- Click the **Browse button** and open the **Diagrams and Organization Charts presentation** from the first hands-on exercise. Select the **organization chart**, then click the **Insert button** to insert this slide into the presentation.

- Click the **Browse button** a second time, but this time select the **Introduction to Charts presentation** from the second exercise. Insert the chart that plots **revenue by quarter** (the second chart). Close the Slide Finder dialog box.

- Save the presentation as **Super Zoo Solution** in the **Exploring PowerPoint folder**.

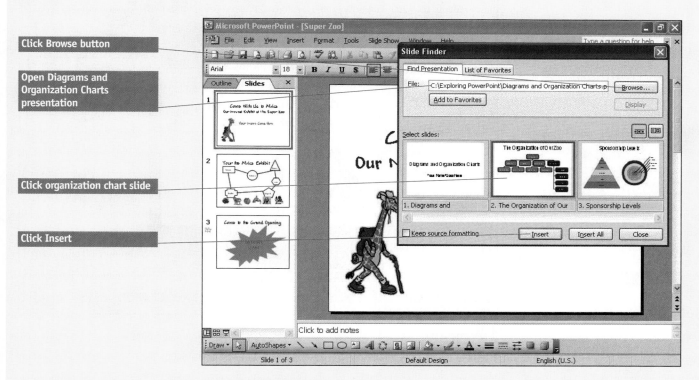

(a) Insert a Slide (step 1)

FIGURE 3.8   Hands-on Exercise 3

CREATE A NEW FOLDER

Pull down the File menu, click the Open or Save As command as appropriate, then click the Create New Folder button to display the New Folder dialog box. Enter the name of the new folder, then click OK. Use the Look In box to change to the new folder the next time you open a document.

Step 2: **Animate the Title Slide**

- The font for the slide titles of the newly inserted slides does not match the font on the title slide. Use the **Format Painter** to copy the font (**Andy, 54-point, blue**) from the title slide to the inserted slides.

- Select the title slide. Pull down the **Slide Show menu** and click the **Custom Animation command** to open the task pane as shown in Figure 3.8b.

- Click anywhere in the title to select the title. Click the **Add Effect button** in the task pane, click **Entrance**, and click the **Fly In** effect. The title flies in from the bottom of the slide (the default position).

- Modify the parameters for the Fly In effect by clicking the **down arrows** in the appropriate list boxes. Set the direction to **From Top** and the speed to **Medium**. Click the **Play button** to see how these parameters modify the animation.

- Select the **giraffe**. Click the **Add Effect button**, choose the **Dissolve In** entrance effect, change the start to **After Previous**, and set the speed to **Fast**. A second effect appears in the task pane.

- Save the presentation.

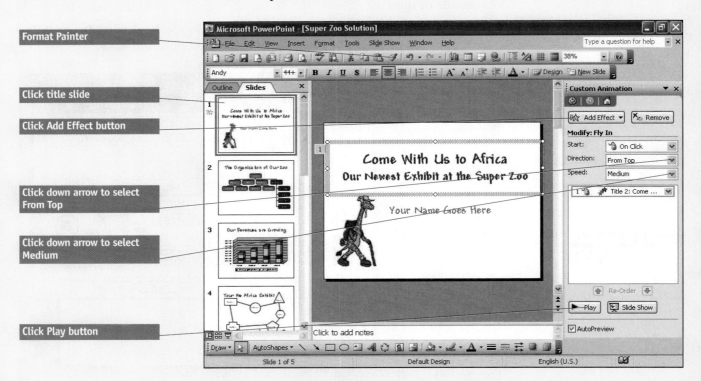

(b) Animate the Title Slide (step 2)

FIGURE 3.8 Hands-on Exercise 3 (*continued*)

YOU'RE THE DIRECTOR

No one ever said that animating a presentation was quick or easy. It takes time, more time than you might expect initially, as each slide has to be choreographed in detail. Think of yourself as the director who must tell the actors (the objects on a slide) when to come on stage and how to make their entrance. Try to think of the overall performance, and then develop one object at a time. Save the presentation continually as you add new effects. Click the Undo command anytime the result is not what you intended it to be.

Step 3: Complete the Animation

- Close the left pane to give yourself more room in which to work as shown in Figure 3.8c. Add the animation effects in the order below. Set each effect to start **After Previous effect**:
  - ❏ A **motion path to the right** for the giraffe at **slow speed**. (Increase the length of the motion path by dragging the line on the red arrow to the right.)
  - ❏ The giraffe should **dissolve out** (exit effect) at a **medium speed**.
  - ❏ Your name should dissolve in at **medium speed**.
  - ❏ Your name should **grow 150 percent** (emphasis effect) at **medium speed**.

- Click the **down arrow** on the last effect in the task pane. Set the option to **Show Advanced timeline**, then click the **left arrow** below the timeline so that you see the entire sequence. Increase the width of the task pane to see the timeline for all animations.

- Select the first effect, then click the **Play button** to view the animation for the entire slide. (You can modify any existing effect by selecting the effect in the task pane, and clicking the **Change button**.)

- Save the presentation.

(c) Complete the Animation (step 3)

FIGURE 3.8 Hands-on Exercise 3 (*continued*)

THE CUSTOM ANIMATION TASK PANE

The icon next to each effect in the custom animation task pane indicates when the effect is to appear within the animation sequence. A Mouse icon indicates that the effect begins with a mouse click, whereas the Clock icon shows that the effect will appear automatically after the previous effect. The absence of an icon means that the effect will start simultaneously with the previous effect. Note, too, that the various effects are color coded, where green, red, and yellow denote an entrance, exit, and emphasis effect, respectively.

Step 4: Animate the Organization Chart

- Press the **PgDn key** to move to the second slide (the slide with the organization chart). Click the **Text Box tool** on the Drawing toolbar, then click and drag to create a text box at the bottom of the slide.

- Enter the text of the box "**And Our Newest Exhibit . . .**" as shown in Figure 3.8d. Change the font to match the font on the title of the slide, albeit in a smaller point size.

- If necessary, open the Custom Animation task pane. Select the text box, and then add the **Fade entrance effect**, at **Medium speed**, to begin **After Previous effect**. Now click anywhere in the organization chart to make it the active object, and add the **Fade entrance effect**.

- Click the **down arrow** next to the Organization Chart animation in the task pane. Click **Effect Options** to display the Fade dialog box as shown in Figure 3.8d, then click the **Diagram Animation tab**. Click the **down arrow** in the Group diagram list box, select **Each branch, shape by shape**, and click **OK**.

- The Organization Chart animation should be selected. Change the start of the animation to **After Previous**. Click the **Play button** to see the animation thus far.

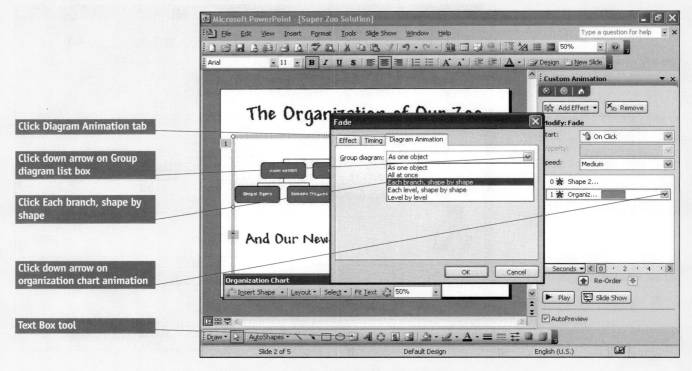

(d) Animate the Organization Chart (step 4)

FIGURE 3.8 Hands-on Exercise 3 (*continued*)

ANIMATING DIAGRAMS

Each shape in an organization chart requires its own animation effect if the shapes are to appear individually. You do not, however, have to apply the effects individually. Select the entire chart and apply an entrance effect, then go to the Custom Animation task pane, click the arrow on the effect, click the Effect Options command, click the Diagram Animation tab, and choose the type of animation. You can animate each branch shape by shape or each level shape by shape.

Step 5: Change the Animation Sequence

- We will change the animation sequence so that the text announcing the new exhibit appears prior to the entrance of the associated branch in the organization chart.

- Click the **double arrow (chevron)** in the animation pane. The single effect for the chart expands to display the animation of the individual boxes as shown in Figure 3.8e.

- Select the animation effect for **Shape 29** (the number on your text box may be different from ours).

- Click the **Reorder down arrow** repeatedly until this effect is immediately above the **African Exhibit**. Click the **Play button** to test the presentation.

- The blocks in the organization chart should come in sequentially (top to bottom, one branch at a time), until you see the box for **Koala Bears**.

- You should then see the text for the newest exhibit, after which you will see the branch for the **African exhibit**.

- Save the presentation.

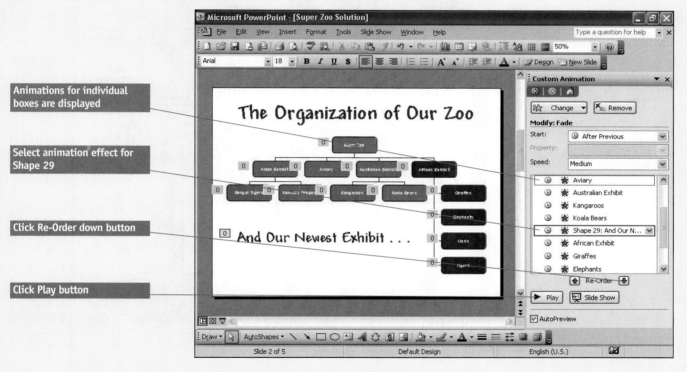

(e) Change the Animation Sequence (step 5)

FIGURE 3.8   Hands-on Exercise 3 (*continued*)

DELETE THE EFFECT NOT THE OBJECT

Click any object on a slide to select the object and display the associated sizing handles. This action also selects the associated animation effect (if any) in the Custom Animation task pane by surrounding the descriptive text with a rectangle. Be careful, however, about pressing the Del key; pressing the Del key when the object is selected deletes both the object and the animation affect. To delete the animation, but retain the object, click off (deselect) the object, click (select) the animation effect, then press the Del key. Use the Undo command if you make a mistake and try again.

Step 6:   **Animate the Chart**

- Press the **PgDn key** to move to the slide containing the chart. Select the chart.

- Click the **Add Effect button** in the task pane and choose the **Fade entrance effect** at **Medium speed**.

- Click the **down arrow** next to the chart animation in the task pane, click **Effect Options** to display the Fade dialog box, and click the **Chart Animation tab**. Click the **down arrow** in the Group chart list box and select **By Category**.

- Clear the box to **animate the grid and legend**. Click **OK**. You should see the columns appear one at a time as the effect is previewed automatically. Click the **chevron** in the animation task pane to see the individual animations.

- Select the title of the slide. Click the **Add effect button**, select **Emphasis**, and then choose the **Grow/Shrink effect** as shown in Figure 3.8f. The default setting is to increase the font size 150%.

- Save the presentation.

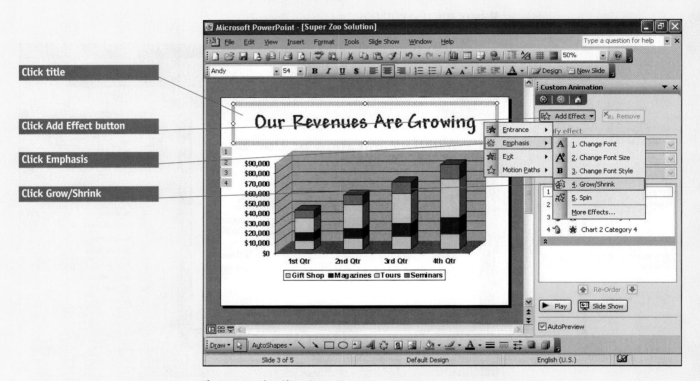

(f) Animate the Chart (step 6)

FIGURE 3.8   Hands-on Exercise 3 (*continued*)

CATEGORY VERSUS SERIES

Choose the effect that will best convey your intended message. Animating by category displays the stacked columns one column at a time, focusing on the difference between columns. Animating by series displays one element at a time from every column, emphasizing the growth of each column. Note, too, that the ability to animate a chart by its components exists only for charts created by Microsoft Graph; you cannot animate a chart that was dynamically linked to an Excel workbook.

Step 7: **Animate Multiple Objects**

- Press the **PgDn key** to move to the next slide. Press and hold the **Shift** (or **Ctrl**) **key** as you click the multiple clip art images that are on the slide.

- Click the **Add Effect button**, click **Entrance**, then click **Random Effects** to apply a different effect to each of the selected objects. The effects have been created, but you still have to set the timing.

- The first effect is set to begin on a mouse click. Press and hold the **Ctrl key** to deselect the first effect. Click the **down arrow** next to the Start list box in the animation task pane. Choose **After Previous** as shown in Figure 3.8g.

- Click and drag each animal to its appropriate place on the slide. Click the **Play button** to test the animation.

- Click the **Slide Show button**, then click the mouse to begin the animation. Note the movement within the elephant and lion after these (animated GIF) objects appear on the screen. Press **Esc** to cancel the show and continue working.

- Save the presentation.

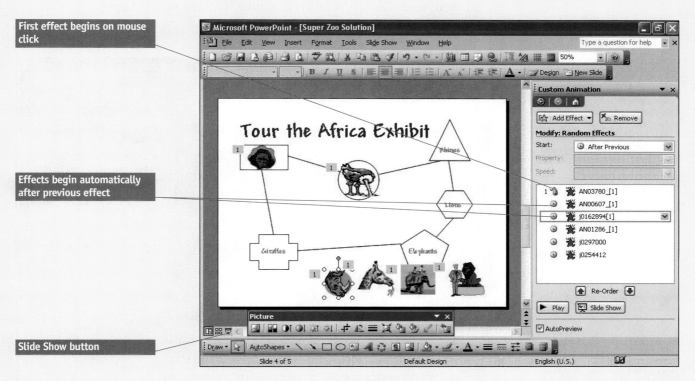

(g) Animate Multiple Objects (step 7)

FIGURE 3.8 Hands-on Exercise 3 (*continued*)

USE ANIMATED GIFS

An animated GIF file, as its name implies, adds motion to the associated clip art. Click the Insert Clip Art button on the Drawing toolbar to open the task pane. Click the down arrow in the Results Should be list box, then clear the check boxes next to all four major categories: clip art, photographs, movies, and sound. Expand the Movie category and check the box for an animated GIF file. Click in the Search text box, type "animal", then click the Go button to look for animated GIF files related to animals. Remember to reset the search criteria (i.e., check the high-level box for all media types) the next time you insert clip art.

Step 8: **Create the Explosion**

- Press the **PgDn key** to move to the last slide. Click in the left pane, click the down arrow in the **Zoom box**, and change the magnification to **33%**. You may be surprised to see that there is an AutoShape above the actual slide as shown in Figure 3.8h.

- The animation effects for this object have been set. The object will zoom in from the screen center, at a very fast speed, to the sound of an explosion, automatically after the previous effect.

- Select the **AutoShape**, click the **Copy button**, then click the **Paste button** to duplicate the shape. The animation effects are copied with the object.

- Click and drag the copied shape away from the original, then click and drag a sizing handle to change its size. Click the **down arrow** on the **Fill Color button** on the Drawing toolbar and change its color. Repeat this process to create 10 to 20 similar AutoShapes around the slide.

- Click the **Play button** to see the completed animation. Experiment with a different sound and/or a different timing for some of the shapes.

- Save the presentation.

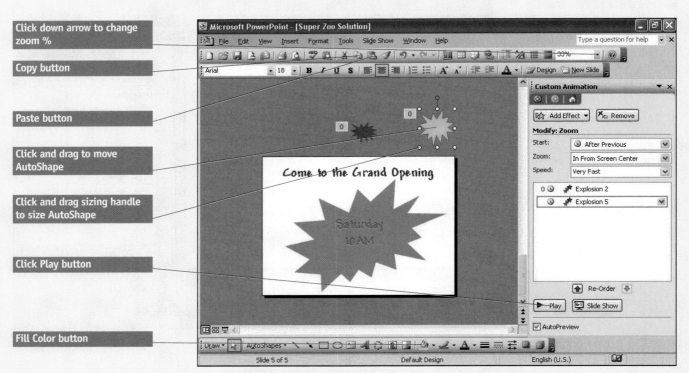

(h) Create the Explosion (step 8)

FIGURE 3.8   Hands-on Exercise 3 (*continued*)

COPY EFFICIENTLY

You start with one object and need a total of 15. You can copy and paste the individual object multiple times, or you can duplicate groups of objects. Copy the first object, then press and hold the Ctrl key to select both objects. Press Ctrl+C to copy, then Ctrl+V to paste. You now have four objects. Click and drag the copied objects to position them on the screen (you may want to select the objects individually). Now select and copy all four objects to get eight, then copy the eight, and so on.

Step 9: **Show Time**

- Close the Animation task pane. Change to the **Slide Sorter view**, where you should see five slides in the completed presentation. (The AutoShapes in the ending slide do not appear in this view, because they are off the slide.)

- Select the first slide, and click the **Slide Show button**. The screen is blank.
  - ❏ Click the mouse, the title appears, the giraffe walks across the screen in Figure 3.8i, and then your name appears.
  - ❏ Click the mouse to move to the next slide and see the animation for the organization chart. Click the mouse to move to the next slide.
  - ❏ You should see an empty chart because we opted not to animate the grid or legend. Click the mouse repeatedly to display the stacked columns for each series, then click the mouse a final time to enlarge the title. Click the mouse to move to the next slide.
  - ❏ Click the mouse to display the animals as you tour the **Africa exhibit**. Click the mouse when you are ready to move to the last slide.
  - ❏ The fireworks begin immediately. Press **Esc** when the presentation ends.

- Exit PowerPoint. Congratulations on a job well done.

Giraffe walks across screen and disappears

Come With Us to Africa
Our Newest Exhibit at the Super Zoo

(i) Show Time (step 9)

FIGURE 3.8 Hands-on Exercise 3 (*continued*)

ANNOTATING A SLIDE AND OTHER KEYBOARD SHORTCUTS

Press Ctrl+P to change the mouse pointer to a point, then click and drag on the slide during the presentation to annotate the slide. Press the letter E to erase the annotations or press Ctrl+A to change the mouse pointer back to an arrow. Press Ctrl+S to display a list of the slides in a presentation, and then double click the slide you want to view. (You can also type the number of a slide followed by the Enter key to go to that slide.) If you can't remember these shortcuts, press the F1 key to see the entire list.

SUMMARY

The Diagram Gallery provides six figure types to describe different types of relationships within an organization. The diagrams include an organization chart (hierarchical relationships), a cycle diagram (continuous cycle), a radial diagram (elements around a core), a pyramid diagram (foundation relationships), a target diagram (steps toward a goal), and a Venn diagram (overlap between elements).

All diagrams are developed within the drawing canvas (an area enclosed within hashed lines) that appears automatically as you create a diagram. Additional (e.g., subordinate) shapes can be inserted, and/or existing shapes can be deleted. The appearance of the diagram as a whole can be changed through the AutoFormat command, and/or individual shapes can be formatted independently.

A chart (or graph) is a graphic representation of data that is based on numeric values called data points and descriptive entries called category labels. The data points are grouped into one or more data series that appear in rows or columns of a spreadsheet. Multiple data series are typically plotted as one of two chart types—side-by-side column charts or stacked column charts.

The choice between plotting data in rows or columns, as well as the decision on the type of chart, depends on the intended message. If the data series are in rows, Microsoft Graph will use the first row in the datasheet for the category labels on the X axis and the first column for the legend. If the data series are in columns, then Microsoft Graph will use the first column in the datasheet for the category labels on the X axis and the first row for the legend. An Excel chart can be imported into a PowerPoint presentation, and/or it can be created within the presentation. The latter is accomplished through Microsoft Graph, the default charting program for Microsoft Office that is installed automatically with PowerPoint.

Custom animation determines when and how objects appear on a slide, what they do after they appear on the screen, and how the objects are to exit. The animation is accomplished in the Custom Animation task pane. The effects in the task pane are color coded—green, red, and yellow to indicate an entrance effect, an exit effect, and an emphasis effect, respectively.

The icon next to each effect indicates when the effect is to appear within the animation sequence. A Mouse icon indicates that the effect begins with a mouse click, whereas the Clock icon shows that the effect will appear automatically after the previous effect. The absence of an icon means that the effect will start simultaneously with the previous effect. The advanced timeline shows the sequence and duration of each effect. Custom animation may be applied to charts and/or organization charts to display the series, branches, or levels individually, as opposed to displaying the entire object at one time.

KEY TERMS

MULTIPLE CHOICE

1. Which diagram type is recommended to show hierarchical relationships?

   (a) Organization chart
   (b) Pyramid diagram
   (c) Venn diagram
   (d) Radial diagram

2. You have created an organization chart with two levels. The president is at the top and there are three vice presidents. How do you add a fourth vice president?

   (a) Click in the President box and add an assistant
   (b) Click in the rightmost vice president's box and add a coworker
   (c) Both (a) and (b)
   (d) Neither (a) nor (b)

3. Which of the following best describes the formatting options for a diagram?

   (a) The entire diagram can be formatted as a single object using AutoFormat
   (b) Individual shapes can be selected and formatted independently
   (c) Both (a) and (b)
   (d) Neither (a) nor (b)

4. Which of the following *cannot* be accomplished using the Change to button on the Diagram toolbar?

   (a) Change an organization chart to a cycle diagram
   (b) Change a cycle diagram to a radial diagram
   (c) Change a radial diagram to a pyramid diagram
   (d) Change a pyramid diagram to a Venn diagram

5. Which of the following is true regarding custom animation?

   (a) An object may have an entrance effect but not an exit effect
   (b) An object may have an exit effect but not an entrance effect
   (c) An object may have both an entrance effect and an exit effect
   (d) An object may have neither an entrance effect nor an exit effect

6. Which of the following best describes the colors associated with custom animation effects?

   (a) Red, green, and yellow for entrance, exit, and emphasis, respectively
   (b) Red, yellow, and green for entrance, exit, and emphasis, respectively
   (c) Green, red, and yellow for entrance, exit, and emphasis, respectively
   (d) Green, yellow, and red for entrance, exit, and emphasis, respectively

7. Which of the following parameters is *not* specified in conjunction with the "Fly in" entrance effect?

   (a) The direction (e.g., top or bottom)
   (b) The speed (e.g., fast or slow)
   (c) The starting time (e.g., on a mouse click or after the previous animation)
   (d) The exit path

8. Which of the following animations is available for an organization chart?

   (a) A branch at a time and shape by shape within the branch
   (b) A level at a time and shape by shape within the level
   (c) As a single object (the entire chart comes in at once)
   (d) All of the above

9. What happens if you click the View Datasheet button on the Microsoft Graph toolbar twice in a row?

   (a) The datasheet is closed (hidden)
   (b) The datasheet is opened (displayed)
   (c) The datasheet is in the same status as it was before it was clicked
   (d) Impossible to determine

10. Which of the following is true of data series that are plotted in rows?

    (a) The first row in the datasheet contains the category names for the X axis
    (b) The first column in the datasheet contains the legend
    (c) Both (a) and (b)
    (d) Neither (a) nor (b)

... continued

11. Which of the following is true of data series that are plotted in columns?

    (a) The first column in the datasheet contains the category names for the X axis

    (b) The first row in the datasheet contains the legend

    (c) Both (a) and (b)

    (d) Neither (a) nor (b)

12. How do you create a new slide containing a chart?

    (a) Add a blank slide, pull down the Insert menu, and click the Chart command

    (b) Add a blank slide, then click the Insert Chart button on the Standard toolbar

    (c) Add a blank slide, select a slide layout that contains a chart, then double click the placeholder for the chart in the Slide view

    (d) All of the above

13. Which effect will display the columns in a stacked column chart one at a time?

    (a) Animation by series

    (b) Animation by category

    (c) Animation by elements in a series

    (d) Animation by elements in a category

14. Custom Animation enables you to:

    (a) Specify a different animation effect for each object on a slide

    (b) Change the order in which the objects appear on a slide

    (c) Both (a) and (b)

    (d) Neither (a) nor (b)

15. You are working on an organization chart. The hashed border surrounds the drawing canvas, but none of the objects in the chart is selected. What happens if you press the Del key?

    (a) The entire organization chart is deleted

    (b) The slide itself is deleted

    (c) The last box selected is deleted

    (d) Nothing, since no objects are selected within the drawing area

16. Which type of diagram is *not available* in the Diagram Gallery?

    (a) Pyramid diagram

    (b) Cycle diagram

    (c) Target diagram

    (d) Periodic table

17. What happens if you click a chart that is not currently selected?

    (a) The chart is selected

    (b) The chart is deleted

    (c) The chart is animated

    (d) The application that created the chart (e.g., Microsoft Graph) is started

18. What happens if you double click a chart that is not currently selected?

    (a) The chart is selected

    (b) The chart is deleted

    (c) The chart is animated

    (d) The application that created the chart (e.g., Microsoft Graph) is started

ANSWERS

1. a	**7.** d	**13.** b
2. b	**8.** d	**14.** c
3. c	**9.** c	**15.** a
4. a	**10.** c	**16.** d
5. c	**11.** c	**17.** a
6. c	**12.** d	**18.** d

PRACTICE WITH POWERPOINT

1. **Animation 101:** You will find a partially completed version of the presentation in Figure 3.9 in the file *Chapter 3 Practice 1* in the Exploring PowerPoint folder. Open the presentation and add the indicated animation effects on each slide. Be sure to include a sound effect where indicated. Use any trigger that you deem appropriate; that is, you can specify that the effect begins on a mouse click or after the previous effect as you see fit. Proceed as follows:

    a. Add your name on the title slide. The slide title should fly in from the top to the accompaniment of a drum roll.

    b. Slide 2 illustrates different entrance effects, each of which is denoted by a green icon in the custom animation task pane. Add sound where indicated, such as the whoosh for the last bullet.

    c. Slide 3 shows different ways to add emphasis to text. Note the specification of a typewriter sound for the last effect, which displays the letters one at a time

    d. Slide 4 contains various effects for emphasis. Once again, you have a sound effect, this time a gentle breeze.

    e. Slide 5 describes how to create motion paths.

    f. Slide 6 contains exit strategies, each of which is indicated by a red icon in the custom animation task pane.

    g. Save the completed presentation. Print the title slide as a full slide to use as a cover sheet for the assignment. Print the audience handouts of the revised presentation (six slides in all) for your instructor.

    h. View the completed presentation. Do you have a better appreciation for custom animation? Summarize your thoughts in a brief note to your instructor. Be sure to mention the different colors that are associated with entrance and exit effects in the custom animation task pane. Describe the timeline and the associated icons that show when an object appears.

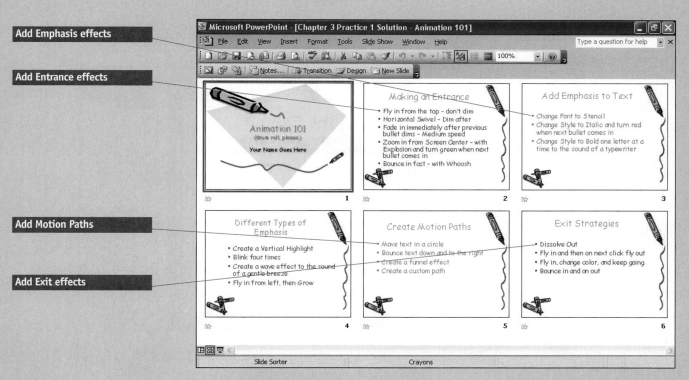

FIGURE 3.9 Animation 101 (exercise 1)

2. **Adding a Timeline:** Create a new slide containing the timeline in Figure 3.10 for the existing Super Zoo presentation from the third hands-on exercise. You do not have to duplicate our slide exactly, but you are required to include the equivalent functionality which includes a table, clip art, and custom animation. Proceed as follows:

   a. Open the Super Zoo presentation from the last hands-on exercise. Insert a new (title only) slide as the fourth slide in the presentation (i.e., insert the new slide after the stacked column chart). Add the title of the slide as shown in the figure.

   b. Click the Insert Table tool on the Standard toolbar to create a 2 × 12 (2 rows and 12 columns) table as shown in Figure 3.10. Click and drag the line separating the two rows in the table so that the top row is much narrower than the bottom. Click in the second row, then press Enter two or three times to increase row size.

   c. Enter the months of the year in the top row. Format the text for January, as you see fit, then use the Format Painter to copy the formatting to the remaining months.

   d. Click the AutoShapes tool on the Drawing toolbar, choose Block Arrows, and create the first arrow. Right click the arrow and click the command to add text, then enter the appropriate text as shown in the figure.

   e. Copy this arrow (or create additional arrows) so that you have four milestones on the slide. Edit the text in each arrow as necessary. Use the same formatting for all four arrows.

   f. Insert an appropriate clip art image under each arrow.

   g. Animate the completed slide so that the individual milestones appear on successive mouse clicks. Use any effects that you deem appropriate. Experiment with different speeds for each animation.

   h. Save the completed presentation. Print the title slide as a full slide to use as a cover sheet for the assignment. Print the audience handouts of the revised presentation (six slides in all) for your instructor.

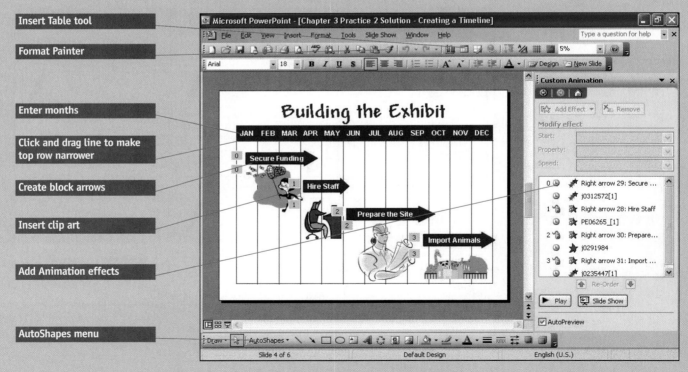

FIGURE 3.10 Adding a Timeline (exercise 2)

3. **Working with Photographs:** The presentation in Figure 3.11 displays a collection of photographs. All of the photographs were obtained by searching the Clip Organizer within Microsoft Office. Click the button to Insert Clip Art to open the task pane, enter "Animals" as the text for your search, then restrict the results to photographs. The command works best with an active Internet connection that extends the search to the Microsoft Web site. Proceed as follows:

a. Start a new presentation. Create a title slide, and then insert a blank slide. Use the Insert Clip Art command as just described to locate multiple photographs for insertion on the slide. Arrange the pictures in an attractive overlapping fashion.

b. Select all of the photographs, then use the Format Picture command to apply a black 4-point border around every picture.

c. Check that all of the photographs are still selected. Click the Compress Photographs tool on the Picture toolbar to compress the pictures and reduce the file sizes.

d. Click on any picture to deselect all of the pictures. Pull down the Slide Show menu, click Custom Animation, and apply individual entrance effects to each of the photographs. Set each entrance so that it begins automatically after the previous animation effect has ended.

e. Insert a second blank slide. Create six separate WordArt objects, each of which is a single letter, (S, A, F, A, R, and I), and each of which uses a different photograph for fill. (You have to save each picture as a separate file in order to use it as background fill for a WordArt object.)

f. Use custom animation so that the objects appear in sequence, one after the other. Include the sound of applause in conjunction with the letter i when "Safari" is spelled out completely.

g. Print the title slide as a full slide to use as a cover sheet for the assignment. Print the presentation as an audience handout (two slides per page) for your instructor. Add a footer at the bottom of the page that includes your name.

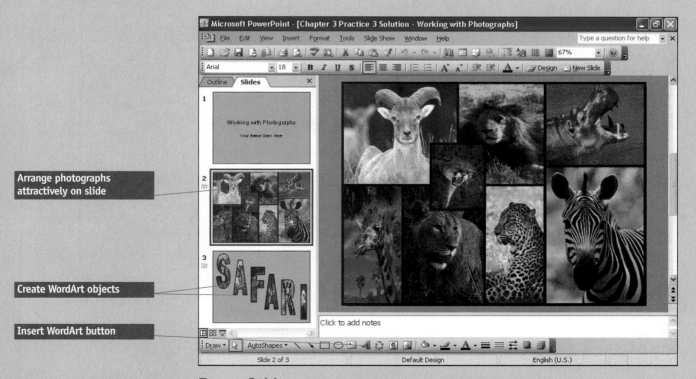

FIGURE 3.11   Working with Photographs (exercise 3)

4. **Organization Charts:** The presentation in Figure 3.12 illustrates various ways in which to format and/or animate an organization chart. Open the partially completed presentation in *Chapter 3 Practice 4* in the Exploring PowerPoint folder and proceed as follows.

a. Add your name to the title slide, then choose any appropriate animation for the two text objects.

b. Go to the second slide and create an organization chart of at least four levels. Each box in the chart should contain a title and the name of an individual. Your instructor should appear at the top of the chart as the president. You should appear at the left of the second level as the first vice president. Use the default formatting that is provided for an organization chart.

c. Copy the chart you just created to the remaining slides in the presentation (slides 3 to 6). Set the formatting for each of these charts to the formatting depicted in Figure 3.12. Note, too, that in addition to changing the color and/or shape of the boxes, you are also to change the style. Slide 3, for example, has left hanging subordinates. Slide 4, however, has right hanging subordinates.

d. Animate each chart according to the instructions that appear at the bottom of the slide. Slides 2 and 3 bring the chart in as a single object. Slides 4 and 5, however, bring in the shapes individually, by branch and level, respectively. Slide 6 brings in one level at a time.

e. Save the completed presentation. Print the title slide as a full slide to use as a cover sheet for the assignment. Print the completed presentation as audience handouts (six per page) for your instructor.

f. Do you have a better understanding of how to create and modify organization charts? Which type of animation is the most effective? Summarize your thoughts in a brief note to your instructor.

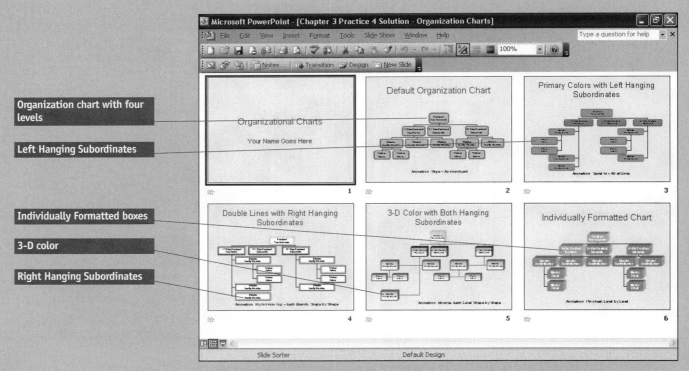

FIGURE 3.12 Organization Charts (exercise 4)

5. **The Diagram Gallery:** Create a six-slide presentation that is similar to the one in Figure 3.13. You do not have to match our presentation exactly, but you are required to include all of the indicated shapes. (The presentation includes all diagram types except for the organization chart.) Proceed as follows:

a. Start a new presentation. The title slide includes the title, "The Diagram Gallery", and your name.

b. The cycle diagram in slide 2 depicts the relationship between faculty, residential assistants (RAs), and administration. The goals of all three groups are to build community, promote personal growth, and support academic success.

c. The target diagram illustrates fund-raising goals and associated milestones. The outer circle has a goal of $250,000 by February 1st. Each successive (smaller) circle has a higher goal in a subsequent month.

d. The pyramid diagram illustrates Maslow's hierarchy of needs. Use your favorite search engine to locate the five levels of the hierarchy if you are unable to read the text in our figure.

e. The Venn diagram illustrates a probability calculation.

f. The radial diagram depicts a simple computer network. Clip art has been placed on top of each circle in the diagram.

g. Use auto formatting and/or custom formatting to make your presentation more attractive. Add animation to each diagram as you see fit.

h. Copy the completed diagrams to the title slide, then move and size each diagram as shown in our figure.

i. Save the completed presentation. Print the title slide as a full slide to use as a cover sheet for the assignment. Print the completed presentation as audience handouts (six per page) for your instructor.

j. Do you have a better understanding of the Diagram Gallery? Which type of diagram(s) will be most useful to you? Summarize your thoughts in a brief note to your instructor.

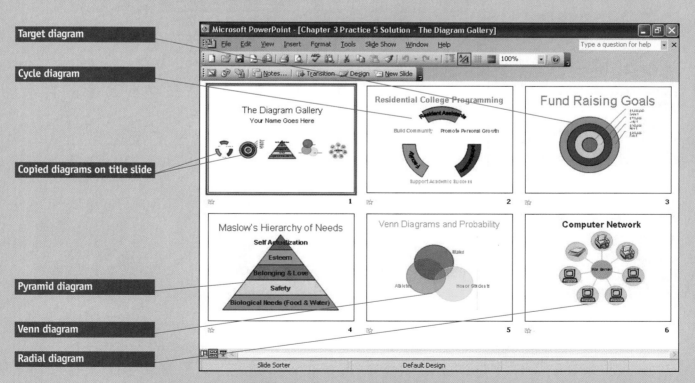

FIGURE 3.13 The Diagram Gallery (exercise 5)

6. **Charts and Animation Effects:** The charts in Figure 3.14 are based on the data in an Excel worksheet. We want to animate the charts by individual series and category, however, and thus you have to create the charts in Microsoft Graph, as opposed to importing charts from Excel. You can, however, import the worksheet on which the charts are based. Open the partially completed presentation in *Chapter 3 Practice 6* in the Exploring PowerPoint folder and proceed as follows:

a. Add your name to the title slide. The font color for both the title and your name is black. Animate both objects to change to red automatically at the beginning of the slide show. (Use the Change Font Color effect.)

b. Select the second slide. Use the Insert Object command to insert the worksheet from the *Chapter 3 Practice 6 Excel workbook* that is found in the Exploring PowerPoint folder. Increase the size of the worksheet as shown in Figure 3.14. Use the Pinwheel animation effect for both the title and the worksheet.

c. Select the third slide and start Microsoft Graph to create the chart. Click in the upper-left area of the datasheet (the cell above row 1 and to the left of column A) to select the entire datasheet, then click the Import Data button on the Microsoft Graph toolbar to display the Import Data dialog box. Select the *Chapter 3 Practice 6 Excel workbook*. (There is only one worksheet in the workbook, and you should import the entire worksheet.)

d. Move and size the chart so that it approximates the slide in Figure 3.14. Change the color of the Appetizers and Beverage series to red and yellow, respectively.

e. Copy the chart that you just created to slides 4, 5, and 6. Modify each chart individually to match those in Figure 3.16. Add animation effects to the individual charts as you see fit.

f. Save the completed presentation. Print the title slide as a full slide to use as a cover sheet for the assignment. Print the completed presentation as audience handouts (six per page) for your instructor.

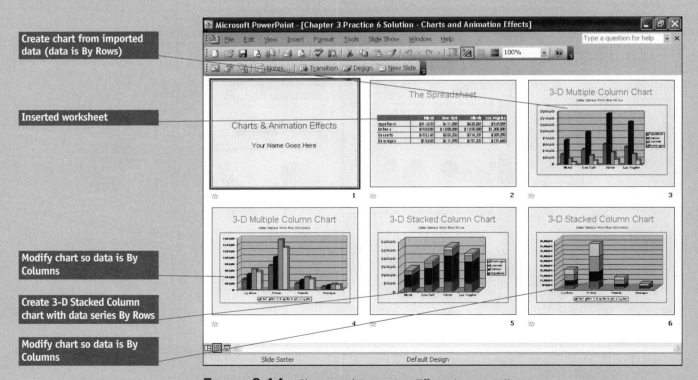

FIGURE 3.14 Charts and Animation Effects (exercise 6)

7. **Left Brain/Right Brain Conflict:** The presentation in Figure 3.15 describes the different modes of thinking in the left and right sides of the brain. The left brain is the logical part and controls speech, language, and mathematical reasoning. The right brain is the creative part and thinks in images and colors, and remembers music and complex pictures. Open the partially completed presentation in *Chapter 3 Practice 7* and proceed as follows:

a. Add your name to the title slide, then animate the slide as you see fit.

b. The three yellow rectangles on slide 2 are intended to emphasize the text behind each rectangle during the presentation. Select all three rectangles and add the Dissolve In entrance effect at slow speed. The first rectangle should start on a mouse click; the next two rectangles should dissolve after the previous animation.

c. Animate slide 3 so that the left and right sides of the brain fly in at medium speed, from the appropriate sides of the slide, on successive mouse clicks. Each column of bulleted text should appear one item at a time as the brain appears on the slide.

d. There is no animation for slide 4. Read the text of this slide carefully, however, because it represents the essence of the presentation. The slide does not contain a typo; that is, the word "blue" appears in red letters. Your right brain tries to say the color (red), but your left brain insists on reading the word (blue).

e. Animate the words on the fifth slide so that they appear automatically, without having to click the mouse. Vary the speed at which the words appear; the first word can appear slowly, the next few at medium speed, then fast, then very fast. Test yourself to see if you can say the written color.

f. Save the completed presentation. Print the title slide to use as a cover sheet for the assignment. Print the completed presentation as audience handouts (six per page).

g. View the presentation. The last slide contains two hyperlinks to Web sites that provide additional information on the brain. Visit both sites and print a page from each site for your instructor. Submit these pages with the printout of your presentation.

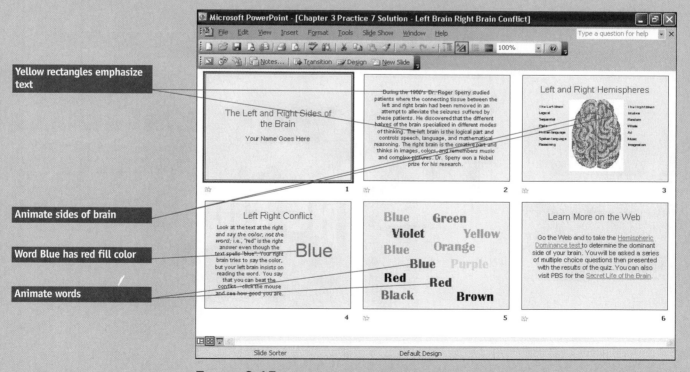

FIGURE 3.15 Left Brain/Right Brain Conflict (exercise 7)

8. **The Grand Finale:** The presentation in Figure 3.16 shows you how to end a presentation with flair. You do not have to duplicate our fireworks exactly, but you are to retain the equivalent functionality. Start a new presentation and enter "The Grand Finale" as its title. Add your name to the title slide. (The title slide is there only to identify the presentation to your instructor when you submit the assignment.)

   a. Add a blank slide after the title and proceed as follows to create the fireworks. Draw and animate a curved (freeform) line to start the show. Sound and motion are important. We used Wipe from bottom as the entrance effect, at a very fast speed, to the sound of a laser. The intent is to represent a flare as it might appear during an actual fireworks display.

   b. Use the AutoShape button to create a series of large 24-point stars that appear one after another to the sound of an explosion. These large bursts are followed by a series of five-point stars that appear to the sound of a chime. The speed of these smaller stars has been manually adjusted to one tenth of a second to create a more realistic effect. (Very fast is only five tenths of a second.)

   c. Use WordArt to create the text. (You may want to use a font color other than white initially, to make it easier to see the object on the slide.) The WordArt should appear automatically when the slide is first displayed. We chose the Dissolve In entrance effect at medium speed. Now add a second effect to increase the size of the WordArt by 25% to the sound of applause, and then add a faded zoom as an exit effect. All three effects should execute automatically, one after another at medium speed.

   d. The entire presentation should then fade to black. We found the easiest way to do this was to create a black rectangle that extended beyond the slide (use the Order command to move the rectangle to the back of the slide, so that you can see the other objects). The rectangle should simply appear after the previous effect.

   e. Print the title slide as a full slide to use as a cover sheet for the assignment. Save the completed presentation. Print the audience handouts of the revised presentation (two slides in all) for your instructor.

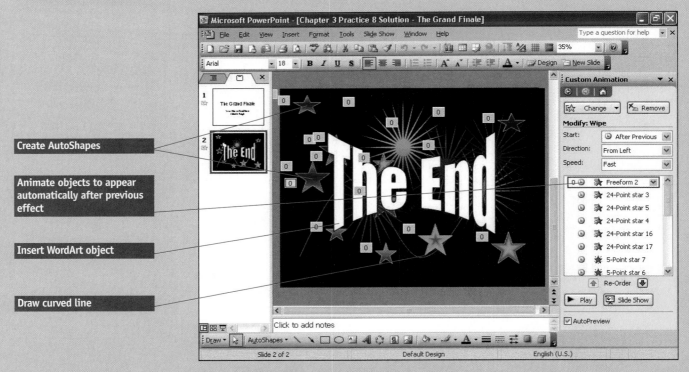

FIGURE 3.16 The Grand Finale (exercise 8)

Digital Cameras

As with all technology, the price of a digital camera has come down significantly while performance has gone up dramatically. What are the most significant capabilities in a digital camera? What is the least amount of money you have to spend to purchase (what you consider) a worthwhile camera? What are the parameters and cost of your ideal camera? Be sure to consider the size and weight of the camera—the more functionality, the larger the camera. The worst picture is the one you do not take because the camera is too big to take with you.

Microsoft Producer

An "add-on" is a supplemental program that extends the capabilities of Microsoft Office by adding custom commands and specialized features. Microsoft Producer is a PowerPoint add-on that makes it easy to capture, synchronize, and publish audio, video, slides, and images. Where do you obtain the Microsoft Producer add-on and how much does it cost? How is it installed? How easy is it to use? Try to obtain a copy in order to experiment with the program, then summarize your findings in a short note to your instructor.

Microsoft Excel versus Microsoft Graph

An Excel chart can be imported into a PowerPoint presentation, and/or a chart can be created from scratch within the presentation using Microsoft Graph. Which technique is easier? Can either type of chart be linked or embedded into the presentation? What capabilities (if any) are present in Microsoft Graph, but not in the charting component of Microsoft Excel?

Movies and Video

Use the Search command on your computer to locate any movie or video files that may exist. It's easiest in Windows XP because you can specify "video," as opposed to a specific file type. How large are these files compared to documents created by other programs? Which program is required to play the video files you find? What is the Windows Movie Maker program? What features does it have, and how does it compare to similar offerings by other vendors? Summarize your findings in a short note to your instructor for class discussion.

4

Advanced Techniques:
Slide Masters, Narration, and Web Pages

OBJECTIVES

After reading this chapter you will:

1. Distinguish between a template and a color scheme.

2. Explain the role of the slide master in formatting a presentation.

3. Add action buttons to each slide for easy navigation.

4. Use the Sound Recorder to create an original sound, then insert that sound on a slide.

5. Insert hyperlinks into a presentation.

6. Save a presentation as a Web document using the Single File Web Page format in Office 2003.

7. Use the Record Narration command to add sound to a presentation.

8. Create a custom slide show; explain the advantage of having multiple shows in one presentation.

hands-on exercises

1. COLOR SCHEMES, SOUND, AND THE SLIDE MASTER
   Input: PowerPoint Quiz
   Output: PowerPoint Quiz Solution

2. PRESENTATIONS ON THE WEB
   Input: Create a Quiz
   Output: Constitution Quiz (Single File Web Page)

3. NARRATING A PRESENTATION
   Input: Welcome to Computers 101
   Output: Welcome to Computers 101 Solution

CASE STUDY
GET UP AND GO

The alarm rings and you struggle to get out of bed. If you are typical of your generation, you may begin your day with some type of hot drink, such as coffee, hot chocolate, or tea, none of which offers significant nutritional value. There should be a better product, and the food products company where you are interning this summer is planning to introduce an alternative beverage. The product is named *Get Up and Go*, and it is slated for introduction into the college market next fall. The company believes that there is a large potential demand for a beverage that contains a significant portion of the daily recommended nutritional requirement as recommended by the FDA (Food and Drug Administration).

The marketing department has conducted a series of focus groups to determine consumer preferences for the precise formulation of the new drink. The study also sought to determine whether consumers would be inclined to give up their morning coffee in favor of the new drink. These sessions are over, and it is your task to complete a PowerPoint presentation that shows the results. The presentation is to be posted to the company's internal Web site for others to view. This is an ideal assignment. You are health conscious, an avid coffee drinker, and you enjoy hot chocolate. It is also a paid internship, and you will get college credit upon completing the presentation. ■

Your assignment is to read the chapter and complete the *Chapter 4 Case Study—Get Up and Go* presentation in the Exploring PowerPoint folder. You are to apply a design template to the existing presentation and add action buttons to the master slide for easy navigation. The presentation is confidential, and this should be indicated at the bottom of every slide. Animate the presentation as you see fit and include limited sound effects. Use the Sound Recorder, if possible, to create an original sound file for added interest. Save the presentation as a Web page, but you are not required to post the presentation to a Web server. Print the completed presentation for your instructor.

Figure 4.1 displays a six-slide presentation in the form of a quiz. Sound is used throughout the presentation although you cannot hear anything by merely looking at our figure. Look closely, however, and you will see a Sound icon next to each potential answer in slides 4 and 5. Click any of these icons and you will hear whether or not you are correct. A sound file is also embedded on the third slide in the form of a reminder to test the speakers and adjust the volume. Custom animation has been added to this slide, so that clicking the clip art (the icon is hidden behind the image of the speakers) will play an appropriate sound.

The use of sound requires additional hardware, namely a sound card, speakers, and a microphone if you want to record your own sound files. Multiple sound files are supplied, however, within Microsoft Windows as well as Microsoft Office. Additional sounds may be imported from the Web and/or created through the **Sound Recorder**, a Windows accessory, which creates a digitized recording of an actual sound.

The Sound Recorder uses a chip in the sound card on your computer to convert the recorded sound into a file, and then stores the file on disk. You can record any type of sound, such as your voice to narrate a presentation, and/or special effects such as the sound of applause. Sound files are stored just like any other type of file and can be moved and copied from one folder to another. The size of a sound file is directly proportional to its duration.

The Crayons template in Figure 4.1 may look familiar, but we have changed the underlying color scheme. A **template** controls every aspect of a presentation's design such as the background, fonts and formatting, and the size and placement of bullets and other elements. Each template has a default **color scheme**, consisting of eight balanced colors that are used for the background, text, slide title, shadows, and other accents. Change the template and you change every aspect of a presentation. Change the color scheme within a template (every template has several alternate color schemes from which to choose) and you retain the overall look, but effect a subtle change in the appearance.

Most presentations are designed for sequential viewing, starting with the first slide and ending with the last. You can also build flexibility into a presentation by including **action buttons** that will take you through the slides in a different sequence. Thus, each slide in Figure 4.1, except the title slide, contains a uniform set of four buttons to move to the first, previous, next, and last slides, respectively. You are under no obligation to use the action buttons, and indeed, you can still move through the presentation sequentially by clicking the left mouse button (or pressing the PgDn key) to move to the next sequential slide. Nevertheless, action buttons (or navigation buttons as they are sometimes called) provide a convenient way to return to the previous slide and/or jump to the last slide, which in this example contains the answer key.

The answer key on the last slide contains three **hyperlinks**, two of which return to earlier slides that contain questions one and two, and a third branches to an external link (www.prenhall.com/grauer). All three hyperlinks are created through the **Insert Hyperlink command**. Hyperlinks, like action buttons, provide flexibility for the speaker; for example, in reviewing the answers, you can click the hyperlink to return to the associated question. You do not have to use the hyperlinks during the presentation, but the more effective public speakers are sensitive to their audience, anticipate potential questions, and take advantage of this flexibility.

Hidden slides provide additional flexibility during delivery in that they do not appear during a regular slide show. The answer key, for example, is hidden, which means that the presenter has to take explicit action to display that slide, such as clicking the appropriate action button. The hidden slide can be displayed during a slide show by right clicking the slide, clicking the Go to Slide command, and then choosing the hidden slide from the list of slides.

(a) Title Slide

(b) Test Your Speakers

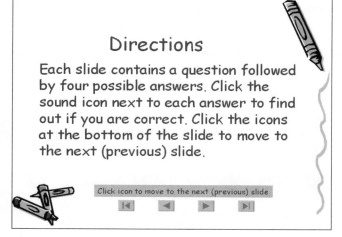

(c) Directions

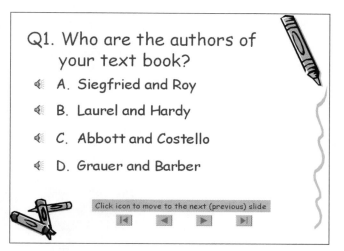

(d) Question 1

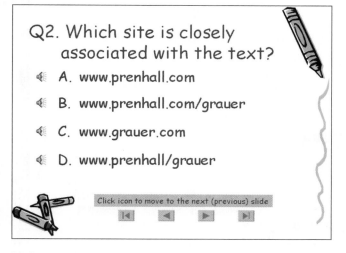

(e) Question 2

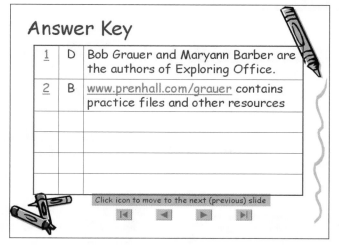

(f) Answer Key with Hyperlinks

FIGURE 4.1 An Online Quiz

The Slide Master

The action buttons in our presentation can be added individually to every slide, but that would be unnecessarily tedious. It is much more efficient to add the buttons to the **slide master**, as opposed to the individual slides shown in Figure 4.2. The slide master stores information about the template, including font styles, placeholder sizes and positions, background design, additional clip art or other elements, and color schemes.

The slide master is the easiest way to make global changes to a presentation. Any change to any element on the slide master is automatically reflected in every existing slide (except the title slide) as well as any new slides that are subsequently added. The title slide has its own master (as seen in Figure 4.2), although it is just as easy to make changes to the title slide itself. Additional masters are available for handouts and speaker notes.

The slide master provided by PowerPoint contains a placeholder for the title of the slide, a second placeholder for the bulleted text, additional placeholders at the bottom of the slide for the date, footer, and slide number, and two clip art images. We also modified the master to include the additional text box and associated action buttons. Change the position of any of these elements on the slide master, and the corresponding element will be changed throughout the presentation. In similar fashion, any change to the font, point size, or alignment within a placeholder also carries through to all of the individual slides.

The slide master is modified by using commands from the appropriate menu or from a toolbar. The action buttons, for example, were created through the Action Buttons command in the Slide Show menu. Clip art, such as a corporate logo, can also be added. Once the objects have been created, they can be moved and sized like any other Windows object. And, as indicated, every slide in the presentation will contain the objects that appear on the slide master. It's easy and powerful, and as you might have guessed, it is time for our first hands-on exercise.

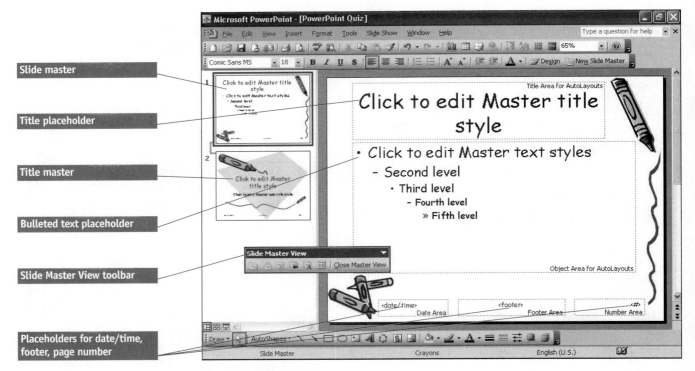

FIGURE 4.2 The Slide Master

1   Color Schemes, Sound, and the Slide Master

Objective   To change a color scheme; to record a sound, then insert the sound onto a slide; to use the slide master to add action buttons to every slide.

Step 1:   **Change the Color Scheme**

■ Open the **PowerPoint Quiz presentation** in the Exploring PowerPoint folder. Add **your name** to the title slide.

■ Save the presentation as **PowerPoint Quiz Solution** so that you can return to the original presentation if necessary.

■ Click the **Design button** to open the task pane, then click the link to **Color Schemes** to display the color schemes for the selected design.

■ Click the **down arrow** next to the second color scheme, then click the **Apply to All Slides** as shown in Figure 4.3a. The accent color on the title slide changes to light purple (the background remains white).

■ Close the task pane.

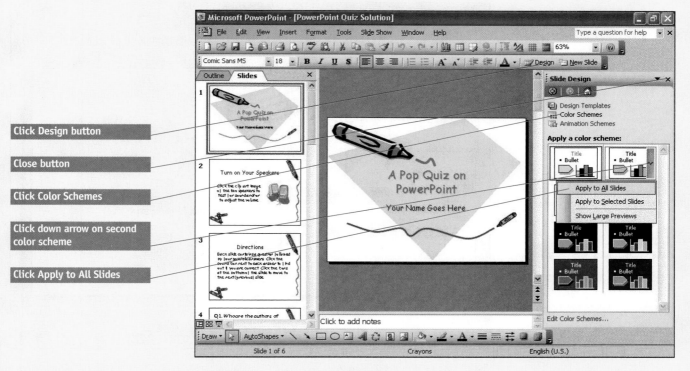

(a) Change the Color Scheme (step 1)

FIGURE 4.3   Hands-on Exercise 1

ADD A FAVORITE

Select the desired folder in the Open or Save As dialog boxes, click the down arrow next to the Tools button, and click the Add to "My Places" command. The next time you open either dialog box, you will be able to click the Folder icon at the left of the dialog box to go directly to the folder, as opposed to having to select the folder from the Look in list box.

Step 2: Record the Sound(s)

- Skip this step if you do not have a microphone to record your own sounds.

- Click the **Start button** on the Windows taskbar. Click **All Programs**, click **Accessories**, click **Entertainment**, then click **Sound Recorder** to display the associated dialog box in Figure 4.3b.

- Click the **red dot** to begin recording, be sure you speak directly into the microphone, and say the word "Incorrect". Click the **Stop button**.

- Click the **Rewind button**, then click the **Play button** to listen to the sound. If you are not satisfied, pull down the **File menu**, click **New**, then click **No** when asked whether to save the file, and start a new recording.

- Pull down the **File menu** (in the Sound Recorder window) and save the file as **Incorrect** in the **Exploring PowerPoint folder**. You should see a message that the file already exists (we created a default file) and asking if you want to replace it. Click **Yes**.

- Record two additional files, **Sorry** and **Try Again**, in similar fashion. Close the Sound Recorder.

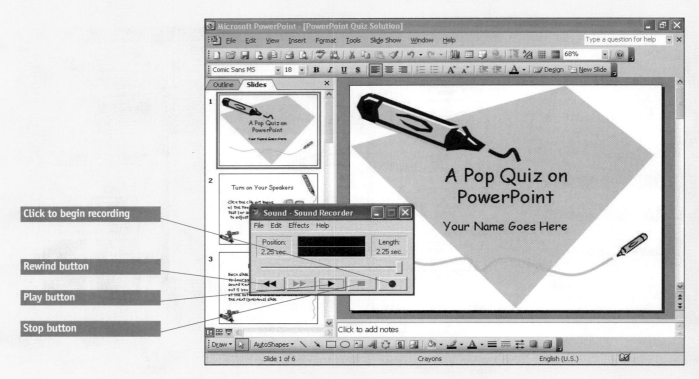

(b) Record the Sound(s) (step 2)

FIGURE 4.3   Hands-on Exercise 1 (*continued*)

YOU DON'T NEED STEREO

A voice can generally be converted to a lesser-quality (smaller) file, without an appreciable difference in quality. Open the Sound Recorder, pull down the File menu and click the Properties command to view the existing parameters. Click the down arrow in the Choose From list box, choose All Formats, and click the Convert Now button. Select 11kHz, 8 bit, Mono, which requires 10K bytes per second. Other settings can require as much as 180K bytes per second.

Step 3: **Insert the Sound**

- Select the fourth slide (the slide containing the first question in our quiz). The Sound icon does not yet appear next to the answer, "Siegfried and Roy". Pull down the **Insert menu**, click **Movies and Sounds**, then click **Sound from File** to display the Insert Sound dialog box.

- Change to the **Exploring PowerPoint folder**, then select the **Incorrect** sound you recorded earlier.

- Click the **OK button** (not visible in the figure) to insert the sound. Click the **When Clicked button** when asked how you want the sound to start. A Sound icon should appear in the middle of the slide. Click and drag the **Sound icon** to the left of the first answer as shown in Figure 4.3c.

- Insert the **Try Again**, **Sorry**, and **Applause** sound files in similar fashion so that the associated Sound icons appear next to answers (b), (c), and (d), respectively. Click the **When Clicked button** when asked how you want the sound to start.

- Press and hold the **Ctrl key** as you select all four **Sound icons**. Pull down the **Format menu**, click **Picture** to display the Format Picture dialog box, then click the **Position tab**. Enter **.75"** in the Horizontal list box. Click **OK**.

- Save the presentation.

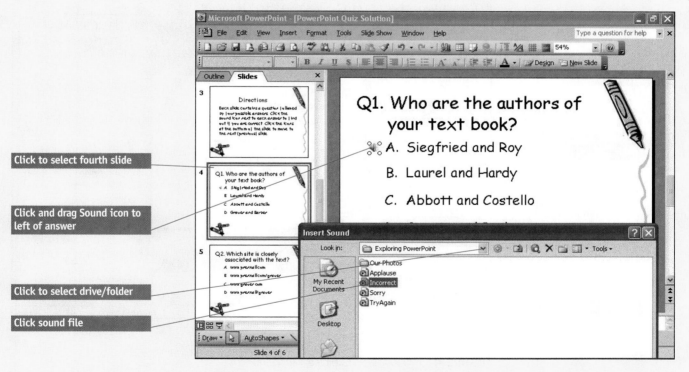

(c) Insert the Sound (step 3)

FIGURE 4.3 Hands-on Exercise 1 (*continued*)

DISCONNECT YOUR MICROPHONE

The speech recognition capabilities in Microsoft Office are quite impressive. There is a downside, however, in that a microphone will often mistake ambient noise for Office commands. You can tell this is happening if menus appear for no reason and/or random characters are continually inserted into a document. Turn the microphone off and the problem should disappear.

Step 4: Check the Answers

- Select the fifth slide (the slide containing the second question in our quiz) and insert an appropriate sound file next to each answer. (The correct answer is (B), **www.prenhall.com/grauer**.) All of the sound files should be in the Exploring PowerPoint folder.

- Position the icons .75″ from the left border as in the previous step.

- Pull down the **Slide Show menu** and click the **Custom Animation command** to open the animation task pane as shown in Figure 4.3d. You should see a trigger next to each animation effect, although the number next to each sound object may be different from ours.

- Click the **Slide Show button** to test the slide. Click the **Sound icon** next to each answer to test the presentation. You can click each icon as often as you like. (You advance to the next slide when you click a blank space on the slide, as opposed to clicking a Sound icon.)

- Press **Esc** when you are satisfied the slide is correct. Close the task pane. Save the presentation.

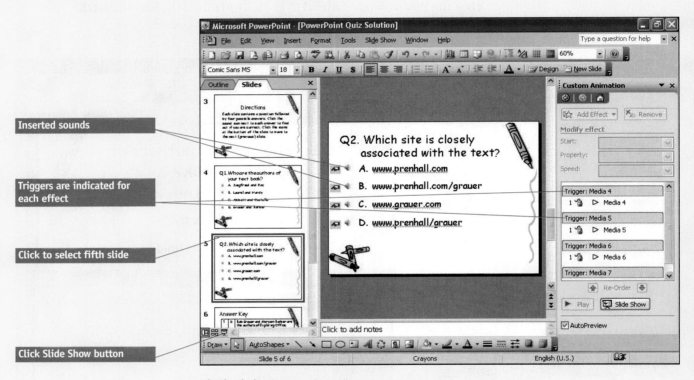

Inserted sounds

Triggers are indicated for each effect

Click to select fifth slide

Click Slide Show button

(d) Check the Answers (step 4)

FIGURE 4.3 Hands-on Exercise 1 (*continued*)

TRIGGERING A SOUND EFFECT

An animation or sound effect can be "triggered" to play in conjunction with clicking a specific object; for example, clicking the clip art image of the microphone plays the associated sound. This differs from simply starting the effect on a mouse click, because you can click the trigger object repeatedly to play the sound as many times as you like. This technique is used on slide 2, where the sound is triggered by clicking the clip art image of the speakers.

Step 5: **Add the Action Buttons**

- Pull down the **View menu**, click the **Master command**, then select the **Slide Master** to display the view in Figure 4.3e. Be sure the bulleted slide is selected, as opposed to the title slide.

- Pull down the **Slide Show menu**, click the **Action buttons command**, and select (click) the beginning ◀ **button** that indicates the first slide. The mouse pointer changes to a tiny crosshair.

- Click in the footer area at the bottom of the slide, then drag the mouse to create an action button. Release the mouse. The Action Settings dialog box is displayed automatically.

- The **Hyperlink to Option button** is selected and the First Slide is specified in the associated list box. Click **OK** to accept the default settings and close the Action Settings dialog box.

- Repeat this process three additional times to create action buttons for the previous, next, and ending slides in that sequence. Do not be concerned about the precise size or location of the buttons at this time. Save the presentation.

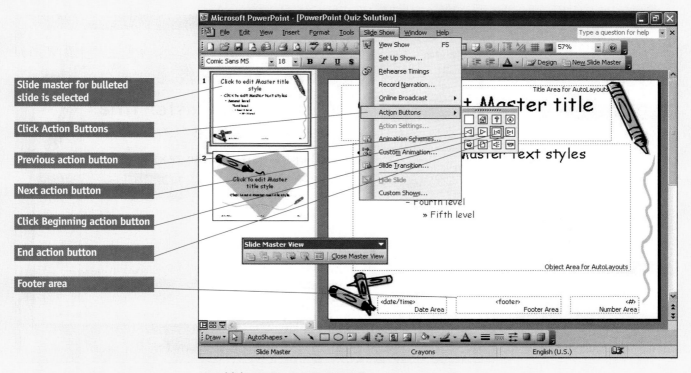

(e) Add the Action Buttons (step 5)

FIGURE 4.3   Hands-on Exercise 1 (*continued*)

THE HEADER AND FOOTER COMMAND

The Header and Footer command provides another way to display information on every slide. Pull down the View menu, click the Header and Footer command, then enter the date of the presentation, a descriptive footer, and/or the slide number in the associated dialog box. Click the Apply to All button to display these fields on every slide (or check the box to suppress the information on the title slide). The contents of these fields do not show on the slide master, but are hidden within the <date/time>, <footer>, <#> fields that appear in the footer area.

Step 6: **Size and Align the Action Buttons**

- Click and drag the individual action buttons so that there is sufficient space between the buttons to increase their size to ½ inch each. Press and hold the **Shift key** as you click each action button to select all four buttons.
- Point to any button, click the **right mouse button** to display a context-sensitive menu, then click **Format AutoShape** to display the Format AutoShape dialog box.
- Click the **Size tab**, then enter **.35** and **.5** as the height and width of each button. Click **OK** to accept the settings and close the dialog box.
- Click the **Draw button** on the Drawing toolbar, select the **Align or Distribute command**, then click **Align Top** to align the buttons.
- Click the **Draw button** a second time, select the **Align or Distribute command**, then click **Distribute Horizontally** to allocate a uniform amount of space between each button.
- Add a **text box** above the action buttons as shown in Figure 4.3f. Change the fill color to match the color of the buttons.
- Click the **Close Master View button** on the Slide Master View toolbar. Save the presentation.

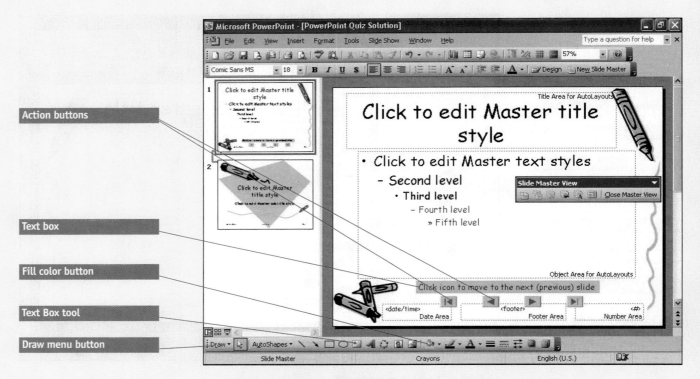

(f) Size and Align the Action Buttons (step 6)

FIGURE 4.3 Hands-on Exercise 1 (*continued*)

MULTIPLE SLIDE MASTERS ARE POSSIBLE

Most presentations use only a single template, but there are occasions when you want to include multiple designs in the same presentation. Change to the Slide Sorter view, then press and hold the Ctrl key to select the slides that will reflect the alternate template. Click the Slide Design button on the Slide Sorter toolbar to open the task pane, click the down arrow next to the desired design, then apply the design to the selected slide(s). Repeat the process to include another design. See problem 4 at the end of the chapter.

Step 7: **Create the Hyperlinks**

- Press **Ctrl+End** to move to the last slide in the presentation. The action buttons appear at the bottom of the slide because you modified the master slide layout in the previous step.

- Click and drag to select the number **1** in the first cell of the table, then click the **Insert Hyperlink button** on the Standard toolbar to display the associated dialog box. Click the **Place in This Document icon** and select the slide containing the first question as shown in Figure 4.3g. Click **OK**.

- The number 1 has been converted to a hyperlink. Create a hyperlink to the second question in similar fashion.

- Click and drag to select the text **www.prenhall.com/grauer** (which appears as a partial explanation for the second question). Press **Ctrl+C** to copy this link to the Windows clipboard.

- Click the **Insert Hyperlink button**, click the icon for **Existing file or Web page**, click in the **Address text box**, then press **Ctrl+V** to enter the actual address. Click **OK** to create the hyperlink. Save the presentation.

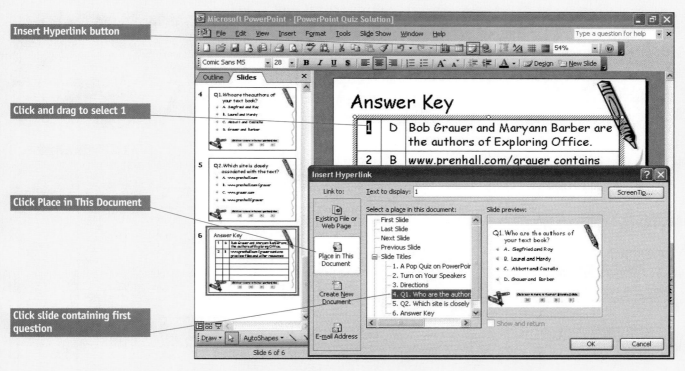

(g) Create the Hyperlinks (step 7)

FIGURE 4.3   Hands-on Exercise 1 (*continued*)

THE TABLES AND BORDERS TOOLBAR

Pull down the View menu, click the Toolbars command, and then display the Tables and Borders toolbar. (Point to any button to display a ToolTip that is indicative of the underlying function.) You can change the line style or thickness, distribute rows and columns evenly within a table, merge or split cells, or add a fill color. Click the down arrow next to the Table command for additional commands to insert or delete rows and columns. The tools and conventions are identical to those in Microsoft Word.

Step 8: **Hide the Answer Key**

■ Change to the **Slide Sorter view**. You should see three hyperlinks on the last slide, one link to each question within the presentation and one link to the Grauer Web site at www.prenhall.com/grauer.

■ Select the last slide. Click the **Hide Slide button** on the Slide Sorter toolbar. The slide will be hidden during the slide show as can be seen from the Hidden Slide icon over the slide number below the slide.

■ The **Hide Slide command** functions as a toggle switch. Click the button, and the slide is marked to be hidden during the presentation. Click the button a second time, and the slide is marked as visible. Set the button to hide the last slide.

■ Check that the last slide is still selected, then click the **Transition button** on the Slide Sorter toolbar to open the task pane. Select a transition effect, a transition speed, and optionally a sound. A Transition icon appears below the slide.

■ Save the presentation.

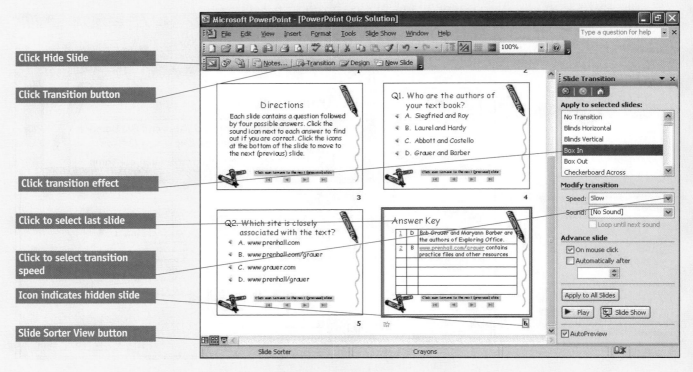

(h) Hide the Answer Key (step 8)

FIGURE 4.3 Hands-on Exercise 1 (*continued*)

DISPLAY THE HIDDEN SLIDE

A hidden slide does not appear during a regular slide show, but it can be displayed at any time using the Go to Slide command. Right click any slide during a presentation and click the Go to Slide command to display a list of every slide. Click any slide (parentheses appear around the number of a hidden slide) to display that slide, and then continue with the presentation from that point.

Step 9: **Take the Quiz**

- Press **Ctrl+Home** to move to the first slide in the presentation. Pull down the **Slide Show menu** and click the **View Show command**.

- You should see the title slide. Click the mouse or press the **PgDn key** to move to the second slide.

- Click the **icon** to test the speakers. Move to the next slide.

- Read the directions. Click the **action button** to move to the next slide.

- You should see the first question as shown in Figure 4.3i. Click the **Sound icon** next to each answer. Move to the next slide.

- Click the **Sound icon** next to each answer. Click a blank area to move to the next slide. You do not see the answer key because the slide is hidden.

- Press **Esc** to return to PowerPoint. Print audience handouts (six per page) for your instructor. Exit PowerPoint if you do not want to continue with the next exercise at this time.

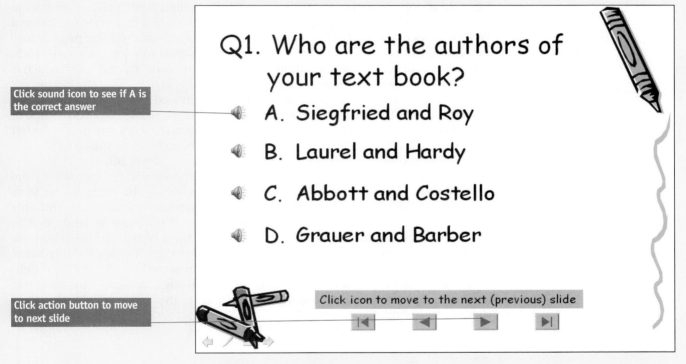

(i) Take the Quiz (step 9)

FIGURE 4.3   Hands-on Exercise 1 (*continued*)

KEYBOARD SHORTCUTS DURING THE SLIDE SHOW

Use the keyboard to gain additional flexibility during a slide show. Press the letter B to toggle between a black screen and the slide show (or the letter W to toggle between a White screen and the slide show). Type a number plus the Enter key to go to a specific slide. Use Ctrl+P to change the mouse pointer to a pen to annotate the slide, then press E to erase the annotations. Press Ctrl+A to change the mouse pointer back to an arrow. And if you can't remember these shortcuts, press the F1 key to see the entire list of shortcuts.

All Web pages are written in a language called **HTML (HyperText Markup Language)**. Initially, the only way to create a **Web page** was to learn HTML. Microsoft Office simplifies the process as it lets you create the document in any Office application, then simply save it as a Web page. In other words, you start PowerPoint in the usual fashion and enter the text of the presentation with basic formatting. However, instead of saving the document in the default format (as a PowerPoint presentation), you use the **Save As Web Page command** to convert the presentation to a Web document. (PowerPoint 2003 introduces the **Single File Web Page** format to store all of the elements of a presentation in a single file.) PowerPoint does the rest and generates the HTML statements for you. You do not have to place the resulting document on the Web, but can view it locally using an Internet browser.

Figure 4.4 displays two different views of the title slide of our next presentation. Figure 4.4a shows the expanded outline and the associated speaker notes (if any) with the selected slide. Figure 4.4b shows only the title of each slide and suppresses the details in the outline. The most significant difference, however, is the location of the presentation. Figure 4.4a displays the presentation from a local drive, whereas Figure 4.4b displays the presentation from a Web server. Viewing a Web page locally is useful for two reasons. First, it lets you test the page before uploading to the Web. Second, you can restrict access to a local area network, which is useful in a corporate setting to view documents on an "Intranet," which is limited to those within the organization.

In any event, the Internet Explorer window is divided into two vertical frames and is similar to the Normal view in PowerPoint. The left frame displays the title of each slide, and these titles function as links; that is, you can click any title in the left frame, and the corresponding slide is displayed in the right pane. You can also click and drag the border separating the panes to change the size of the panes.

The buttons above the status bar provide additional options for viewing the presentation. (The buttons were created automatically in conjunction with the Save As Web Page command when the presentation was saved initially.) The Show/Hide Outline button toggles the left (outline) pane on and off. The Expand/Collapse Outline button appears to the right of the outline when the outline is visible and lets you vary the detail of the outline. The Show/Hide Notes button toggles a notes pane on and off at the bottom of the slide. The left and right arrows move to the previous and next slide, respectively. The Slide Show button at the lower right creates a slide show on the Internet that is identical to the slide show viewed within PowerPoint.

Uploading a Presentation

Creating a Web document is only the beginning in that you may want to place the page on the Web, so that other people will be able to access it. This in turn requires you to obtain an account on a Web server, which is a computer with Internet access and adequate disk space to hold the various pages you create. You need to check with your system administrator at school or work, or with your local Internet provider, to determine how to submit your Web page when it is complete.

As indicated earlier, you can still view a Web page locally, even if you do not place it on a Web server. This is the approach we follow in the next hands-on exercise, which has you create a Web document. Your document is stored on a local drive (e.g., on drive A or drive C) rather than on a Web server, but it can still be viewed through Internet Explorer (or any other browser). After you have completed the exercise, you (and/or your instructor) can determine if it is worthwhile to place your page on your school or university's server, where it can be accessed by anyone.

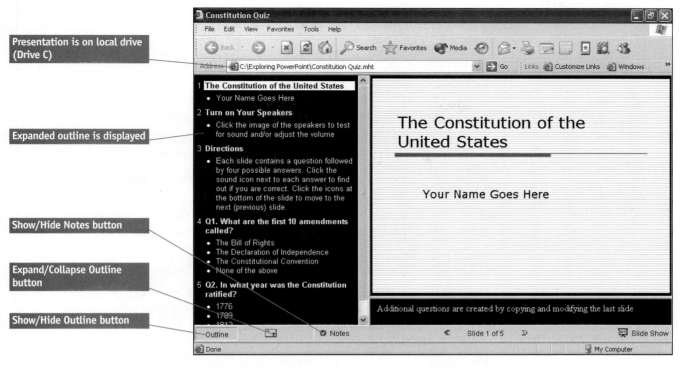

Presentation is on local drive (Drive C)

Expanded outline is displayed

Show/Hide Notes button

Expand/Collapse Outline button

Show/Hide Outline button

(a) Viewed Locally

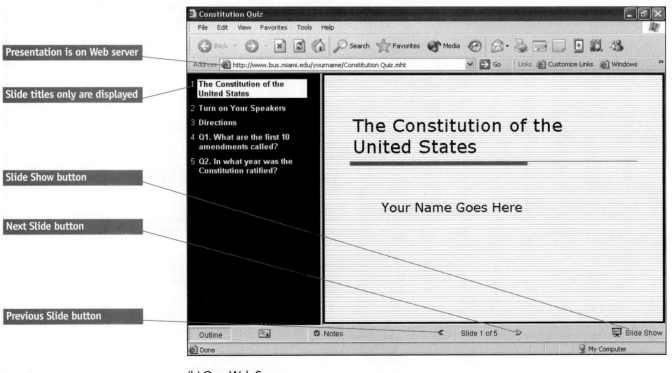

Presentation is on Web server

Slide titles only are displayed

Slide Show button

Next Slide button

Previous Slide button

(b) On a Web Server

FIGURE 4.4   PowerPoint Web Pages

2   Presentations on the Web

Objective   To save a presentation as a Web page, then view the result in Internet Explorer; to modify the newly created Web document in PowerPoint.

Step 1:   **Create the Web Page**

- Open the **Create a Quiz presentation** in the **Exploring PowerPoint folder**. Change the title to **The Constitution of the United States**.

- Add your name to the title slide. Click in the **Speaker Notes** area and enter the text shown in Figure 4.5a.

- Pull down the **File menu** and click the **Save As Web Page command** to display the Save as dialog box. Select the **Exploring PowerPoint folder**.

- Save the file as **Constitution Quiz**. The file type should be specified as **Single File Web Page**, which was introduced in Office 2003.

- Click the **Save button** to save the presentation as a Web page. The title bar changes to the name of the Web page (Constitution Quiz), but the display does not change in any other way.

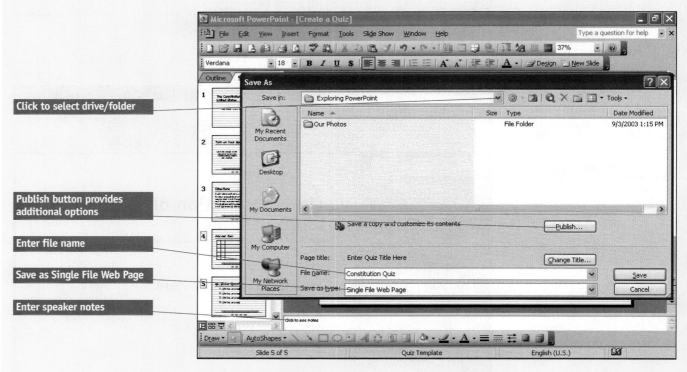

Click to select drive/folder

Publish button provides additional options

Enter file name

Save as Single File Web Page

Enter speaker notes

(a) Create the Web Page (step 1)

FIGURE 4.5   Hands-on Exercise 2

PUBLISHING OPTIONS

Click the Publish button in the Save as dialog box to display the Publish as Web page dialog box, where you view and/or modify the various options associated with an HTML document. The default publishing options work well, and you have total control over your Web pages.

Step 2: Add the Additional Slides

- The Create a Quiz Presentation, with which we began the exercise, is generic, and thus specific questions have to be added. This will be accomplished by copying the last (empty question) slide multiple times, and modifying each slide accordingly.

- Change to the **Slide Sorter view**. Press **Ctrl+End** to move to the last slide. Press and hold the **Ctrl key** as you drag the last slide to the left of the answer key. Release the mouse to duplicate the slide.

- The newly copied slide should still be selected. Click the **Hide Slide button** on the Slide Sorter toolbar to unhide this slide as shown in Figure 4.5b.

- Click the **Copy button** or press **Ctrl+C** to copy the new (and unhidden) slide to the clipboard. Click the **Paste button** or press **Ctrl+V** to paste the copied slide into the presentation.

- The presentation should now contain a total of seven slides (the original five slides plus the two you just added).

- Save the presentation.

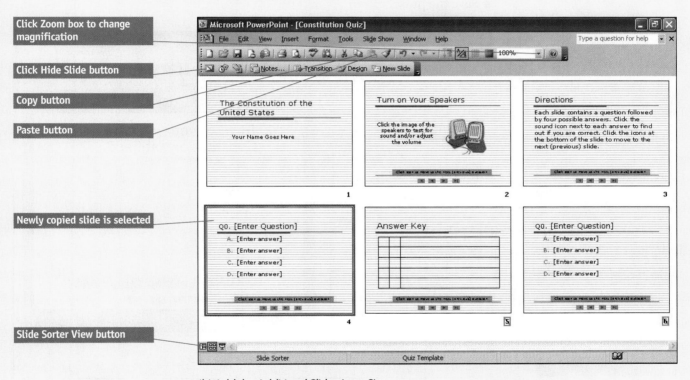

(b) Add the Additional Slides (step 2)

FIGURE 4.5   Hands-on Exercise 2 (*continued*)

CHANGE THE MAGNIFICATION

Click the down arrow on the Zoom box to change the display magnification, which in turn determines the size of individual slides. The higher the magnification, the easier it is to read the text of an individual slide, but the fewer slides you see at one time. Conversely, changing to lower magnification decreases the size of the individual slides, but enables you to see more of the presentation. You can also change the size of either pane in the Normal view in similar fashion.

Step 3: Create the Questions

■ Change to the **Normal view** and select the fourth slide. Change Q0 to **Q1**. Replace the default text with the question and answers on the first 10 amendments to the Constitution as shown in Figure 4.5c.

■ Pull down the **Insert menu**, click **Movies and Sounds**, then click **Sound from File** to display the Insert Sound dialog box. Select the **Applause** sound and click **OK**. Click the **When Clicked button** when asked how you want the sound to start. A Sound icon should appear in the middle of the slide.

■ Click and drag the **Sound icon** to the left of the first answer, **The Bill of Rights**, which is the correct answer. Insert the other sounds to signify an erroneous answer next to the remaining choices.

■ Press and hold the **Ctrl key** as you select all four **Sound icons**. Pull down the **Format menu**, click **Picture** to display the Format Picture dialog box, then click the **Position tab**. Enter **.75″** in the Horizontal list box. Click **OK**.

■ Create the second question as shown in Figure 4.5c. Insert the appropriate sound files next to each answer, placing the Applause file next to part (b). Align the sound icons **.75 inch** from the left edge of the slide.

■ Save the presentation.

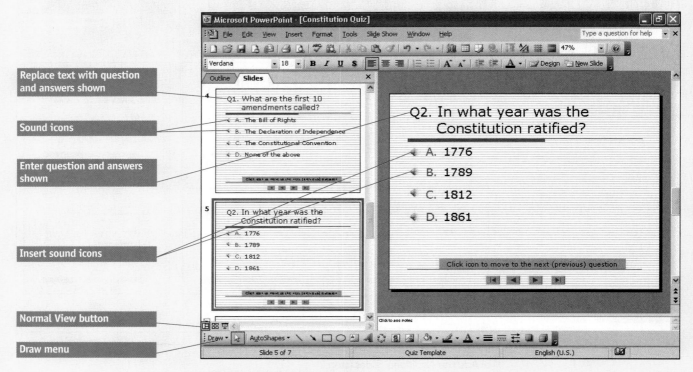

(c) Create the Questions (step 3)

FIGURE 4.5 Hands-on Exercise 2 (*continued*)

ALIGN, DISTRIBUTE, AND NUDGE

You can align objects left, center, or right (vertical stack), or top, middle, or bottom (horizontal row). Press and hold the Ctrl key as you select multiple objects on a slide, then click the down arrow on the Draw button within the Drawing toolbar to align the selected objects. You can also create uniform space between the objects by distributing horizontally or vertically. You can even nudge the objects by moving them slightly in the desired direction.

Step 4: Open the Web Page

- You can view the Web page you just created even if it has not been saved on a Web server. Start **Internet Explorer** if it is not already open, or click its button on the Windows taskbar.

- Pull down the **File menu** and click the **Open command** to display the Open dialog box in Figure 4.5d.

- Click the **Browse button**, then select the folder and drive (e.g., **Exploring PowerPoint** on drive C) where you saved the Web page.

- Select **Constitution Quiz** and click **Open**, which closes the dialog box. The selected file name has been inserted into the original Open dialog box. Click **OK** to open the presentation.

- You should see the presentation that was created earlier, except that you are viewing it in Internet Explorer rather than PowerPoint. The Address bar reflects the local address (the Exploring PowerPoint folder) of the presentation.

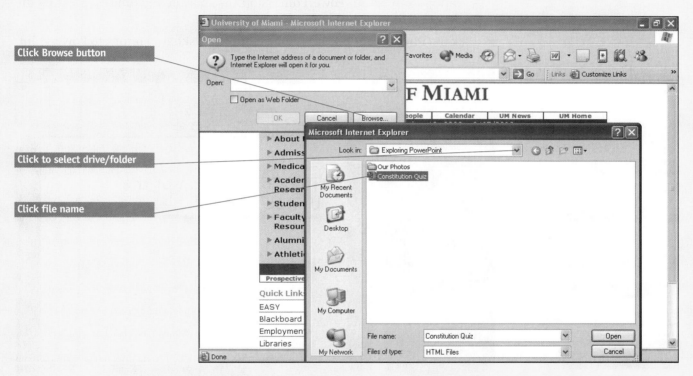

Click Browse button

Click to select drive/folder

Click file name

(d) Open the Web Page (step 4)

FIGURE 4.5   Hands-on Exercise 2 (*continued*)

SINGLE FILE WEB PAGE

Microsoft Office 2003 introduces a Single File Web Page format that saves all of the elements of a Web page, including text and graphics, in a single file. The new MHTML format lets you upload your page to a Web server as a single file, as opposed to sending multiple files and folders. It also lets you send the entire page as a single e-mail attachment. The new file format is supported by Internet Explorer 4.0 and higher.

Step 5: **View the Presentation**

- Explore the navigation controls that appear at the bottom of the Internet Explorer window as shown in Figure 4.5e. (If you do not see these controls, return to step 3 and save the presentation with these controls. Click the **Publish button** in the Save as dialog box, click the **Web Options command button**, click **General**, then check the appropriate box.)

- Click the **Show/Hide Outline button** at the bottom left to show or hide the outline. Click the **Expand/Collapse Outline button** (when the outline is visible) to vary the detail of the outline.

- Click the **Notes button** to show/hide the Notes pane at the bottom of the window. The title page is the only slide that contains a note.

- Click the **Slide Show button** at the lower right of the Internet Explorer window to start the slide show.

- This is the identical slide show that you would see if you were viewing the presentation from within PowerPoint. Stop the show at any time by pressing the **Esc key** to return to the view in Figure 4.5e.

- Click the **PowerPoint button** on the Windows taskbar to return to PowerPoint.

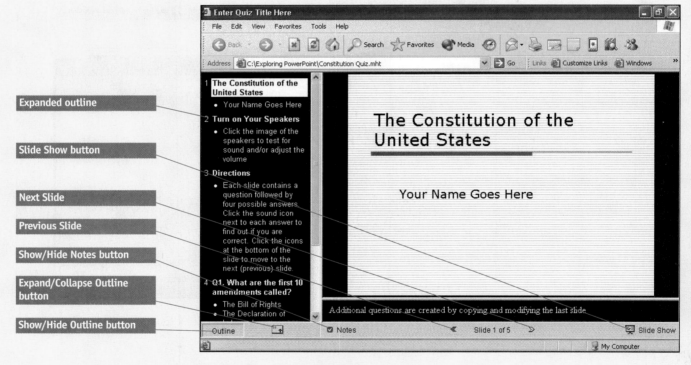

(e) View the Presentation (step 5)

FIGURE 4.5 Hands-on Exercise 2 (*continued*)

TWO WAYS TO NAVIGATE

The Previous and Next Slide buttons within the Internet Explorer window may appear redundant with the corresponding action buttons that were added explicitly to the PowerPoint slides. Note, however, that you can click the Slide Show button within Internet Explorer to show a presentation on the Web, which in turn (temporarily) closes Internet Explorer and reverts to a true PowerPoint presentation in which the action buttons are useful.

Step 6: Modify the Presentation

- You should be back in PowerPoint. If necessary, change to the **Normal view**, and then select the sixth slide (the slide containing the answer key). Enter the answers to the first two questions as shown in Figure 4.5f.

- Click and drag to select the number of the first question, click the **Insert Hyperlink button** on the Standard toolbar, click **Places in this Document**, and set the link to slide 4 (the slide containing the first question). Create a hyperlink for the second question in similar fashion.

- Click the **Slides tab** in the left pane. Right click the slide containing the answer key to display a context-sensitive menu as shown in Figure 4.5f, then click the **Hide Slide command** to display the slide during a slide show. The icon next to the slide will change to show that the slide is no longer hidden.

- **Save the presentation.** This is very important, because if you do not save the presentation, these changes will not be visible when you return to Internet Explorer.

- Click the **Internet Explorer button** on the Windows taskbar to return to the Web presentation.

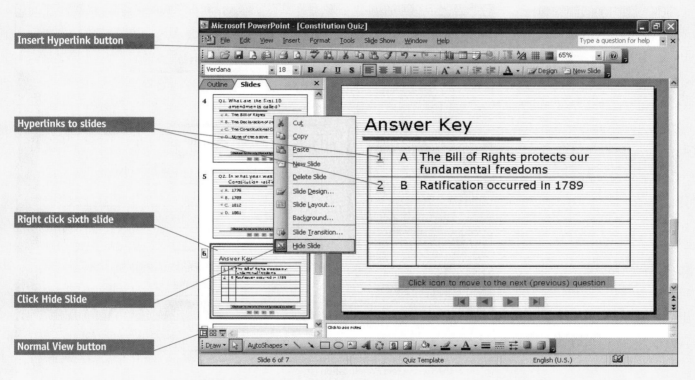

(f) Modify the Presentation (step 6)

FIGURE 4.5 Hands-on Exercise 2 (*continued*)

ROUND TRIP HTML

All applications in Microsoft Office enable you to open an HTML or MHTML document in the Office application that created it. In other words, you can start with a PowerPoint presentation, use the Save as Web page command to convert the presentation to a Web document, then view that document in a Web browser. You can then reopen the Web document in PowerPoint (the original Office application) and have full access to all PowerPoint commands in order to edit the presentation.

Step 7: **View the Corrected Presentation**

- Close Internet Explorer, then reopen Internet Explorer and reload the **Constitution Quiz** presentation.

- Select the **Answer Key slide** in the left pane to display the associated slide in the right pane. Click the **hyperlink** to the first question to test the link. Return to the slide containing the answer key. Test the hyperlink to the second question in similar fashion.

- You can improve the presentation further by changing the text of the title bar (which currently says, "Enter Quiz Title Here"). Return to PowerPoint.

- Pull down the **File menu** and click the **Save As Web Page command** to display the associated dialog box. Click the **Change Title button** to display the Set Page Title dialog box, enter **Constitution Quiz**, and click **OK**. Click **Save** to save the page. Click **Yes** if asked whether to replace the existing presentation.

- Close Internet Explorer, then reopen Internet Explorer and reload the **Constitution Quiz** presentation. The title bar should reflect the new title as shown in Figure 4.7g.

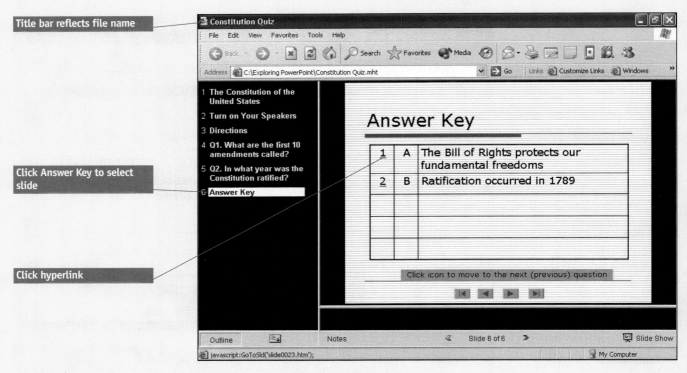

(g) View the Corrected Presentation (step 7)

FIGURE 4.5   Hands-on Exercise 2 (*continued*)

WHY REFRESH DOESN'T WORK

A Web browser cannot display an MHTML document directly, but must expand it to one or more temporary HTML documents. Thus, if you update a presentation that is saved in MHTML format and then click the Refresh button in Internet Explorer, the browser simply reloads the previous HTML documents. You have to close Internet Explorer, reopen Internet Explorer, and then open the updated MHTML file. The file then expands to display an updated set of HTML documents that show the modified presentation.

Step 8: Print the Web Page

- Select the first slide. Pull down the **File menu** (in Internet Explorer) and click the **Print Preview command** to display the screen in Figure 4.5h. If necessary, click the **down arrow** on the zoom box to adjust the magnification so that you can read the page header.

- Click the **Page Setup button** on the Print Preview toolbar to display the associated dialog box.

- Click the **question mark** (Help button) in the Page Setup dialog box, then point to the header list box to see an explanation of the associated codes, then compare these codes to the appearance of the printed page. The default settings display the title and the number of pages at the top of the page.

- Close the Page Setup dialog box. Print the title page of the presentation for your instructor to show that you have created the Web page.

- Close Internet Explorer and return to PowerPoint. Print the audience handouts, six per page, to show the completed presentation.

- Save the presentation. Exit PowerPoint if you do not want to continue with the next exercise at this time.

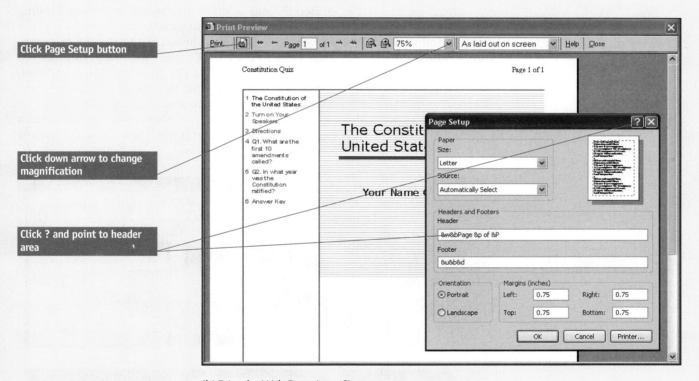

(h) Print the Web Page (step 8)

FIGURE 4.5 Hands-on Exercise 2 (*continued*)

PRINT FROM POWERPOINT

Internet Explorer is great for viewing Web pages, but less than ideal for printing them. PowerPoint provides far more flexibility. Click the PowerPoint button on the Windows taskbar to return to PowerPoint, then pull down the File menu and click the Print command. You can print individual slides, audience handouts, a presentation outline, and/or speaker notes.

NARRATING A PRESENTATION

The presentations thus far have used limited sound, which was played on demand by the viewer. This section describes how to add narration (or voiceover) that plays automatically when a presentation is delivered. Narration is very useful to create a self-running presentation for a trade show or kiosk and/or to embellish a Web-based presentation.

Figure 4.6 displays a six-slide presentation in the Slide Sorter view that represents a hypothetical introduction to this course as it might be delivered by your professor. The **Record Narration command** creates a specific narrative (sound file) for each slide and also records the required time for that narrative. Look closely, and you will see a sound icon on each slide as well as the associated time. Once the narrative has been created, you can set the presentation to play automatically, advancing from one slide to the next, in conjunction with your voice.

We recommend that you create a script and rehearse the presentation prior to recording it, so that the narrative flows smoothly, but if necessary you can rerecord the entire presentation as often as you like. You can also delete the sound file on an individual slide, use the Windows Sound Recorder to create a new file for just that slide, and then use the Custom Animation command to substitute the new recording.

Sound files can grow very large as the duration increases, and thus you are given the choice to link or embed the narration at the time of recording. Linking creates individual sound files for each slide, which in turn decreases the size of the presentation itself. Linking makes it more difficult, however, to copy the presentation to another computer (or upload it to the Web) because you must remember to take all of the files (the presentation as well as the individual sound files). Embedding creates a larger presentation, but results in a single file. Either technique is acceptable, however, and the choice is up to you.

Our next exercise also describes how to create a **custom show**, consisting of a subset of slides within the presentation, to play for a specific audience. Multiple custom shows can be created within one presentation.

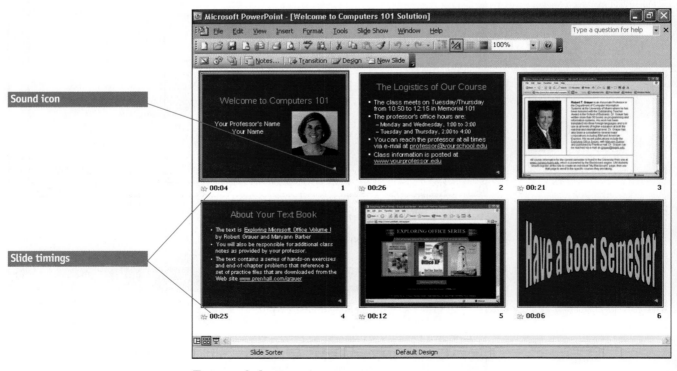

FIGURE 4.6 Narrating a Presentation

Any presentation, including video and audio, can be delivered as a **Web broadcast**. The **broadcast** can be live or recorded. A live broadcast is scheduled at a precise time, and invitations are sent to a designated list of attendees. A recorded broadcast is uploaded to a Web server and configured for on-demand viewing. Either type of broadcast is ideal for reaching large and/or geographically dispersed audiences. PowerPoint alone is sufficient to deliver a broadcast to groups of 10 or fewer individuals. Additional software, such as Microsoft Windows Media Server, is required to reach larger audiences.

PowerPoint also supports **online meetings** in addition to Web broadcasts. A broadcast is a one-way connection in which you speak, and the audience listens. An online meeting is a two-way connection in which everyone can communicate with everyone else. Online meetings are limited to 10 or fewer attendees and require the Microsoft NetMeeting software.

Figure 4.7 displays the opening slide in a hypothetical Web broadcast. A Web broadcast is viewed in Internet Explorer and is similar in appearance to a presentation that is saved as a Web page. The controls for the presentation appear in the left pane. You can start and stop the presentation at will and/or adjust the volume of the narration. The links at the top of the right pane let you return to previous slides and/or e-mail the author of the presentation. The broadcast is stored on a Web server, where it is accessed by the invited audience. (Our presentation is stored locally, however, because it has not yet been uploaded to the Web.)

A live broadcast, like any other presentation, should be rehearsed several times prior to the actual delivery. This is accomplished entirely on a stand-alone computer without having to upload the broadcast pages to the Web. Note, however, that a broadcast contains its own audio, which means that the associated PowerPoint presentation should not contain its own sound files.

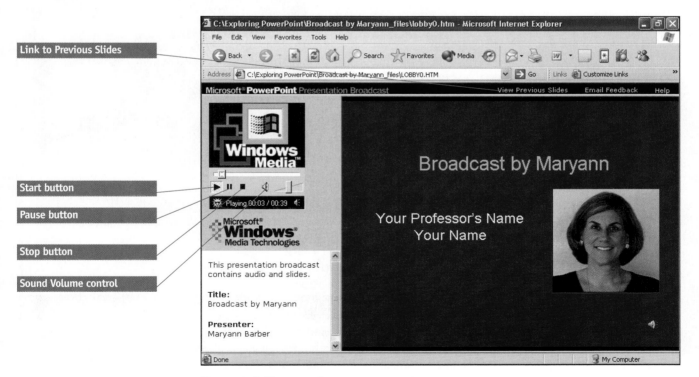

FIGURE 4.7 Broadcasting a Presentation

3 Narrating a Presentation

Objective Add narration to a presentation; create a custom show within an existing presentation. Use Figure 4.8 as a guide in doing the exercise.

Step 1: **Open the Presentation**

■ Open the **Welcome to Computers 101** presentation in the **Exploring PowerPoint folder** as shown in Figure 4.8a. The presentation consists of six slides that describe an introductory computer course.

■ Add **your name** and **your professor's name** to the title slide. Replace Maryann's picture with your own or with that of an instructor if a photo is available.

■ Change the text of the second slide so that the information corresponds to the logistics of your specific course. The remaining slides can be used without any modification.

■ Save the presentation as **Welcome to Computers 101 Solution**.

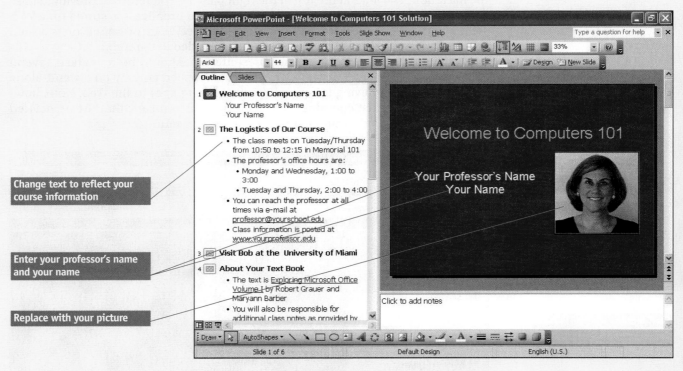

Change text to reflect your course information

Enter your professor's name and your name

Replace with your picture

(a) Open the Presentation (step 1)

FIGURE 4.8 Hands-on Exercise 3

REHEARSE THE PRESENTATION

You should create a script and rehearse your presentation before recording so that the narrative flows smoothly. Even if you are well rehearsed, you can still make a mistake, in which case you can simply rerecord the entire presentation. You can also delete the sound file on an individual slide, then use the Windows Sound Recorder to create a new file for just that slide.

Step 2: **Record the Narration**

- Press **Ctrl+Home** to move to the first slide. Pull down the **Slide Show menu** and click the **Record Narration command** to display the Record Narration dialog box.

- Click the **Change Quality command button** to display the Sound Selection dialog box in Figure 4.8b.

- Click the **down arrow** in the Name box and select **Telephone Quality**. Click **OK.** You do not need CD quality if you are recording a speaking voice.

- It's easier to embed the sound files into the presentation, as opposed to linking to individual files. Thus, the box to link narration should be clear.

- Click the **Set Microphone Level command button** to test the microphone. Read the text into the mike. You should see a set of green squares to indicate that the microphone is working properly. Click **OK** to close the Microphone Check dialog box.

- Click **OK** to begin recording your presentation. You should see the first slide in your presentation. Speak naturally and introduce yourself as the instructor.

- Pause briefly when you have finished recording the first slide, then click the mouse to move to the next slide. Continue speaking into the microphone as you move from one slide to the next. Press **Esc** when finished.

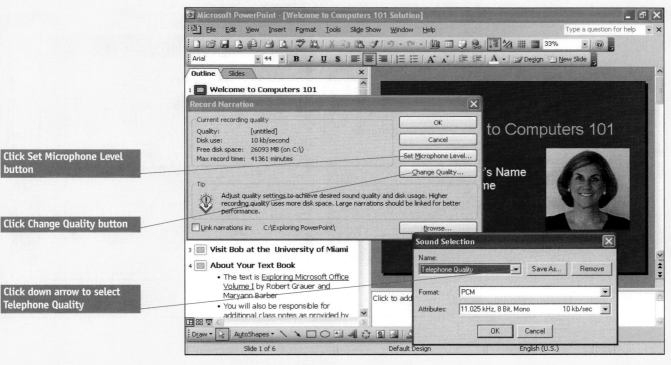

(b) Record the Narration (step 2)

FIGURE **4.8** Hands-on Exercise 3 (*continued*)

CHOOSE THE APPROPRIATE OPTIONS

A two-minute voice recording will require approximately 1,200 kilobytes or 1.2 megabytes of storage, given a recording rate of 10kb per second. At CD quality, however, the same recording requires almost 20 megabytes, given a recording rate of 172 kb/second, and you will be hard pressed to hear the difference. Be sure to select telephone quality prior to recording.

Step 3: Set Up the Presentation

- You will see a message indicating that the narrations have been saved with each slide and asking whether you want to save the slide timings as well. Click the **Save button**.

- You should see a screen similar to Figure 4.8c. The time required for each slide appears under the slide within the Slide Sorter view.

- Pull down the **Slide Show menu** and click the **Set Up Show command** to display the associated dialog box. The check boxes in the Show options area should be clear. Be sure the option to Advance slides Using timings is selected.

- Click **OK**. Select the first slide, then click the **Slide Show button** above the status bar to begin the presentation. The slides should advance automatically, and you should hear the associated narration as each slide appears on the screen.

- You can replace the narration for the entire presentation by repeating step 2 on the previous page. Alternatively, you can replace the narration (sound file) for an individual slide as described in step 4.

- Save the presentation.

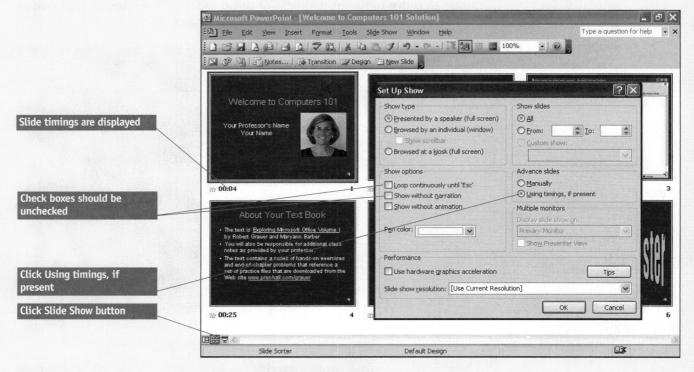

(c) Set Up the Presentation (step 3)

FIGURE 4.8   Hands-on Exercise 3 (*continued*)

THE REHEARSE TIMINGS COMMAND

The Record Narration command is similar in concept to the Rehearse Timings command, except that the latter does not include recorded sound. The Rehearse Timings command does, however, display a Rehearsal toolbar that lets you pause and catch your breath as you practice your speech for each slide. The Rehearsal toolbar also displays the amount of time spent on each slide as well as the total time for the presentation. Unfortunately, the toolbar is not available in conjunction with the Record Narration command.

Step 4: Modify the Narration

- Skip this step if you are satisfied with the narration for the entire presentation. Otherwise, return to the **Normal view** and select the slide where you want to replace the narration. Select the **Sound icon**.

- Pull down the **Slide Show menu** and open the Custom Animation task pane as shown in Figure 4.8d. Click the **Play button** to hear the narration to be sure you want to replace it. The Sound icon should still be selected. Press the **Del key**.

- Start the Sound Recorder (see boxed tip), click the **red dot** to begin recording, and click the **Stop button** when you are finished. Click the **Rewind button**, then click the **Play button** to listen to the sound. Save this file in the same folder as the other sounds for this presentation. Close the Sound Recorder.

- Pull down the **Insert menu**, click **Movies and Sounds**, then click **Sound from File** to display the Insert Sound dialog box. Locate the new narration, click **OK**, then click **Automatically** when asked how you want the sound to start. Move the Sound icon to the lower-right corner of the slide.

- The Animation task pane should show that the sound object (Welcome Message on our slide) will play automatically after the previous effect; in other words, the narration plays automatically when the slide is displayed. Close the task pane.

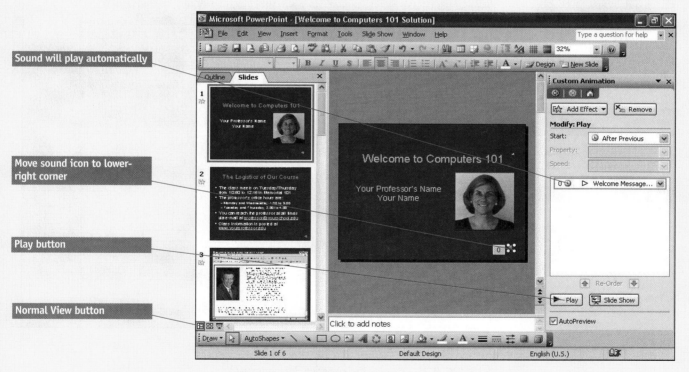

(d) Modify the Narration (step 4)

FIGURE 4.8   Hands-on Exercise 3 (*continued*)

THE SOUND RECORDER

Click the Start button, click All Programs, click Accessories, click Entertainment, then click Sound Recorder to display the associated dialog box. Pull down the File menu, click the Properties command and select All Formats in the Choose From list box. Click the Convert Now button. Select telephone quality as both the recording and playback format. Be sure to save the recorded file in the appropriate folder.

Step 5: Create the Custom Shows

- Pull down the **Slide Show menu** and click the **Custom Shows command** to display the Custom Shows dialog box. Click the **New button** to display the Define Custom Show dialog box in Figure 4.8e.

- Enter **Grauer on the Web** as the name of the new show. Select (click) **slide 3**, **Visit Bob Grauer at the University of Miami**, then click the **Add button**. The selected slide appears in the left column as the first slide in the custom show.

- Double click **slide 5**, **The Grauer Web Site**, to add this slide as well. Both slides should now appear in the left column. Click **OK** to close this dialog box. The newly created show, Grauer on the Web, should appear in the Custom Shows dialog box.

- Click the **New button** to create a second custom show. Enter **Logistics and Text** as the name of the second custom show. Double click **slides 2 and 4** to add these slides to this show. Click **OK** to create the show.

- Click the **Close button** to close the Custom Shows dialog box. Save the presentation.

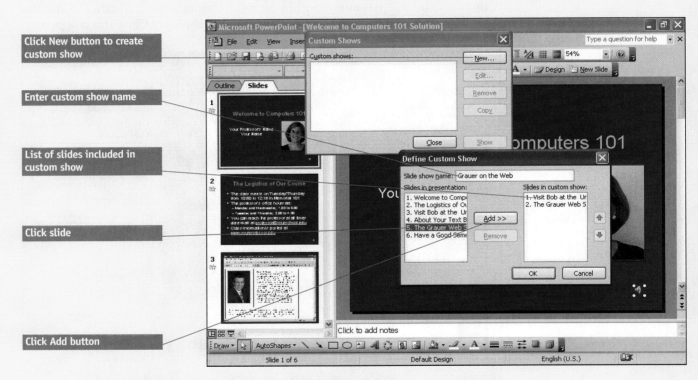

Click New button to create custom show

Enter custom show name

List of slides included in custom show

Click slide

Click Add button

(e) Create the Custom Shows (step 5)

FIGURE 4.8   Hands-on Exercise 3 (*continued*)

DIFFERENT SHOWS FOR DIFFERENT AUDIENCES

Many presenters are faced with the task of creating nearly identical shows for different audiences. There is a "basic show" common to every audience, followed by a few special slides for each audience. You could create multiple presentations and store each presentation in its own file. It is much more efficient, however, to create custom shows within a single presentation. This saves time and effort, especially if you have to update information on a basic slide, in that you would make the change only once.

Step 6: **Show Time**

- Pull down the **Slide Show menu** and click the **Custom Shows command**. Select the first custom show, **Grauer on the Web**. Click the **Show button**.

- You should see the slide containing Bob's home page at the University of Miami as shown in Figure 4.8f. You should also hear the accompanying narration.

- The next slide in the custom show, **The Grauer Web site**, should appear automatically with its narration, after which the presentation ends. Press **Esc** to return to PowerPoint.

- Pull down the **Slide Show menu** and click **Custom Shows** to view the second custom show, **Logistics and Text**, which also contains two slides. Press the **Esc key** at the end of the show to return to PowerPoint.

- Exit PowerPoint if you do not want to continue with the next exercise at this time.

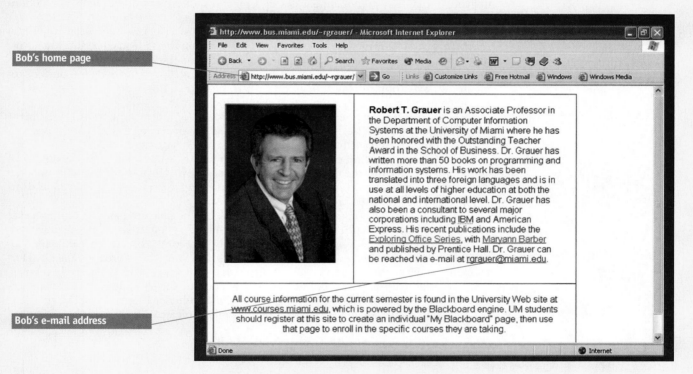

(f) Show Time (step 6)

FIGURE 4.8   Hands-on Exercise 3 (*continued*)

ADD HYPERLINKS TO YOUR CUSTOM SHOWS

Create a table of contents in the form of hyperlinks to the various custom shows in your presentation. Press Ctrl+Home to move to the title slide, insert a text box, then enter the name of each custom show on a separate line. Click and drag to select the name of the first custom show, click the Insert Hyperlink button to display the associated text box, and click the Place in this Document icon at the left. Scroll, if necessary, until you can select the appropriate custom show. Check the box to show and return, and click OK. Do this for each custom show. Click the Slide Show button, then view your custom shows from the title slide.

SUMMARY

The use of sound requires additional hardware, namely, a sound card and speakers. A microphone is necessary to record a sound file, although multiple sounds are supplied within Microsoft Windows as well as Microsoft Office. All sounds are created through the Sound Recorder (a Windows accessory), which creates a WAV file or digitized recording of an actual sound. Sound files are stored just like any other type of file and can be moved and copied from one folder to another.

A template controls every aspect of a presentation's design, such as the background, the fonts and formatting of the text, and the size and placement of bullets and other elements. Each template has a default color scheme, consisting of eight balanced colors that are used for the background, text, slide title, shadows, and other accents. Change the template, and you change every aspect of a presentation. Change the color scheme within a template (each template has several alternate color schemes from which to choose), and you retain the overall look, but effect a subtle change in the appearance.

Action buttons build flexibility into a presentation by enabling easy access to the first, previous, next, and/or last slide in a presentation. Hyperlinks to specific slides provide another means of alternate navigation. Hidden slides provide additional flexibility during delivery in that they do not appear during a regular slide show without deliberate action by the presenter.

The slide master enables you to modify the design of a presentation. Select the slide master from the View menu, then change any element on the slide master, and you automatically change that element on every slide in the presentation. The slide master is frequently used to add a unifying element such as a corporate logo and/or action buttons to facilitate navigation during the slide show. You can also fine-tune a presentation by changing its color scheme.

The Save As Web page command converts a PowerPoint presentation to a Web document, after which it can be uploaded to a Web server, where it can be accessed through an Internet Browser such as Internet Explorer or Netscape Navigator.

The Record Narration command creates a narrative (sound file) for each slide and simultaneously records the time required for that narrative. The narration can be made to play automatically to create a self-running presentation for a trade show or kiosk and/or to embellish a Web-based presentation.

Any presentation, including video and audio, can be delivered as a Web broadcast. The broadcast can be live or recorded. A live broadcast is scheduled at a precise time, and invitations are sent to a designated list of attendees. A recorded broadcast is uploaded to a Web server and configured for on-demand viewing. Either type of broadcast is ideal for reaching large and/or geographically dispersed audiences.

PowerPoint also supports online meetings in addition to Web broadcasts. A broadcast is a one-way connection in which you speak, and the audience listens. An online meeting is a two-way connection in which everyone can communicate with everyone else.

KEY TERMS

MULTIPLE CHOICE

1. How do you insert a corporate logo or other identifying information on every slide in a presentation?

   (a) Select the object, change to the Slide Sorter view, then paste the object on every slide

   (b) Insert the object on the title slide, then pull down the View menu and specify every slide

   (c) Insert the object on the title and slide masters

   (d) Insert the object on the title and handouts masters

2. Which of the following is true?

   (a) PowerPoint supplies many different templates, but each template has only one color scheme

   (b) PowerPoint supplies many different templates, and each template in turn has multiple color schemes

   (c) You cannot change the template of a presentation once it has been selected

   (d) You cannot change the color scheme of a presentation

3. Which of the following is true?

   (a) A color scheme specifies eight different colors, one color for each element in a presentation

   (b) You can change any color within a color scheme

   (c) A given template may have many different color schemes

   (d) All of the above

4. What happens if you click the Hide Slide button twice in a row?

   (a) The slide is hidden

   (b) The slide is visible

   (c) The slide has the same status as before the button was clicked initially

   (d) The slide has the opposite status as before the button was clicked initially

5. What is the best way to switch between PowerPoint and Internet Explorer if both are open?

   (a) Click the appropriate button on the taskbar

   (b) Click the Start button, click Programs, then choose the appropriate program from the displayed list

   (c) Minimize all applications to display the Windows desktop, then double click the icon for the appropriate application

   (d) All of the above are equally convenient

6. Internet Explorer can display a Web page stored on:

   (a) A local area network

   (b) A Web server

   (c) Drive A or drive C of a stand-alone PC

   (d) All of the above

7. How do you save a presentation as a Web page?

   (a) Click the Save button on the Standard toolbar

   (b) Pull down the File menu and click the Save As Web Page command

   (c) Both (a) and (b)

   (d) Neither (a) nor (b)

8. Which of the following requires an Internet connection?

   (a) Using Internet Explorer to view the Microsoft home page

   (b) Using Internet Explorer to view a Web page that is stored locally

   (c) Both (a) and (b)

   (d) Neither (a) nor (b)

9. A Record Narration command that checks the box to link narrations will:

   (a) Create a separate sound file for each slide

   (b) Record the time required to narrate each slide

   (c) Both (a) and (b)

   (d) Neither (a) nor (b)

... continued

10. You are using Internet Explorer to view a presentation saved as a Single File Web Page when you notice an error. You return to PowerPoint and fix the presentation. Which of the following must you do in order to see the changes in Internet Explorer?

    (a) Save the PowerPoint presentation after the changes have been made

    (b) Close Internet Explorer, then reload the MHTML document

    (c) Both (a) and (b)

    (d) Nothing at all; the changes will be visible as soon as you return to Internet Explorer

11. What sound quality and approximate storage requirement was recommended for recording a voice to narrate a presentation?

    (a) CD quality at 172 kb/sec

    (b) Telephone quality at 172 kb/sec

    (c) CD quality at 10 kb/sec

    (d) Telephone quality at 10 kb/sec

12. Which of the following is true?

    (a) You can replace the narration for the entire presentation by executing the Record Narration command a second time

    (b) You delete the narration associated with a specific slide, then use the Sound Recorder to replace the narration for just that slide

    (c) Both (a) and (b)

    (d) Neither (a) nor (b)

13. Which of the following is true about a custom slide show?

    (a) It contains a subset of the slides in a presentation

    (b) There can be only one custom show within a specific presentation

    (c) It must contain narration

    (d) All of the above

14. Which of the following was introduced in Office 2003?

    (a) The Save As Web Page command

    (b) The Single File Web Page format

    (c) Both (a) and (b)

    (d) Neither (a) nor (b)

15. Which vehicle is best to deliver a live presentation to 100 people in different locations?

    (a) A broadcast

    (b) An online meeting

    (c) A Web discussion

    (d) All of the above are equally suitable

16. Which technique should you use to minimize the file size of a presentation that contains multiple sound files?

    (a) Embed each sound file directly into the presentation

    (b) Link each sound file to the presentation

    (c) Display a sound icon on every slide

    (d) All of the above

17. Which of the following can be easily accomplished with action buttons?

    (a) Jumping to the first or last slide

    (b) Advancing to the next slide

    (c) Returning to the previous slide

    (d) All of the above

18. In which view is a hidden slide truly hidden (i.e., you do not see it unless you take special action)?

    (a) Slide Sorter

    (b) Normal

    (c) Slide Show

    (d) All of the above

ANSWERS

1.	c	**7.**	b	**13.**	a
2.	b	**8.**	a	**14.**	b
3.	d	**9.**	c	**15.**	a
4.	c	**10.**	c	**16.**	b
5.	a	**11.**	d	**17.**	d
6.	d	**12.**	c	**18.**	c

PRACTICE WITH POWERPOINT

1. **A Modified Quiz:** The presentation in Figure 4.9 is based on the completed PowerPoint quiz from the first hands-on exercise. The modified presentation contains three additional questions and a slightly modified design. Your assignment is to open the *PowerPoint Quiz Solution* presentation as it existed at the end of the first hands-on exercise and proceed as follows:

   a. Insert three additional slides, each containing a multiple choice question, so that the completed presentation contains a total of nine slides, as opposed to the six slides in the original presentation. You can select questions from the list of multiple choice questions for this chapter and/or you can make up your own. Be sure, however, that the text for the question fits on two lines and that each answer takes only a single line.

   b. Add the appropriate Sound icon next to each choice. Position the icons uniformly from the left edge of the slide.

   c. Modify the slide containing the answer key to reflect the new questions. Include hyperlinks next to each answer to return you to the slide with the corresponding question.

   d. Use the slide master to add a second small crayon at the bottom right of each slide. In addition, delete the large crayon that appears at the upper right of each slide. (You will have to press the Del key multiple times since the crayon comprises multiple ungrouped objects.)

   e. Change the font on the master slide to Arial. In addition, create a shadow effect for the title of each slide.

   f. Restore the color scheme of the presentation to the default color scheme for the Crayons template.

   g. Print the completed presentation for your instructor as follows. Print the title slide as a slide to use as a cover page, then print the entire presentation as audience handouts (six per page).

   h. Exchange your presentation with at least one other classmate. Are you able to answer his or her questions? Is this exercise a good way to review the conceptual material in the chapter?

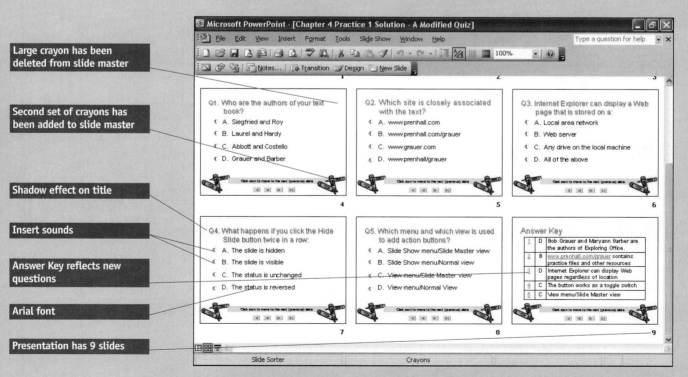

FIGURE 4.9 A Modified Quiz (exercise 1)

2. **Expanded Constitution Quiz:** Open the Constitution Quiz solution from the second hands-on exercise. (This is a Web document, so you will need to click the PowerPoint button on the taskbar to return to PowerPoint.) Proceed as follows:

a. Create three additional multiple choice questions (slides 6, 7, and 8) as shown in Figure 4.10. Add the appropriate Sound icon next to each answer to indicate whether the answer is correct or not. Position the icons uniformly from the left edge of the slide.

b. Modify the answer key to reflect the new questions. Include hyperlinks next to each answer to return you to the slide with the corresponding question.

c. Print the completed presentation from PowerPoint for your instructor. Print the title slide as a slide to use as a cover page, then print the entire presentation as audience handouts (six per page).

d. Exchange your presentation with at least one other classmate. Are you able to answer his or her questions? Did you learn anything about the United States Constitution?

e. Open the presentation from Internet Explorer, then print the slide containing the answer key to show that you have successfully created a Web document. Is printing from a browser limited compared to printing from PowerPoint?

f. The Web pages corresponding to this presentation can be viewed locally as was done in the hands-on exercise. What additional steps have to be taken to upload the presentation to a Web server? What additional software (if any) is required for uploading? Summarize the procedure to upload your presentation in a short note to your instructor.

g. Explain how to convert the Web page to a recorded broadcast. How do you schedule the broadcast so that it runs at a designated time? Would the sound files and action buttons continue to work in a Web broadcast? Do you need additional software to broadcast the presentation?

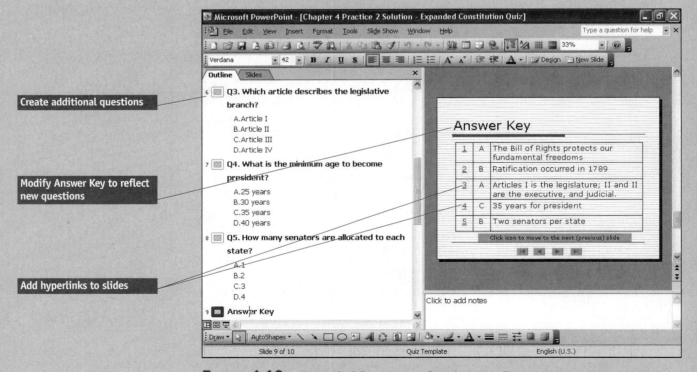

FIGURE 4.10   Expanded Constitution Quiz (exercise 2)

3. **Nutrition Quiz:** Create a PowerPoint presentation, consisting of at least five multiple choice questions, on any desired topic. Our quiz is on nutrition, and the end result is shown in Figure 4.11. (Slides 7 and 8 contain two additional questions. Slide 9 contains the answer key.) Proceed as follows:

a. Open the *Create a Quiz* presentation in the Exploring PowerPoint folder that was used in the second hands-on exercise. Save the presentation as *Chapter 4 Practice 3 Solution.*

b. Copy the last slide in the presentation (containing the sample question) several times, moving the copied slides to their appropriate places in the presentation. Add the text and suggested answers for each question. Try to keep the questions and answers brief so that they fit attractively on the slide.

c. Add the appropriate sound file next to each answer. Align the icons uniformly from the left edge of the slide.

d. Create the answer key for your quiz with hyperlinks to the corresponding question next to each answer. At least one of your answers should contain a hyperlink to an external Web site.

e. Insert clip art as appropriate next to the individual questions.

f. Change the template and/or the associated color scheme as you see fit. Set a time limit, or else you will spend too much time with your selection.

g. Print the completed presentation for your instructor as follows. Print the title slide as a slide to use as a cover page, then print the entire presentation as audience handouts (six per page).

h. Save the completed presentation as a Web page. You do not have to upload the presentation to the Web. Print the first slide in the presentation from Internet Explorer to show that you have successfully created a Web document.

i. Exchange your presentation with at least one other classmate. Are you able to answer his or her questions? Was the quiz interesting? Did you learn anything?

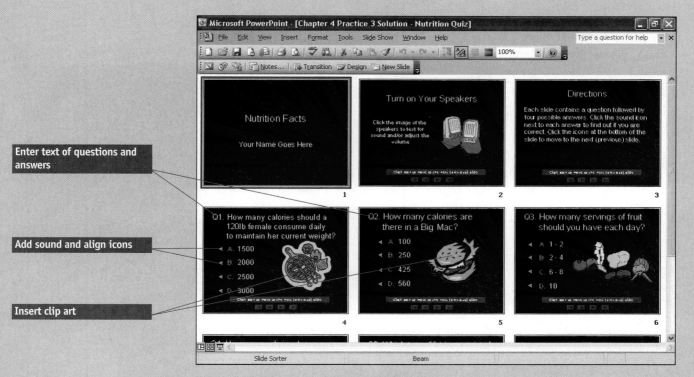

FIGURE 4.11   Nutrition Quiz (exercise 3)

4. **A Business Plan:** The presentation in Figure 4.12 was created from the AutoContent Wizard and saved as a Web page. The presentation can be viewed locally as in Figure 4.12, or it can be uploaded to the Web. Either way, it is a sophisticated presentation that can be created in a matter of minutes.

a. Use the AutoContent Wizard to create a presentation for a business plan. Change the title slide to include a specific name for the business, such as Widgets of America. Add your name to the title page. On every slide (except the title slide) include a footer that contains the date, your school, and the slide number.

b. The default presentation contains 12 slides as can be seen from Figure 4.12. Modify the text on three or four slides to make the business plan your own.

c. Print the completed presentation as audience handouts (six per page). Be sure to frame the slides.

d. Save the completed presentation as a Single File Web page. (This file format was not available in previous versions of Microsoft Office.)

e. Close PowerPoint. Start Internet Explorer and open the presentation as shown in Figure 4.12. Experiment with the various controls at the bottom of the Internet Explorer window to view the presentation. How do you go to a specific slide? What happens if you click the Outline button? What happens if you click the Slide Show button in Internet Explorer?

f. Print the title slide from Internet Explorer to prove to your instructor that you have created the Web page. How does this page differ from the same page printed within PowerPoint? What additional steps are necessary if you want to place your presentation on the Web so that it can be viewed by others?

g. Attach the audience handouts that you printed in part (c) and submit the completed assignment to your instructor.

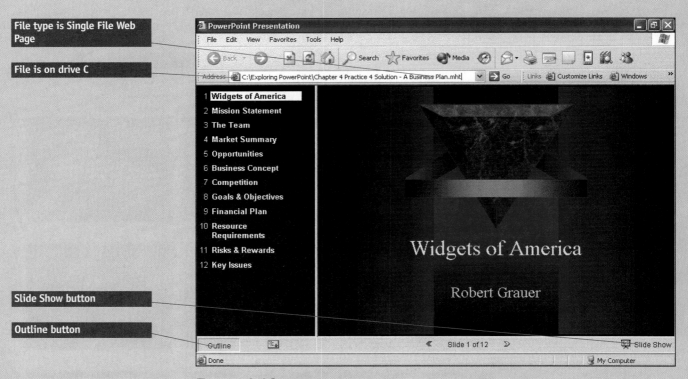

FIGURE 4.12 A Business Plan (exercise 4)

5. **Photographs on the Web:** Choose any collection of photographs to create a Web-based presentation similar to the one in Figure 4.13. You can select your own pictures, download photographs from the Microsoft Design Gallery, and/or use the photographs we supply in the Exploring PowerPoint folder. Each photograph must be saved as a separate file. (The photographs can be stored in different folders.)

   a. Start a new presentation. Create a title slide containing your name. Insert five or six new slides (choose the title only layout) for the photographs.

   b. Select the second slide in your presentation (the slide that will contain the first photograph). Pull down the Format menu, click Background to display the Background dialog box, click the down arrow in the background fill list box, and choose Fill Effects. Click the Picture tab, click the Select Picture button, insert the desired picture, and apply it to this slide. The photograph should fill the entire slide, a technique that adds interest to any presentation.

   c. Enter an appropriate title for the picture in the title placeholder, changing the font color and/or the position of the placeholder as necessary in order to read the title.

   d. Repeat steps b and c to insert additional photographs and the associated titles on the remaining slides.

   e. Change to the Slide Sorter view after all of the pictures have been inserted into the presentation. Press and hold the Shift key to select multiple slides, pull down the Slide Show menu, and click the Transition command. Add a transition effect for each slide, which includes the camera sound.

   f. Print the audience handouts (six per page) for your instructor. You must specify color (even if you do not have a color printer) within the Color/Grayscale list box within the Print dialog box in order to see the slide backgrounds.

   g. Save the completed presentation as a Single File Web Page as shown in Figure 4.13. You do not have to upload the presentation to the Web. Print the first slide in the presentation from Internet Explorer to show that you have successfully created a Web document.

FIGURE 4.13   Photographs on the Web (exercise 5)

6. **Brainstorming Session:** The presentation in Figure 4.14 was created using the AutoContent Wizard, which provided the design as well as the content. The wizard "jump starts" the creative process by asking you a series of leading questions, then it creates the presentation for you. Proceed as follows:

a. Start PowerPoint, close any open presentations, then pull down the File menu and click the New command. The task pane opens automatically. Select the link to the AutoContent Wizard. Click the Next button when you see the first screen.

b. Select the Brainstorming Session presentation. Click Next. Select the onscreen presentation. Click Next. Enter Brainstorming Session as the title of the presentation. Clear the check boxes that include specific information on each slide. Click Next. Click Finish.

c. The wizard pauses a second, then it creates a very general presentation similar to Figure 4.14. This is a good start, but you have to modify the presentation.

d. Delete the third slide (overview) because the information on this slide is redundant with the agenda slide that is displayed in the figure. Delete the overview bullet on the agenda slide as well.

e. Open the slide master. Use the Text Box tool on the Drawing toolbar to create the text box for the first action button. Create five additional buttons, each of which contains the title of another slide in the presentation.

f. Add the appropriate hyperlink to each of the action buttons you just created. Move and size the action buttons as appropriate. All of the buttons should be the same size and should be a uniform distance from the bottom of the slide.

g. Add your name to the title slide. Print the completed presentation for your instructor as follows. Print the first slide as a slide to use as a cover page. Print the entire presentation as audience handouts (six per page).

h. How many additional presentations are available from the AutoContent Wizard? Do you see the value of the wizard in jump-starting the creative process? How much time did you save by using the wizard?

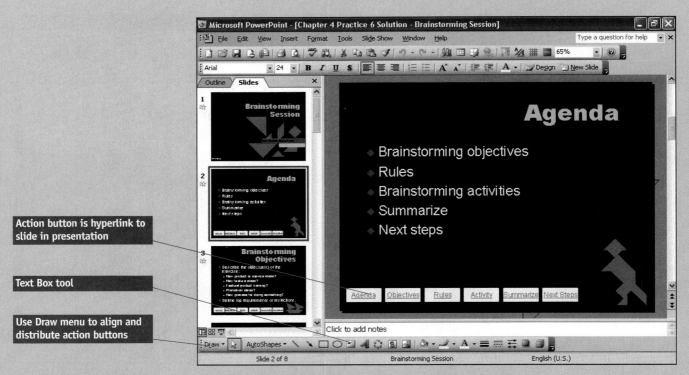

FIGURE 4.14 Brainstorming Session (exercise 6)

7. **Copyright and the Law:** The 10-slide presentation in Figure 4.15 contains useful information about copyrights and software piracy. Open the partially completed presentation in *Chapter 4 Practice* 7. Add your name to the title slide, then proceed as follows to complete the presentation:

   a. Select an appropriate template and a color scheme within that template. (We used default color scheme for the Network template.) Limit the time that you spend searching for a template.

   b. Add action buttons to the slide master that go to the first, previous, next, and last slides, respectively. Copy the copyright symbol that appears on the title slide and add it to the slide master as well.

   c. Insert the hyperlinks on the last slide so that the displayed text for each link is the Web address of that link. Visit at least one of the Web sites. Did you learn anything about copyright law?

   d. Create three custom shows as follows:

      (i) The Basics of Copyright Law (slides 2, 3, and 4)

      (ii) Infringement and Piracy (slides 5, 6, and 9)

      (iii) Using Copyright Material (slides 7 and 8)

   e. View each custom show. Press the Esc key at the end of each show to return to PowerPoint. Do the action buttons function differently within a custom show, as opposed to the entire presentation?

   f. Print each custom show separately as audience handouts (three slides per page).

   g. Save the completed presentation as a Web page. You do not have to upload the presentation to the Web.

   h. Print the first slide in the presentation from Internet Explorer to show that you have successfully created a Web document.

   i. Print the title slide as a slide to use as a cover page. Submit all of the printed pages to your instructor.

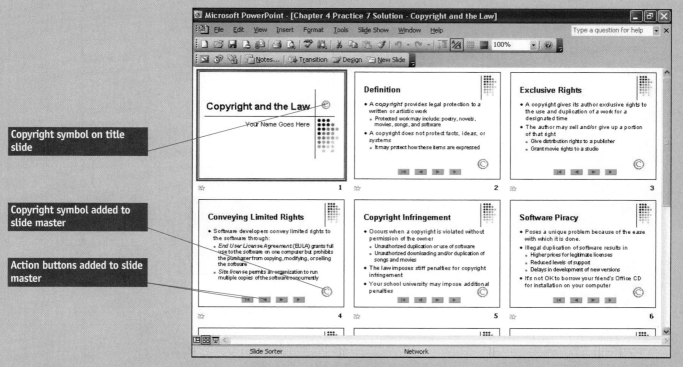

FIGURE 4.15   Copyright and the Law (exercise 7)

8. **Navigating within a Presentation:** The presentation in Figure 4.16 depicts a different way to navigate through a presentation in which hyperlinks to other slides appear in a menu on the title slide. The hyperlinks are the equivalent of a table of contents as they provide immediate access to every other slide. Open the partially completed presentation in *Chapter 4 Practice 8*, click Update Links, and proceed as follows.

a. Switch to the Normal view. Move the placeholders containing the title of the presentation and your name to the top of the title slide. Add a new text box and enter the titles of the other slides in the presentation. The slide titles should appear in two columns within the text box, which was achieved simply by pressing the Tab key as appropriate.

b. Select the title of each slide as it appears on the title slide, pull down the Insert menu, and select the Hyperlink command. Click the icon for a Place in This Document and select the appropriate slide to complete the hyperlink.

c. The navigation (action) buttons that appear at the bottom of every slide (except the title slide) were created on the slide master. Pull down the View menu, change to the Slide Master, click the Slide Show menu, click Action Buttons, then select the button you want. Click and drag to create the button on the slide master, then supply the necessary link (such as the next or previous slide). Select all four action buttons and size them uniformly. Place the buttons a uniform distance from the bottom of the slide.

d. Every slide except the title also contains today's date as well as the number of the slide within the presentation. Pull down the View menu, click the Header and Footer command, then complete the associated dialog box to display this information.

e. Go to the Slide Show view and test the navigation. Print the audience handouts (six per page) of the completed presentation for your instructor. Print the title slide as a full slide to use as a cover page for this assignment.

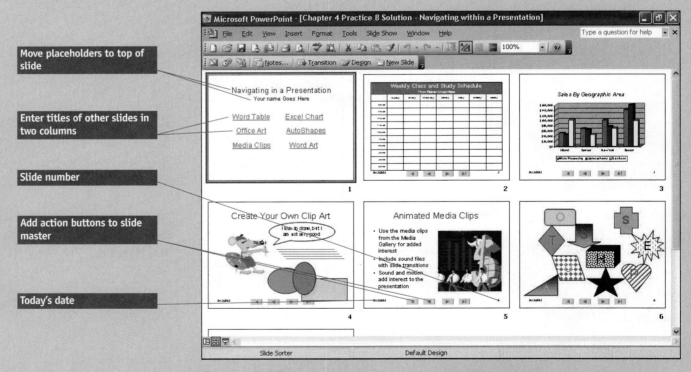

FIGURE 4.16 Navigating within a Presentation (exercise 8)

FTP for Windows

Microsoft Office simplifies the process of uploading a page to a Web server by including a basic FTP (File Transfer Protocol) capability. That is the good news. The bad news is that the capability is limited when compared to stand-alone FTP programs. One advantage of the latter is the ability to display the progress of a file transfer. In PowerPoint you click the Save button to upload your presentation, then you wait several seconds (or longer) before the system displays any additional information. An FTP program, however, will display the progress of the file transfer as it takes place.

Use your favorite search engine to locate an FTP program. There are many such programs available, and many permit a free trial period. Locate a specific program, then compare its capabilities to the FTP capability in Office NET. Summarize your findings in a short note to your instructor.

Speech Recognition

Explore the speech recognition capability that is built into Microsoft Office. Use the Help command to distinguish between the Voice Command mode and the Dictation mode. What is the language bar? How do you display or hide this toolbar? How long does it take to train your computer to recognize your voice? What drawbacks, if any, are there to using this feature? Summarize your findings in a short note to your instructor.

Windows Media Player

The Windows Media Player combines the functions of a radio, a CD or DVD player, and an information database into a single program. You can copy selections from a CD to your computer, organize your music by artist and album, and then create a customized playlist to play the music in a specified order. The playlist may include as many songs from as many albums as you like and is limited only by the size of your storage device. The Media Player will also search the Web for audio or video files and play clips from a favorite movie. Is the Media Player (or an equivalent program) installed on your computer? If not, how do you obtain the Media Player and how much does it cost? Experiment with the software, then summarize your findings in a short note to your instructor.

Searching for Sound

Click the Start button on the Windows taskbar to access the Search command, then search for the sound files that have been installed on your machine. (The installation of Microsoft Windows automatically includes several sound files.) Go to the Web (e.g., the Microsoft Design Gallery) to search for and download at least two additional sound files. Describe your experience in a short note to your instructor.

APPENDIX A

Toolbars for Microsoft® Office PowerPoint® 2003

TOOLBARS

Standard

Formatting

3-D settings

Control Toolbox

Diagram

Drawing

Drawing Canvas

Formatting

Organization Chart

Outlining

Picture

Reviewing

Shadow Settings

Shortcut Menus

Slide Show

Standard

Tables and Borders

Visual Basic

Web

WordArt

OVERVIEW

Microsoft PowerPoint has 18 predefined toolbars that provide access to commonly used commands. The toolbars are displayed in Figure A.1 and are listed here for convenience. They are the Standard, Formatting, 3-D Settings, Control Toolbox, Diagram, Drawing, Drawing Canvas, Organization Chart, Outlining, Picture, Reviewing, Shadow Settings, Shortcut Menus, Slide Show, Tables and Borders, Visual Basic, Web, and WordArt. The Standard and Formatting toolbars are displayed by default and appear on the same row immediately below the menu bar. The other predefined toolbars are automatically displayed with various views (e.g., the Slide Sorter View) or are displayed (hidden) at the discretion of the user.

The buttons on the toolbars are intended to be indicative of their function. Clicking the Printer button, for example (the sixth button from the left on the Standard toolbar), executes the Print command. If you are unsure of the purpose of any toolbar button, point to it, and a ScreenTip will appear that displays its name.

You can display multiple toolbars at one time, move them to new locations on the screen, customize their appearance, or suppress their display.

- To separate the Standard and Formatting toolbars and simultaneously display all of the buttons for each toolbar, pull down the Tools menu, click the Customize command, click the Options tab, then check the box to show the toolbars on two rows. Alternatively, the toolbars appear on the same row so that only a limited number of buttons are visible on each toolbar and hence you may need to click the double arrow at the end of the toolbar to view additional buttons. Additional buttons will be added to either toolbar as you use the associated feature, and conversely, buttons will be removed from the toolbar if the feature is not used.

- To display (or hide) a toolbar, pull down the View menu and click the Toolbars command. Select (deselect) the toolbar that you want to display (hide). The selected toolbar will be displayed in the same position as when last displayed. You may also point to any toolbar and click with the right mouse button to bring up a shortcut menu, after which you can select the toolbar to be displayed (hidden). If the toolbar to be displayed is not listed, click the Customize command, click the Toolbars tab, check the box for the toolbar to be displayed, and then click the Close button.

209

- To change the size of the buttons, suppress the display of the ScreenTips, or display the associated shortcut key (if available), pull down the View menu, click Toolbars, and click Customize to display the Customize dialog box. If necessary, click the Options tab, then select (deselect) the appropriate check box. Alternatively, you can right click on any toolbar, click the Customize command from the context-sensitive menu, then select (deselect) the appropriate check box from within the Options tab in the Customize dialog box.

- Toolbars are either docked (along the edge of the window) or floating (in their own window). A toolbar moved to the edge of the window will dock along that edge. A toolbar moved anywhere else in the window will float in its own window. Docked toolbars are one tool wide (high), whereas floating toolbars can be resized by clicking and dragging a border or corner as you would with any window.
  - ❏ To move a docked toolbar, click anywhere in the background area and drag the toolbar to its new location. You can also click and drag the move handle (the single vertical line) at the left of the toolbar.
  - ❏ To move a floating toolbar, drag its title bar to its new location.

- To customize one or more toolbars, display the toolbar on the screen. Then pull down the View menu, click Toolbars, and click Customize to display the Customize dialog box. Alternatively, you can click on any toolbar with the right mouse button and select Customize from the shortcut menu.
  - ❏ To move a button, drag the button to its new location on that toolbar or any other displayed toolbar.
  - ❏ To copy a button, press the Ctrl key as you drag the button to its new location on that toolbar or any other displayed toolbar.
  - ❏ To delete a button, drag the button off the toolbar and release the mouse button.
  - ❏ To add a button, click the Commands tab in the Customize dialog box, select the category (from the Categories list box) that contains the button you want to add, then drag the button to the desired location on the toolbar.
  - ❏ To restore a predefined toolbar to its default appearance, pull down the View menu, click Toolbars, click Customize, click the Toolbars tab, select (highlight) the desired toolbar, and click the Reset command button.

- Buttons can also be moved, copied, or deleted without displaying the Customize dialog box.
  - ❏ To move a button, press the Alt key as you drag the button to the new location.
  - ❏ To copy a button, press the Alt and Ctrl keys as you drag the button to the new location.
  - ❏ To delete a button, press the Alt key as you drag the button off the toolbar.

- To create your own toolbar, pull down the View menu, click Toolbars, click Customize, click the Toolbars tab, then click the New command button. Alternatively, you can click on any toolbar with the right mouse button, select Customize from the shortcut menu, click the Toolbars tab, and then click the New command button.
  - ❏ Enter a name for the toolbar in the dialog box that follows. The name can be any length and can contain spaces.
  - ❏ The new toolbar will appear on the screen. Initially it will be big enough to hold only one button. Add, move, and delete buttons following the same procedures as outlined above. The toolbar will automatically size itself as new buttons are added and deleted.
  - ❏ To delete a custom toolbar, pull down the View menu, click Toolbars, click Customize, and click the Toolbars tab. *Verify that the custom toolbar to be deleted is the only one selected (highlighted).* Click the Delete command button. Click Yes to confirm the deletion. (Note that a predefined toolbar cannot be deleted.)

MICROSOFT OFFICE POWERPOINT 2003 TOOLBARS

Standard

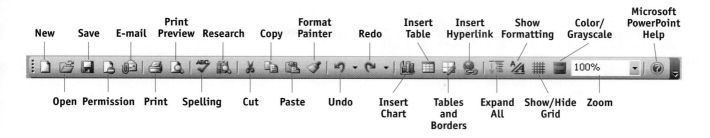

Formatting

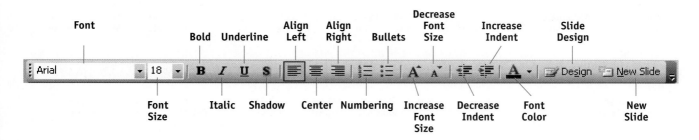

3-D Settings

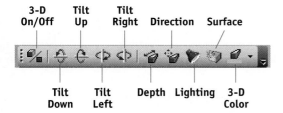

Control Toolbox

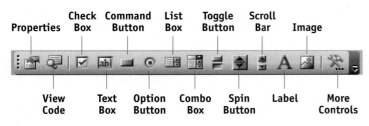

FIGURE A.1   Toolbars

Diagram

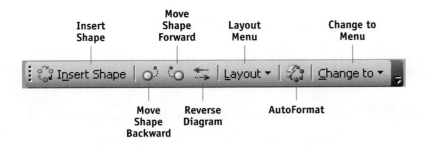

Drawing

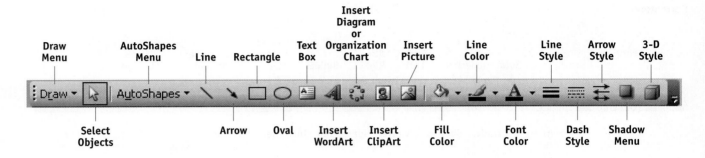

Drawing Canvas

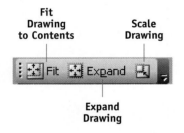

Organization Chart

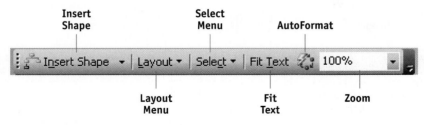

FIGURE A.1 Toolbars (*continued*)

Outlining

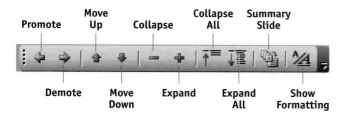

Promote
Move Up
Collapse
Collapse All
Summary Slide

Demote
Move Down
Expand
Expand All
Show Formatting

Picture

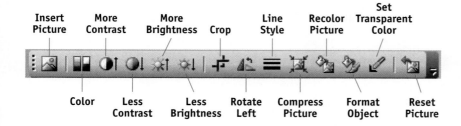

Insert Picture
More Contrast
More Brightness
Crop
Line Style
Recolor Picture
Set Transparent Color

Color
Less Contrast
Less Brightness
Rotate Left
Compress Picture
Format Object
Reset Picture

Reviewing

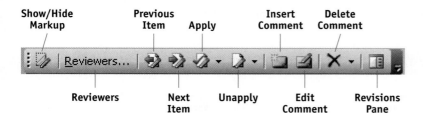

Show/Hide Markup
Previous Item
Apply
Insert Comment
Delete Comment

Reviewers
Next Item
Unapply
Edit Comment
Revisions Pane

Shadow Settings

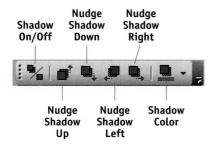

Shadow On/Off
Nudge Shadow Down
Nudge Shadow Right

Nudge Shadow Up
Nudge Shadow Left
Shadow Color

FIGURE A.1   Toolbars (*continued*)

Shortcut Menus

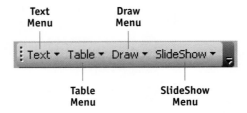

Slide Sorter

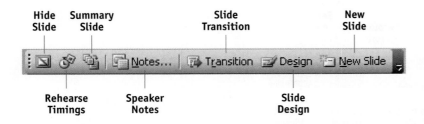

Tables and Borders

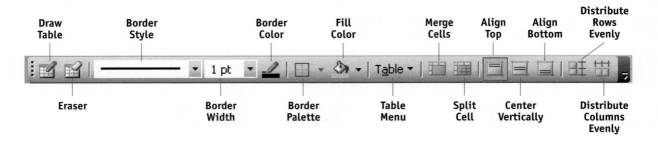

Visual Basic

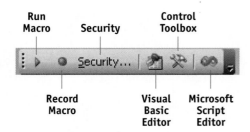

FIGURE A.1   Toolbars (*continued*)

Web

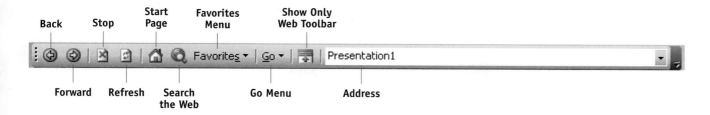

WordArt

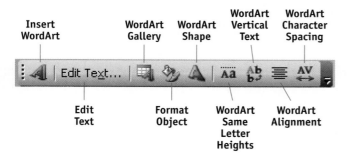

FIGURE A.1 Toolbars (*continued*)

1

Getting Started with Microsoft® Windows® XP

CASE STUDY
UNFORESEEN CIRCUMSTANCES

Steve and his wife Shelly have poured their life savings into the dream of owning their own business, a "nanny" service agency. They have spent the last two years building their business and have created a sophisticated database with numerous entries for both families and nannies. The database is the key to their operation. Now that it is up and running, Steve and Shelly are finally at a point where they could hire someone to manage the operation on a part-time basis so that they could take some time off together.

Unfortunately, their process for selecting a person they could trust with their business was not as thorough as it should have been. Nancy, their new employee, assured them that all was well, and the couple left for an extended weekend. The place was in shambles on their return. Nancy could not handle the responsibility, and when Steve gave her two weeks' notice, neither he nor his wife thought that the unimaginable would happen. On her last day in the office Nancy "lost" all of the names in the database—the data was completely gone!

Nancy claimed that a "virus" knocked out the database, but after spending nearly $1,500 with a computer consultant, Steve was told that it had been cleverly deleted from the hard drive and could not be recovered. Of course, the consultant asked Steve and Shelly about their backup strategy, which they sheepishly admitted did not exist. They had never experienced any problems in the past, and simply assumed that their data was safe. Fortunately, they do have hard copy of the data in the form of various reports that were printed throughout the time they were in business. They have no choice but to manually reenter the data. ■

Your assignment is to read the chapter, paying special attention to the information on file management. Think about how Steve and Shelly could have avoided the disaster if a backup strategy had been in place, then summarize your thoughts in a brief note to your instructor. Describe the elements of a basic backup strategy. Give several other examples of unforeseen circumstances that can cause data to be lost.

Windows® XP is the newest and most powerful version of the Windows operating system. It has a slightly different look than earlier versions, but it maintains the conventions of its various predecessors. You have seen the Windows interface many times, but do you really understand it? Can you move and copy files with confidence? Do you know how to back up the Excel spreadsheets, Access databases, and other documents that you work so hard to create? If not, now is the time to learn.

We begin with an introduction to the desktop, the graphical user interface that lets you work in intuitive fashion by pointing at icons and clicking the mouse. We identify the basic components of a window and describe how to execute commands and supply information through different elements in a dialog box. We stress the importance of disk and file management, but begin with basic definitions of a file and a folder. We also introduce Windows Explorer and show you how to move or copy a file from one folder to another. We discuss other basic operations, such as renaming and deleting a file. We also describe how to recover a deleted file (if necessary) from the Recycle Bin.

Windows XP is available in different versions. Windows *XP Home Edition* is intended for entertainment and home use. It includes a media player, new support for digital photography, and an instant messenger. Windows *XP Professional Edition* has all of the features of the Home Edition plus additional security to encrypt files and protect data. It includes support for high-performance multiprocessor systems. It also lets you connect to your computer from a remote station.

The login screen in Figure 1 is displayed when the computer is turned on initially and/or when you are switching from one user account to another. Several individuals can share the same computer. Each user, however, retains his or her individual desktop settings, individual lists of favorite and recently visited Web sites, as well as other customized Windows settings. Multiple users can be logged on simultaneously, each with his or her programs in memory, through a feature known as *fast user switching*.

Multiple users can be logged on

Accounts can be password-protected

FIGURE 1 Windows XP Login

Windows XP, as well as all previous versions of Windows, creates a working environment for your computer that parallels the working environment at home or in an office. You work at a desk. Windows operations take place on the *desktop*. There are physical objects on a desk such as folders, a dictionary, a calculator, or a phone. The computer equivalents of those objects appear as icons (pictorial symbols) on the desktop. Each object on a real desk has attributes (properties) such as size, weight, and color. In similar fashion, Windows assigns properties to every object on its desktop. And just as you can move the objects on a real desk, you can rearrange the objects on the Windows desktop.

Windows XP has a new interface, but you can retain the look and feel of earlier versions as shown in Figure 2. The desktop in Figure 2a uses the default ***Windows XP theme*** (the wallpaper has been suppressed), whereas Figure 2b displays the "same" desktop using the ***Windows Classic theme***. The icons on either desktop are used to access specific programs or other functions.

The ***Start button***, as its name suggests, is where you begin; it works identically on both desktops. Click the Start button to see a menu of programs and other functions. The Windows XP ***Start menu*** in Figure 2a is divided into two columns. The column on the left displays the most recently used programs for easy access, whereas the column on the right contains a standard set of entries. It also shows the name of the individual who is logged into the computer. The ***Classic Start menu*** in Figure 2b contains only a single column. (Note the indication of the Windows XP Professional operating system that appears at the left of the menu.)

Do not be concerned if your desktop is different from ours. Your real desk is arranged differently from those of your friends, just as your Windows desktop will also be different. Moreover, you are likely to work on different systems—at school, at work, or at home; what is important is that you recognize the common functionality that is present on all desktops.

Look now at Figure 2c, which displays an entirely different desktop, one with four open windows that is similar to a desk in the middle of a working day. Each window in Figure 2c displays a program or a folder that is currently in use. The ability to run several programs at the same time is known as ***multitasking***, and it is a major benefit of the Windows environment. Multitasking enables you to run a word processor in one window, create a spreadsheet in a second window, surf the Internet in a third window, play a game in a fourth window, and so on. You can work in a program as long as you want, then change to a different program by clicking its window.

The ***taskbar*** at the bottom of the desktop contains a button for each open window, and it enables you to switch back and forth between the open windows by clicking the appropriate button. A ***notification area*** appears at the right end of the taskbar. It displays the time and other shortcuts. It may also provide information on the status of such ongoing activities as a printer or Internet connection.

The desktop in Figure 2d is identical to the desktop in Figure 2c except that it is displayed in the Windows Classic theme. The open windows are the same, as are the contents of the taskbar and notification area. The choice between the XP theme or Windows Classic (or other) theme is one of personal preference.

Moving and Sizing a Window

A window can be sized or moved on the desktop through appropriate actions with the mouse. To ***size a window***, point to any border (the mouse pointer changes to a double arrow), then drag the border in the direction you want to go—inward to shrink the window or outward to enlarge it. You can also drag a corner (instead of a border) to change both dimensions at the same time. To ***move a window*** while retaining its current size, click and drag the title bar to a new position on the desktop.

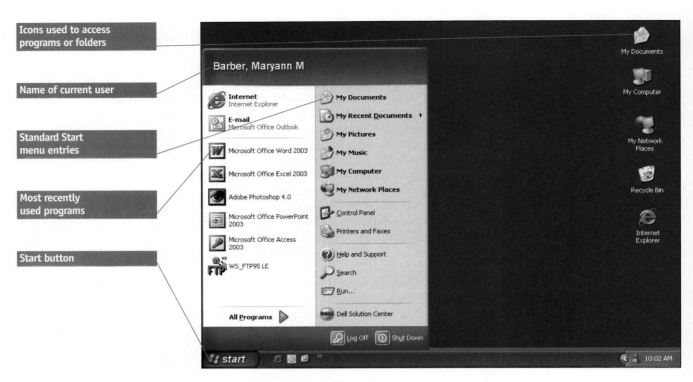

Icons used to access programs or folders

Name of current user

Standard Start menu entries

Most recently used programs

Start button

(a) Windows XP Theme and Start Menu

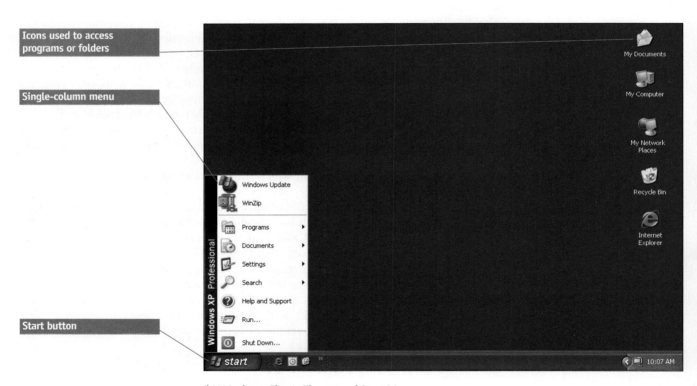

Icons used to access programs or folders

Single-column menu

Start button

(b) Windows Classic Theme and Start Menu

FIGURE 2 The Desktop and Start Menu

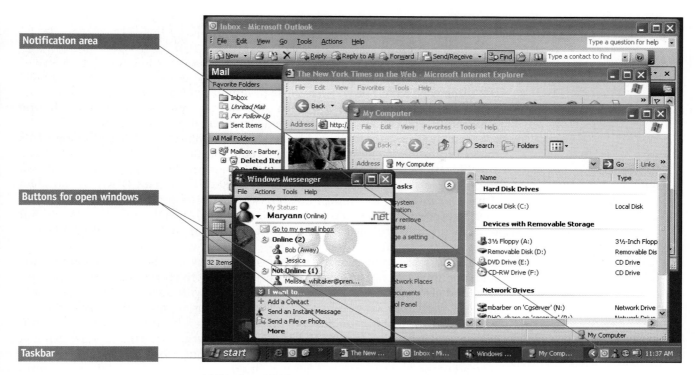

Notification area

Buttons for open windows

Taskbar

(c) Windows XP Theme

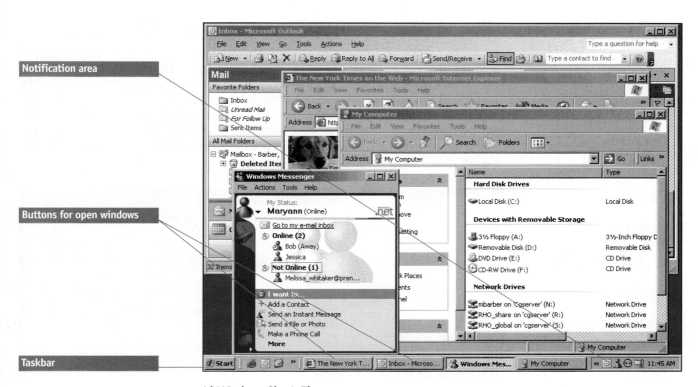

Notification area

Buttons for open windows

Taskbar

(d) Windows Classic Theme

FIGURE 2 The Desktop and Start Menu (*continued*)

All Windows applications share a common user interface and possess a consistent command structure. This means that every Windows application works essentially the same way, which provides a sense of familiarity from one application to the next. In other words, once you learn the basic concepts and techniques in one application, you can apply that knowledge to every other application.

The **My Computer folder** in Figure 3 is used to illustrate basic technology. This folder is present on every system, and its contents depend on the hardware of the specific computer. Our system, for example, has one local disk, a floppy drive, a removable disk (an Iomega Zip® drive), a DVD drive, and a CD-RW (recordable) drive. Our intent at this time, however, is to focus on the elements that are common to every window. A **task pane** (also called a task panel) is displayed at the left of the window to provide easy access to various commands that you might want to access from this folder.

The **title bar** appears at the top of every window and displays the name of the folder or application. The icon at the extreme left of the title bar identifies the window and also provides access to a control menu with operations relevant to the window, such as moving it or sizing it. Three buttons appear at the right of the title bar. The **Minimize button** shrinks the window to a button on the taskbar, but leaves the window in memory. The **Maximize button** enlarges the window so that it takes up the entire desktop. The **Restore button** (not shown in Figure 3) appears instead of the Maximize button after a window has been maximized, and restores the window to its previous size. The **Close button** closes the window and removes it from memory and the desktop.

The **menu bar** appears immediately below the title bar and provides access to pull-down menus. One or more **toolbars** appear below the menu bar and let you execute a command by clicking a button, as opposed to pulling down a menu. The **status bar** at the bottom of the window displays information about the window as a whole or about a selected object within a window.

A vertical (or horizontal) **scroll bar** appears at the right (or bottom) border of a window when its contents are not completely visible and provides access to the unseen areas. The vertical scroll bar at the right of the task panel in Figure 3 implies that there are additional tasks available that are not currently visible. A horizontal scroll bar does not appear since all of the objects in the My Computer folder are visible at one time.

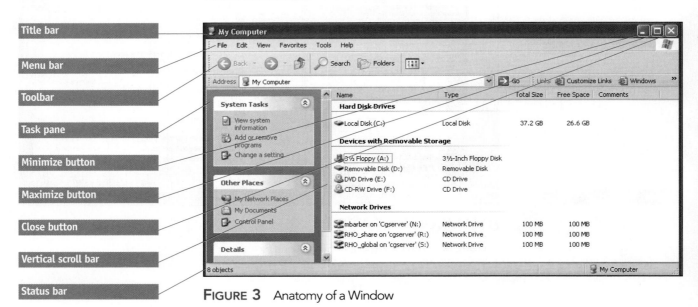

FIGURE 3 Anatomy of a Window

Pull-down Menus

The menu bar provides access to ***pull-down menus*** that enable you to execute commands within an application (program). A pull-down menu is accessed by clicking the menu name or by pressing the Alt key plus the underlined letter in the menu name; for example, press Alt+V to pull down the View menu. (You may have to press the Alt key to see the underlines.) Figure 4 displays three pull-down menus that are associated with the My Computer folder.

Commands within a menu are executed by clicking the command or by typing the underlined letter. Alternatively, you can bypass the menu entirely if you know the equivalent shortcuts shown to the right of the command in the menu (e.g., Ctrl+X, Ctrl+C, or Ctrl+V to cut, copy, or paste as shown within the Edit menu). A dimmed command (e.g., the Paste command in the Edit menu) means the command is not currently executable, and that some additional action has to be taken for the command to become available.

An ellipsis (. . .) following a command indicates that additional information is required to execute the command; for example, selection of the Format command in the File menu requires the user to specify additional information about the formatting process. This information is entered into a dialog box (discussed in the next section), which appears immediately after the command has been selected.

A check next to a command indicates a toggle switch, whereby the command is either on or off. There is a check next to the Status Bar command in the View menu of Figure 4, which means the command is in effect (and thus the status bar will be displayed). Click the Status Bar command and the check disappears, which suppresses the display of the status bar. Click the command a second time and the check reappears, as does the status bar in the associated window.

A bullet next to an item, such as Icons in the View menu, indicates a selection from a set of mutually exclusive choices. Click a different option within the group—such as Thumbnails—and the bullet will move from the previous selection (Icons) to the new selection (Thumbnails).

An arrowhead after a command (e.g., the Arrange Icons by command in the View menu) indicates that a submenu (also known as a cascaded menu) will be displayed with additional menu options.

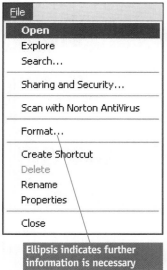

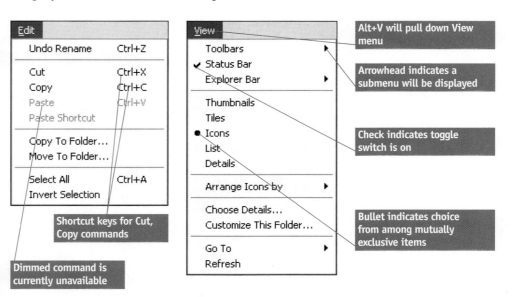

FIGURE 4   Pull-down Menus

Dialog Boxes

A **dialog box** appears when additional information is necessary to execute a command. Click the Print command in Internet Explorer, for example, and you are presented with the Print dialog box in Figure 5, requesting information about precisely what to print and how. The information is entered into the dialog box in different ways, depending on the type of information that is required. The tabs at the top of the dialog box provide access to different sets of options. The General tab is selected in Figure 5.

Option (radio) buttons indicate mutually exclusive choices, one of which *must* be chosen, such as the page range. In this example you can print all pages, the selection (if it is available), the current page (if there are multiple pages), or a specific set of pages (such as pages 1–4), but you can choose *one and only one* option. Any time you select (click) an option, the previous option is automatically deselected.

A **text box** enters specific information such as the pages that will be printed in conjunction with selecting the radio button for pages. A **spin button** is another way to enter specific information such as the number of copies. Click the up or down arrow to increase or decrease the number of pages, respectively. You can also enter the information explicitly by typing it into a spin box, just as you would a text box.

Check boxes are used instead of option buttons if the choices are not mutually exclusive or if an option is not required. The Collate check box is checked, whereas the Print to file box is not checked. Individual options are selected and cleared by clicking the appropriate check box, which toggles the box on and off. A **list box** (not shown in Figure 5) displays some or all of the available choices, any one of which is selected by clicking the desired item.

The **Help button** (a question mark at the right end of the title bar) provides help for any item in the dialog box. Click the button, then click the item in the dialog box for which you want additional information. The Close button (the X at the extreme right of the title bar) closes the dialog box without executing the command.

All dialog boxes also contain one or more **command buttons**, the function of which is generally apparent from the button's name. The Print button in Figure 5, for example, initiates the printing process. The Cancel button does just the opposite and ignores (cancels) any changes made to the settings, then closes the dialog box without further action.

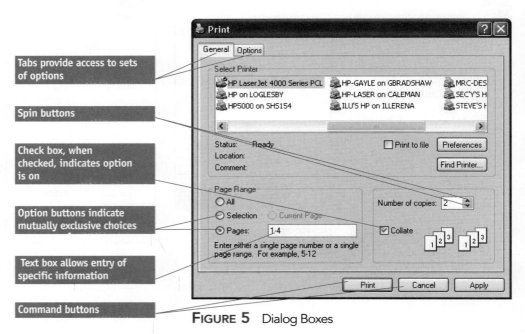

FIGURE 5 Dialog Boxes

HELP AND SUPPORT CENTER

The **Help and Support Center** combines such traditional features as a search function and an index of help topics. It also lets you request remote help from other Windows XP users, and/or you can access the Microsoft Knowledge base on the Microsoft Web site. Click the Index button, type the keyword you are searching for, then double click the subtopic to display the associated information in the right pane. The mouse is essential to Windows, and you are undoubtedly familiar with its basic operations such as pointing, clicking, and double clicking. Look closely, however, at the list of subtopics in Figure 6 and you might be surprised at the amount of available information. Suffice it to say, therefore, that you will find the answer to almost every conceivable question if only you will take the trouble to look.

The toolbar at the top of the window contains several buttons that are also found in **Internet Explorer 6.0**, the Web browser that is built into Windows XP. The Back and Forward buttons enable you to navigate through the various pages that were viewed in the current session. The Favorites button displays a list of previously saved (favorite) help topics from previous sessions. The History button shows all pages that were visited in this session.

The Support button provides access to remote sources for assistance. Click the Support button, then click the link to ask a friend to help, which in turn displays a Remote Assistance screen. You will be asked to sign in to the Messenger service (Windows Messenger is discussed in more detail in a later section). Your friend has to be running Windows XP for this feature to work, but once you are connected, he or she will be able to view your computer screen. You can then chat in real time about the problem and proposed solution. And, if you give permission, your friend can use his or her mouse and keyboard to work on your computer. Be careful! It is one thing to let your friend see your screen. It is quite a leap of faith, however, to give him or her control of your machine.

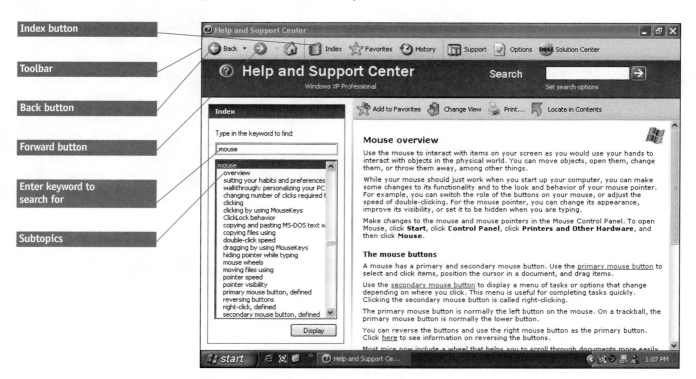

FIGURE 6   Help and Support Center

1 Welcome to Windows XP

Objective To log on to Windows XP and customize the desktop; to open the My Computer folder; to move and size a window; to format a floppy disk and access the Help and Support Center. Use Figure 7 as a guide.

Step 1: **Log On to Windows XP**

- Turn on the computer and all of the peripheral devices. The floppy drive should be empty prior to starting your machine.

- Windows XP will load automatically, and you should see a login screen similar to Figure 7a. (It does not matter which version of Windows XP you are using.) The number and names of the potential users and their associated icons will be different on your system.

- Click the icon for the user account you want to access. You may be prompted for a password, depending on the security options in effect.

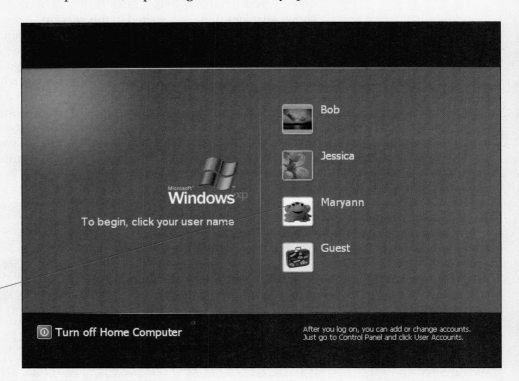

Click icon for user account to be accessed

(a) Log On to Windows XP (step 1)

FIGURE 7 Hands-on Exercise 1

USER ACCOUNTS

The available user names are created automatically during the installation of Windows XP, but you can add or delete users at any time. Click the Start button, click Control Panel, switch to the Category view, and select User Accounts. Choose the desired task, such as creating a new account or changing an existing account, then supply the necessary information. Do not expect, however, to be able to modify user accounts in a school setting.

Step 2: **Choose the Theme and Start Menu**

- Check with your instructor to see if you are able to modify the desktop and other settings at your school or university. If your network administrator has disabled these commands, skip this step and go to step 3.

- Point to a blank area on the desktop, click the **right mouse button** to display a context-sensitive menu, then click the **Properties command** to open the Display Properties dialog box. Click the **Themes tab** and select the **Windows XP theme** if it is not already selected. Click **OK**.

- We prefer to work without any wallpaper (background picture) on the desktop. **Right click** the desktop, click **Properties**, then click the **Desktop tab** in the Display Properties dialog box. Click **None** as shown in Figure 7b, then click **OK**. The background disappears.

- The Start menu is modified independently of the theme. **Right click** a blank area of the taskbar, click the **Properties command** to display the Taskbar and Start Menu Properties dialog box, then click the **Start Menu tab**.

- Click the **Start Menu option button**. Click **OK**.

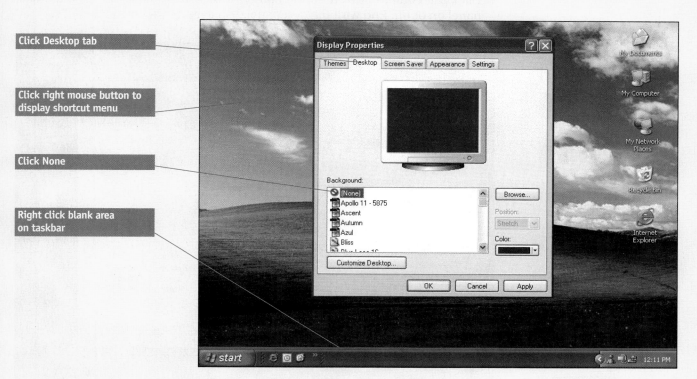

(b) Choose the Theme and Start Menu (step 2)

FIGURE 7 Hands-on Exercise 1 (*continued*)

IMPLEMENT A SCREEN SAVER

A screen saver is a delightful way to personalize your computer and a good way to practice with basic commands in Windows XP. Right click a blank area of the desktop, click the Properties command to open the Display Properties dialog box, then click the Screen Saver tab. Click the down arrow in the Screen Saver list box, choose the desired screen saver, then set the option to wait an appropriate amount of time before the screen saver appears. Click OK to accept the settings and close the dialog box.

Step 3: **Open the My Computer Folder**

■ Click the **Start button** to display a two-column Start menu that is characteristic of Windows XP. Click **My Computer** to open the My Computer folder. The contents of your window and/or its size and position on the desktop will be different from ours.

■ Pull down the **View menu** as shown in Figure 7c to make or verify the following selections. (You have to pull down the View menu each time you make an additional change.)
  ❑ The **Status Bar command** should be checked. The Status Bar command functions as a toggle switch. Click the command and the status bar is displayed; click the command a second time and the status bar disappears.
  ❑ Click the **Tiles command** to change to this view. Selecting the Tiles view automatically deselects the previous view.

■ Pull down the **View menu**, then click (or point to) the **Toolbars command** to display a cascaded menu. If necessary, check the commands for the **Standard Buttons** and **Address Bar**, and clear the other commands.

■ Click the **Folders button** on the Standard Buttons toolbar to toggle the task panel on or off. End with the task panel displayed as shown in Figure 7c.

(c) Open the My Computer Folder (step 3)

FIGURE 7 Hands-on Exercise 1 (*continued*)

DESIGNATING THE DEVICES ON A SYSTEM

The first (usually only) floppy drive is always designated as drive A. (A second floppy drive, if it were present, would be drive B.) The first hard (local) disk on a system is always drive C, whether or not there are one or two floppy drives. Additional local drives, if any, such as a zip (removable storage) drive, a network drive, a CD and/or a DVD, are labeled from D on.

Step 4: **Move and Size a Window**

- Move and size the My Computer window on your desktop to match the display in Figure 7d.
  - ❏ To change the width or height of the window, click and drag a border (the mouse pointer changes to a double arrow) in the direction you want to go; drag the border inward to shrink the window or outward to enlarge it.
  - ❏ To change the width and height at the same time, click and drag a corner rather than a border.
  - ❏ To change the position of the window, click and drag the title bar.

- Click the **Minimize button** to shrink the My Computer window to a button on the taskbar. My Computer is still active in memory although its window is no longer visible. Click the **My Computer button** on the taskbar to reopen the window.

- Click the **Maximize button** so that the My Computer window expands to fill the entire screen. Click the **Restore button** (which replaces the Maximize button and is not shown in Figure 7d) to return the window to its previous size.

- Practice these operations until you can move and size a window with confidence.

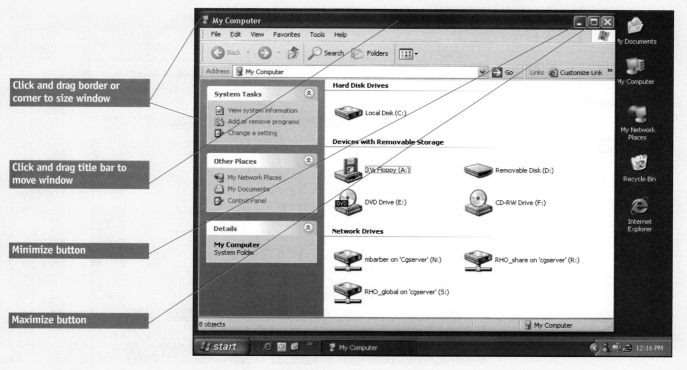

(d) Move and Size a Window (step 4)

FIGURE 7 Hands-on Exercise 1 (*continued*)

MINIMIZING VERSUS CLOSING AN APPLICATION

Minimizing a folder or an application leaves the object open in memory and available at the click of the appropriate button on the taskbar. Closing it, however, removes the object from memory, which also causes it to disappear from the taskbar. The advantage of minimizing an application or folder is that you can return to it immediately with the click of the mouse. The disadvantage is that too many open applications will eventually degrade the performance of a system.

Step 5: Capture a Screen

- Prove to your instructor that you have sized the window correctly by capturing the desktop that currently appears on your monitor. Press the **Print Screen key** to copy the current screen display to the **clipboard**, an area of memory that is available to every application.

- Nothing appears to have happened, but the screen has in fact been copied to the clipboard and can be pasted into a Word document. Click the **Start button**, click the **All Programs command**, then start **Microsoft Word** and begin a new document.

- Enter the title of your document (I Did My Homework) followed by your name as shown in Figure 7e. Press the **Enter key** two or three times to leave blank lines after your name.

- Pull down the **Edit menu** and click the **Paste command** (or click the **Paste button** on the Standard toolbar) to copy the contents of the clipboard into the Word document.

- Print this document for your instructor. There is no need to save this document. Exit Word.

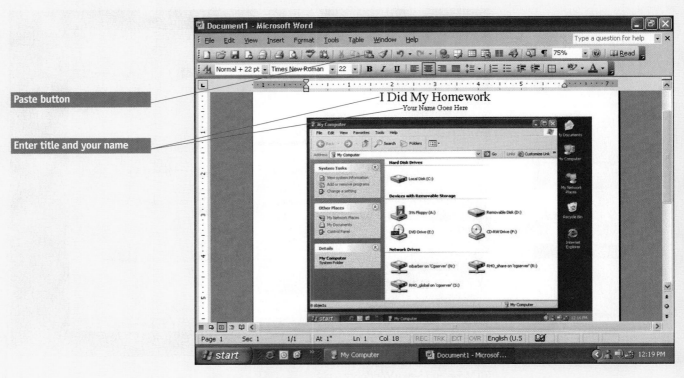

(e) Capture a Screen (step 5)

FIGURE 7   Hands-on Exercise 1 (*continued*)

THE FORMAT PICTURE COMMAND

Use the Format Picture command to facilitate moving and/or sizing an object within a Word document. Right click the picture to display a context-sensitive menu, then click the Format Picture command to display the associated dialog box. Click the Layout tab, choose any layout other than Inline with text, and click OK. You can now click and drag the picture to position it elsewhere within the document.

Step 6: Format a Floppy Disk

- Place a floppy disk into drive A. Select (click) **drive A** in the My Computer window, then pull down the **File menu** and click the **Format command** to display the Format dialog box in Figure 7f.
    - ❏ Set the **Capacity** to match the floppy disk you purchased (1.44MB for a high-density disk and 720KB for a double-density disk. The easiest way to determine the type of disk is to look for the label HD or DD, respectively.).
    - ❏ Click the **Volume label text box** if it's empty, or click and drag over the existing label if there is an entry. Enter a new label (containing up to 11 characters), such as **Bob's Disk**.
    - ❏ You can check the **Quick Format box** if the disk has been previously formatted, as a convenient way to erase the contents of the disk.
- Click the **Start button,** then click **OK**—after you have read the warning message—to begin the formatting operation. The formatting process erases anything that is on the disk, so be sure that you do not need anything on the disk.
- Click **OK** after the formatting is complete. Close the dialog box, then save the formatted disk for the next exercise. Close the My Computer window.

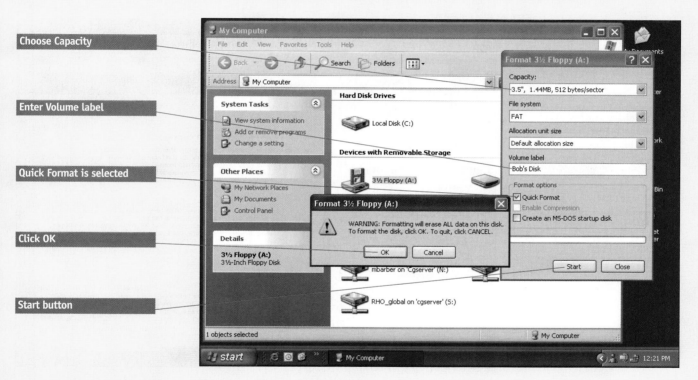

(f) Format a Floppy Disk (step 6)

FIGURE 7   Hands-on Exercise 1 (*continued*)

THE DEMISE OF THE FLOPPY DISK

You may be surprised to discover that your system no longer has a floppy disk drive, but it is only the latest victim in the march of technology. Long-playing records have come and gone. So too have 8-track tapes and the laser disk. The 3½-inch floppy disk has had a long and successful run, but it, too, is slated for obsolescence with Dell's recent announcement that it will no longer include a floppy drive as a standard component in desktop systems. Still, the floppy disk will "live forever" in the Save button that has the floppy disk as its icon.

Step 7: **The Help and Support Center**

- Click the **Start button**, then click the **Help and Support command** to open the Help and Support Center. Click the **Index button** to open the index pane. The insertion point moves automatically to the text box where you enter the search topic.

- Type **help**, which automatically moves you to the available topics within the index. Double click **central location for Help** to display the information in the right pane as shown in Figure 7g.

- Toggle the display of the subtopics on and off by clicking the plus and minus sign, respectively. Click the **plus sign** next to Remote Assistance, for example, and the topic opens. Click the **minus sign** next to Tours and articles, and the topic closes.

- Right click anywhere within the right pane to display the context-sensitive menu shown in Figure 7g. Click the **Print command** to print this information for your instructor.

- Close the Help and Support window.

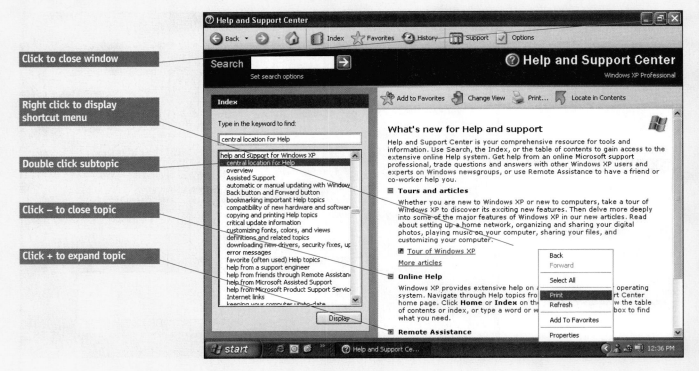

(g) The Help and Support Center (step 7)

FIGURE 7   Hands-on Exercise 1 (*continued*)

THE FAVORITES BUTTON

Do you find yourself continually searching for the same information? If so, you can make life a little easier by adding the page to a list of favorite help topics. Start the Help and Support Center, use the Index button to display the desired information in the right pane, and then click the Add to Favorites button to add the topic to your list of favorites. You can return to the topic at any time by clicking the Favorites button at the top of the Help and Support window, then double clicking the bookmark.

Step 8: **Log (or Turn) Off the Computer**

- It is very important that you log off properly, as opposed to just turning off the power. This enables Windows to close all of its system files and to save any changes that were made during the session.

- Click the **Start button** to display the Start menu in Figure 7h, then click the **Log Off button** at the bottom of the menu. You will see a dialog box asking whether you want to log off or switch users.
  - ❑ Switching users leaves your session active. All of your applications remain open, but control of the computer is given to another user. You can subsequently log back on (after the new user logs off) and take up exactly where you left off.
  - ❑ Logging off ends your session, but leaves the computer running at full power. This is the typical option you would select in a laboratory setting at school.

- To turn the computer off, you have to log off as just described, then select the **Turn Computer Off command** from the login screen. Welcome to Windows XP!

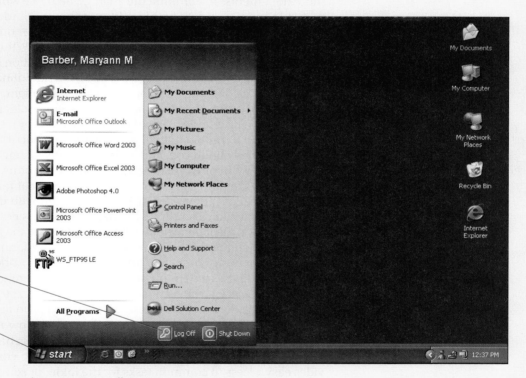

(h) Log (or Turn) Off Computer (step 8)

FIGURE 7 Hands-on Exercise 1 (*continued*)

THE TASK MANAGER

The Start button is the normal way to exit Windows. Occasionally, however, an application may "hang"—in which case you want to close the problem application but continue with your session. Press Ctrl+Alt+Del to display the Windows Task Manager dialog box, then click the Applications tab. Select the problem application (it will most likely say "not responding"), and click the End Task button. This capability is often disabled in a school setting.

A *file* is a set of instructions or data that has been given a name and stored on disk. There are two basic types of files, *program files* and *data files*. Microsoft Word and Microsoft Excel are examples of program files. The documents and workbooks that are created by these programs are data files. A program file is executable because it contains instructions that tell the computer what to do. A data file is not executable and can be used only in conjunction with a specific program. In other words, you execute program files to create and/or edit the associated data files.

Every file has a *filename* that identifies it to the operating system. The filename can contain up to 255 characters and may include spaces and other punctuation. (Filenames cannot contain the following characters: \, /, :, *, ?, ", <, >, and |.) We find it easier, however, to restrict the characters in a filename to letters, numbers, and spaces, as opposed to having to remember the special characters that are not permitted.

Files are kept in *folders* to better organize the thousands of files on a typical system. A Windows folder is similar to an ordinary manila folder that holds one or more documents. To continue the analogy, an office worker stores his or her documents in manila folders within a filing cabinet. Windows stores its files in electronic folders that are located on a disk, CD-ROM, or other device.

Many folders are created automatically by Windows XP, such as the My Computer or My Documents folders that are present on every system. Other folders are created whenever new software is installed. Additional folders are created by the user to hold the documents he or she creates. You might, for example, create a folder for your word processing documents and a second folder for your spreadsheets. You could also create a folder to hold all of your work for a specific class, which in turn might contain a combination of word processing documents and spreadsheets. The choice is entirely up to you, and you can use any system that makes sense to you. A folder can contain program files, data files, or even other folders.

Figure 8 displays the contents of a hypothetical folder with nine documents. Figure 8a displays the folder in *Tiles view*. Figure 8b displays the same folder in *Details view*, which also shows the date the file was created or last modified. Both views display a file icon next to each file to indicate the *file type* or application that was used to create the file. *Introduction to E-mail*, for example, is a PowerPoint presentation. *Basic Financial Functions* is an Excel workbook.

The two figures have more similarities than differences, such as the name of the folder (*Homework*), which appears in the title bar next to the icon of an open folder. The Minimize, Restore, and Close buttons are found at the right of the title bar. A menu bar with six pull-down menus appears below the title bar. The Standard Buttons toolbar is below the menu, and the Address bar (indicating the drive and folder) appears below the toolbar. Both folders also contain a task pane that provides easy access to common tasks for the folder or selected object.

Look closely and you will see that the task panes are significantly different. This is because there are no documents selected in Figure 8a, whereas the *Milestones in Communications* document is selected (highlighted) in Figure 8b. Thus, the File and Folder Tasks area in Figure 8a pertains to folders in general, whereas the available tasks in Figure 8b are pertinent to the selected document. The Details areas in the two task panes are also consistent with the selected objects and display information about the Homework folder and selected document, respectively. A status bar appears at the bottom of both windows and displays the contents of the selected object.

The last difference between the task panes reflects the user's preference to open or close the Other Places area. Click the upward chevron in Figure 8a to suppress the display and gain space in the task pane, or click the downward chevron in Figure 8b to display the specific links to other places. The task pane is new to Windows XP and did not appear in previous versions of Windows.

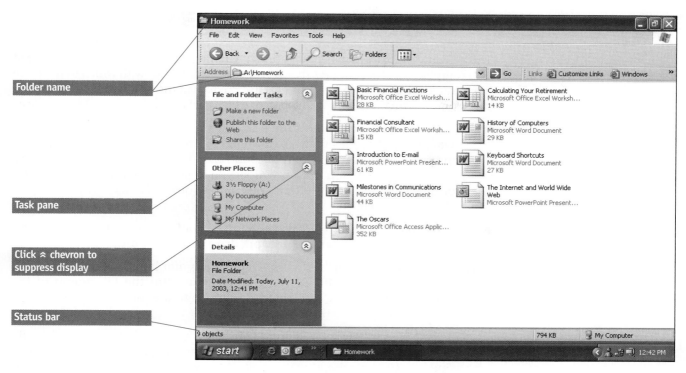

Folder name

Task pane

Click ≈ chevron to
suppress display

Status bar

(a) Tiles View

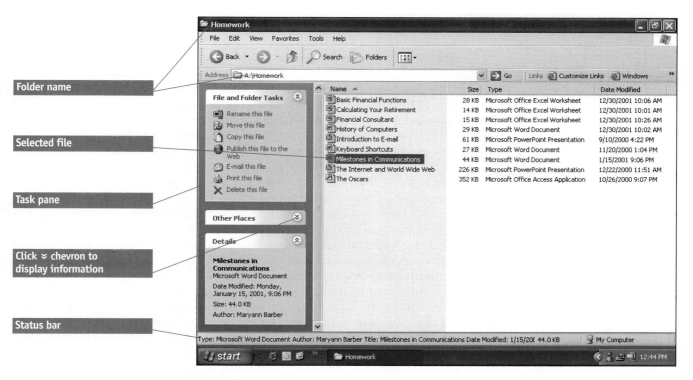

Folder name

Selected file

Task pane

Click ≈ chevron to
display information

Status bar

(b) Details View

FIGURE 8 Files and Folders

THE EXPLORING OFFICE PRACTICE FILES

There is only one way to master disk and file management and that is to practice at the computer. To do so requires that you have a series of files with which to work. We have created these files for you, and we use the files in the next two hands-on exercises. Your instructor will make the practice files available to you in different ways:

■ The files can be downloaded from our Web site at www.prenhall.com/grauer. Software and other files that are downloaded from the Internet are typically compressed (made smaller) to reduce the amount of time it takes to transmit the file. In essence, you will download a single *compressed file* and then uncompress the file into multiple files onto a local drive as described in the next hands-on exercise.

■ The files may be on a network drive at your school or university, in which case you can copy the files from the network drive to a floppy disk.

■ There may be an actual "data disk" in the computer lab. Go to the lab with a floppy disk, then use the Copy Disk command (on the File menu of My Computer when drive A is selected) to duplicate the data disk and create a copy for yourself.

It doesn't matter how you obtain the practice files, only that you are able to do so. Indeed, you may want to try different techniques to gain additional practice with Windows XP. Note, too, that Windows XP provides a *firewall* to protect your computer from unauthorized access while it is connected to the Internet. (See exercise 2 at the end of the chapter.)

CONNECTING TO THE INTERNET

The easiest way to obtain the practice files is to download the files from the Web, which requires an Internet connection. There are two basic ways to connect to the Internet—from a local area network (LAN) or by dialing in. It's much easier if you connect from a LAN (typically at school or work) since the installation and setup have been done for you, and all you have to do is follow the instructions provided by your professor. If you connect from home, you will need a modem, a cable modem, or a DSL modem, and an Internet Service Provider (or ISP).

A *modem* is the hardware interface between your computer and the telephone system. In essence, you instruct the modem, via the appropriate software, to connect to your ISP, which in turn lets you access the Internet. A cable modem provides high-speed access (20 to 30 times that of an ordinary modem) through the same type of cable as used for cable TV. A DSL modem also provides high-speed access through a special type of phone line that lets you connect to the Internet while simultaneously carrying on a conversation.

An *Internet Service Provider* is a company or organization that maintains a computer with permanent access to the Internet. America Online (AOL) is the largest ISP with more than 30 million subscribers, and it provides a proprietary interface as well as Internet access. The Microsoft Network (MSN) is a direct competitor to AOL. Alternatively, you can choose from a host of other vendors who provide Internet access without the proprietary interface of AOL or MSN.

Regardless of which vendor you choose as an ISP, be sure you understand the fee structure. The monthly fee may entitle you to a set number of hours per month (after which you pay an additional fee), or it may give you unlimited access. The terms vary widely, and you should shop around for the best possible deal. Price is not the only consideration, however. Reliability of service is also important. Be sure that the equipment of your provider is adequate so that you can obtain access whenever you want.

Objective   To download a file from the Web and practice basic file commands. The exercise requires a formatted floppy disk and access to the Internet. Use Figure 9 as a guide.

Step 1:   **Start Internet Explorer**

- Click the **Start button**, click the **All Programs command**, and then click **Internet Explorer** to start the program. If necessary, click the **Maximize button** so that Internet Explorer takes the entire desktop.

- Click anywhere within the **Address bar**, which automatically selects the current address (so that whatever you type replaces the current address). Enter **www.prenhall.com/grauer** (the http:// is assumed). Press **Enter**.

- You should see the Exploring Office Series home page as shown in Figure 9a. Click the book for **Office 2003**, which takes you to the Office 2003 home page.

- Click the **Student Downloads tab** (at the top of the window) to go to the Student Download page.

Enter
www.prenhall.com/grauer
in Address bar

Click book for Office 2003

(a) Start Internet Explorer (step 1)

FIGURE 9   Hands-on Exercise 2

A NEW INTERNET EXPLORER

The installation of Windows XP automatically installs a new version of Internet Explorer. Pull down the Help menu and click the About Internet Explorer command to display the current release (version 6.0). Click OK to close the About Internet Explorer window.

Step 2: Download the Practice Files

- You should see the Student Download page in Figure 9b. Place the formatted floppy disk from the first exercise in drive A. Be sure there are no files on this disk.

- Scroll down the page until you see the link to the student data disk for **Windows XP**. Click the link to download the practice files.

- You will see the File Download dialog box, asking what you want to do. Click the **Save button** to display the Save As dialog box. Click the **drop-down arrow** on the Save in list box, and select (click) **drive A**.

- Click **Save** to download the file. The File Download window may reappear and show you the status of the downloading operation as it takes place.

- If necessary, click **Close** when you see the dialog box indicating that the download is complete. Minimize Internet Explorer.

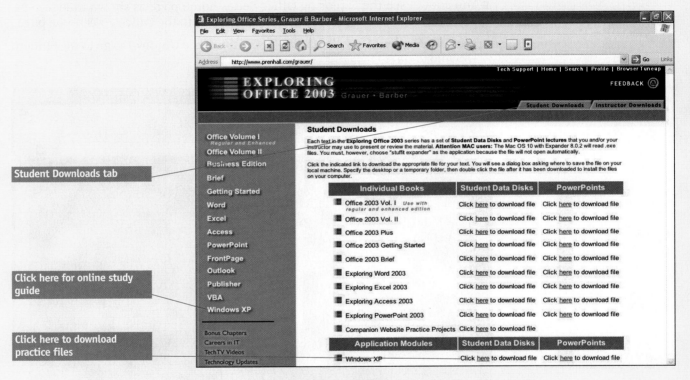

(b) Download the Practice Files (step 2)

FIGURE 9 Hands-on Exercise 2 (*continued*)

EXPLORE OUR WEB SITE

The Exploring Office Series Web site offers an online study guide (multiple-choice, true/false, and matching questions) for each individual textbook to help you review the material in each chapter. You can take practice quizzes by yourself and/or e-mail the results to your instructor. These online study guides are available via the tabs in the left navigation bar. You can return to the Student Download page at any time by clicking the tab toward the top of the window and/or you can click the link to Home to return to the home page for the Office 2003 Series. And finally, you can click the Feedback button at the top of the screen to send a message directly to Bob Grauer.

Step 3: Install the Practice Files

- Click the **Start button**, then click the **My Computer command** on the menu to open the My Computer folder. If necessary, click the Maximize button so that the My Computer window takes up the entire desktop. Change to the **Details view**.

- Click the icon for **drive A** to select it. The description of drive A appears at the left of the window. Double click the icon for **drive A** to open this drive. The contents of the My Computer window are replaced by the contents of drive A as shown in Figure 9c.

- Double click the **XPData file** to install the practice files, which displays the dialog box in Figure 9c. When you have finished reading, click **OK** to continue the installation and display the WinZip Self-Extractor dialog box.

- Check that the Unzip To Folder text box specifies **A:** to extract the files to the floppy disk. Click the **Unzip button** to extract (uncompress) the practice files and copy them onto the designated drive.

- Click **OK** after you see the message indicating that the files have been unzipped successfully. Close the WinZip dialog box.

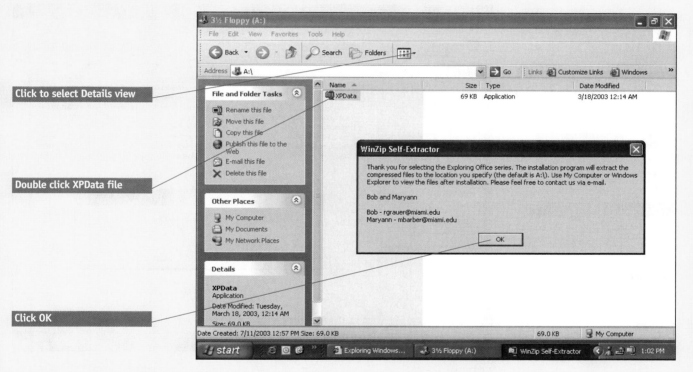

(c) Install the Practice Files (step 3)

FIGURE 9 Hands-on Exercise 2 (*continued*)

DOWNLOADING A FILE

Software and other files are typically compressed (made smaller) to reduce the amount of storage space the files require on disk and/or the time it takes to download the files. In essence, you download a compressed file (which may contain multiple individual files), then you uncompress (expand) the file on your local drive to access the individual files. After the file has been expanded, it is no longer needed and can be deleted.

Step 4: **Delete the Compressed File**

■ The practice files have been extracted to drive A and should appear in the Drive A window. If you do not see the files, pull down the **View menu** and click the **Refresh command**.

■ If necessary, pull down the **View menu** and click **Details** to change to the Details view in Figure 9e. You should see a total of eight files in the drive A window. Seven of these are the practice files on the data disk. The eighth file is the original file that you downloaded earlier. This file is no longer necessary, since it has been already been expanded.

■ Select (click) the **XPData file**. Click the **Delete this file command** in the task pane (or simply press the **Del key**). Pause for a moment to be sure you want to delete this file, then click **Yes** when asked to confirm the deletion as shown in Figure 9d.

■ The XPData file is permanently deleted from drive A. (Items deleted from a floppy disk or network drive are not sent to the Recycle bin, and cannot be recovered.)

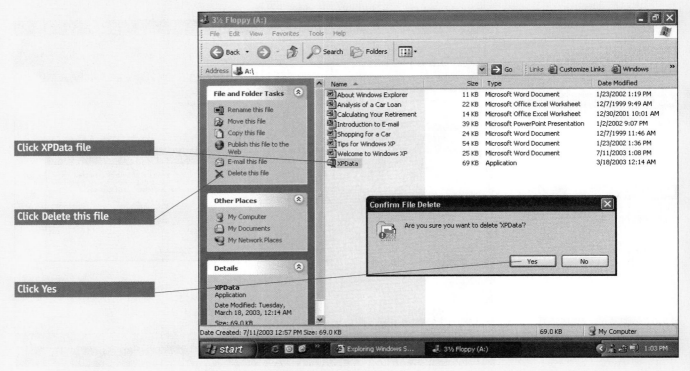

(d) Delete the Compressed File (step 4)

FIGURE 9 Hands-on Exercise 2 (*continued*)

SORT BY NAME, DATE, FILE TYPE, OR SIZE

The files in a folder can be displayed in ascending or descending sequence, by name, date modified, file type, or size, by clicking the appropriate column heading. Click Size, for example, to display files in the order of their size. Click the column heading a second time to reverse the sequence; that is, to switch from ascending to descending, and vice versa. Click a different column heading to display the files in a different sequence.

Step 5: **Modify a Document**

■ Double click the **Welcome to Windows XP** document from within My Computer to open the document as shown in Figure 9e. (The document will open in the WordPad accessory if Microsoft Word is not installed on your machine.)

■ Maximize the window for Microsoft Word. Read the document, and then press **Ctrl+End** to move to the end of the document. Do not be concerned if your screen does not match ours exactly.

■ Add the sentence shown in Figure 9e, press the **Enter key** twice, then type your name. Click the **Save button** on the Standard toolbar to save the document.

■ Pull down the **File menu**, click the **Print command**, and click **OK** (or click the **Print button** on the Standard toolbar) to print the document and prove to your instructor that you did the exercise.

■ Pull down the **File menu** and click **Exit** to close Microsoft Word. You should be back in the My Computer folder.

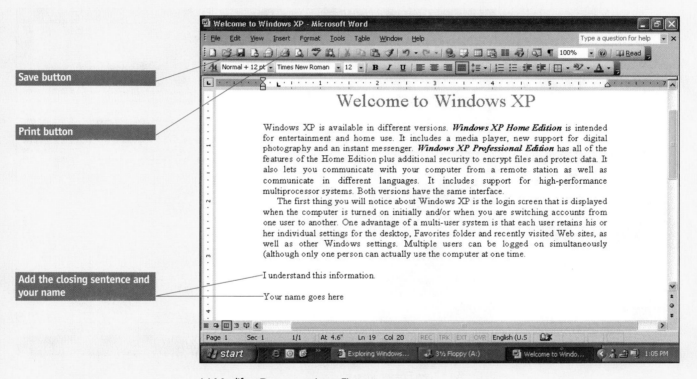

(e) Modify a Document (step 5)

FIGURE 9 Hands-on Exercise 2 (*continued*)

THE DOCUMENT, NOT THE APPLICATION

The Windows operating system is document oriented, which means that you are able to think in terms of the document rather than the application that created it. You can still open a document in traditional fashion, by starting the application that created the document, then using the File Open command in that program to retrieve the document. It's often easier, however, to open the document from within a folder by double clicking its icon. Windows will start the associated application and then open the document for you.

Step 6: Create a New Folder

- Look closely at the date and time that are displayed next to the Welcome to Windows XP document in Figure 9f. It should show today's date and the current time (give or take a minute) because that is when the document was last modified. Your date will be different from ours.

- Look closely and see that Figure 9f also contains an eighth document, called "Backup of Welcome to Windows XP." This is a backup copy of the original document that will be created automatically by Microsoft Word if the appropriate options are in effect. (See the boxed tip below.)

- Click **a blank area** in the right pane to deselect the Welcome to Windows XP document. The commands in the File and Folder Tasks area change to basic folder operations.

- Click the command to **Make a New folder**, which creates a new folder with the default name "New Folder". Enter **New Car** as the new name. You will move files into this folder in step 7.

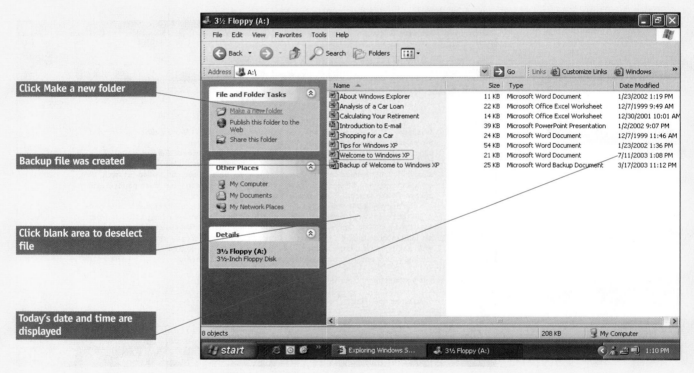

Click Make a new folder

Backup file was created

Click blank area to deselect file

Today's date and time are displayed

(f) Create a New Folder (step 6)

FIGURE 9   Hands-on Exercise 2 (*continued*)

USE WORD TO CREATE A BACKUP COPY

Microsoft Word enables you to automatically keep the previous version of a document as a backup copy. The next time you are in Microsoft Word, pull down the Tools menu, click the Options command, click the Save tab, then check the box to Always create backup copy. Every time you save a file from this point on, the previously saved version is renamed "Backup of document," and the document in memory is saved as the current version. The disk will contain the two most recent versions of the document, enabling you to retrieve the previous version if necessary.

Step 7: Move the Files

- There are different ways to move a file from one folder to another. The most basic technique is to
  - ❑ Select (click) the **Analysis of a Car Loan** workbook to highlight the file, then click the **Move this file command** in the task pane.
  - ❑ You will see the Move Items dialog box in Figure 9g. Click the plus sign (if it appears) next to the 3½ floppy disk to expand the disk and view its folders. Click the **New Car folder**, then click the **Move button**.
  - ❑ The selected file is moved to the New Car folder and the dialog box closes. The Analysis of a Car Loan document no longer appears in the right pane of Figure 9g because it has been moved to a new folder.

- If the source and destination folders are both on the same drive, as in this example, you can simply click and drag the file to its new destination. Thus, click and drag the **Shopping for a Car** Word document to the New Car folder. Release the mouse when the file is directly over the folder to complete the move.

- Double click the **New Car folder** to view the contents of this folder, which should contain both documents. The Address bar now says A:\New Car.

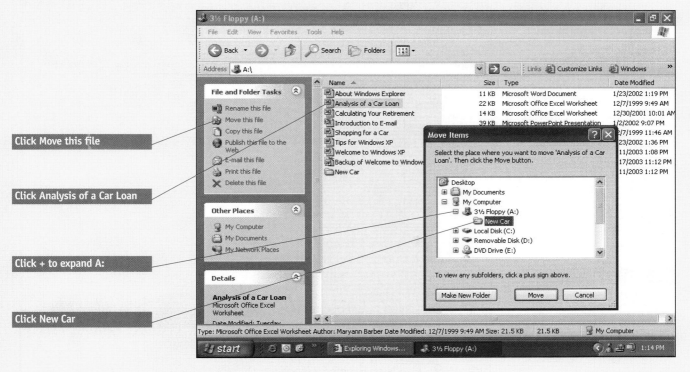

Click Move this file

Click Analysis of a Car Loan

Click + to expand A:

Click New Car

(g) Move the Files (step 7)

FIGURE 9   Hands-on Exercise 2 (*continued*)

THE PLUS AND MINUS SIGNS

Any drive, be it local or on the network, may be expanded or collapsed to display or hide its folders. A minus sign indicates that the drive has been expanded and that its folders are visible. A plus sign indicates the reverse; that is, the device is collapsed and its folders are not visible. Click either sign to toggle to the other. Clicking a plus sign, for example, expands the drive, then displays a minus sign next to the drive to indicate that the folders are visible. Clicking a minus sign has the reverse effect.

Step 8: **A Look Ahead**

■ Click the **Folders button** to display a hierarchical view of the devices on your computer as shown in Figure 9h. This is the same screen that is displayed through Windows Explorer, a program that we will study after the exercise.

■ The Folders button functions as a toggle switch; click the button a second time and the task pane (also called task panel) returns. Click the **Folders button** to return to the hierarchical view.

■ The New Car folder is selected (highlighted) in the left pane because this is the folder you were working in at the previous step. The contents of this folder are displayed in the right pane.

■ Click the icon for the **3½ floppy drive** to display the contents of drive A. The right pane displays the files on drive A as well as the New Car folder.

■ Close the My Computer folder. Close Internet Explorer. Log off if you do not want to continue with the next exercise at this time.

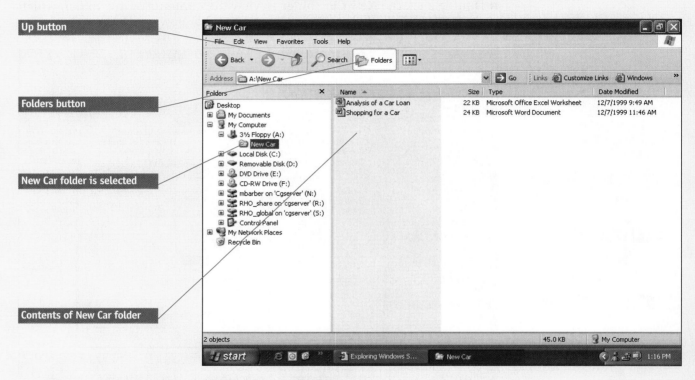

(h) A Look Ahead (step 8)

FIGURE 9 Hands-on Exercise 2 (*continued*)

NAVIGATING THE HIERARCHY

Click the Up button on the Standard Buttons toolbar to move up one level in the hierarchy in the left pane and display the associated contents in the right pane. Click the Up button when you are viewing the New Car folder, for example, and you are returned to drive A. Click the Up button a second time and you will see the contents of My Computer. Note, too, how the contents of the Address bar change each time you view a different folder in the right pane.

WINDOWS EXPLORER

Windows Explorer is a program that displays a hierarchical (tree) structure of the devices on your system. Consider, for example, Figure 10a, which displays the contents of a hypothetical Homework folder as it exists on our computer. The hierarchy is displayed in the left pane, and the contents of the selected object (the Homework folder) are shown in the right pane. The advantage of viewing the folder in this way (as opposed to displaying the task pane) is that you see the location of the folder on the system; that is; the Homework folder is physically stored on drive A.

Let's explore the hierarchy in the left pane. There is a minus sign next to the icon for drive A to indicate that this drive has been expanded and thus you can see its folders. Drive C, however, has a plus sign to indicate that the drive is collapsed and that its contents are not visible. Look closely and you see that both drive A and drive C are indented under My Computer, which in turn is indented under the desktop. In other words, the desktop is at the top of the hierarchy and it contains the My Computer folder, which in turn contains drive A and drive C. The desktop also contains a My Documents folder, but the plus sign next to the My Documents folder indicates the folder is collapsed. My Computer, on the other hand, has a minus sign and you can see its contents, which consist of the drives on your system as well as other special folders (Control Panel and Shared Documents).

Look carefully at the icon next to the Homework folder in the left pane of the figure. The icon is an open folder, and it indicates that the (Homework) folder is the active folder. The folder's name is also shaded, and it appears in the title bar. Only one folder can be active at one time, and its contents are displayed in the right pane. The Milestones in Communications document is highlighted (selected) in the right pane, which means that subsequent commands will affect this document, as opposed to the entire folder. If you wanted to work with a different document in the Homework folder, you would select that document. To see the contents of a different folder, such as Financial Documents, you would select (click) the icon for that folder in the left pane (which automatically closes the Homework folder). The contents of the Financial Documents folder would then appear in the right pane.

You can create folders at any time just like the Homework and Financial Documents folders that we created on drive A. You can also create folders within folders; for example, a correspondence folder may contain two folders of its own, one for business correspondence and one for personal letters.

Personal Folders

Windows automatically creates a set of personal folders for every user. These include the ***My Documents folder*** and the ***My Pictures folder*** and ***My Music folder*** within the My Documents folder. The My Documents folder is collapsed in Figure 10a, but it is expanded in Figure 10b, and thus its contents are visible. The My Music folder is active, and its contents are visible in the right pane.

Every user has a unique set of personal folders, and thus Windows has to differentiate between the multiple "My Documents" folders that may exist. It does so by creating additional folders to hold the documents and settings for each user. Look closely at the Address bar in Figure 10b. Each back slash indicates a new folder, and you can read the complete path from right to left. Thus, the My Music folder that we are viewing is contained in My Documents folder within Maryann's folder, which in turn is stored in a Documents and Settings folder on drive C.

Fortunately, however, Windows does the housekeeping for you. All you have to do is locate the desired folder—for example, My Music or My Pictures—in the left pane, and Windows does the rest. ***Personal folders*** are just what the name implies—"personal," meaning that only one person has access to their content. Windows also provides a ***Shared Documents folder*** for files that Maryann may want to share with others.

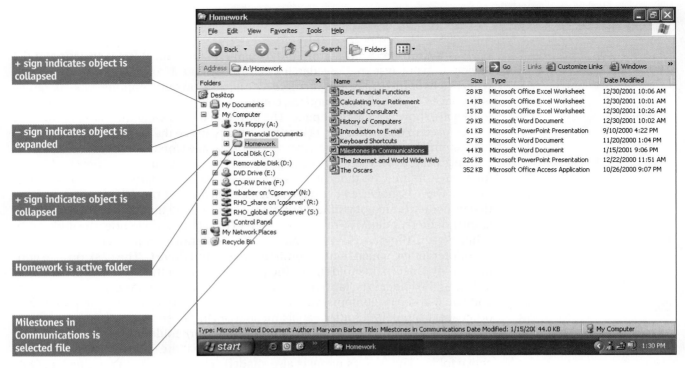

+ sign indicates object is collapsed

– sign indicates object is expanded

+ sign indicates object is collapsed

Homework is active folder

Milestones in Communications is selected file

(a) Homework Folder

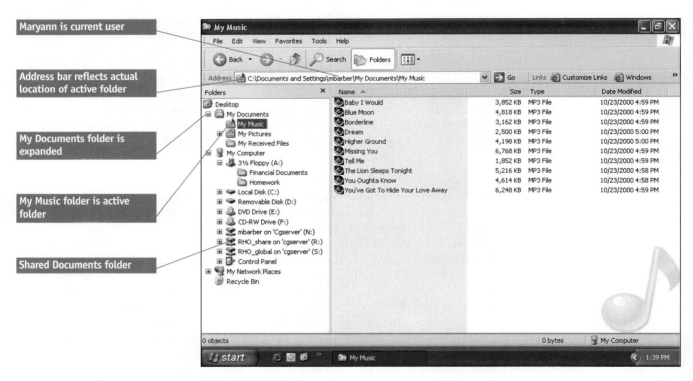

Maryann is current user

Address bar reflects actual location of active folder

My Documents folder is expanded

My Music folder is active folder

Shared Documents folder

(b) My Music Folder

FIGURE 10 Windows Explorer

Moving and Copying a File

The essence of file management is to **move** and **copy a file** or folder from one location to another. This can be done in different ways. The easiest is to click and drag the file icon from the source drive or folder to the destination drive or folder, within Windows Explorer. There is one subtlety, however, in that the result of dragging a file (i.e., whether the file is moved or copied) depends on whether the source and destination are on the same or different drives. Dragging a file from one folder to another folder on the same drive moves the file. Dragging a file to a folder on a different drive copies the file. The same rules apply to dragging a folder, where the folder and every file in it are moved or copied, as per the rules for an individual file.

This process is not as arbitrary as it may seem. Windows assumes that if you drag an object (a file or folder) to a different drive (e.g., from drive C to drive A), you want the object to appear in both places. Hence, the default action when you click and drag an object to a different drive is to copy the object. You can, however, override the default and move the object by pressing and holding the Shift key as you drag.

Windows also assumes that you do not want two copies of an object on the same drive, as that would result in wasted disk space. Thus, the default action when you click and drag an object to a different folder on the same drive is to move the object. You can override the default and copy the object by pressing and holding the Ctrl key as you drag. It's not as complicated as it sounds, and you get a chance to practice in the hands-on exercise, which follows shortly.

Deleting a File

The **Delete command** deletes (erases) a file from a disk. The command can be executed in different ways, most easily by selecting a file, then pressing the Del key. It's also comforting to know that you can usually recover a deleted file, because the file is not (initially) removed from the disk, but moved instead to the Recycle Bin, from where it can be restored to its original location. Unfortunately, files deleted from a floppy disk are not put into the Recycle Bin and hence cannot be recovered.

The **Recycle Bin** is a special folder that contains all files that were previously deleted from any hard disk on your system. Think of the Recycle Bin as similar to the wastebasket in your room. You throw out (delete) a report by tossing it into a wastebasket. The report is gone (deleted) from your desk, but you can still get it back by taking it out of the wastebasket as long as the basket wasn't emptied. The Recycle Bin works the same way. Files are not deleted from the hard disk per se, but moved instead to the Recycle Bin from where they can be restored to their original location. (The protection afforded by the Recycle Bin does not extend to files deleted from a floppy disk.)

Backup

It's not a question of *if* it will happen, but *when*—hard disks die, files are lost, or viruses may infect a system. It has happened to us and it will happen to you, but you can prepare for the inevitable by creating adequate backup *before* the problem occurs. The essence of a **backup strategy** is to decide which files to back up, how often to do the backup, and where to keep the backup.

Our strategy is very simple—back up what you can't afford to lose, do so on a daily basis, and store the backup away from your computer. You need not copy every file, every day. Instead, copy just the files that changed during the current session. Realize, too, that it is much more important to back up your data files than your program files. You can always reinstall the application from the original disks or CD, or if necessary, go to the vendor for another copy of an application. You, however, are the only one who has a copy of the term paper that is due tomorrow. Once you decide on a strategy, follow it, and follow it faithfully!

3 Windows Explorer

Objective	Use Windows Explorer to move, copy, and delete a file; recover a deleted file from the Recycle Bin. Use Figure 11 as a guide.

Step 1: **Create a New Folder**

- Place the floppy disk from the previous exercise into drive A. Click the **Start Button**, click the **All Programs command**, click **Accessories**, then click **Windows Explorer**. Click the **Maximize button**.

- Expand or collapse the various devices on your system so that My Computer is expanded, but all of the devices are collapsed.

- Click (select) **drive A** in the left pane to display the contents of the floppy disk. You should see the New Car folder that was created in the previous exercise.

- Point to a blank area anywhere in the **right pane**, click the **right mouse button**, click the **New command**, then click **Folder** as the type of object to create.

- The icon for a new folder will appear with the name of the folder (New Folder) highlighted. Type **Windows Information** to change the name. Press **Enter**.

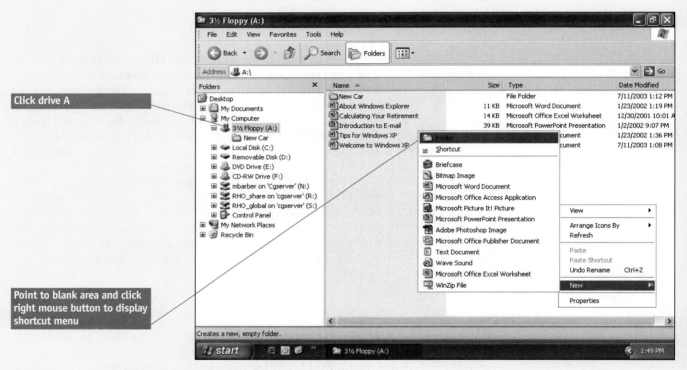

Click drive A

Point to blank area and click right mouse button to display shortcut menu

(a) Create a New Folder (step 1)

FIGURE 11 Hands-on Exercise 3 (*continued*)

THE RENAME COMMAND

Right click the file or a folder whose name you want to change to display a context-sensitive menu, and then click the Rename command. The name of the folder will be highlighted with the insertion point at the end of the name. Enter (or edit) the new (existing) name and press Enter.

Step 2: **Move the Files**

- If necessary, change to the **Details view** and click the **plus sign** next to drive A to expand the drive as shown in Figure 11b. Note the following:
  - ❑ The left pane shows that drive A is selected. The right pane displays the contents of drive A (the selected object in the left pane). The folders are shown first and appear in alphabetical order. If not, press the **F5 (Refresh) key** to refresh the screen.
  - ❑ There is a minus sign next to the icon for drive A in the left pane, indicating that it has been expanded and that its folders are visible. Thus, the folder names also appear under drive A in the left pane.

- Click and drag the **About Windows Explorer** document in the right pane to the **Windows Information folder** in the left pane, to move the file into that folder.

- Click and drag the **Tips for Windows XP** and the **Welcome to Windows XP** documents to move these documents to the **Windows Information folder**.

- Click the **Windows Information folder** in the left pane to select the folder and display its contents in the right pane. You should see the three files that were just moved.

- Click the **Up button** to return to drive A.

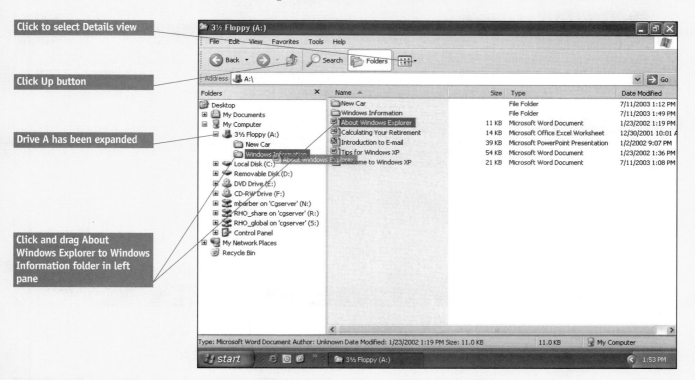

(b) Move the Files (step 2)

FIGURE 11 Hands-on Exercise 3 *(continued)*

SELECT MULTIPLE FILES

Selecting (clicking) one file automatically deselects the previously selected file. You can, however, select multiple files by clicking the first file, then pressing and holding the Ctrl key as you click each additional file. Use the Shift key to select multiple files that are adjacent to one another by clicking the icon of the first file, then pressing and holding the Shift key as you click the icon of the last file.

Step 3: Copy a Folder

- Point to the **Windows Information folder** in the right pane, then **right click and drag** this folder to the **My Documents folder** (on drive C) in the left pane. Release the mouse to display a context-sensitive menu.

- Click the **Copy Here command** as shown in Figure 11c.
  - ❏ You may see a Copy files message box as the individual files within the Windows Information folder are copied to the My Documents folder.
  - ❏ If you see the Confirm Folder Replace dialog box, it means that you (or another student) already copied these files to the My Documents folder. Click the **Yes to All button** so that your files replace the previous versions in the My Documents folder.

- Click the **My Documents folder** in the left pane. Pull down the **View menu** and click the **Refresh command** (or press the **F5 key**) so that the hierarchy shows the newly copied folder. (Please remember to delete the Windows Information folder from drive C at the end of the exercise.)

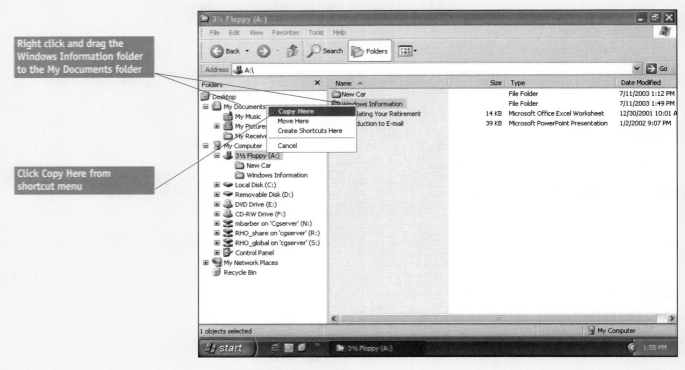

(c) Copy a Folder (step 3)

FIGURE 11   Hands-on Exercise 3 (*continued*)

RIGHT CLICK AND DRAG

The result of dragging a file with the left mouse button depends on whether the source and destination folders are on the same or different drives. Dragging a file to a folder on a different drive copies the file, whereas dragging the file to a folder on the same drive moves the file. If you find this hard to remember, and most people do, click and drag with the right mouse button to display a context-sensitive menu asking whether you want to copy or move the file. This simple tip can save you from making a careless (and potentially serious) error. Use it!

Step 4: Modify a Document

- Click the **Windows Information folder** within the My Documents folder to make it the active folder and to display its contents in the right pane. Change to the **Details view**.

- Double click the **About Windows Explorer** document to start Word and open the document. Do not be concerned if the size and/or position of the Microsoft Word window are different from ours. Read the document.

- If necessary, click inside the document window, then press **Ctrl+End** to move to the end of the document. Add the text shown in Figure 11d.

- Pull down the **File menu** and click **Save** to save the modified file (or click the **Save button** on the Standard toolbar). Pull down the **File menu** and click **Exit** to exit from Microsoft Word.

- Pull down the **View menu** and click the **Refresh command** (or press the **F5 key**) to update the contents of the right pane. The date and time associated with the About Windows Explorer document (on drive C) have been changed to indicate that the file has been modified.

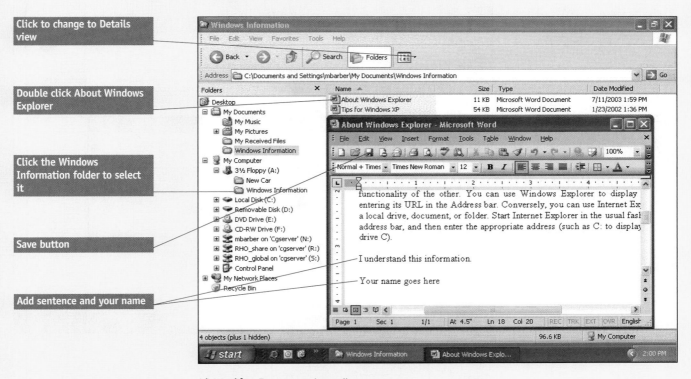

(d) Modify a Document (step 4)

FIGURE 11 Hands-on Exercise 3 (*continued*)

KEYBOARD SHORTCUTS

Most people begin with the mouse, but add keyboard shortcuts as they become more proficient. Ctrl+B, Ctrl+I, and Ctrl+U are shortcuts to boldface, italicize, and underline, respectively. Ctrl+X (the X is supposed to remind you of a pair of scissors), Ctrl+C, and Ctrl+V correspond to Cut, Copy, and Paste, respectively. Ctrl+Home and Ctrl+End move to the beginning or end of a document. These shortcuts are not unique to Microsoft Word, but are recognized in virtually every Windows application.

Step 5: Copy (Back up) a File

■ Verify that the **Windows Information folder** (on drive C) is the active folder, as denoted by the open folder icon. Click and drag the icon for the **About Windows Explorer** document from the right pane to the **Windows Information folder** on **drive A** in the left pane.

■ You will see the message in Figure 11e, indicating that the folder (on drive A) already contains a file called About Windows Explorer and asking whether you want to replace the existing file.

■ Click **Yes** because you want to replace the previous version of the file on drive A with the updated version from the My Documents folder.

■ You have just backed up a file by copying the About Windows Explorer document from a folder on drive C to the disk in drive A. In other words, you can use the floppy disk to restore the file to drive C should anything happen to it.

■ Keep the floppy disk in a safe place, away from the computer.

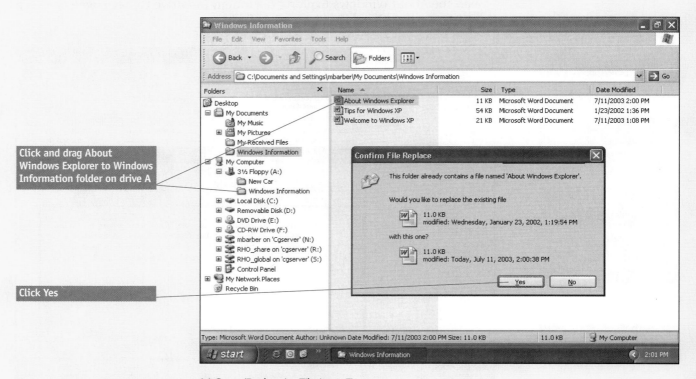

(e) Copy (Back up) a File (step 5)

FIGURE 11   Hands-on Exercise 3 (*continued*)

THE MY DOCUMENTS FOLDER

The My Documents folder is created by default with the installation of Windows XP. There is no requirement that you store your documents in this folder, but it is convenient, especially for beginners who may lack the confidence to create their own folders. The My Documents folder is also helpful in a laboratory environment where the network administrator may prevent you from modifying the desktop and/or from creating your own folders on drive C, in which case you will have to use the My Documents folder.

Step 6: **Delete a Folder**

- Select (click) **Windows Information folder** within the My Documents folder in the left pane. Pull down the **File menu** and click **Delete** (or press the **Del key**).

- You will see the dialog box in Figure 11f, asking whether you are sure you want to delete the folder and send its contents to the Recycle Bin, which enables you to restore the folder at a later date.

- Click **Yes** to delete the folder. The folder disappears from drive C. Note that you have deleted the folder and its contents.

- Now pretend that you do not want to delete the folder. Pull down the **Edit menu**. Click **Undo Delete**.

- The deletion is cancelled and the Windows Information folder reappears in the left pane. If you do not see the folder, pull down the **View menu** and click the **Refresh command** (or press the **F5 key**).

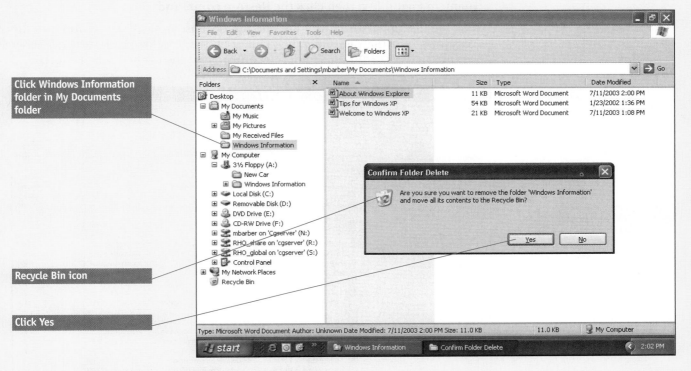

Click Windows Information folder in My Documents folder

Recycle Bin icon

Click Yes

(f) Delete a Folder (step 6)

FIGURE 11   Hands-on Exercise 3 (*continued*)

CUSTOMIZE WINDOWS EXPLORER

Increase or decrease the size of the left pane within Windows Explorer by dragging the vertical line separating the left and right panes in the appropriate direction. You can also drag the right border of the various column headings (Name, Size, Type, and Modified) in the right pane to increase or decrease the width of the column and see more or less information in that column. And best of all, you can click any column heading to display the contents of the selected folder in sequence by that column. Click the heading a second time and the sequence changes from ascending to descending and vice versa.

Step 7: **The Recycle Bin**

- If necessary, select the **Windows Information folder** within the My Documents folder in the left pane. Select (click) the **About Windows Explorer** file in the right pane. Press the **Del key**, then click **Yes** when asked to delete the file.

- Click the **down arrow** in the vertical scroll bar in the left pane until you can click the icon for the **Recycle Bin**.

- The Recycle Bin contains all files that have been previously deleted from the local (hard) disks, and hence you will see a different number of files than those displayed in Figure 11g.

- Change to the **Details view**. Pull down the **View menu**, click (or point to) **Arrange Icons by**, then click **Date Deleted** to display the files in this sequence. Execute this command a second time (if necessary) so that the most recently deleted file appears at the top of the window.

- Right click the **About Windows Explorer** file to display the context-sensitive menu in Figure 11g, then click the **Restore command**.

- The file disappears from the Recycle bin because it has been returned to the Windows Information folder. You can open the Windows Information folder within the My Documents folder to confirm that the file has been restored.

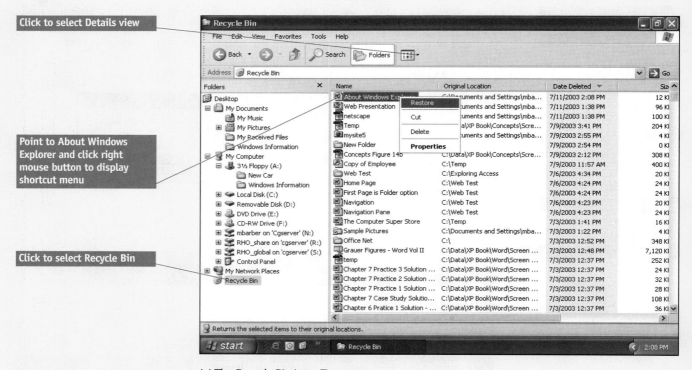

Click to select Details view

Point to About Windows Explorer and click right mouse button to display shortcut menu

Click to select Recycle Bin

(g) The Recycle Bin (step 7)

FIGURE 11 Hands-on Exercise 3 (*continued*)

TWO WAYS TO RECOVER A FILE

The Undo command is present in Windows Explorer. Thus, you do not need to resort to the Recycle Bin to recover a deleted file provided you execute the Undo command immediately (within a few commands) after the Delete command was issued. Some operations cannot be undone (in which case the Undo command will be dimmed), but Undo is always worth a try.

Step 8: **The Group By Command**

- Select (click) the **Windows Information folder** on drive A. You should see the contents of this folder (three Word documents) in the right pane.

- Pull down the **View menu**, (click or) point to the **Arrange Icons by command**, then click the **Show in Groups command** from the cascaded menu.

- You see the same three files as previously, but they are displayed in groups according to the first letter in the filename. Click the **Date Modified** column, and the files are grouped according to the date they were last modified.

- The Show in Groups command functions as a toggle switch. Execute the command and the files are displayed in groups; execute the command a second time and the groups disappear.

- Select (click) the icon for **drive A** in the left pane to display the contents of drive A. You should see two folders and two files. Pull down the **View menu**, (click or) point to the **Arrange Icons by command**, and then click the **Show in Groups command** from the cascaded menu.

- Change to the **Details view**. Click the **Type column** to group the objects by folder and file type.

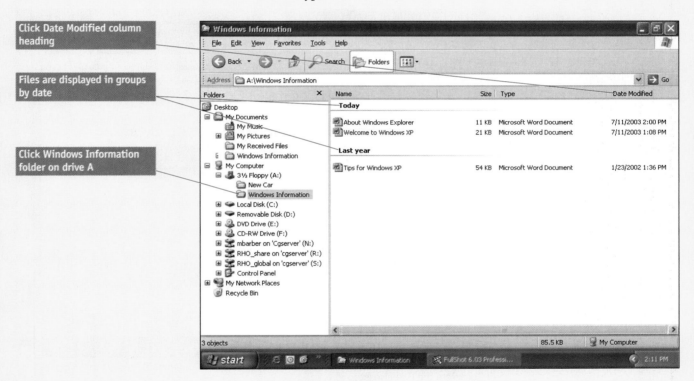

(h) The Group By Command (step 8)

FIGURE 11 Hands-on Exercise 3 (*continued*)

KEEP THE VIEW

Once you set the desired view in a folder, you may want to display every other folder according to those parameters. Pull down the Tools menu, click the Folder Options command, and click the View tab. Click the button to Apply to All folders, then click Yes when prompted to confirm. Click OK to close the Folder Options dialog box. The next time you open another folder, it will appear in the same view as the current folder.

Step 9: Complete the Exercise

■ Prove to your instructor that you have completed the exercise correctly by capturing the screen on your monitor. Press the **Print Screen key**. Nothing appears to have happened, but the screen has been copied to the clipboard.

■ Click the **Start button**, click the **All Programs command**, then start Microsoft Word and begin a new document. Enter the title of your document, followed by your name as shown in Figure 11i. Press the **Enter key** two or three times.

■ Pull down the **Edit menu** and click the **Paste command** (or click the **Paste button** on the Standard toolbar) to copy the contents of the clipboard into the Word document.

■ Print this document for your instructor. There is no need to save this document. Exit Word.

■ Delete the **Windows Information folder** from the My Documents folder as a courtesy to the next student. Close Windows Explorer.

■ Log off if you do not want to continue the next exercise at this time. (Click the **Start button**, click **Log Off**, then click **Log Off** a second time to end your session.)

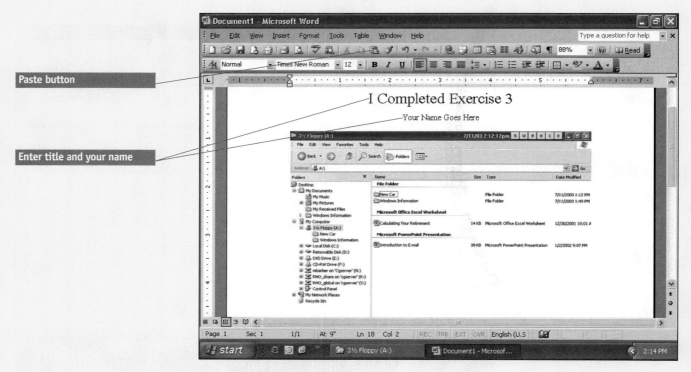

Paste button

Enter title and your name

(i) Complete the Exercise (step 9)

FIGURE 11 Hands-on Exercise 3 (*continued*)

SWITCHING USERS VERSUS LOGGING OFF

Windows XP gives you the choice of switching users or logging off. Switching users leaves all of your applications open, but it relinquishes control of the computer to another user. This lets you subsequently log back on (after the new user logs off) and take up exactly where you were. Logging off, on the other hand, closes all of your applications and ends the session, but it leaves the computer running at full power and available for someone else to log on.

You have learned the basic concepts of disk and file management, but there is so much more. Windows XP has something for everyone. It is easy and intuitive for the novice, but it also contains sophisticated tools for the more knowledgeable user. This section describes three powerful features to increase your productivity. Some or all of these features may be disabled in a school environment, but the information will stand you in good stead on your own computer.

The Control Panel

The *Control Panel* affects every aspect of your system. It determines the appearance of your desktop, and it controls the performance of your hardware. You can, for example, change the way your mouse behaves by switching the function of the left and right mouse buttons and/or by replacing the standard mouse pointers with animated icons that move across the screen. You will not have access to the Control Panel in a lab environment, but you will need it at home whenever you install new hardware or software. You should be careful about making changes, and you should understand the nature of the new settings before you accept any of the changes.

The Control Panel in Windows XP organizes its tools by category as shown in Figure 12. Point to any category and you see a Screen Tip that describes the specific tasks within that category. The Appearance and Themes category, for example, lets you select a screen saver or customize the Start menu and taskbar. You can also switch to the Classic view that displays every tool in a single screen, which is consistent with all previous versions of Windows.

The task pane provides access to the *Windows Update* function, which connects you to a Web site where you can download new device drivers and other updates to Windows XP. You can also configure your system to install these updates automatically as they become available. Some updates, especially those having to do with Internet security, are absolutely critical.

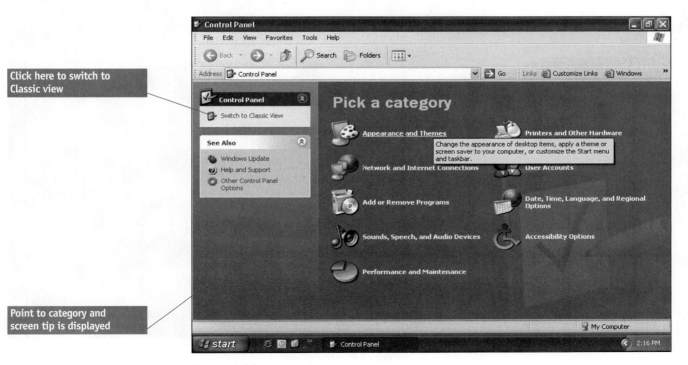

FIGURE 12 The Control Panel

Shortcuts

A ***shortcut*** is a link to any object on your computer, such as a program, file, folder, disk drive, or Web page. Shortcuts can appear anywhere, but are most often placed on the desktop or on the Start menu. The desktop in Figure 13 contains a variety of shortcuts, each of which contains a jump arrow to indicate a shortcut icon. Double click the shortcut to Election of Officers, for example, and you start Word and open this document. In similar fashion, you can double click the shortcut for a Web page (Exploring Windows Series), folder, or disk drive (drive A) to open the object and display its contents.

Creating a shortcut is a two-step process. First, you use Windows Explorer to locate the object such as a file, folder, or disk drive. Then you select the object, use the right mouse button to drag the object to the desktop, and then click the Create Shortcut command from the context-sensitive menu. A shortcut icon will appear on the desktop with the phrase "shortcut to" as part of the name. You can create as many shortcuts as you like, and you can place them anywhere on the desktop or in individual folders. You can also right click a shortcut icon after it has been created to change its name. Deleting the icon deletes the shortcut and not the object.

Windows XP also provides a set of predefined shortcuts through a series of desktop icons that are shown at the left border of the desktop in Figure 13. Double click the My Computer icon, for example, and you open the My Computer folder. These desktop icons were displayed by default in earlier versions of Windows, but not in Windows XP. They were added through the Control Panel as you will see in our next exercise.

Additional shortcuts are found in the ***Quick Launch toolbar*** that appears to the right of the Start button. Click any icon and you open the indicated program. And finally, Windows XP will automatically add to the Start menu shortcuts to your most frequently used programs. Desktop shortcuts are a powerful technique that will increase your productivity by taking you directly to a specified document or other object.

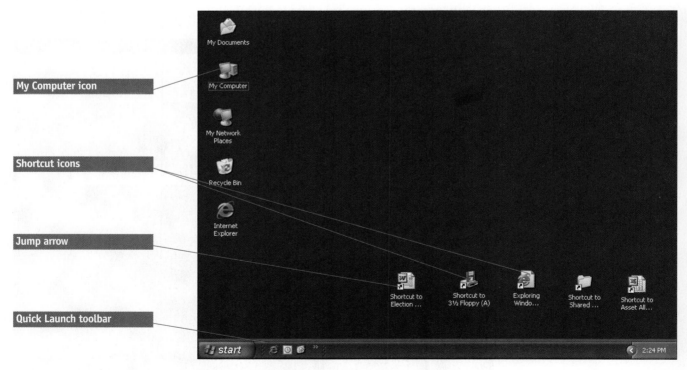

FIGURE 13 Desktop with Shortcuts

The Search Companion

Sooner or later you will create a file, and then forget where (in which folder) you saved it. Or you may create a document and forget its name, but remember a key word or phrase in the document. Or you may want to locate all files of a certain file type—for example, all of the sound files on your system. The **Search Companion** can help you to solve each of these problems and is illustrated in Figure 14.

The Search Companion is accessed from within any folder by clicking the Search button on the Standard Buttons toolbar to open the search pane at the left of the folder. You are presented with an initial search menu (not shown in Figure 14) that asks what you want to search for. You can search your local machine for media files (pictures, music, or video), documents (such as spreadsheets or Word documents), or any file or folder. You can also search the Help and Support Center or the Internet.

Once you choose the type of information, you are presented with a secondary search pane as shown in Figure 14. You can search according to a variety of criteria, each of which will help to narrow the search. In this example we are looking for any document on drive C that has "Windows" as part of its filename and further, contains the name "Maryann" somewhere within the document. The search is case sensitive. This example illustrates two important capabilities, namely that you can search on the document name (or part of its name) and/or its content.

Additional criteria can be entered by expanding the chevrons for date and size. You can, for example, restrict your search to all documents that were modified within the last week, the past month, or the last year. You can also restrict your search to documents of a certain size. Click the Search button after all of the criteria have been specified to initiate the search. The results of the search (the documents that satisfy the search criteria) are displayed in the right pane. You can refine the search if it is unsuccessful and/or you can open any document in which you are interested. The Search Companion also has an indexing service to make subsequent searches faster.

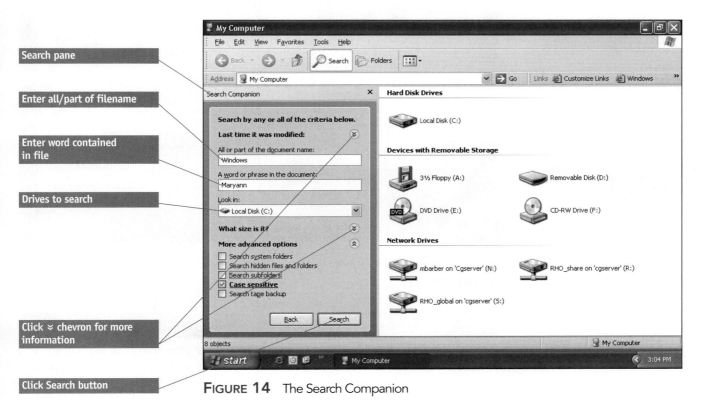

FIGURE 14 The Search Companion

Increasing Productivity

Objective   To create and use shortcuts; to locate documents using the Search Companion; to customize your system using the Control Panel; to obtain a passport account. The exercise requires an Internet connection. Use Figure 15 as a guide.

Step 1:   **Display the Desktop Icons**

■ Log on to Windows XP. Point to a blank area on the desktop, click the **right mouse button** to display a context-sensitive menu, then click the **Properties command** to open the Display Properties dialog box in Figure 15a.

■ Click the **Desktop tab** and then click the **Customize Desktop button** to display the Desktop Items dialog box.

■ Check the boxes to display all four desktop icons. Click **OK** to accept these settings and close the dialog box, then click **OK** a second time to close the Display Properties dialog box.

■ The desktop icons should appear on the left side of your desktop. Double click any icon to execute the indicated program or open the associated folder.

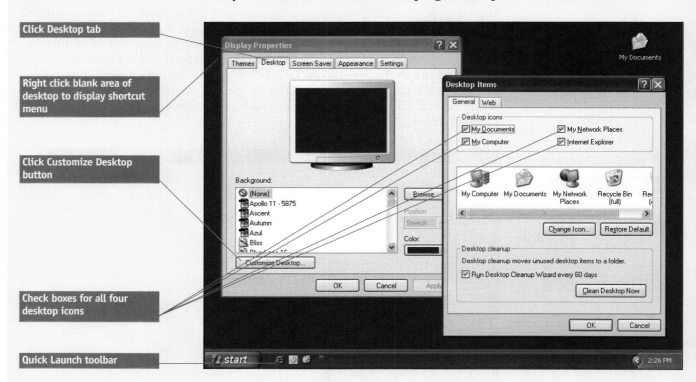

Click Desktop tab

Right click blank area of desktop to display shortcut menu

Click Customize Desktop button

Check boxes for all four desktop icons

Quick Launch toolbar

(a) Display the Desktop Icons (step 1)

FIGURE 15   Hands-on Exercise 4

THE QUICK LAUNCH TOOLBAR

The Quick Launch toolbar is a customizable toolbar that executes a program or displays the desktop with a single click. Right click a blank area of the taskbar, point to (or click) the Toolbars command, then check the Quick Launch toolbar to toggle its display on or off.

Step 2: Create a Web Shortcut

- Start Internet Explorer. You can double click the newly created icon at the left of the desktop, or you can single click its icon in the Quick Launch toolbar. Click the **Restore button** so that Internet Explorer is not maximized, that is, so that you can see a portion of the desktop.

- Click in the Address bar and enter the address **www.microsoft.com/ windowsxp** to display the home page of Windows XP. Now that you see the page, you can create a shortcut to that page.

- Click the **Internet Explorer icon** in the Address bar to select the entire address, point to the Internet Explorer icon, then click and drag the icon to the desktop (you will see a jump arrow as you drag the text). Release the mouse to create the shortcut in Figure 15b.

- Prove to yourself that the shortcut works. Close Internet Explorer, and then double click the shortcut you created. Internet Explorer will open, and you should see the desired Web page. Close (or minimize) Internet Explorer since you do not need it for the remainder of the exercise.

(b) Create a Web Shortcut (step 2)

FIGURE 15   Hands-on Exercise 4 (*continued*)

WORKING WITH SHORTCUTS

You can work with a shortcut icon just as you can with any other icon. To move a shortcut, drag its icon to a different location on the desktop. To rename a shortcut, right click its icon, click the Rename command, type the new name, then press the enter key. To delete a shortcut, right click its icon, click the Delete command, and click Yes in response to the confirming prompt. Deleting a shortcut deletes just the shortcut and not the object to which the shortcut refers.

Step 3:   Create Additional Shortcuts

■ Double click the **My Computer icon** to open this folder. Place the floppy disk from hands-on exercise 3 into the floppy drive. Double click the icon for **drive A** to display the contents of the floppy disk as shown in Figure 15c.

■ The contents of the Address bar have changed to A:\ to indicate the contents of the floppy disk. You should see two folders and two files.

■ Move and size the window so that you see a portion of the desktop. Right click and drag the icon for the **Windows Information folder** to the desktop, then release the mouse. Click the **Create Shortcuts Here command** to create the shortcut.

■ Look for the jump arrow to be sure you have created a shortcut (as opposed to moving or copying the folder). If you made a mistake, right click a blank area of the desktop, then click the **Undo command** to reverse the unintended move or copy operation.

■ Right click and drag the icon for the **PowerPoint presentation** to the desktop, release the mouse, and then click the **Create Shortcuts Here command**.

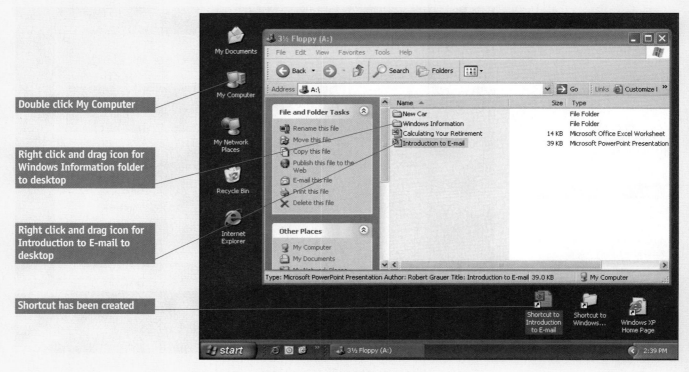

(c) Create Additional Shortcuts (step 3)

FIGURE 15   Hands-on Exercise 4 (*continued*)

THE ARRANGE ICONS COMMAND

The most basic way to arrange the icons on your desktop is to click and drag an icon from one place to another. It may be convenient, however, to have Windows arrange the icons for you. Right click a blank area of the desktop, click (or point to) the Arrange Icons by command, then click Auto Arrange. All existing shortcuts, as well as any new shortcuts, will be automatically aligned along the left edge of the desktop. Execute the Auto Arrange command a second time to cancel the command, and enable yourself to manually arrange the icons.

Step 4: **Search for a Document**

■ Maximize the My Computer window. Click the **Search button** on the Standard Buttons toolbar to display the Search pane. The button functions as a toggle switch. Click the button and the Search pane appears. Click the button a second time and the task pane replaces the Search Companion.

■ The initial screen (not shown in Figure 15d) in the Search Companion asks what you are searching for. Click **Documents (word processing, spreadsheet, etc.)**.

■ You may be prompted to enter when the document was last modified. Click the option button that says **Don't Remember**, then click **Use advanced search options**. You should see the screen in Figure 15d.

■ Enter the indicated search criteria. You do not know the document name and thus you leave this text box blank. The other criteria indicate that you are looking for any document that contains "interest rate" that is located on drive A, or in any subfolder on drive A.

■ Click the **Search button** to initiate the search. You will see a Search dialog box to indicate the progress of the search, after which you will see the relevant documents.

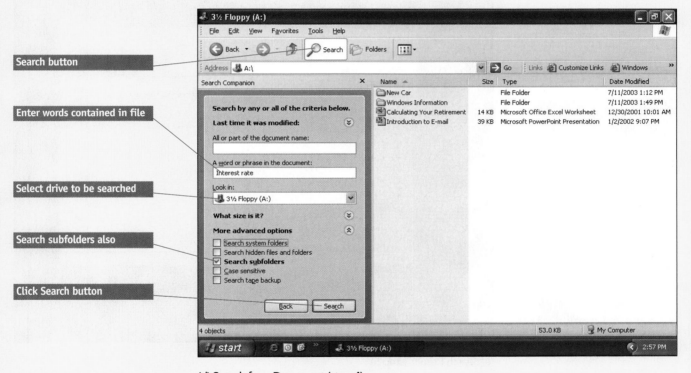

(d) Search for a Document (step 4)

FIGURE 15   Hands-on Exercise 4 (*continued*)

YOU DON'T NEED THE COMPLETE FILENAME

You can enter only a portion of the filename, and the Search Companion will still find the file(s). If, for example, you're searching for the file "Marketing Homework," you can enter the first several letters such as "Marketing" and Windows will return all files whose name begins with the letters you've entered—for example, "Marketing Homework" and "Marketing Term Paper."

Step 5: Search Results

- The search should return two files that satisfy the search criteria as shown in Figure 15e. Click the **Views button** and select **Tiles view** if you want to match our figure. If you do not see the same files, it is for one of two reasons:
  - ❏ You did not specify the correct search criteria. Click the **Back button** and reenter the search parameters as described in step 4. Repeat the search.
  - ❏ Your floppy disk is different from ours. Be sure to use the floppy disk as it existed at the end of the previous hands-on exercise.

- Click the **Restore button** so that you again see a portion of the desktop. Right click and drag the **Calculating Your Retirement** workbook to the desktop to create a shortcut on the desktop.

- Close the Search Results window, close the My Documents window, then double click the newly created shortcut to open the workbook.

- Retirement is a long way off, but you may want to experiment with our worksheet. It is never too early to start saving.

- Exit Excel when you are finished.

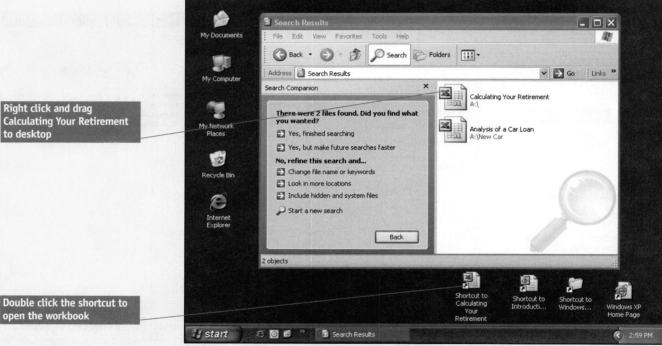

(e) Search Results (step 5)

FIGURE 15 Hands-on Exercise 4 (*continued*)

SHORTCUT WIZARD

Shortcuts can be created in many ways, including the use of a wizard. Right click a blank area of the desktop, click (or point) to the New command, then choose Shortcut to start the wizard. Enter the Web address in the indicated text box (or click the Browse button to locate a local file). Click Next, then enter the name for the shortcut as it is to appear on the desktop. Click the Finish button to exit the wizard. The new shortcut should appear on the desktop.

Step 6: **Open the Control Panel Folder**

- Click the **Start button**, then click **Control Panel** to open the Control Panel folder. Click the command to **Switch to Classic View** that appears in the task pane to display the individual icons as shown in Figure 15f. Maximize the window.

- Double click the **Taskbar and Start Menu icon** to display the associated dialog box. Click the **Taskbar tab**, then check the box to **Auto-hide the taskbar.** Your other settings should match those in Figure 15f. Click **OK** to accept the settings and close the dialog box.

- The taskbar (temporarily) disappears from your desktop. Now point to the bottom edge of the desktop, and the taskbar reappears. The advantage of hiding the taskbar in this way is that you have the maximum amount of room in which to work; that is, you see the taskbar only when you want to.

- Double click the **Fonts folder** to open this folder and display the fonts that are installed on your computer. Change to the **Details view**.

- Double click the icon of any font other than the standard fonts (Arial, Times New Roman, and Courier New) to open a new window that displays the font. Click the **Print button**. Close the Font window.

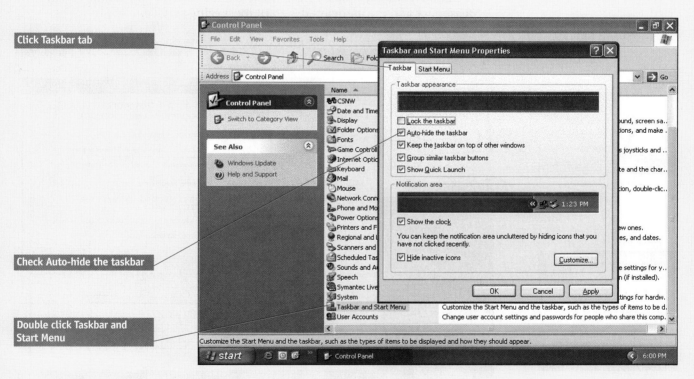

(f) Open the Control Panel Folder (step 6)

FIGURE 15 Hands-on Exercise 4 (*continued*)

MODIFY THE START MENU

Click and drag a shortcut icon to the Start button to place the shortcut on the Start menu. It does not appear that anything has happened, but the shortcut will appear at the top of the Start menu. Click the Start button to display the Start menu, then press the Esc key to exit the menu without executing a command. You can delete any item from the menu by right clicking the item and clicking the Unpin from the Start menu command.

Step 7: Obtain a .NET Passport

- Click the **Back button** to return to the Control Panel, then double click the **User Accounts icon** in the Control Panel folder. Maximize the User Accounts window so that it takes the entire desktop.

- Click the icon corresponding to the account that is currently logged to display a screen similar to Figure 15g. Click the command to **Set up my account to use a .NET passport**. You will see the first step in the Passport Wizard.

- Click the link to **View the privacy statement**. This starts Internet Explorer and goes to the .NET Passport site on the Web. Print the privacy agreement. It runs nine pages, but it contains a lot of useful information.

- Close Internet Explorer after you have printed the agreement. You are back in the Passport Wizard. Click **Next** to continue.

- Follow the instructions on the next several screens. You will be asked to enter your e-mail address and to supply a password. Click **Finish** when you have reached the last screen.

- You will receive an e-mail message after you have registered successfully. You will need your passport in our next exercise when we explore Windows Messenger and the associated instant messaging service.

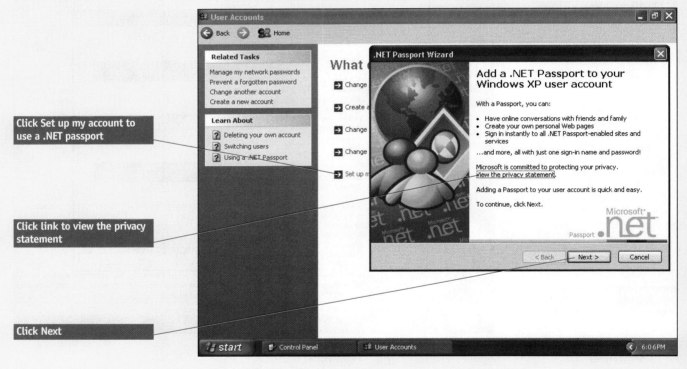

(g) Obtain a .NET Passport (step 7)

FIGURE 15 Hands-on Exercise 4 *(continued)*

UPDATING YOUR PASSPORT

You can modify the information in your passport profile at any time. Open the Control Panel, click User Accounts, select your account, then click the command to Change Your .NET passport. You can change your password, change the question that will remind you about your password should you forget it, and/or change the information that you authorize the passport service to share with others.

Step 8: **Windows Update**

- Close the User Accounts window to return to the Control Panel folder. Click the link to **Windows Update** to display a screen similar to Figure 15h.

- Click the command to **Scan for updates**. (This command is not visible in our figure.) This command will take several seconds as Windows determines which (if any) updates it recommends. Our system indicates that there are no critical updates but that additional updates are available.

- Click the link(s) to review the available updates. You do not have to install the vast majority of available updates. It is essential, however, that you install any updates deemed critical. One critical update appeared shortly after the release of Windows XP and closed a hole in the operating system that enabled hackers to break into some XP machines.

- Click the link to **View installation history** to see which updates were previously installed. Print this page for your instructor.

- Close the Update window. Log off the computer if you do not want to continue with the next exercise at this time.

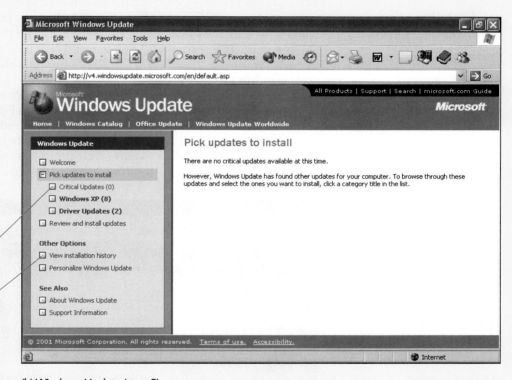

(h) Windows Update (step 8)

FIGURE 15   Hands-on Exercise 4 (*continued*)

THE SHOW DESKTOP BUTTON

The Show Desktop button or command minimizes every open window and returns you immediately to the desktop. You can get to this command in different ways, most easily by clicking the Show Desktop icon on the Quick Launch toolbar. The button functions as a toggle switch. Click it once and all windows are minimized. Click it a second time and the open windows are restored to their position on the desktop.

The "XP" in Windows XP is for the experience that Microsoft promises individuals who adopt its operating system. Windows XP makes it easy to enjoy music and video, work with *digital photographs*, and chat with your friends. This section describes these capabilities and then moves to a hands-on exercise in which you practice at the computer. All of the features are available on your own machine, but some may be disabled in a laboratory setting. It's not that your professor does not want you to have fun, but listening to music or engaging in instant messaging with your friends is not practical in a school environment. Nevertheless, the hands-on exercise that follows enables you to practice your skills in disk and file management as you work with multiple files and folders.

Windows Media Player

The *Windows Media Player* combines the functions of a radio, a CD, or DVD player, and an information database into a single program. It lets you listen to radio stations anywhere in the world, play a CD, or watch a DVD movie (provided you have the necessary hardware). You can copy selections from a CD to your computer, organize your music by artist and album, and then create a customized *playlist* to play the music in a specified order. The playlist may include as many songs from as many albums as you like and is limited only by the size of your storage device. The Media Player will also search the Web for audio or video files and play clips from a favorite movie.

The buttons at the left of the Media Player enable you to switch from one function to the next. The Radio Tuner button is active in Figure 16, and the BBC station is selected. Think of that—you are able to listen to radio stations from around the world with the click of a button. The Media Guide button connects you to the home page of the Windows Media Web site, where you can search the Web for media files and/or play movie clips from your favorite movies.

FIGURE 16 Windows Media Player

Digital Photography

Windows XP helps you to organize your pictures and share them with others. The best place to store photographs is in the My Pictures folder or in a subfolder within this folder as shown in Figure 17. The complete path to the folder appears in the Address bar and is best read from right to left. Thus, you are looking at pictures in the Romance Folder, which is in the My Pictures folder, which in turn is stored in a My Documents folder. Remember that each user has his or her unique My Documents folder, so the path must be further qualified. Hence, you are looking at the My Documents folder, within a folder for Jessica (one of several users), within the Documents and Settings folder on drive C. The latter folder maintains the settings for all of the users that are registered on this system.

The pictures in Figure 17 are shown in the *Thumbnails view*, which displays a miniature image of each picture in the right pane. (Other views are also available and are accessed from the View menu or Views button.) The Picture Tasks area in the upper right lists the functions that are unique to photographs. You can view the pictures as a slide show, which is the equivalent of a PowerPoint presentation without having to create the presentation. You can print any picture, use it as the background on your desktop, or copy multiple pictures to a CD, provided you have the necessary hardware. You can also order prints online. You choose the company; select print sizes and quantities, supply the billing and shipping information, and your photographs are sent to you.

One photo is selected (BenWendy) in Figure 17, and the associated details are shown in the Details area of the task pane. The picture is stored as a JPG file, a common format for photographs. It was created on January 21, 2002.

The File and Folder Tasks area is collapsed in our figure, but you can expand the area to gain access to the normal file operations (move, copy, and delete). You can also e-mail the photograph from this panel. Remember, too, that you can click the Folders button on the Standard Buttons toolbar to switch to the hierarchical view of your system, which is better suited to disk and file management.

FIGURE 17 Working with Pictures

Windows Messenger

Windows Messenger is an instant messaging system in which you chat with friends and colleagues over the Internet. (It is based on the same technology as the "buddies list" that was made popular by America Online.) You need an Internet connection, a list of contacts, and a **Microsoft passport** that is based on your e-mail address. The passport is a free Microsoft service that enables you to access any passport-enabled Internet site with a single user name and associated password. (Step 7 in the previous hands-on exercise described how to obtain a passport.)

You can initiate a conversation at any time by monitoring the contacts list to see who is online and starting a chat session. Up to four people can participate in the same conversation. It is easy, fun, and addictive. You know the instant someone signs on, and you can begin chatting immediately. The bad news, however, is that it is all too easy to chat incessantly when you have real work to do. Hence you may want to change your status to indicate that you are busy and unable to participate in a conversation.

Figure 18 displays a conversation between Maryann and Bob. The session began when Maryann viewed her contact list, noticed that Bob was online, and started a conversation. Each person enters his or her message at the bottom of the conversation window, and then clicks the Send button. Additional messages can be sent without waiting for a response. Emoticons can be added to any message for effect. Note, too, the references to the file transfer that appear within the conversation, which are the result of Maryann clicking the command to send a file or photo, then attaching the desired file.

Windows Messenger is more than just a vehicle for chatting. If you have speakers and a microphone, you can place phone calls from your computer without paying a long distance charge. The most intriguing feature, however, is the ability to ask for remote assistance, whereby you can invite one of your contacts to view your desktop as you are working in order to ask for help. It is as if your friend were in the room looking over your shoulder. He or she will see everything that you do and can respond immediately with suggestions.

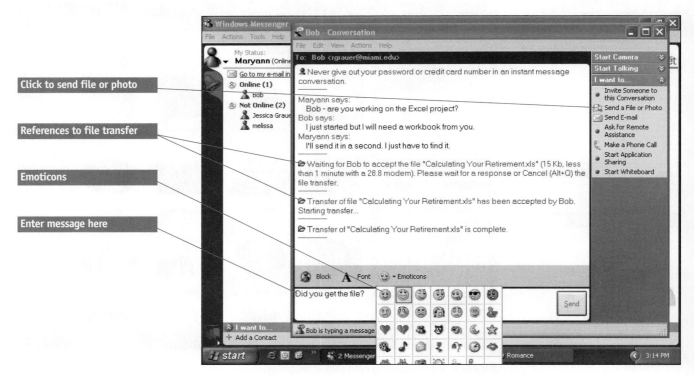

FIGURE 18 Windows Messenger

5 Fun with Windows XP

Objective To use Windows Media Player, work with photographs, and experiment with Windows Messenger. Check with your professor regarding the availability of the resources required for this exercise. Use Figure 19.

Step 1: **Open the Shared Music Folder**

- Start Windows Explorer. Click the **Folders button** to display the tree structure. You need to locate some music to demonstrate the Media Player.

- The typical XP installation includes some files within the Shared Documents folder. Expand the My Computer folder to show the **Shared Documents folder**, expand the **Shared Music folder**, and then open the **Sample Music folder** as shown in Figure 19a.

- Point to any file (it does not matter if you have a different selection of music) to display the ScreenTip describing the music. Double click the file to start the Media Player and play the selected music.

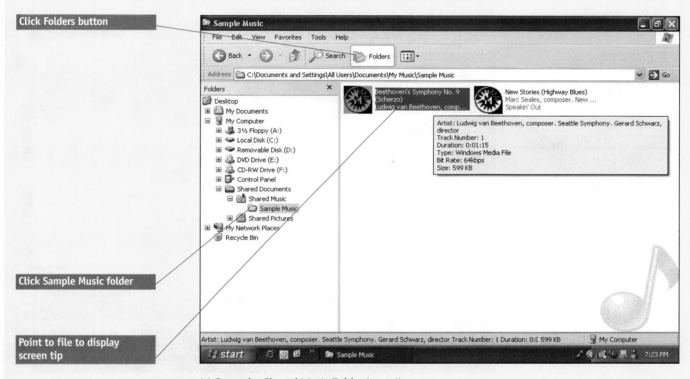

(a) Open the Shared Music Folder (step 1)

FIGURE 19 Hands-on Exercise 5

SHARED FOLDERS VERSUS PERSONAL FOLDERS

Windows XP automatically creates a unique My Documents folder for every user, which in turn contains a unique My Pictures folder and My Music folder within the My Documents folder. These folders are private and cannot be accessed by other users. Windows also provides a Shared Documents folder that is accessible to every user on a system.

Step 2: **Listen to the Music**

- You should hear the music when the Windows Media Player opens in its own window as shown in Figure 19b. The controls at the bottom of the window are similar to those on any CD player.
  - ❏ You can click the **Pause button**, then click the **Play button** to restart the music at that point.
  - ❏ You can click the **Stop button** to stop playing altogether.
  - ❏ You can also drag the slider to begin playing at a different place.

- You can also adjust the volume as shown in Figure 19b. Double click the **Volume Control icon** in the notification area at the right of the taskbar to display the Volume Control dialog box. Close this window.

- Click the **Radio Tuner button** at the side of the Media Player window. The system pauses as it tunes into the available radio stations.

- Select a radio station (e.g., **BBC World**) when you see the list of available stations, then click the **Play button** after you choose a station.

- You will see a message at the bottom of the window indicating that your computer is connecting to the media, after which you will hear the radio station.

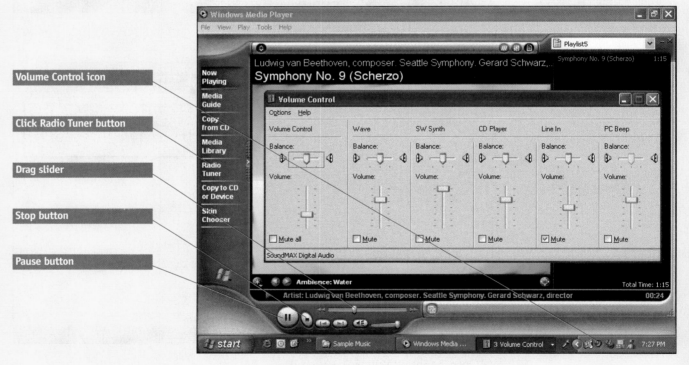

(b) Listen to the Music (step 2)

FIGURE 19 Hands-on Exercise 5 (*continued*)

OTHER MEDIA PLAYERS

If you double click a music (MP3) file, and a program other than Windows Media starts to play, it is because your system has another media player as its default program. You can still use the Windows Media Player, but you will have to start the program explicitly from the Start menu. Once the Media Player is open, pull down the File menu and click the Open command, then select the music file you want to play.

Step 3: Create a Playlist

- Click the **Media Library button** at the side of the Media player to display the media files that are currently on your computer.
  - ❏ The left pane displays a tree structure of your media library. Thus, you click the plus or minus sign to collapse or expand the indicated folder.
  - ❏ The right pane displays the contents of the selected object (the My Music playlist) in Figure 19c.
- Do not be concerned if your media library is different from ours. Click the **New playlist button**, enter **My Music** as the name of the new list, and click **OK**.
- Click the newly created playlist in the left pane to display its contents in the left pane. The playlist is currently empty.
- Start **Windows Explorer**. Open the **My Music Folder** within the My Documents folder. If necessary, click the **Restore button** to move and size Windows Explorer so that you can copy documents to the Media library.
- Click and drag one or more selections from the My Music folder to the right pane of the Media library to create the playlist. Close Windows Explorer.
- Click the **down arrow** in the list box at the upper right of the Media Gallery and select the My Music playlist to play the songs you have selected.

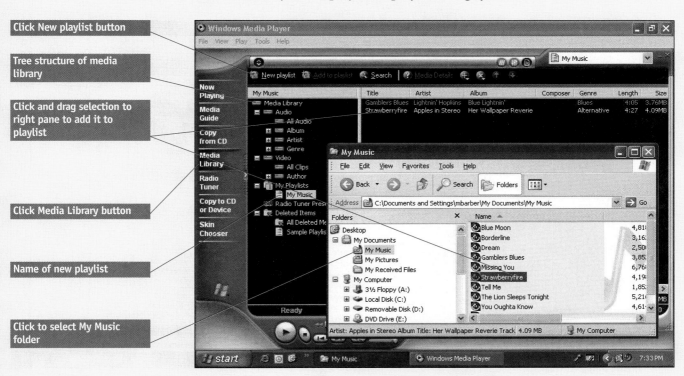

Click New playlist button

Tree structure of media library

Click and drag selection to right pane to add it to playlist

Click Media Library button

Name of new playlist

Click to select My Music folder

(c) Create a Playlist (step 3)

FIGURE 19   Hands-on Exercise 5 (continued)

THE MEDIA GUIDE

Click the Media Guide button at the left of the Media Player to display the home page of the Windows Media Site. You can also get there by starting Internet Explorer and entering windowsmedia.com in the Address bar. Either way, you will be connected to the Internet and can search the Web for media files and/or play clips from your favorite movie.

Step 4: **Create a Pictures Folder**

- You can use your own pictures, or if you don't have any, you can use the sample pictures provided with Windows XP. Start (or maximize) Windows Explorer. Open the **My Pictures folder** within the **My Documents folder**.

- Do not be concerned if the content of your folder is different from ours. Our folder already contains various subfolders with different types of pictures in each folder.

- Click the **Views button** and change to the **Thumbnails view**. This view is especially useful when viewing folders that contain photographs because (up to four) images are displayed on the folder icon.

- Right click anywhere in the right pane to display a context-sensitive menu as shown in Figure 19d. Click **New**, and then click **Folder** as the type of object to create.

- The icon for a new folder will appear with the name of the folder (New Folder) highlighted. Enter a more appropriate name (we chose **Romance** because our pictures are those of a happy couple), and press **Enter**.

- Copy your pictures from another folder, a CD, or floppy disk to the newly created folder.

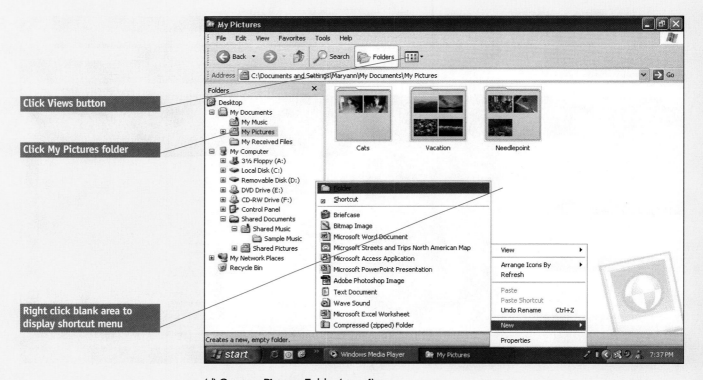

(d) Create a Pictures Folder (step 4)

FIGURE 19 Hands-on Exercise 5 (continued)

DESIGN GALLERY LIVE

The Microsoft Design Gallery is an excellent source of photographs and other media. Start Internet Explorer and go to the Design Gallery at dgl.microsoft.com. Enter the desired topic in the Search for text box, indicate that you want to search everywhere, and specify that the results should be photos. Download one or more of the photos that are returned by the search and use those pictures to complete this exercise.

Step 5: **Display Your Pictures**

- Double click the newly created folder to display its contents. Click the **Folders button** to display the Windows Explorer task pane, as opposed to the hierarchy structure. Click the **Views button** and change to the **Filmstrip view** as shown in Figure 19e.

- Click the **Next Image** or (**Previous Image**) **button** to move from one picture to the next within the folder. If necessary, click the buttons to rotate pictures clockwise or counterclockwise so that the pictures are displayed properly within the window.

- Click the command to **View as a slide show**, then display your pictures one at a time on your monitor. This is a very easy way to enjoy your photographs. Press the **Esc key** to stop.

- Choose any picture, then click the command to **Print this picture** that appears in the left pane. Submit this picture to your instructor.

- Choose a different picture and then click the command to **Set as desktop background**. Minimize Windows Explorer.

(e) Display Your Pictures (step 5)

FIGURE 19   Hands-on Exercise 5 (*continued*)

CHANGE THE VIEW

Click the down arrow next to the Views button on the Standard toolbar to change the way files are displayed within a folder. The Details view provides the most information and includes the filename, file type, file size, and the date that the file was created or last modified. (Additional attributes are also possible.) Other views are more visual. The Thumbnails view displays a miniature image of the file and is best used with clip art, photographs, or presentations. The Filmstrip view is used with photographs only.

Step 6:   Customize the Desktop

- Your desktop should once again be visible, depending on which (if any) applications are open. If you do not see the desktop, right click a blank area of the taskbar, then click the **Show Desktop command**.

- You should see the picture you selected earlier as the background for your desktop. The picture is attractive (you chose it), but it may be distracting.

- To remove the picture, **right click** the background of the desktop and click the **Properties command** to display the Display Properties dialog box in Figure 19f.

- Click the **Desktop tab**, then click **None** in the Background list box. Click **OK** to accept this setting and close the dialog box. The picture disappears.

- Regardless of whether you keep the background, you can use your pictures as a screen saver. Redisplay the Display Properties dialog box. Click the **Screen Saver tab** in the Display Properties box, then choose **My Picture Slideshow** from the screen saver list box.

- Wait a few seconds and the picture within the dialog box will change, just as it will on your desktop. Click **OK** to accept the screen saver and close the Display Properties dialog box.

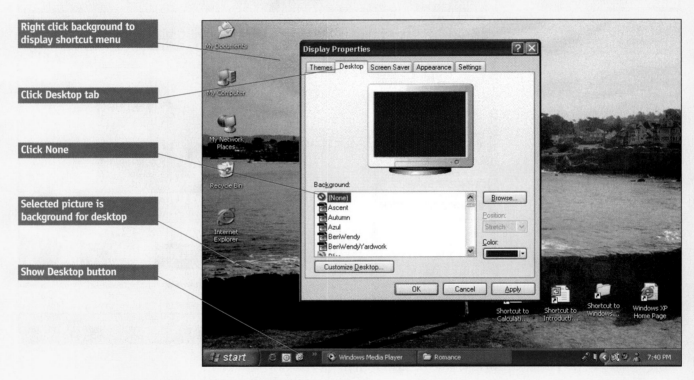

(f) Customize the Desktop (step 6)

FIGURE 19   Hands-on Exercise 5 *(continued)*

CHANGE THE RESOLUTION

The resolution of a monitor refers to the number of pixels (picture elements or dots) that are displayed at one time. The higher the resolution, the more pixels are displayed, and hence you see more of a document at one time. You can change the resolution at any time. Right click the desktop, click the Properties command to show the Display Properties dialog box, then click the Settings tab. Drag the slider bar to the new resolution, then click OK.

Step 7: **Start Windows Messenger**

- You need a passport to use Windows Messenger. Double click the **Windows Messenger icon** in the notification area of the taskbar to sign in.

- Maximize the Messenger window. You will see a list of your existing contacts with an indication of whether they are online.

- Add one or more contacts. Pull down the **Tools menu**, click the command to **Add a Contact**, then follow the onscreen instructions. (The contact does not have to have Windows XP to use instant messaging.)

- Double click any contact that is online to initiate a conversation and open a conversation window as shown in Figure 19g.

- Type a message at the bottom of the conversation window, then click the **Send button** to send the message. The text of your message will appear immediately on your contact's screen. Your friend's messages will appear on your screen.

- Continue the conversation by entering additional text. You can press the **Enter key** (instead of clicking the **Send button**) to send the message. You can also use **Shift + enter** to create a line break in your text.

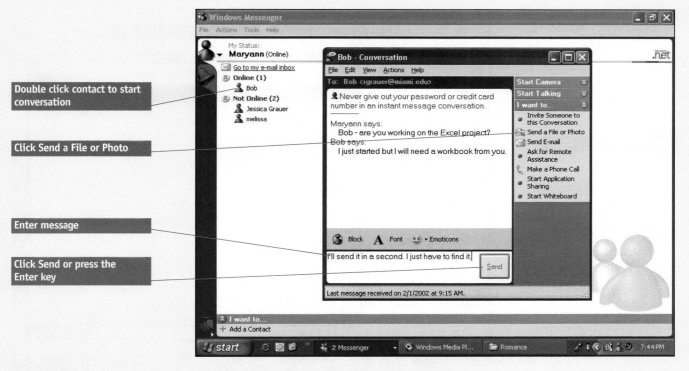

(g) Start Windows Messenger (step 7)

FIGURE 19 Hands-on Exercise 5 *(continued)*

CHANGE YOUR STATUS

Anyone on your contact list knows immediately when you log on; thus, the larger your contact list, the more likely you are to be engaged in idle chitchat when you have real work to do. You can avoid unwanted conversations without being rude by changing your status. Click the down arrow next to your name in the Messenger window and choose a different icon. You can appear offline or simply indicate that you are busy. Either way you will be more likely to get your work done.

Step 8: Attach a File

- Click the command to **Send a File or Photo**, which displays the Send a File dialog box in Figure 19h. It does not matter which file you choose, since the purpose of this step is to demonstrate the file transfer capability.

- A series of three file transfer messages will appear on your screen. Windows Messenger waits for your friend to accept the file transfer, then it indicates the transfer has begun, and finally, that the transfer was successful.

- Click the command to **Invite someone to this conversation** if you have another contact online. You will see a second dialog box in which you select the contact.

- There are now three people in the conversation. (Up to four people can participate in one conversation.) Your friends' responses will appear on your screen as soon as they are entered.

- Send your goodbye to end the conversation, then close the conversation window to end the chat session. You are still online and can participate in future conversations.

- Close Windows Messenger. You will be notified if anyone wants to contact you.

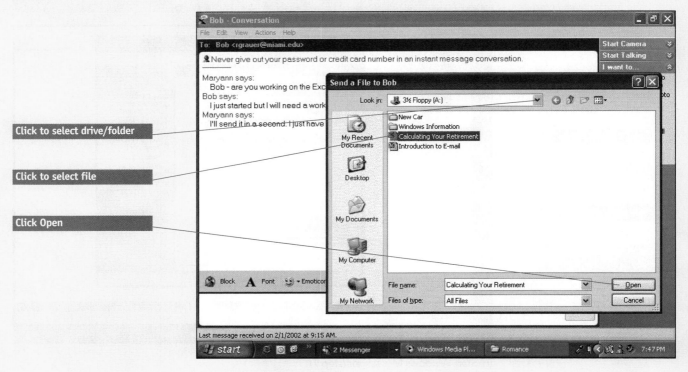

(h) Attach a File (step 8)

FIGURE 19 Hands-on Exercise 5 *(continued)*

E-MAIL VERSUS INSTANT MESSAGING

E-mail and instant messaging are both Internet communication services, but there are significant differences. E-mail does not require both participants to be online at the same time. E-mail messages are also permanent and do not disappear when you exit your e-mail program. Instant messaging, however, requires both participants to be online. Its conversations are not permanent and disappear when you end the session.

Step 9: **Ask for Assistance**

- Your contacts do not require Windows XP to converse with you using Windows Messenger. Windows XP is required, however, to use the remote assistance feature.

- Click the **Start button**, then click the **Help and Support command** to display the home page of the Help and Support Center. Click the **Support button**, then click the command to **Ask a friend to help**.

- A Remote Assistance screen will open in the right pane. Click the command to **Invite someone to help**, which will display your contact list as shown in Figure 19i. You can choose any contact who is online, or you can enter the e-mail address of someone else.

- You will see a dialog box indicating that an invitation has been sent. Once your friend accepts the invitation, he or she will be able to see your screen. A chat window will open up in which you can discuss the problem you are having. Close the session when you are finished.

- Pull down the **File menu** and click the command to **Sign out**. The Windows Messenger icon in the notification will indicate that you have signed out.

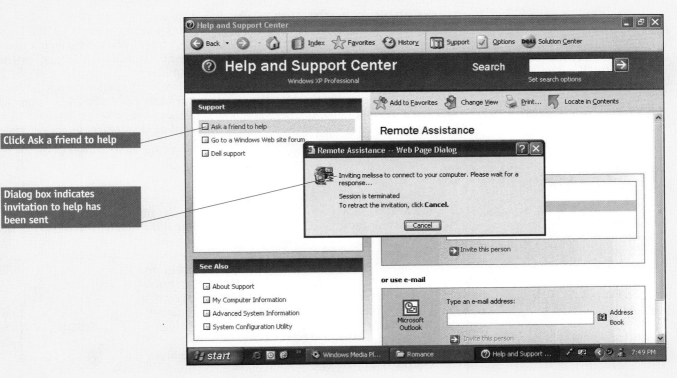

(i) Ask for Assistance (step 9)

FIGURE 19 Hands-on Exercise 5 *(continued)*

SUPPORT ONLINE

Microsoft provides extensive online support in a variety of formats. Start at the Windows XP home page (www.microsoft.com/windowsxp), then click the Support button to see what is available. You will be able to search the Microsoft Knowledge Base for detailed information on virtually any subject. You can also post questions and participate in threaded discussions in various newsgroups. Support is available for every Microsoft product.

SUMMARY

Windows XP is the newest and most powerful version of the Windows operating system. It has a slightly different look than earlier versions, but it maintains the conventions of its predecessors. All Windows operations take place on the desktop. Every window contains the same basic elements, which include a title bar, a Minimize button, a Maximize or Restore button, and a Close button. All windows may be moved and sized. The taskbar contains a button for each open program and enables you to switch back and forth between those programs by clicking the appropriate button. You can obtain information about every aspect of Windows through the Help and Support Center.

A file is a set of data or set of instructions that has been given a name and stored on disk. There are two basic types of files, program files and data files. A program file is an executable file, whereas a data file can be used only in conjunction with a specific program. Every file has a filename and a file type.

Files are stored in folders to better organize the hundreds (or thousands) of files on a disk. A folder may contain program files, data files, and/or other folders. Windows automatically creates a set of personal folders for every user. These include the My Documents folder and the My Pictures folder and My Music folder within the My Documents folder. Windows also provides a Shared Documents folder that can be accessed by every user. The My Computer folder is accessible by all users and displays the devices on a system.

Windows Explorer facilitates every aspect of disk and file management. It presents a hierarchical view of your system that displays all devices and, optionally, the folders on each device. Any device may be expanded or collapsed to display or hide its folders.

Windows XP contains several tools to help you enjoy your system. The Windows Media Player combines the functions of a radio, CD player, DVD player, and an information database into a single program. Windows Messenger is an instant messaging system in which you chat with friends and colleagues over the Internet.

The Control Panel affects every aspect of your system. It determines the appearance of your desktop and it controls the performance of your hardware. A shortcut is a link to any object on your computer, such as a program, file, folder, disk drive, or Web page. The Search Companion enables you to search for a file according to several different criteria.

KEY TERMS

MULTIPLE CHOICE

1. Which of the following is true regarding a dialog box?

   (a) Option buttons indicate mutually exclusive choices

   (b) Check boxes imply that multiple options may be selected

   (c) Both (a) and (b)

   (d) Neither (a) nor (b)

2. Which of the following is the first step in sizing a window?

   (a) Point to the title bar

   (b) Pull down the View menu to display the toolbar

   (c) Point to any corner or border

   (d) Pull down the View menu and change to large icons

3. Which of the following is the first step in moving a window?

   (a) Point to the title bar

   (b) Pull down the View menu to display the toolbar

   (c) Point to any corner or border

   (d) Pull down the View menu and change to large icons

4. Which button appears immediately after a window has been maximized?

   (a) The Close button

   (b) The Minimize button

   (c) The Maximize button

   (d) The Restore button

5. What happens to a window that has been minimized?

   (a) The window is still visible but it no longer has a Minimize button

   (b) The window shrinks to a button on the taskbar

   (c) The window is closed and the application is removed from memory

   (d) The window is still open but the application has been removed from memory

6. What is the significance of a faded (dimmed) command in a pull-down menu?

   (a) The command is not currently accessible

   (b) A dialog box appears if the command is selected

   (c) A Help window appears if the command is selected

   (d) There are no equivalent keystrokes for the particular command

7. The Recycle Bin enables you to restore a file that was deleted from

   (a) Drive A

   (b) Drive C

   (c) Both (a) and (b)

   (d) Neither (a) nor (b)

8. Which of the following was suggested as essential to a backup strategy?

   (a) Back up all program files at the end of every session

   (b) Store backup files at another location

   (c) Both (a) and (b)

   (d) Neither (a) nor (b)

9. A shortcut may be created for

   (a) An application or a document

   (b) A folder or a drive

   (c) Both (a) and (b)

   (d) Neither (a) nor (b)

10. What happens if you click the Folders button (on the Standard Buttons toolbar in the My Computer folder) twice in a row?

    (a) The left pane displays a task pane with commands for the selected object

    (b) The left pane displays a hierarchical view of the devices on your system

    (c) The left pane displays either a task pane or the hierarchical view depending on what was displayed prior to clicking the button initially

    (d) The left pane displays both the task pane and a hierarchical view

... continued

11. The Search Companion can

   (a) Locate all files containing a specified phrase

   (b) Restrict its search to a specified set of folders

   (c) Both (a) and (b)

   (d) Neither (a) nor (b)

12. Which views display miniature images of photographs within a folder?

   (a) Tiles view and Icons view

   (b) Thumbnails view and Filmstrip view

   (c) Details view and List view

   (d) All views display a miniature image

13. Which of the following statements is true?

   (a) A plus sign next to a folder indicates that its contents are hidden

   (b) A minus sign next to a folder indicates that its contents are hidden

   (c) A plus sign appears next to any folder that has been expanded

   (d) A minus sign appears next to any folder that has been collapsed

14. Ben and Jessica are both registered users on a Windows XP computer. Which of the following is a *false statement* regarding their personal folders?

   (a) Ben and Jessica each have a My Documents folder

   (b) Ben and Jessica each have a My Pictures folder that is stored within their respective My Documents folders

   (c) Ben can access files in Jessica's My Documents folder

   (d) Jessica cannot access files in Ben's My Documents folder

15. When is a file permanently deleted?

   (a) When you delete the file from Windows Explorer

   (b) When you empty the Recycle Bin

   (c) When you turn the computer off

   (d) All of the above

16. What happens if you (left) click and drag a file to another folder on the same drive?

   (a) The file is copied

   (b) The file is moved

   (c) The file is deleted

   (d) A shortcut menu is displayed

17. How do you shut down the computer?

   (a) Click the Start button, then click the Turn Off Computer command

   (b) Right click the Start button, then click the Turn Off Computer command

   (c) Click the End button, then click the Turn Off Computer command

   (d) Right click the End button, then click the Turn Off Computer command

18. Which of the following can be accomplished with Windows Messenger?

   (a) You can chat with up to three other people in the conversation window

   (b) You can place telephone calls (if you have a microphone and speaker) without paying long-distance charges

   (c) You can ask for remote assistance, which enables your contact to view your screen as you are working

   (d) All of the above

ANSWERS

1. c	**7.** b	**13.** a
2. c	**8.** b	**14.** c
3. a	**9.** c	**15.** b
4. d	**10.** c	**16.** b
5. b	**11.** c	**17.** a
6. a	**12.** b	**18.** d

PRACTICE WITH WINDOWS XP

1. **Two Different Views:** The document in Figure 20 is an effective way to show your instructor that you understand the My Computer folder, the various views available, the task pane, and the hierarchy structure. It also demonstrates that you can capture a screen for inclusion in a Word document. Proceed as follows:

   a. Open the My Computer folder, click the Views button, and switch to the Tiles view. Click the Folders button to display the task pane. Size the window as necessary so that you will be able to fit two folders onto a one-page document as shown in Figure 20.

   b. Press and hold the Alt key as you press the Print Screen key to copy the My Computer window to the Windows clipboard. (The Print Screen key captures the entire screen. Using the Alt key, however, copies just the current window.) Click the Start menu, click Programs, and then click Microsoft Word to start the program. Maximize the window.

   c. Enter the title of the document, press Enter, and type your name. Press the Enter key twice in a row to leave a blank line.

   d. Pull down the Edit menu. Click the Paste command to copy the contents of the clipboard to the document. Press the Enter key to add a figure caption, then press the Enter key two additional times.

   e. Click the taskbar to return to the My Computer folder. Change to the Details view. Click the Folders button to display the hierarchy structure, as opposed to the task pane. Expand My Computer in the left pane, but collapse all of the individual devices. Press Alt+Print Screen to capture the My Computer folder in this configuration.

   f. Click the taskbar to return to your Word document. Press Ctrl+V to paste the contents of the clipboard into your document. Enter an appropriate caption below the figure. Save the completed document and print it for your instructor.

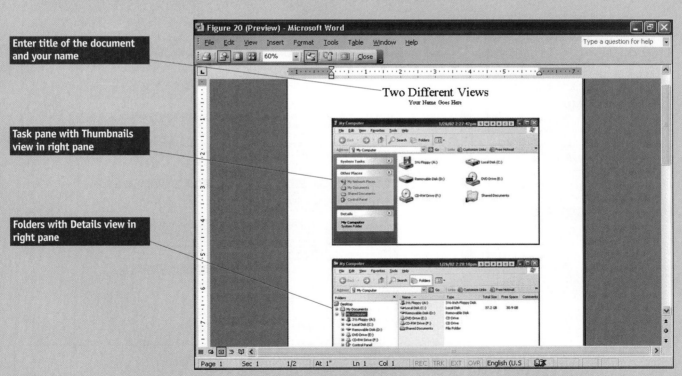

FIGURE 20 Two Different Views (exercise 1)

2. **Network Connections:** The document in Figure 21 displays the network connections on our system as well as the status of one of those connections. Your assignment is to create the equivalent document for your computer. Proceed as follows:

   a. Open the Control Panel, switch to the Classic view, then double click the Network Connections icon to display the Network Connections folder. (You can also get to this folder from My Computer, by clicking the link to My Network Places, and then clicking Network Connections from within the Network Tasks area.)

   b. Maximize the Network Connections folder so that it takes the entire desktop. Change to the Tiles view. Click the Folders button to display the task pane. Select (click) a connection, then click the link to View status of the connection, to display the associated dialog box.

   c. Press the Print Screen key to print this screen. Start Microsoft Word and open a new document. Press the Enter key several times, then click the Paste button to copy the contents of the clipboard into your document.

   d. Press Ctrl+Home to return to the beginning of the Word document, where you can enter the title of the document and your name. Compose a paragraph similar to the one in our figure that describes the network connections on your computer. Print this document for your instructor.

   e. Experiment with the first two network tasks that are displayed in the task pane. How difficult is it to set up a new connection? How do you set a firewall to protect your system from unauthorized access when connected to the Internet? How do you establish a home or small office network?

   f. Use the Help and Support Center to obtain additional information. Print one or two Help screens for your instructor.

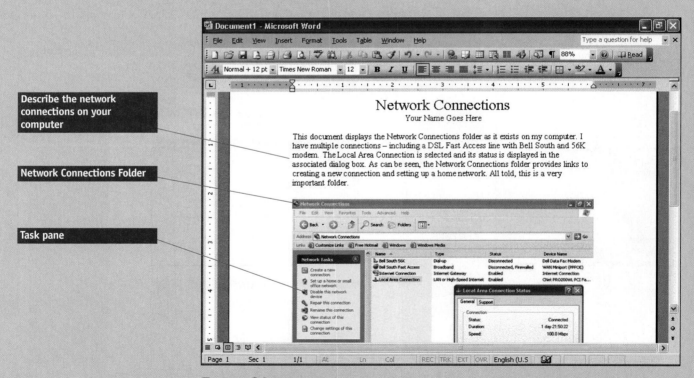

FIGURE 21 Network Connections (exercise 2)

3. **Create Your Own Folders:** Folders are the key to the Windows storage system. Folders can be created at any time and in any way that makes sense to you. The My Courses folder in Figure 22, for example, contains five folders, one folder for each class you are taking. In similar fashion, the Correspondence folder in this figure contains two additional folders according to the type of correspondence. Proceed as follows:

a. Place the floppy disk from hands-on exercise 3 into drive A. Start Windows Explorer. Click the Folders button to display the hierarchy structure in the left pane. Change to the Details view.

b. Create a Correspondence folder on drive A. Create a Business folder and a Personal folder within the Correspondence folder.

c. Create a My Courses folder on drive A. Create a separate folder for each course you are taking within the My Courses folder. The names of your folders will be different from ours.

d. Pull down the View menu, click the Arrange Icons by command, and click the command to Show in Groups. Click the Date Modified column header to group the files and folders by date. The dates you see will be different from the dates in our figure.

e. The Show in Groups command functions as a toggle switch. Execute the command, and the files are displayed in groups; execute the command a second time, and the groups disappear. (You can change the grouping by clicking the desired column heading.)

f. Use the technique described in problems 1 and 2 to capture the screen in Figure 22 and incorporate it into a document. Add a short paragraph that describes the folders you have created, then submit the document to your instructor.

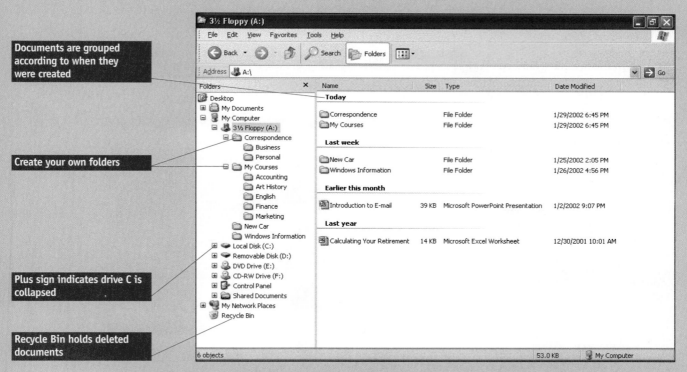

FIGURE 22   Create Your Own Folders (exercise 3)

4. **What's New in Windows XP:** Anyone, whether an experienced user or a computer novice, can benefit from a quick overview of new features in Windows XP. Click the Start button, click Help and Support, and then click the link to What's New in Windows XP. Click the second link in the task pane (taking a tour or tutorial), select the Windows XP tour, and choose the desired format. We chose the animated tour with animation, music, and voice narration.

a. Relax and enjoy the show as shown in Figure 23. The task bar at the bottom of the figure contains three buttons to restart the show, exit, or toggle the music on and off. Exit the tutorial when you are finished. You are back in the Help and Support window, where you can take a tour of the Windows Media Player. Try it. Click the Close button at the upper right of any screen or press Escape to exit the tour. Write a short note to your instructor with comments about either tour.

b. Return to the Help and Support Center and find the topic, "What's New in Home Networking." Print two or three subtopics that describe how to create a home network. Does the task seem less intimidating after you have read the information?

c. Locate one or more topics on new features in digital media such as burning a CD or Windows Movie Maker. Print this information for your instructor.

d. Return once again to the Help and Support Center to explore some of the other resources that describe new features in Windows XP. Locate the link to Windows News Groups, and then visit one of these newsgroups online. Locate a topic of interest and print several messages within a threaded discussion. Do you think newsgroups will be useful to you in the future?

e. You can also download a PowerPoint presentation by the authors that describes new features in Windows XP. Go to www.prenhall.com/grauer, click the text for Office XP, then click the link to What's New in Windows XP, from where you can download the presentation.

FIGURE 23 What's New in Windows XP (exercise 4)

5. **Keyboard Shortcuts:** Almost every command in Windows can be executed in different ways, using either the mouse or the keyboard. Most people start with the mouse and add keyboard shortcuts as they become more proficient. There is no right or wrong technique, just different techniques, and the one you choose depends entirely on personal preference. If, for example, your hands are already on the keyboard, it is faster to use the keyboard equivalent if you know it.

There is absolutely no need to memorize these shortcuts, nor should you even try. A few, however, have special appeal and everyone has favorites. You are probably familiar with general Windows shortcuts such as Ctrl+X, Ctrl+C, and Ctrl+V to cut, copy, and paste, respectively. (The X is supposed to remind you of a pair of scissors.) Ctrl+Z is less well known and corresponds to the Undo command. You can find additional shortcuts through the Help command.

a. Use the Help and Support Center to display the information in Figure 24, which shows the available shortcuts within a dialog box. Two of these, Tab and Shift+Tab, move forward and backward, respectively, from one option to the next within the dialog box. The next time you are in a physician's office or a dentist's office, watch the assistant as he or she labors over the keyboard to enter information. That person will typically type information into a text box, then switch to the mouse to select the next entry, return to the keyboard, and so on. Tell that person about Tab and Shift+Tab; he or she will be forever grateful.

b. The Help and Support Center organizes the shortcuts by category. Select the Natural keyboard category (not visible in Figure 24), then note what you can do with the ⊞ key. Press the ⊞ key at any time, and you display the Start menu. Press ⊞+M and you minimize all open windows. There are several other, equally good shortcuts in this category.

c. Select your five favorite shortcuts in any category, and submit them to your instructor. Compare your selections to those of your classmates. Do you prefer the mouse or your newly discovered shortcuts?

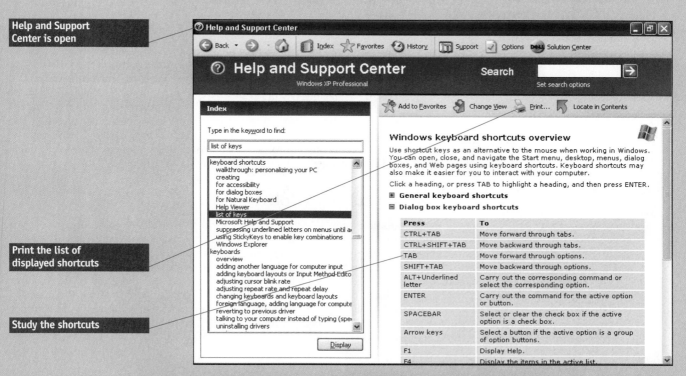

FIGURE 24 Keyboard Shortcuts (exercise 5)

Planning for Disaster

Do you have a backup strategy? Do you even know what a backup strategy is? You had better learn, because sooner or later you will wish you had one. You will erase a file, be unable to read from a floppy disk, or worse yet, suffer a hardware failure in which you are unable to access the hard drive. The problem always seems to occur the night before an assignment is due. The ultimate disaster is the disappearance of your computer, by theft or natural disaster. Describe, in 250 words or less, the backup strategy you plan to implement in conjunction with your work in this class.

Tips for Windows XP

Print the *Tips for Windows XP* document that was downloaded as one of the practice files in the hands-on exercises. This document contains many of the boxed tips that appeared throughout the chapter. Read the document as a review and select five of your favorite tips. Create a new document for your instructor consisting of the five tips you selected. Add a cover page titled, "My Favorite Tips." Include your name, your professor's name, and a reference to the Grauer/Barber text from where the tips were taken.

File Compression

You've learned your lesson and have come to appreciate the importance of backing up all of your data files. The problem is that you work with large documents that exceed the 1.44MB capacity of a floppy disk. Accordingly, you might want to consider the acquisition of a file compression program to facilitate copying large documents to a floppy disk in order to transport your documents to and from school, home, or work. You can download an evaluation copy of the popular WinZip program at www.winzip.com. Investigate the subject of file compression and submit a summary of your findings to your instructor.

The Threat of Virus Infection

A computer virus is an actively infectious program that attaches itself to other programs and alters the way a computer works. Some viruses do nothing more than display an annoying message at an inopportune time. Most, however, are more harmful, and in the worst case, erase all files on the disk. Use your favorite search engine to research the subject of computer viruses to answer the following questions. When is a computer subject to infection by a virus? What precautions does your school or university take against the threat of virus infection in its computer lab? What precautions, if any, do you take at home? Can you feel confident that your machine will not be infected if you faithfully use a state-of-the-art anti-virus program that was purchased in June 2002?

Your First Consultant's Job

Go to a real installation such as a doctor's or attorney's office, the company where you work, or the computer lab at school. Determine the backup procedures that are in effect, then write a one-page report indicating whether the policy is adequate and, if necessary, offering suggestions for improvement. Your report should be addressed to the individual in charge of the business, and it should cover all aspects of the backup strategy; that is, which files are backed up and how often, and what software is used for the backup operation. Use appropriate emphasis (for example, bold italics) to identify any potential problems. This is a professional document (it is your first consultant's job), and its appearance should be perfect in every way.

Index